THE PRACTICE OF CONFLICT MANAGEMENT AMONG TEXTILE MILL MANAGERS

Subramanian.K   MBA, Ph.D.

Published by

Centre for Conflict Management Studies

India

2020

<h1>ACKNOWLEDGEMENT</h1>

This book is one of the resultants of a series of studies to attempt to understand the greater world of conflict and its management among business organisations. There exists a dearth of literature directly dealing and pertaining to the field of conflict management in India. This book address the research gaps in theorising conflict management by exploring various theories, models and assumptions, thereby synchronising and presenting before the reader. Learned academicians and practitioners will certainly feel informed and substantially gained when and only when conflict management theories are presented in a synthesised manner. This is an attempt to bring forth the forte of conflict management theories and models. This work also postulate integrated models and explore suggestive scenarios. I am sure this will be beneficial for executives, managerial workforce, business consultants, academicians and policy makers.

Whether I need to thank the fruit for it gave its taste when I was in great need of it, or the branch which sustained the fruit or the twigs or the tree or the root or the seed or the soil or the earth? I thank the exponential reality we may experience through the creative explorations, sustainable reinventions and the creative destructions when we say we are living. Probably that is how I am in receipt of few glimpses of the essence of old, yet matchless word-GOD.

I intend to dedicate this work to those unsung and forgotten heroes- *odorous orphans* who experienced the essence of management with its most beautiful rainbows. Some of them are still underrepresented and consciously ignored by modern management thinkers and practitioners. Those unsung heroes are part of a *grand plan* to give the simple solutions to our complex conflicts. When we receive the answers as simple as they can be from those Mahatmas, we may reassure that they are coming out directly from God to the humanity. I heard some of it from the likes of life and works of Mahatma Gandhi, *uncommonness in few common men* and attempting to express so as to be in this world upon. Voices of eternal truth from those great souls will certainly be constant motivations as like the grand banyan tree of Gandhigram university- both representing the creating, nourishing, sustaining and integrating principles that elevate human beings to higher non-dual consciousness.

I wish a great success to YOU the reader for considering this research work robust enough to attempt to examine.

K.SUBRAMANIAN

Executive Summary

A necessary part of addressing the issues concerning conflict management seems to be learning about the conditions under which people can be blossomed to perform work in organisations despite the conflicts and or create a better conflict situation/level to enhance the performance constructively. Conflict management as a key component of successful managerial strategy has been researched in this study from different directions. One of the primary responsibilities of this academic research resembles to attempt to find a pathway that better expresses the management of conflicts among the textile mill managers from the selected textile mills in the Coimbatore region. Along with finding the integral and integrative path, an attempt to modelise the effectiveness of managing occupational conflicts of the study group with the input from synthesised circles of Gandhian conflict management were carried out.

Attitudinal sample survey research was carried out as the method of gathering quantitative/quantifiable data from respondents. Modest attempts along the lines of triangulation are included in the form of essay documentation primarily supplied through the data widely accrued by focus group interviews, supplementary in-depth interviews, behavioural case fundamentals, semi structured observations, content analysis and expert opinions. This exploratory analysis of the data collected in tandem brings a modulating and pragmatic appraisal model to the research dynamics. Hypothetico-deductive mechanism is used judiciously in the present research design and study encompassing the representative factorial dimensions.

Distinct philosophies that refer to different managerial attitudes toward conflicts have been identified and the emerging view of conflict, called as interactionist view, reverses many of the cozy nostrums of human relations management. This study presumes conflict– not as an organisational abnormality and it is as a normal aspect of organisational intercourse. The fundamental assumptions regarding conflicts that are necessarily different from the prejudiced positions among the managers and the related organisational characteristics are all explored. Critical for conflict management behaviour is how managers think their goals are predominantly linked; these perceptions influence their expectations and actions, and thereby the outcomes of the conflict management. Approaching the phenomenon of conflict management along these lines will evoke far-reaching implications both for the theory of conflict as well as for the practice of conflict management. Suggestive training modules are designed for conflict management. The management of conflicts could in integrative way be understood together in terms of the same general notion of order; the way would be opened to comprehending their relationship on the basis of some common ground. This study postulates that with the advent of concepts like integral, integrated and interactionist conflict management models as well as conflict management strings; understanding the dynamics of conflict management in organisational sphere in these days are all helpful to practice these prescribed notions so as to enhance the scenario of conflict management among the textile mill managers.

Key Words: Conflict Management, Textile Management, Organisational Development

TABLE OF CONTENTS

Chapter	Description	Page No
ONE	INTRODUCTION	1
TWO	REVIEW OF THE LITERATURE	21
THREE	RESEARCH METHODOLOGY	45
FOUR	CONFLICT MANAGEMENT- A THEORETICAL FRAMEWORK	66
FIVE	ANALYSIS OF DATA AND INTERPRETATION	112
SIX	MAJOR FINDINGS, SUGGESTIONS AND CONCLUSION	262

BIBLIOGRAPHY

CONTENTS IN DETAIL

CHAPTER ONE

1.1 PREAMBLE OF THE STUDY

In an organisation, there seems to be an array of exclusive activities and practices which are deemed to be progressive and fruitful for the organisational development and effectiveness. The dynamic pendulum of change will pave the way to initiate a conscious managerial awakening among the workforce. Any occupational turbulence will necessitate detailed conscious or otherwise psychological notations among the organisational human essentials. The managerial understanding flocks through interesting problems. Managers are held responsible for countless tasks performed in an organisation. But a manager alone cannot complete the tasks at hand and the contributed efforts are indispensable. A manager must induce people to contribute their efforts to the performance of the task at hand. Widespread humanistic activities resulting from organisational interactions generate friction among the workforce and the resultant can be described in a common term-Conflicts. Organisations often face a turbulent, ambiguous and even hostile environment containing forces that generates or revolve into the complex fabric of conflict.

A necessary part of learning management therefore, is learning about the conditions under which people can be motivated to perform work in organisations despite the conflicts and or create a better conflict situation/level to enhance the performance constructively. The engineer cannot expect water to run uphill, the physician cannot assume that an ailment will disappear and a manager cannot expect people to contribute their efforts to organisational tasks, all merely for the asking. Yet each can achieve the desired results by and only by, harnessing the lawful course of processes involved. Engineers who would have water run uphill increase the chances of its doing so when they understand gravity, pressure and flows. Physicians who would cure patients increase their chances of doing so when they understand anatomy, physiology and biochemistry and what more. Managers who would constructively administer their employees increase the chances of positive resultants when they understand the work related etiquette, constraints, needs, beliefs and expectations both self and others' in conflict situations. The results show that the very individuals who regularly and successfully help the human elements in their organisations to solve hot conflicts (carried out openly and with great emotion) themselves suffer from many cold conflicts (expressed covertly) in their own organisations, and generally fail to deal with these in a professional manner. Instead, such conflicts are deflected or allowed to drag on, and have destructive ramifications and or potentials on the human relations' climate in the field of conflict.

In some cases, the stress of this situation can even lead to burn-out problems and retreat from this field of occupation. Protagonists in conflicts are also faced with similar stresses. It is for this reason that a proper understanding of conflict potential within team members and organisations is imperative. This theory gap to understand the dynamics of conflict and its managerial initiation is especially apparent when it comes to stipulating the yardsticks by which the success of individual activities or programmes of intervention are to be measured. Because of the organisational complexities, it is extraordinarily difficult to establish a causal link between micro-measures and macro-effects. It is therefore all the more necessary that we find a way to explicitly address the gap and to isolate and examine the unspoken assumptions underlying a large part of organisational managerial practices and research. There lies a real danger that management, in cases of commotion will be equated either with the stabilisation of relationships of dominance or with the mere smoothing over of human relations if in any way the organisations in the limelight make less grades.

The image of 'conflict' is often double edged. It generally evokes a scenario of in-house fighting, hostility, and painful divisiveness. But also of 'real people' discussing issues in-depth and honesty and creating a common ground with shared values. Hard-charging people run over others for self-aggrandisement, but also 'get things done' and 'create wealth'. Conflicts provoke fears of chaotic revolutions and excitement of revolutionary innovation. Issues of what is just, right and wrong are all debated. People argue about what to do and how to do it for every organisation. They protect their interests yet reach out to understand and accommodate (adjust!) the needs and hopes of others. With such heavy stakes, one is often excited and anxious and may be outraged and despairing. To say the real fact-Conflict tests people in their organisations. To deal with conflicts effectively, we need understanding, introspective reaching out and effective management of feelings-be it from an individual or an organisation.

It may not be possible to compress the essential ingredients of the term 'conflict' in a precise definition because it occurs in many different settings and may take several forms-an enemy to be defeated, an ally to be protected, a moral dilemma to be resolved, a contract to be enacted, a production quota to be beaten up, a client to be won, etc. Often, it is fantasised in such a colourful expressions like–controversy, strife, battle, clash and internecine warfare. But the essence of conflict appears to be disagreement, dissonance, contradiction, incompatibility or even disengagement.

More specifically, on the interrelationship scenario, it was observed that "conflict is a process which begins when one party perceives that another party has frustrated, or is about to frustrate, some concern of his" (Thomas, 1976). Thus, it can be extended as a process/situation in which person A/need A deliberately tries to offset the efforts of person B/need B by some form of blocking that will result in frustrating person B/dissatisfaction of attaining need B or furthering interests. The above definition acknowledges awareness (perceptual), opposition, scarcity and blockage in its core.

People with divergent personalities, perceptions, attitudes and values occupy the positions in organisations. These positions often have differing or contrasting job charts, different levels of status attached to them and also foster occupational anomalies. Individuals experience conflict due to many pressures exerted on him by many groups to which he belongs and demands of various roles he must play in the organisational framework. The higher the organisational interactions, the greater would be the chances for occupational distortions. Managers are usually trying to find ways to get organisational synergy to work and induce people to contribute their efforts to the performance of the task in hand. A necessary part of learning management therefore is learning about the conditions under which people handle their occupational conflicts and it would be quite natural to start that with the most facilitating, influential and decision making group in the organisation- managers. Effectiveness of managers depends on how well they understand the underlying dynamics of the conflict, which may be all together different from its expression, and whether they can identify the crucial tactical points for intervention. This is the challenge of Conflict management.

Conflicts can be viewed as a dynamic process which generates energy for the organisation to deal with uncertain situations. It is always a challenge facing by employees and their associates. In the state of ongoing tensions and conflicts which occur naturally in organisations, some people may act in ways that manage these conflicts and creates more room for organisational creative learning, while others may act in ways that leave conflicts unaddressed, unresolved and get precipitated in antagonistic behaviours. Given two employees in the same job with the same peers and bosses and the same number of initial disputes, the degree of conflict in their respective environment may still be quite different. That calls for better managerial understanding of the dynamics of conflict management and the proactive as well as responsive strategies with which a manager can get accustomed.

1.1 CONFLICT POTENTIAL AND ORGANISATIONAL LEVELS

In a theoretical perspective, the potential for the conflicts to occur in every organisational level is alarmingly high. The historical importance attached to the conflicts at the interpersonal levels/individual levels alone may not bring the desired results in these days. The better we understand the potentials for the conflict in all the organisational levels the better we can frame a decent mechanism to cope up with those situations. Although it has been widely acclaimed that a conflict arises in one level can spawn or moves to another or other levels and vice versa.

1.2.1 Individual group member

A group member/team member experiences the constant intra-psychological struggles and conflicts and he express these externally for he seeks to cooperate with the other team members. The known conflict mechanisms in this context usually appear within individuals and corrupt their perceptions, thinking, feelings and their external behaviour. The perception capability of the individual can be strongly impaired through the effects of stress, tension and pressure. The result can lead to selective or distorted perception or even the fading out of perceptions that do not conform to the preconceived picture. This is how prejudices occur and become fixed, since all evidence, which might contradict previous perceptions, are suppressed and discarded. The concepts and ideas which people form on the basis of such distorted perceptions are likely to become into one-sided black and white pictures, which can no longer easily corrected by further evidence or perceptions. The members take only information that confirms the prejudice.

In the emotional sector, empathy dries up. People become encapsulated one from another, prisoner of their own feelings. Sympathy and antipathy serve to create a polarised emotional picture. If the conflict escalates, the picture seems to be more dramatic as all point of reference to the outside world is lost. Unconscious or semiconscious driving forces and motives become dominant in those situations. Perceiving, thinking and willing all mutually reinforce one another in a vicious spiral and the tension can be even more difficult when they contradict each other. In the external behaviour of these individuals, a noticeable change will preoccupy. Stereotypes, rumor spreading and compulsiveness control their actions.

1.2.2 The interaction or psychosocial level

Each group will need to organise itself around certain roles if it is to achieve its goals and also to maintain cohesion as a team. Conflicts tend to occur when a group member –

- ◘ Feels pressure from the group to assume a role in which he does not want and to which he/other members objects the same or vice versa
- ◘ Experiences the allocated roles as constraining and decelerating his development
- ◘ Feel avoidance / covert sanctions imposed by other elements of a team
- ◘ Hierarchical constraints, especially the leadership dilemmas and formal/informal authority.

1.2.3 The content or the issue level

Rational individuals often assume that conflicts arise and keep it as long as everybody remains objective. However, as a conflict escalates, issue related and psycho-social issues become increasingly mixed. Potential for conflict can be easily arise at this level if managers fail to recognise that any issue can be perceived and asserted differently by different task groups/team members. Unfortunately, concepts can only rarely be clarified to everyone's satisfaction. The result would be misunderstandings and misinterpretations. There may be a failure to identify the real issues thus producing conflicts.

1.2.4 The procedural / method level

Teams in the organisations are expected to learn and familiarise themselves with a variety of working procedures and methods and must become good at reaching right decisions. Conflicts are often initially experienced as relation-specific, even though the problems can actually be traced to a poor selection of work methods.

1.2.5 External relations and outreach

The relations between a team and its organisational setting can also contain many seeds of conflict. One important aspect is to specify the degree of participation of the team in defining itself against higher-ranking levels or other teams within the organisation. In that sense the extraneous variables for the organisation and its prominent impact on the team members shall play a key role in defining the conflict potentials. These extraneous factors include the social, economic, cultural, political, industrial, technical and other superfluous dimensions that instill the dynamics of change or at least a positional alteration in the organisational setup. External relations and its influences are multitudinal and calls for a holistic and expanded study of conflict potentials. Interestingly, this seems to be the most damaging type of conflicts which are of innumerable in characteristics yet not been able to make positions of.

1.3 TYPES OF CONFLICT

Conflict comes in a variety of forms. Regardless of the form, the essence of conflict seems to be the distortion it causes for the better or the worse in every sphere of organisational life. The vicious circle of conflict is supported and or supplemented by the great potentialities that it inculcates in the organisational development and change clearly indicates that it can give positive returns apart from the usually branded one sided view of its prevarication. Various forms of conflict include the following ones. The fundamental element of every form of conflict seems to be the perceived situation or the initial reactionary means that is exercised by the parties involved in the conflict situation. Conflict has been classified in different ways. Following are the some of the classifications.

1.3.1 Perceived, latent and manifest conflicts

- Perceived conflicts exist in individuals when they perceive that there is a conflict in the work environment, which may truly be existing or not. Perceived conflict may give rise to real conflict.
- Latent conflicts are one that does not emerge in open i.e. individuals involved in conflict do not show it openly although the conflict exists.
- Manifest conflicts is open conflict where in parties involved in conflict recognise and openly explicitly express the conflict.

1.3.2 Realistic and non-realistic conflicts

Realistic conflict arises when participants clash in the pursuit of claims and expectation of gain. It is viewed as a means towards the achievement of specific goals that might be abandoned if other means appear to be more effective. Non-realistic conflict arises from aggressive impulses that seek expression no matter what the object, allows no functional alternative of means. Since it is not aimed at the attainment of concrete results, but at the expression of aggressive impulses in an individual, it draws managerial attention.

1.3.3 Organised and unorganised conflicts

Organised and unorganised conflicts exist in organisations. It can be called organised conflict when parties involved in conflict express it in organised manner like strike or lock out, as there are no contraventions of any of the provisions laid down by the organisational framework. Unorganised conflicts are expressed through absenteeism, late coming etc and are essentially system transgressions. While there are different kinds of conflicts explained above, all conflicts in organisation – both organised and unorganised fall within one of six categories mentioned below–

- External (conflicts related to competition, the marked place, regulation, or on adversarial take over).
- Management process and style (conflicts stemming from leadership style, the decision making process, or organisational structure.
- Strategic direction (conflicts over the company's mission direction, objectives and strategies).
- Operational (conflicts related to issue such as 'quality verses schedule' or 'design-to-production transition').
- Interdepartmental (conflicts that occur when divisions compete with themselves rather than with other companies.
- Value system (conflicts over business philosophy).

1.3.4 Bargaining, Bureaucratic and Systems conflicts

- Bargaining conflicts occur among the interest groups in competition for scarce resources, this is appropriate for the analysis of labour–management relations, budgeting processes and staff-line conflicts.
- Bureaucratic conflicts between the parties to a superior, subordinate relationship particularly concerned with the problems caused by institutional attempts to control behaviour and the organisations' reaction to such control.
- Systems conflicts occur among parties to a lateral or working relationship or a functional relationship. Analysis of the problems of coordination is the special prefecture of this model.

1.3.5 Organisational conflicts

Intra-individual, inter personal and inter group conflicts are all inherent in organisational conflicts. The various shades of organisational conflicts are in effect exercise their combined options.

1.3.5.1 *Intrapersonal conflicts*

Intrapersonal conflicts occur within an individual, and often involve some form of frustration and or dissonance felt by an individual. Goal, cognitive, affective and role conflicts and ambiguity are common denominations of the intrapersonal conflicts. Frustration occurs when goal-directed behaviour is blocked.

Goal conflicts occur when two or more desired or expected outcomes are seemed and or perceived to be incompatible. Goal conflict may involve inconsistencies between the individual's or group's values and norms and the demands or goals assigned by higher levels in the organisation. More frequently, goal conflict occurs when an individual or group is assigned or selects incompatible goals according to their understanding. The concept of goal difficulty is in fact the essence of goal conflicts. And it refers to the extent to which an individual's or group's goal is at odds with the capacity to achieve the goal. Goal conflict occurs when a goal has either positive and negative features; or when an individual has two or more competing goals thus blocking, one another. Three types of goal conflicts are generally identified.

- *Approach – approach conflict*, where the individual is motivated to approach two or more positive but mutually exclusive goals.
- *Approach – avoidance conflict*, where a single goal has both positive and negative characteristics and individual is motivated to approach and avoid it at the same time. This has relevance to the analysis of organisational behaviour.
- *Avoidance – avoidance conflict*, where the individual is motivated to avoid two or more negative but mutually exclusive goals.

Cognitive conflicts occur when the ideas and thoughts within an individual or between individuals are incompatible. The relative perceptions about the task at hand or the means to achieve the desired results are at the crossroads and the fundamental distortions in the minds of the human elements are vital to be ignored as cognitive dissonance fuels conflicts. Cognitive conflict is sometimes beneficial because it requires teams to engage in activities that are essential to a team's effectiveness. Cognitive conflict focuses attention on assumptions that may underlie a particular issue and which are often ignored. Cognitive conflict improves the quality of team decisions.

Intrapersonal conflicts may also be a consequence of cognitive dissonance, which occurs when individuals recognise inconsistencies in their own thoughts and or behaviour. The existence of substantial and recognised inconsistencies is usually stressful and uncomfortable. Both goal conflict and cognitive conflict causes or triggers the dissonance and accompany many important decision making scenario. The greater the goal conflict before the decision, the greater the cognitive dissonance is likely to be after the decision. The more difficulty individuals have in arriving at the original decision, the greater is their need to justify the decision afterward. Some cognitive dissonances are inevitable as there seems to be a perceptual distinction exists between the actual and the expected world views exercised by the individuals. Cognitive dissonance can fuel role conflict and ambiguity as an individual is expected to play various roles and a clash there from.

The personality mechanism can also be a distinguishable factor that instigates inner conflict among the individuals. Neurotic tendencies are irrational personality mechanisms that an individual uses often unconsciously, which create inner conflict. In turn, inner conflict often results in behaviours that lead to conflict with others. The psychological sources of neurotic tendencies are beyond the scope of discussion but it has been pointed out by many thinkers that neurotic managers might make excessive use of tight organisational controls because they distrust people. A few may be fearful of uncertainty and risk, not just distrustful of others. Those managers may be predisposed to rely on hunches and impressions rather than seek out available facts. Such managers may not use participation and consultation in their decision making unless extremely required to do so. Individuals with neurotic tendencies will always be affected by their cognitive dissonance and usually struggle unsuccessfully with their intrapersonal conflicts. Because they cannot manage their own problems, they often trigger conflict with the others. The excessive distrust and need to control exhibited by neurotic managers is likely trigger conflict with others, especially subordinates who come to feel over controlled and distrusted. Open or covert aggression and hostility will be an out growth creating the vicious circle of conflicts in psycho-social relations of organisational dealings.

Affective conflicts occur when the feelings and emotions within an individual or even between individuals are incompatible. The expressive components as well the intra emotive feelings experienced by every party and its reactionary cognition are important to determine the nature of the conflict in this regard. Affective conflict lowers team effectiveness by provoking hostility, distrust, cynicism, and apathy among team members. Most affective conflicts are focused on personalised anger or resentment, usually directed at specific individuals rather than specific ideas. Affective conflict undermines team effectiveness by preventing teams from engaging in the kinds of activities that are critical to team effectiveness.

Role conflicts occur when expectations of a role are materially different or even opposite from the behaviour anticipated by that person in that role. The wings of role conflict have its sway in the intrapersonal level as well as to other levels particularly to the interpersonal level. A role is a set of expectations people have about the behaviour of a person in a position. Such behaviour may be formally prescribed by job description, delegation, organisational manuals, and the likes and is derived from the tasks, missions, procedures, or instructions. Roles may also be derived from the informal activities in which members may be engaged. An individual may feel role conflict because there is no way to meet on expectation without rejecting other. Mutually exclusive expectations may arise from a persons' behaviour in many ways. Some of them can be identified as follows–

- When an individual is asked to do a job for which he is not capable of doing or time and resources are not just sufficient to do the job,
- When an individual is asked to do a job which does not fit with his own value system,
- When an individual receives roles from different sources and if those sources prescribe different behaviour,
- When an individual holds two or more roles and their expectations are different and even mutually exclusive as perceived by that individual.

Normally all those factors which are associated with the determination of role expectations may be responsible for role conflict because role conflict arises due to mutually exclusive role expectations. Role ambiguity, organisational positions, personal characteristics are all contributory channels to the role conflicts amongst the individuals. *Role ambiguity* arises when uncertainty or lack of clarity surrounding expectations about a single role. Like role conflict, severe role ambiguity may cause stress and subsequent coping behaviours. The coping behaviours may includes– aggressive actions and hostile communications, ignoring and conscious avoidance causing withdrawal from the situations and seeking guidance through organisational mechanisms. Research findings are not clear cut on the relationships among the role conflict, role ambiguity, and their outcomes. However they indicate stress reactions, aggression, hostility, and withdrawal among others.

1.3.5.2 *Interpersonal conflicts*

Interpersonal conflict arises from personal differences, information deficiency, role incompatibility and environmental stress. It usually involves two or more individuals who believe that their attitudes, behaviours, or preferred goals are in opposition. Many interpersonal conflicts are based on some type of role conflict and or role ambiguity. They may stem out of the intrapersonal levels that precipitates as a visible component through the conflict mechanism.

Inter-psychic conflicts exist within an individual when she or he feels drawn to two or more divergent desires or actions ignited through external situations and activates conflicts at psycho-social levels. Psycho-social conflicts exist between people or between a person and a group or vice versa and is present when a person must choose in favour of one course of action, at the expense of an equally desirable course of action (e.g. personal goals at the expense of groups/organisational goals). Conflict of interest is present when parties involved in conflict share the same understanding of the situation but prefers a different and incompatible solution to problem. Conflict of understanding occurs when parties involved in conflict do not share the same conceptualisation of the situation. This may occur because of divergent ideologies, cultures, values or cognitive structures.

1.3.5.3 *Intragroup conflicts*

Intragroup conflict occurs when the actions or beliefs of one or more members of the group are unacceptable to – and hence are resisted by *one or more* of the other group members. Intragroup conflict involves clashes among some or all of the group's members, which often affect the groups' processes and effectiveness. In many instances conflict in a group occurs because members must compete for limited resources. Once the conflict begins, it often intensifies before it begins abate. This conflict spiral is produced by a host of factors, including misperceptions, commitment, entrapment, behavioural provocations, reciprocity, and coalitions.

1.3.5.4 *Intergroup conflicts*

Intergroup conflict can be expressed as the behaviour that occurs among organisational groups when participants identify with one group and perceive that other groups may block their group's achievement or expectations. Intergroup conflict requires four ingredients- group identification, observable group differences, competition and frustration. The employees have to perceive themselves as part of an identifiable group or department, the presence of observable difference of some form and the third ingredient of the frustration should be felt by the group members. The element of competition plays an important role and creates the platform to express intergroup conflicts. Intergroup conflict within organisations can occur horizontally across departments or vertically between different levels of the organisation. Conflict can also occur between different divisions or business units with an organisation. Some of the major sources of intergroup conflict can be identified as goal incompatibility, differentiation, task interdependence and limited resources.

1.3.6 Inter-organisational conflicts

Another visible conflict dominion does exist in the inter-organisational levels where multiple groups from more than one organisation may also be part of the conflict continuum. The groups in the organisations perceive that other groups may block their group's achievement or expectations' conflicts. This is fueled through the organisational aspirations arising from the macro business environment when organisations compete for market share, economical compulsions, business priorities, value promotion or to satisfy organisation's self promotive leniency.

1.3.7 Procedural conflicts

Procedural conflicts occur when people differ over the process to use for managing an organisational *decision- inviting* situation. It can be regarded as the style or the method with which the human elements want to achieve the desired results.

1.3.8 Structural conflicts

The very nature of the structure of an organisation also gives rise to conflict. Modern organisations are not immune to the structural conflicts even though they sometimes incorporate the matrix structure and try to pool logically the available resources through under the project banner. In classical organisation there are several types of structural conflicts as indicated below.

- ◘ Hierarchical conflicts – exist between various levels in the hierarchy of the organisation like board of director and top management, middle management with supervising personnel, management vs. workers.
- ◘ Functional conflicts – exists between various functional departments in every organisation like marketing, personnel, financial, production etc.
- ◘ Line vs staff conflicts – Intra organisational functional experts and other officials may have their conflicts with the line managers who are primarily delegators of the task assigned.
- ◘ Formal – informal conflicts exists between formal and informal organisational structure and set up among the workforce.
- ◘ Diversity- based conflicts can occur because of the differences existing and or felt by the workforce regarding age, gender, religion, caste, traditions and other cultural background.

1.3.9 Innovative conflicts

Innovative conflict is the most dramatic form of conflict in complex organisation and has its generous hands in ground-breaking movements that challenge the very legitimacy of the organisation or in some cases, the present anomalies in the organisational structure. This is different from other kinds of conflict that it does not ask for a greater share of the scarce resources but they demand that all the resources be redistributed to new organisation and that the old systems cease to exist.

1.4 PERSPECTIVES ON ORGANISATIONAL CONFLICTS AND ITS MANAGEMENT

The complex variables of conflict fabric had historically initiated the managerial thinkers to formulate a decent idea with which the practicing managers can approach the conflict situation and act upon. Fortunately or unfortunately the perspectives on organisational conflict among the theoretical exponents reflected the ever undergoing process regarding the management of the conflict affairs. Three distinguishable perspectives emerged out of the managerial interactions with the conflict associations and they are interestingly complementary towards each other in certain proportions.

1.4.1 Traditional (unitary) perspectives

This perspective holds that conflict represents a malfunction within the individual, group, department or the organisation. Within it, conflict is seen as bad and harmful and hence should be avoided if possible and eradicated if it erupts .This perspective is called traditional because it has its roots in the Hawthorne studies which were conducted in the United States in the 1924-32 period. It is also referred to as unitary because of its endorsement by managerial thinkers of pre 1970's including Elton Mayo, Dalton, Barrett and Cosier among others. Organisation as a fundamentally harmonious, cooperative structure where no systematic conflict of interest occurs seems to be at the core that lies beneath in this perspective. Common goals are assumed and organisational success or failure is seen as leading to success or failure for the entire human elements that are present in that organisation. Managers are advised by this perspective to see their organisation as analogous to teams with all the team members striving towards the achievement of common goals. The concept of the 'pulling together in the same direction' and that of the 'espirit de corps' are followed unquestioningly and in a flattened view of the same preferences, values beliefs and attitude predispositioned among the human workforce.

Explaining conflict from unitary perspective is difficult rather problematic because, as all the members of the organisation are held to share common objectives and values which unite them; while managerial prerogative is accepted with unified authority and there is organisational loyalty; perhaps too much that a manager has to assume to apply this perspective in the real situation. The unitary perspective sees consensus especially the non conflict in essence as the ideal and natural state. When conflict occurs its existence tends to be explained in one of three ways. Most commonly it is attributed to poor communication. Management accepts responsibility for failing to get its intended message through to its employees and to meet their needs and aspirations.

Conflict is thus seen as being caused by misunderstandings. The instability which led to the conflict breaking out is held to be the result of a lack of trust, openness and adequate communications which are necessarily to be rectified. In other ways, conflict may be seen as a failure by management to design an organisational structure that allows individuals, units or departments to cooperate to achieve organisational objectives. In the third dimension, management may claim that it has shown the workforce the right perspective and that was irreparably sabotaged by a few unrepresented minorities that are essentially unwanted in the workforce, hence the conflict propels as the outcome. Irrespective of which of the three explanations is adopted by the practicing manager the core issues that are advocated to act upon remains the same, eliminating the causes of the conflicts and to reestablish the satisfactory situation that was prevailing in the organisation. The traditional perspective is viewed as the resultant of the historical conflict that was visible throughout the industrial revolution and its immediate aftermath in every economy ranging from European to the Latin American. The class warfare and the industrial schools had their influence on shaping the unitary thoughts which seems to be highly flattened by its own wishes to remain encircled by insulating the changed scenarios.

1.4.2 Pluralist perspectives

It may be noted that the glimpses of this perspective was early identified by many managerial thinkers but the promulgation of pluralist perspective starts with Alan Fox(1966) in United States, an old advocate of unitarian conflict thinker later aloofed himself from the pitfalls of traditional viewpoints. It is called pluralist because it rejects the view that individual employees have the same interests as the management on the other hand and that an organisation is best seen as one big team on the other. Instead it holds that individuals have unique and different interests that they form into cliques on the basis of these and that an organisation is best seen as consisting of many separate but related interest camps each pursuing their own objectives. If however the interests coincide or rather collide whilst others they will clash and the frictional basis can develop into the conflict envisaged. The obvious clashes may be between or among the organisational workforce in every level possible. The contributory expansion of this perspective attained was that it recognised a fact that the conflict may not necessarily among the two parties in the organisation; even more the disagreement among three or more parties in the organisational sphere was visualised and deemed to be imperative in determining the detrimental value of the conflicts. The job of the management becomes one of keeping the balance between potentially conflicting goals and managing the differences between the differing interest groups.

Acceptance of the pluralist perspective implies that conflict is inevitable. Indeed given the organisational relationships, it will be endemic. However unlike the traditional perspective which sees conflict as harmful and something to be eliminated, in the pluralistic view conflict should be accepted since in certain circumstances it may even enhance the relationships and promote the organisational efficiency. Underlying the pluralist perspective ids the belief that conflict can be resolved through compromise to the benefit of all. However it requires all parties to limit their claims to a level which is at least tolerable to the others and which allows further collaboration to continue. Lewis Pondy (1967, p.320) wrote that, "Conflict is not necessarily good or bad, but must be evaluated in terms of its individual organisational functions and dysfunctions. In general, conflict generates pressure to reduce conflict, but chronic conflict persists and is endured under certain conditions and consciously created and managed by the politically astute administrator". For the pluralist the organisation is indeed a system of interrelationships between the individuals and groups within it each pursuing their own goals. Conflicts in an organisation acts as the safety-valve and keeps the organisational elements responsible and even responsive to the internal and external changes. The inevitable conflict has to be managed so that organisational goals are reconciled with the group interests to the benefit of organisational prosperity.

1.4.3 Interactionist perspectives

The interactionist perspective goes beyond the pluralist school's toleration and the management of the conflict. It actually in a way promotes a healthy conflict level by stimulating the conflict situation advocating conscious organisational interventions. It encourages the conflict stimulation and conflict resolution in equal ways. This perspective argues that an individual, group or department that seems to be too peaceful harmonious and or cooperative in some cases can become apathetic and unresponsive to the changing needs. Such extreme cohesion, be it blossoming from an individual thought or that from a group can lead to the stagnation phenomenon that are visibly disconcerted by any changes encouraging a reactionary shield of opposing every change and leniency towards maintaining the status quo would not be a sought-after measure for the organisational set up.

The interactionist view recognises that the conflict occurs as a process or sequence of events. These events take place in conflict episodes between the parties. Whenever the interactions happen, there exist a wider scope for conflict and its management of the same in organisational context was highly appreciated by this perspective. The process of conflict does not occur in a vacuum. Rather they are shaped by structural parameters of the system, the relatively fixed or slow changing conditions influencing events at the interface between the parties. These structural conditions include the properties of the parties as well as the context in which they interact. Most organisational conflicts are managed primarily by the principal parties of the conflict. However one or more third parties may also play a role in managing the conflict. Depending on the system and the interface where the conflict occurs, the third party could be a manager, board of directors, consultant or a mediator etc. The interventions that are exercised by the third parties and subsequent changes in the interrelationship scenario is identified and recognised in the interactionist perspective. The unwinding of the negative outlook regarding the conflicts and to give a more pragmatic vision towards dealing the conflicts in the organisation seems to be the major intransigent force though it was really propelled by the interactionist view.

1.5 FUNCTIONAL AND DYSFUNCTIONAL ASPECTS OF CONFLICT AND ITS MANAGEMENT

The perspectives on organisational conflicts seem to differ in terms of their evaluation of conflict with regard to its functionality aspects. The traditional view sees all conflict as bad, while the pluralist and interactionist perspectives hold that certain conflicts can be good. In other words whether a conflict is functional or disturbs the smooth functioning of the organisational workings is put under litmus test. From 1970's the basic question that arises among the managerial exponents regarding the functional and or dysfunctional aspects of the conflicts are addressed constructively in these days. It has been suggested that under some situations conflict can generate positive response in the organisation. Thus a conflict may have both positive and negative aspects. Boulding has recognised that some optimum level and associated personal stress and tension are necessary for progress and productivity but he portrays conflict primarily as a potential social cost.

Similarly Kahn and others view that one might well make a case for interpreting some conflict as essential for the continued development of mature and competent human beings and they feel that conflict is necessarily a social cost. It has been widely acclaimed as a conflict is functional if it improves the quality of decisions, stimulates creativity and innovation, encourages interest and curiosity amongst the group members, provides a way of airing grievances, releases tensions and encourages self evaluation and change. It is dysfunctional if it breeds discontent, dissolves common ties, leads to the destruction of the group, retards communication, reduces group cohesion, individual interests supplant group goals, reduces group effectiveness and threatens group survival. Functionality is thus defined at the level of the group as a whole in terms of outcomes, rather than in its effects on the individual members. In essence the conflict is functional when it supports the goals of an individual / group /organisation and improves her/his/its performance. It is by this idea amalgamation that functional conflicts are sometimes referred as constructive and or cooperative conflicts. Those conflict situations are regarded as necessarily dysfunctional when it hinders individual's/group's performance towards attaining organisational goals.

1.6 CONFLICT CONTINUUM

Notion and ideas about managing conflict underwent an interesting evolution during the twentieth century among management thinkers. Initially scientific management experts like Frederick Winslow Taylor of United States believed that all conflicts ultimately threaten management's authority and thus had to be avoided or to be quickly resolved. 'Bostonian' Follett, the only leading lady in the whole gamut of management thinkers shifted the spotlight to the man at the centre stage. Perhaps she was the first advocate of constructive conflict practices for the organisation and a dynamic promoter of integration as the leading way for managing the conflicts. Later Elton Mayo and his associates of human relations school recognised the inevitability of conflicts and advised managers to learn to live with it. Emphasis however remained on the resolution of the conflict whenever possible. From the 1970's, organisational experts like, M.A.Rahim, K.W.Thomas, S.P.Robbins among others began to realise that conflicts had both positive and negative outcomes, depending upon its nature and intensity and advocated the balancing views of conflict in the organisations. In addendum to the appreciation of the conflict in its totality a revolutionary idea cropped among the mainstream management thinkers and practitioners that organisations could suffer from too little conflict. Thereafter the intensity of the conflict and its relationship with the outcomes were studied exclusively with a rejuvenated spirit by the exponents of management literature.

Individuals, work groups, departments or organisations that experience too little conflict tend to be plagued by apathy, lack of creativity, indecision and missed work schemas. Excessive conflict, on the other hand, can corrode organisational performance because of in-house fighting, dissatisfaction among the workforce, lack of teamwork, and attrition tendencies. Workplace aggression and active violence can be manifestations of excessive and non productive conflicts. Appropriate types and levels of conflict energise people in more constructive directions. It seems that the conflict continuum advocating a decent conflict energy that is adorable for the organisational performance and it can be directed towards more positive channels by the conscious organisational interventions by the managerial practitioners.

1.7 NEED AND SIGNIFICANCE OF THE PRESENT STUDY

One of the major challenge counted by practicing managers and other stakeholders of contemporary management ethos, is the expressive development of a body of theory to explain why organisational conflicts take the form they do, and why they/others behave as they do, including various stratum of the managerial responses towards conflict dynamics. Outlining some aspects of this emerging line of research on organisations and to call attention to a number of related methodological issues that play an important role in these areas of research – the relation between situational processes, handling strategies and theories, the importance to the research effort of the choice of tautologies and definitions, the nature of evidence, behavioural reengineering, process realignment, organisational preparedness/ adaptability/receptivity and the role of personality-structure interplays among other related domains enshrine the expanding horizons.

Something is *common knowledge* if it is known to each person, and in addition, each person knows that she or he has this knowledge; knows that the other person/s knows the person knows it; and so forth. If in any case, a crevice in this structure entitles a need to acquire the *savoir faire* and to transform the relationship to new heights. It exactly suits for the expanding domains of conflict management studies. Present study is a modest attempt to promote *common knowledge* about conflict management and to share the intricacies of the practice of conflict management with a special emphasise on managerial modes.

1.8 RESEARCH FRAMEWORK

Research evolves in a sequence of steps, which are closely interrelated. Qualitative and exploratory elements in the conflict management ethos makes the success of research depends upon the successful completion or extension of ordered strides in research framework. Conscious identification of the research areas in physical, mental and appraising levels deeply evolves the strengthening of the research frame. An inquiry on the domains of conflict management with special emphasis on the textile mill managers stationed at Coimbatore district in Tamilnadu, India requires a scientific transmission of research observations. Rationale behind conscious/ unconscious expediency in selecting the area and population were explained in detailed methodological discussion. Defining research problems, identifying the conceptual and theoretical framework of conflict management, approaching and collecting data studded with hypothetical assumptions through well defined procedures, appraising thus explored outputs and document the process outcomes, constitutes the adorable initial ingredients of the research framework of the present study.

1.8.1 Broad objectives

Broad objectives of the present study include –

- to evaluate the constructive and/or vicious conflict management practices among the Coimbatore textile managerial workforce;
- to identify potential causative, remedial, collateral and other organisational psycho-social factors that are influenced by the conflict response patterns of the study group, and;
- to make an attempt to explore integrating conflict management mechanism imbibing Gandhian values and spirit of situation handling.

1.8.2 Scope and Limitations

At first glance, it is tempting to take a stand that the systematic research on conflict management unearths an array of opportunities and a plethora of managerial explicabilities. Surely, it does but with applied qualms. The assessment of innumerable ways of managing conflicts requires at least a couple of dozens of well drawn studies from every sphere including academia. Smartly intertwined components that are primarily responsible for conflicts in organisations, fixes the scales of managing the state of affairs in every sense. Leniency in a way or other, towards the overbearing human elements of an organisation may sometimes unwarranted or even unwanted to explicitly communicate through this research process. Multi-faceted assessment of issues concerning conflict management may or may not exclusively reflect an extensional propensity in a strictly non-longitudinal study. A study on micro-issues, that too, too complex like conflict issues and its subsequent macro-causal determination may have its toll. Further, a particulistic focus group study cannot be generalised to various tunes.

The present study, part of an academic exercise had not insulated itself from various constraints from every possible and thinkable quarters. Despite all this, the research study modestly attempt to integrate every channels of information flows with a genuine quest for knowledge management proclaiming transformative principles to the domains of conflict management – as planting a sapling and visualising a greeny ,thicker forest.

1.9 PRELIMINARY STUDY AND FEASIBILITY ANALYSIS

Systematic field visits were made to the textile mills in the Coimbatore area and had sequential in-depth discussions with the authorities and the experts. Exclusive investigative analyses were carried out in the textile unit to the better understanding of the organisational structure and the systematic work procedures they are practicing. Formal and informal meetings with an array of Governmental and other officials rendering their services in the textile sector had expanded the operational necessities of the research enquiry. It has been necessitated by the fact that the better understanding of the organisational set up can improve the research scope of the study and can remove the ill-represented responses from the study group. Further, when researcher seek out people who are well informed on the topic, especially those who have clearly stated positions on controversial aspects of the problem, research questions can be addressed effectively and the study would reflect the real expositions on the field. The responses from the individual units were very positive and their input had certainly broadened and fine-tuned the research inputs. The feasibility analyses expounded the strengthening and necessary ramifications regarding the i) management problems, ii) exploring the research questions and iii) creating an effective research design and they are encouragingly integrated into the research fold.

1.10 CHAPTER SCHEME

The background introductory schema concerning the componential expositions constitutes major elements in the present chapter, *chapter-one*. Primary resultants of the library research, enhanced conceptual framework, and the critical observations endowed in the name of literature review in *chapter two*. The methodological considerations, procedural approach and the research tool descriptions were all part and parcel of *chapter three*. The theoretical considerations and the framework are explained in *chapter four*. Analysis and the general interpretation, including the testing of the guided hypotheses constitutes *chapter five*. Identifiable and expressive measures of the research process find its right place in *chapter six*. Referential studies integrated in the respective portions with detailed source identification in appendices.

CHAPTER TWO

REVIEW OF THE LITERATURE

Review of the literature constitutes the critical, exponential, and an endeavor for a summarisation of previous / contemporary / relevant studies towards enhancing conceptual understanding. Accordingly, with due consideration to the management questions, research problem emerges operationally as to study the conflict management mechanism among the managerial study group. Preliminary explorations were undertaken to fine tune the research questions through concurrent field visits and theoretical studies. Preliminary feasibility analyses were also done with the help of various didactic aids. The present study constitutes of primarily 'qualitative descriptive' and partially 'exploratory' elements, thus making review of literature, an obligatory component. Hence a review of literature in this area, focusing on the main ideas about conflict behaviour, controversies and findings, seems appropriate to situate the problem in a variety of situations from intra-individualistic to the group/systems spheres of influence. The major objective of this review of literature is to throw sufficient light on the factors responsible for the arousal of conflict and the course normally sought by the conflicting parties.

Primary focus of the review of literature was strengthening the conceptual framework of the study by exercising an essential review of conflict and conflict management among business and industrial organisations, various theories, approaches, models, major outcomes of previous explorations and practices related to conflict and conflict management, within the scope of the research framework and emphasising the literature available after the advent of Management as a discipline. Primary topic being the conflict management which is multidisciplinary in nature - domains of management, individual psychology, conflict studies, anthropology, social psychology, sociology, group studies, ethology and many special interdisciplinary endeavors deal with the complex aspects of conflict behaviour and its management among individuals, within and between groups as well as in broader levels were critically reviewed.

Human interactions on all levels in an organisation necessitates a basic differentiation of the literature review along the lines of the two themes-personality and structure, although these two are still too broad to be useful for a full fledged, detailed examination and description of a conflict situation. If we depict the two dimensions of conflict as clusters of personality and structural variables, we are able to list the major components of this multivariate phenomenon.

In the examination of the role of personality for conflict approach preferential, such issues as– motives, the cognitive structure, value-orientation, self/other perception, etc, does matter the most. The study of the structure of the conflict managerial mechanism includes the basic preconditions of interaction within/between/among the party/parties, specific conflict situation, conflict functionaries, the wider environment and, the dynamics of conflict process from its very inception to various metamorphic impulsions.

In the process of review of the existing literature pertaining to research questions, no conscious attempts were made to include all the theories/models/components to be put into analyses and include in the documentation purposes. However a modest attempt was made to include those highly relevant constituents of conflict management that were necessitated by research considerations of the present study. The studies and inputs from the predominantly English speaking world seem to have an immense presence than others in the review process. Further, the present chapter constitutes major literature review concerning to the research questions. In no way it is the exhaustive representative of the review process of the present study and as and when required, relatively relevant portions of review were documented in other chapters also.

The review presented here reflects the domains of conflict and conflict management recognised by the research framework and their managerial relevance to the present study. The limelight consciously swings to the individuals' managerial reflections in group/ organisational contexts. Connotations of conflict and conflict management in various dimensions, theories/models pertaining to the study of it, major research findings from the past – both from international arena and in Indian context, were critically revisited. Further, this made an attempted exploration in the spirit of genuine interdisciplinary approach, and a judicious documentation in germane propositions.

2.1 CONFLICT DEFINITION

The Latin word *conflictus*, as "striking together with force" implies disagreement, discord, and friction among the members of a group. It indicates those interactions in which words, emotions, and actions "strike together" to produce disruptive effects. Conflict has been defined in many ways depending upon the suitability, focus and group interest. Some conflicts are characterised as intrapersonal, while others have been described as interpersonal. Some manifestations of conflict have also been recognised in the organisational context.

As it emerges mainly between two groups, conflict is characterised in terms of overall group interest and union-management conflict has been popular term particularly coined to describe similar phenomena in different organisations. Although there are many definitions available in the literature, it is necessary to restrict ourselves to definitions that best describe organisational conflict with emphasis on managerial sphere. A sample of definitions describing varying manifestations of conflict in organisations are quoted below-

- "Conflict is a breakdown in the standard mechanism of decision-making, so that an individual or a group experiences difficulty in selecting an action alternative" (March and Simon, 1958).This definition views the organisation primarily as a decision making body, whereas all agents are engaged in making big or small decisions. Conflict occurs when the parties do not agree on which alternative should be chosen for implementation. The scope of this definition is more or less confined to the decision-making process.

- "Conflict is a struggle of values, or claims to status, power and scarce resources in which the aims of the conflicting parties are not only to gain desired values but also to neutralise or injure or eliminate their rivals" (Coser, 1967). Although conflicts do arise from the factors such as values, power and status, there are a host of other factors that are as potent. In that sense, Coser's definition seems to be more limited and more appropriate to the general social context.

- "A situation in which the conditions, practices or goals for the different participants, are inherently incompatible" (Smith, 1966.p.511). "Conflict is described as a resultant of antecedent conditions, affective states of the individuals involved, cognitive states of the individuals and conflictual behaviour ranging from positive resistance to overt aggression" (Pondy, 1967). Pondy has mentioned four stages of conflict and distinguished a conflict aftermath which means that if the conflict is not resolved to the satisfaction of the parties, the basis for more conflict may be established. These two definitions in question are quite wide and embrace both the process and the structural aspects of the conflict.

- "Conflict is viewed as the active striving for one's own preferred outcome which, if attained, precludes the attainment by others of their own preferred outcome, thereby producing hostility" (Likert and Likert, 1976). Conflict occurs when party forces its views over others to see that their preferred outcomes are achieved. Here the needs and the personalities are actively involved. Conflicts are seen to be unidirectional in that one party strives without caring the outcome or the end result. The scope of this definition seems to be rather limited.

- "Some type of incompatibility, one goal stands in the way of another…further conflict can be seen as the expression of objective, structural dichotomy especially of the asymmetrical relationships" (Galtung, 1992.p.2)
- "A conflict is brought about between two or more parties when they perceive incompatible goals, scarce rewards, and interference in achieving the goals" (Folger & Poole, 1984).
- "A situation or state between at least two interdependent parties, which characterised by perceived differences that the parties evaluate as negative. This often results in negative emotional states and behaviours intended to overcome the opposition" (Katz & Lawyer, 1993, p.7).
- "A feature of normal and frequently collaborative and creative relationships, an integral part of competitive system… conflicts… are deeply-rooted in human needs, and… frequently require major environmental and policy restructuring for their resolution" (Burton,1990,p.1).
- "The process that begins when one party perceives that the other party has negatively affected something that he or she cares about" (Thomas, 1992, p.653).
- "An interactive process manifested in incompatibility, disagreement, or dissonance within or between social entities (i.e., individual, group, organisation, etc)" (Rahim, 1992.p.16).
- "Conflict occurs as incompatibility of behaviours, cognitions and/or affect among the individuals or groups that may lead to aggressive expression of social incompatibility" (Boardman and Horowitz, 1994).

2.2 HOT AND COLD CONFLICTS

Conflict can be both a cold (cognitive) and a hot (emotional and cognitive) experience (Rahim, 1992.p.17). Cold conflict mainly involves the cognitive experiences of seeking information, examining alternatives, evaluating options, and the deciding between two or more alternatives. In cold conflict, the experience is primarily adult (mature), computational, and without emotion. On the other hand, hot conflict involves a mix of cognitive and emotional experiences within and between conflicting persons that can erupt into hurtful or extremely harmful behaviours by either party. In cold conflict, people are usually considerate, calculating, and well intentioned when they attempt to handle the conflict and to optimise their outcomes. In hot conflict, people are usually angry, frustrated, and sad and may be malicious or even murderous if the dynamics of the conflict go beyond acceptable rational and organisational constraints.

2.3 TASK, RELATIONSHIP AND PROCESS CONFLICTS

Research has shown conflict to be multidimensional (e.g. Amason, 1996; Cosier & Schwenck, 1990; Jehn, 1995; Van de Vliert & De Dreu, 1994). Thus, it is possible for one dimension of conflict to enhance effectiveness whereas another hinders consensus and commitment between group members. Based on past research (Amason & Sapienza, 1997; Cosier & Rose, 1977; Guetzkow & Gyr, 1954; Jehn, 1997; Pelled, 1996; Pinkley, 1990; Wall & Nolan, 1986) conflict in work groups is often categorised into three types – relationship, task, or process conflict and these types have tended to have different effects on team performance.

Numerous studies have investigated the relationships between different types of conflict and several personal, group and organisational outcomes–such as satisfaction, tension or commitment. Task conflict is positively related to the quality of ideas and innovation (West and Anderson, 1996), the increase of constructive debate (Jehn, Northcraft & Neale, 1999), the affective acceptance of group decisions (Amason, 1996), or the prevention of groupthink (Turner & Pratkanis, 1997). In contrast, relationship conflict is negatively associated with such variables (for a revision, see De Dreu & Van Viannen, 2001). In turn, it has been found that relationship conflict affects group climate and reduces team effectiveness (Jehn, 1997).Relationship conflict is defined as an awareness of interpersonal incompatibilities, which includes affective components such as feeling tension and friction. Empirical studies tend to show that relationship, or affective conflict is detrimental to individual and group performance, member satisfaction, and the likelihood the group will work together in the future (Jehn, 1995; Shah & Jehn, 1993). Research findings indicate that the anxiety produced by interpersonal animosity may inhibit cognitive functioning (Roseman, Wiest, & Swartz, 1994; Staw, Sandelands, & Dutton, 1981), as well as distract team members from the task, causing them to work less effectively and produce sub-optimal products (Argyris, 1962; Kelley, 1979).

By contrast, task conflict is an awareness of differences in viewpoints and opinions pertaining to the group's task. It pertains to conflict about ideas and differences of opinion about the task, similar to cognitive conflict (Amason & Sapienza, 1997). Moderate levels of task conflict have been shown to be beneficial to group performance in certain types of tasks (Jehn & Shah, 1997). Task conflict is thought to improve decision quality because the synthesis that emerges from the conflict is generally superior to the individual perspectives themselves (Mason & Mitroff, 1981; Schweiger & Sandberg, 1989; Schwenk, 1990).

These conclusions about the positive function of task conflict and the negative function of relationship conflict, has been based on research that only examined how one type of conflict affects team performance regardless of the other type (e.g. Amason, 1996; Jehn, 1994, 1995). Consistent with this perspective, scholars have tended to recommend management teams to stimulate task conflict and mitigate relationship conflict during team decision making. Nevertheless, the link between task conflict and performance is not perfect. Both kinds of conflict are related. Amason & Mooney (1999) argue that, for some time, researchers have expressed doubt that decision-making could effectively embrace one type of conflict, while simultaneously resisting the other. Evidence exists that high levels of task conflict can reduce satisfaction and commitment within the team (e.g. Amason & Sapienza, 1997). High levels of task conflict may also cause tension, antagonism, and unhappiness between group members, and an indisposition to work together in the future (Jehn, 1995).

Almost all studies, with the exception of Jehn (1995) that measured task and relationship conflict in groups, have shown positive correlations between the two types of conflict (Amason, 1996; De Dreu, 1997; Friedman, Tidd, Currall & Tsai, 2000; Janssen, Van de Vliert & Veenstra, 1999; Jehn, 1995; Jehn & Mannix, 2001; Jehn & Chatman, 2000; Pelled, Eisenhardt & Xin, 1999). A possible explanation for this incongruity is that task-related conflict may turn into relationship conflict (Jehn, 1997). Amason (1996) pointed out that cognitive criticism might easily be interpreted as a personal disapproval or a strategy to enhance one's own position at the expense of someone else's. Baron (1990) showed that a critical evaluation produced negative affective reactions regardless of performance.

Jehn and Chatman (2000), and Janssen, Van de Vliert & Veenstra (1999) view conflict as a complex system of conflict types. In this sense, conflict resolution means that one has to address relative levels of each type of conflict, rather than concentrating on one single type of conflict. Research by Simons and Peterson (2000) provides evidence that task conflict generates relationship conflict. Friedman's study (2000) seems to suggest that the relationship between task conflict and affective variables such as tension at work, are mediated by relationship conflict. However the sign of the relation is not clear; since this effect could work in either direction. For instance, a team member might try to cause difficulties or sabotage the work of a co-worker for personal motives (Jehn, 1995). While it is also possible that certain factors that arouse cognitive conflict might also trigger affective conflict (Amason, 1999).

Recent studies have sometimes identified a third, unique type of conflict, labelled process conflict. It is defined as an awareness of controversies about aspects of how task accomplishment will proceed. More specifically, process conflict pertains to issues of duty and resource delegation such as who should do what or how much one should get. For example, when group members disagree about whose responsibility it is to complete a specific duty, they are experiencing process conflict. Of the three conflict types, process conflict is the least well examined and understood. Indeed, process conflict is not always reliably distinguished from task or relationship conflict (cf. Jehn, 1997; Jehn & Mannix, 2001). In a small number of cross sectional studies, high levels of process conflict have been negatively related to performance and satisfaction (Jehn, 1997; Jehn, Northcraft, & Neale, 1999; Porter & Lilly, 1996). However, in a recent study of conflict patterns over time, high performing teams were found to have significantly higher levels of process conflict toward the end of the group interaction (but not at the beginning or middle) compared with low performing teams (Jehn & Mannix, 2001). Thus, the findings regarding process conflict are limited, and somewhat contradictory. In addition, the relationship between process conflict and lower levels of performance (at least in some studies) is problematic, especially for leaderless or self-managed teams. In such teams, some level of process conflict seems inevitable. When a team leader is present, typical process decisions made by team managers or leaders are aimed at decreasing conflict over roles and resources (Pondy, 1967), including delegating tasks and responsibilities, setting goals and deadlines, creating schedules, monitoring progress toward goals, dealing with conflicts, and making final decisions on controversial issues (Edelmann, 1993; Pondy, 1967; Wall & Callister, 1995). Because self-managing teams lack a legitimate authority, they must arrive at some agreement about how to handle these procedural matters. As such, they may be prone to repeated or escalating conflicts about process, resulting in potential performance liabilities.

2.4 INTRODUCTION TO CONFLICT MANAGEMENT

One of the most outstanding aspects of organisational conflict is that it is practically intrinsic to the life and dynamics of organisations. Conflict is present in interpersonal relations (Pruitt & Carnevale, 1993), in intragroup and intergroup relations (Jehn, 1995), in strategic decision-making (Amason, 1996), and other organisational episodes. As many authors have pointed out (De Dreu & Van de Vliert, 1997; Pondy, 1967), conflict is a phenomenon that may give rise to both beneficial and functional consequences, as well as having important positive and negative effects on individuals, groups and organisations. Therefore, it is necessary to exercise managerial aura and to have access to diagnosis and intervention tools that may allow it to handle conflicts appropriately.

Brown (1983) has suggested that, "conflict management can require intervention to reduce conflict if there is too much or intervention to promote conflict if there is too little". Argyris (1976, 1980) and, Argyris and Schon (1978) have argued that an intervention for conflict management should promote double-loop rather than single-loop learning. "Learning that results in the detection and correction of error without changing the underlying policies, assumptions, and goals may be called single-loop. Double-loop learning occurs when the detection and correction of error requires changes in the underlying policies, assumptions, and goals" (Argyris, 1980, p. 291). Along these lines Eric Neilsen (1972) outlines seven general strategies for managing intergroup conflict, which vary in the degree to which they address the particular conflict behaviours (the symptoms of the conflict) or the underlying attitudes that provoke the conflict in the first place.

Within organisational settings, managing conflict is, simply put, "doing everything in our power to ensure that its positive effects are maximised while its negative and potentially disruptive effects are minimised" (Baron, 1990.p.1). Kottler (1994) defined conflict management as diagnostic processes, interpersonal styles, negotiating strategies, and other interventions that are designed to avoid unnecessary conflict and reduce or resolve excessive conflict.

In the words of Bloomfield and Reilly, "Conflict management is the positive and constructive handling of difference and divergence. Rather than advocating methods for removing conflict, it addresses the more realistic question of managing conflict- how to deal with it in a constructive way, how to bring opposing sides together in a cooperative process, how to design a practical, achievable, cooperative system for the constructive management of difference" (Bloomfield and Reilly, 1998).

2.5 CONFLICT MANAGEMENT AND CONFLICT RESOLUTION

The difference between resolution and management of conflict is more than semantic (Boulding, 1968, p. 410; Robbins, 1978). Conflict resolution and conflict management represent current differing viewpoints of the preferred outcomes of any conflict. Conflict resolution is based on the underlying notion that conflict is essentially negative and destructive and has the primary focus of ending a specific conflict (Kottler, 1994). Conflict management operates on the basis that conflict can be positive and thus focuses on directing conflict toward constructive dialogue (Nemeth & Owens, 1996; Rybak & Brown, 1997; Tjosvold, 1991).

Conflict resolution implies reduction or elimination of conflict, whereas the management of conflict does not necessarily imply reduction in the amount of conflict. The process of conflict management is the foundation for more effective conflict resolution. A distinction between conflict management and conflict resolution is, however, needed as a starting point as the concepts often are confused or integrated in an inappropriate manner. Conflict resolution refers to the resolution of the underlying incompatibilities in a conflict and mutual acceptance of each party's existence, while conflict management refers to measures that limit, mitigate and/or contain a conflict without necessary solving it. Fred Tanner (1992) had defined conflict management as the limitation, mitigation and/or containment of a conflict without necessarily solving it. Given that conflict management is not merely the application of conflict resolution methods, it becomes obvious that the tendency to resolve once and for all the conflict is no longer valid. The actual method chosen to handle the conflict must also be appropriate to the situation. As a result, conflict management requires a contingency approach (Robbins, 1984).

The preoccupation with the industrial conflicts leads to the embezzlement or undue appropriation of conflict management methods to be not more than that of dispute resolution in many cases (Saiyaddhin, 2001). Traditional forms of dispute resolution ranging from maintaining dialogues to the active negotiated settlements and like are all address the procedural way of handling the conflicts, thus maintaining an arm's length with the other resolution/managerial practices.

2.6 CONFLICT MANAGEMENT IN PSYCHOLOGICAL LITERATURE

The study of conflict as an important variable in interactional behaviour has relatively recent antecedents in the psychological literature, although individual and social psychological theory and research began in the early decades of the twentieth century. Among these approaches and conceptions are the stimulus-response theory, the Gestalt psychology, the notion of perception and its relationship on conflict and the immediate environment, the theory of stereotypes, perception as learning, the theorem of cognitive dissonance, and the transactional psychology. One way to get access to these studies is to ask what determines and shapes conflict mechanism. Many authors suggests that three main elements- (a) functional factors-predispositions, needs, values, attitudes, etc; (b) structural factors or stimulus factors-like organisation of the stimuli, etc; (c) learning and conditioning are responsible for conflict behaviour.

Looking at the same problem from the angle of personality structure and behaviour potentials, several other classifications emphasises on motivation, cognitive structure and value orientation of general trust/mistrust. The traditional theories of perception, personality and cognitive structure, leadership, motivation, frustration, stress, anger, aggression and learning are all constituents of the psychological understanding of the conflict phenomenon. The extended psychological domains like social psychology, psychotherapy, abnormal psychology and other eulogies expand the individualistic behavioural patternalisation of the conflict behaviour.

In an effort to understand the motivations behind varying styles of conflict management (regardless of gender), researchers have refined the identification of a number of different personality traits and corresponding behavioural styles, although no clear-cut consensus is evident in the literature. Moberg (1995) posited that, "Research . . . has yet to incorporate the dominant contemporary view of personality, the five-factor model (FFM) (1998, Head note section) in relating personality to conflict management behaviours". He noted that the 'stylistic' view indicated that individuals consistently exhibited one form of dispute resolution, regardless of the circumstance or venue. Conversely, Moberg noted, Rahim (1992) contended that "contingent strategies" were employed that were *circumstance-dependent.*

Research conducted over the decade prior to publication, however, "converged around a five-factor model (FFM), proposed by Fiske (1949), Tupes and Christal (1961), and Norman (1963) in earlier writing (Digman, 1990)" (1998). These five factors were labeled as emotional stability, urgency, culture, agreeableness, and will or dependability. According to Moberg, this model became the "dominant paradigm" and "most widely accepted contemporary model of personality". Yet, as noted previously, Moberg held that researchers have not integrated this model with conflict-management styles.

2.7 EMOTIONAL EXPERIENCE AND CONFLICT MANAGEMENT

Three underlying components of emotional experience have been proposed by many psychological thinkers- Behavioural, physiological and cognitive (Brodtker & Jameson, 2001; Jones, 2000). The behavioural element refers to the way individuals express their emotional experiences. The physiological dimension pertains to the bodily experience of emotion. Finally, the cognitive component entails perception and appraisal of the particular situation in which the emotional experience has emerged.

According to appraisal theories of emotion (e.g., Lazarus, 1991), negative emotional experience stems from perceived obstruction of one's expectations and goals, whereas positive feelings result from perception of attaining one's goals or receiving unexpected gains. The current study examined the cognitive element of emotional experience, particularly its relationship with the process of conflict management.

Recent research on conflict has emphasised the role of emotions in the processes of dispute management. Specifically, several empirical studies have investigated the effect of emotions on negotiations. Druckman & Broome (1991) showed that both likings as well as familiarity were related to negotiators' flexibility and strategic choice in prenegotiation. In a similar vein, Carnevale & Isen (1986), Baron et al. (1990) and Forgas (1998) found that induction of positive mood led to more cooperative and to less competitive behaviour in negotiation than either neutral mood or negative mood. Other studies, focusing on the effects of specific emotions, demonstrated the negative impact of anger on individuals' attitudes towards the opponent, their actual behaviour in the course of conflict and on negotiation outcomes (Allred, 1999; Allred, Mallozzi, Matsui, & Raia, 1997; Baron, 1993).

Conceivably, positive emotional experience within the work team facilitated open discussion of differences, which has been found to facilitate constructive conflict management (Ayoko et al., 2002; Hobman, et al., 2003; Kay, Shapiro, & Weingart, 2001). Conversely, adverse emotional experience hindered open communication about disparities and disagreements, which in turn mitigated problem solving (Allred et al., 1997; Ayoko et al., 2002). Jones (2000) and Brodtker & Jameson (2001) have considered the role of emotional experience in conflict much more fundamental than merely serving as a moderating effect. Unlike previous research, which has treated emotions as a discrete variable, Brodtker & Jameson contended, "…that conflict is an emotionally defined and driven process, and that recognising this fact fundamentally alters one's approach to conflict management." (p. 263). Following the above argument, we considered individuals' emotional intra-team experience as a major predictor of their overall orientation to conflict management within this particular social unit. Due to the centrality of emotions in the processes of conflict, it deemed important to account for the two opposing emotional experiences towards teammates. Kelley (2001) has argued that the intra-group emotional experience results from the combination of the individual characteristics composition and the group's affective context.

2.8 SELF-EFFICACY AND CONFLICT MANAGEMENT

Self-efficacy was also found to be associated with decision-making and performance. Thus, Bandura (1997) reported that people tend to select tasks for which they believe to have high ability, while refraining from performance of activities for which they perceive having low self-efficacy. In a similar vein, Betz & Luzzo (1996) showed that individuals with a high sense of career-self-efficacy tend to set higher career aspirations, regard wider spectrum of career opportunities and attempt to muster more resources in pursuing their career goals than their counterparts with low sense of career self-efficacy.

Similar mechanisms may operate in conflict situations and negotiation processes. Presumably, individuals with a high sense of self-efficacy concerning their capabilities to manage conflicts, set high goals for negotiation outcomes and actively pursue them. In line with this contention, Brett, Pinkley, & Jackofsky (1996) showed that subjects with high self-efficacy who suggested an alternative for conflict resolution achieved higher individual or joint profit than individuals with low self-efficacy. Likewise, O'Connor & Arnold (2002) found that individuals with high self-efficacy concerning their conflict management capacities persisted in searching for a solution and were highly resistant to concessions even when negotiations reached an impasse or the conflict appeared intractable.

Moreover, two specific negotiation related efficacy beliefs - integrative self-efficacy and distributive self-efficacy predicted tactical choice at the initial negotiation stages, which in turn influenced negotiation outcomes (Sullivan, O'Connor, & Buris, 2003). Studies concerning conflict management in intact work teams showed that the level of global self-efficacy was associated with active - both constructive (integrating) as well as destructive (dominating), conflict management patterns (Eizen & Desivilya, 2003).

2.9 CONFLICT MANAGEMENT IN SOCIO-POLITICAL ADMINISTRATIVE THEMES

If we adopt the notion that conflict and its management are a central fact of every sphere of human interactions or intra-actions and search tradition for materials relevant to it, a great richness is available. Every society requires a minimum realism about its conflicts to survive in its broader sense. The analysis of the organisation and society from the standpoint of its typical conflicts is neither new nor confined to the west. For objective realism, probably, Kautilya's Arthasastra has yet to get a competent rival to surpass.

If we compare the early conflict theorists with the thinkers who laid the foundations of the organismic view of society, some interesting similarities and contrasts are evident. The ancient intellectual was nearly always drawn from the upper strata. This was almost inevitable, since except for unusual circumstances only these strata had access to the literary educations of their times. However, among the founders of conflict theory there was a far greater preponderance of secular men of affairs than among the idealistic predecessor of positivistic organicism. Even in oriental countries like India and China, thinkers like Kautilya, Fei-Tzu and Li Ssu were active men of state affairs. And in the reviving west, Heraclitus, Polybius, Ibn khaldun, and Machiavelli were all influential statesmen and proponents of innovative jurisprudence. Hellenistic thinkers including Plato, Aristotle among others, with their tangential perspectives enshrine even in these days in the academia. The conflict theorists of the past tend to develop ideas more immediately based on actual social experience and less 'out of this world'. However, such close involvement in actual affairs has its own risks. The man of affairs tends to be more skeptical of abstract conceptualisation, which appears to him to be more speculative armchair philosophising. Their thinking was likely to be dominated by the crises of the day. Much of their thoughts turn automatically, to the task of getting the job done rather than pondering its meaning- probably a leaf out of Management in these days.

Conflict theories in socio-dynamical sense are hazy, omnibus term, as we see if we consider the list of its historical representatives in western sense – Ibn Khaldun, Machiavelli, Bodin, Hobbes, Hume, Ferguson, Smith, and Malthus among others. The intellectual differences among these thinkers are at least as important as the similarities. And if we also include several varieties of Social Darwinism as well as the ideas of Gumplowicz, Ratzenhoffer, Sumner, Martindale and Small, not to speak about the works of Coser, Dahrendorf, Mills and others ;it is not difficult to see that the heading covers several heterogeneous and even contradictory perspectives for the background literature of the present study.

Conflict sociological theories tend to be only a step away from ideology, which may be defined as the organisation of ideas for the promotion of social movements or for the defense of social institutions. An ideology is a system of ideas intended to serve practice rather than to promote the aims of understanding. It may, to be sure, raise the level of understanding, but this is not the whole schema of its exclusive functionaries.

Three major forms of conflict ideology arose in the last two centuries; Marxian socialism and two forms of Social Darwinism. In this respect it is of great importance for the understanding of conflict theory to distinguish between ideology and scientific theory though they can be complimentary at most of the times. Marxism was unique among the various types of socialism in that the starting point for its development was found in the romantic idealism of Fichte (who developed the dialectic of the moral experience), Schelling (who developed a dialectic of artistic experience) and Hegel (who developed a spiritual dialectic of human history and civilisation, 1896). These idealistic and romantic philosophers popularised the concept of human society as a developing spiritual process in which every aspect was related to every other in an evolving whole. Although the process was mystically conceived, it did lead to the systematic search for new interrelations between social phenomena. There was in fact a direct kinship between Comte and Hegel in this regard.

While Marxian socialism represented a conflict ideology advanced in the name of the proletariat, both forms of Social Darwinism were developed as ideologies of the business groups of modern society. The first form of social Darwinism, already partly evident in the writings of Charles Darwin conceived human society as a product of the struggle for existence and survival of the fittest. In the works of Spencer, William Graham and others, this led to the notion that the captains of modern industry represented the fittest members of the society. The possible relevance of individual differences to social conduct was formulated and great strides were made with these three ideologies of individual differences although in a divergent scale of thought process. The on-going enterprise of the study, research, teaching and or implementing ideas concerning conflict sociology (if we can use the term in its many folded respects) had its roots in the common sense thinking about interhuman life instances even in the simplest of societies.

2.10 GANDHIAN APPROACHES TO CONFLICT MANAGEMENT

Gandhian social philosophy finds its place in recent conflict management literature. While there seems to be no direct causal link between the two bodies of knowledge, conflict management literature in the guise of modern problem-solving and win-win (as opposed to power-based and zero-sum) approaches leading to integrative conflict management (as opposed to mere compromise and distributive outcomes) strongly echoes Gandhi's own writings and the analyses of few Gandhian scholars. This is especially true in the case of non-mainstream writings that see conflict management practices as potentially being about more than the solution of immediate problems that see a broader personal and organisational transformation as the ultimate goal. It can be explored and certain theoretical connections argue that Gandhian *Satyagraha* should be squarely located within conflict management discourse. Consequently, to handle conflicts, Gandhi conceived of a novel technique which he called *Satyagraha*. Literally it means *Satya* (Truth) with *Agraha* (Firmness) or, *Unwavering search for the Truth* (Weber.T, 2001). And since the only way of getting to Truth is by Non-violence (or Love as it seems), it follows that *Satyagraha* implies an *Unwavering search for the Truth using Non-violence*. Gandhi was fond of pointing out that Satyagraha can be used in broader fields, as it can in the everyday domestic situation; however, he was careful to add "that he who fails in the domestic sphere and seeks to apply it only in the political and social sphere will not succeed". Satyagraha builds its strength upon non-violence as an essential element. Non-violence is the vital ingredient of any 'trust' – "a feeling of security and self-identity is acquired through developing a sense of security in responses of others removed in time and space." (Giddens, A.,1992).Non-violence also remains actively engaged in creating a situation that may lead to the emancipation from fear cultivating the capacity for sacrifice of the highest type in order to be free from fear. It helps in developing social capital in organisations and enables conflict management in its true and positive ways.

Thomas Weber (1999) had expressed that parts of Gandhi's norms 'seem to have given rise to or have been derived from the integrative conflict resolution literature'. The first norm relates to goals and conflicts, and states that one should act in conflicts (for one's own group or self, out of identity and out of conviction); define the conflict well (state your goals clearly, try to understand the opponent's goals, emphasise common and compatible goals, state conflict relevant facts objectively); and have a positive approach to the conflict. The second norm relates to conflict struggle and enjoins one to act non-violently in conflicts (do not harm or hurt with words, deeds or thoughts, prefer violence to cowardice, do good even to the evil doer); to act in a goal-consistent manner (by including constructive elements, acting openly rather than secretly, and by aiming the struggle at the correct point); not to cooperate with evil to be willing to sacrifice (by not escaping from punishment and being willing to die if necessary); not to polarise the situation (by provoking the opponent)and so on. The third and final norm relates to conflict resolution, and it directs that conflicts should be solved (do not continue the struggle forever, always seek negotiation, seek positive social transformation and seek transformation of both the self and the opponent); that one should insist on essentials rather than non-essentials (do not trade with essentials, be willing to compromise on non-essentials).

2.11 MAJOR COMPONENTIAL CONFLICT MANAGEMENT STUDIES IN INTERNATIONAL ARENA

Conflict is popularly believed to have its source in personal processes. The individual's personality plays a significant role in giving rise to conflict and tension (Baron 1989; Chanin and Schneer, 1984). A survey (*Accoumtemps Survey*, 1992) in which more than 200 executives participated from the 1000 largest companies in the United States found that managers spend 6.5 work weeks each year or 13.4 percent of their time dealing with personality conflicts with the employees. This figure was an increase from 5 years previously when managers devoted 9.2 percent of their time to resolving the conflict.

However, it must be remembered that conflict is caused in an interpersonal context where interpersonal variables, and communication processes contribute to a large extent (Barefoot and Strickland, 1982). Amason et al's (1995) study found that the ability to discourage interpersonal conflict, while encouraging issue related conflict is critically important to team success. Two types of conflict were identified, based on interviews with executive decision making teams in 48 small to mid size firms. C-type (Cognitive conflict) relates to substantive differences of opinion, airs concerns for different perspectives and leads to better decisions, while A-type (affective)conflict steaming from impersonal issues tends to harm team cohesiveness and hampers team consensus. It was emphasised that to reduce the impact of interpersonal conflict, team culture is essential.

Corroborating this view Cappozoli (1995) suggested that in order for an organisation to benefit from the conflict, all of its members must be taught and encouraged to use a positive conflict resolution process. Conflict is believed to be caused by groups within the organisation such as union and management (Stagner and Rosen, 1965) or two and more interest groups such as staff and line (Nelson, 1984). It was also pointed out that certain types of conflicts are unique to a given culture (Kozan, 1989). In addition, there has been a theoretical corollary put forth and illustrated by a long-term participant observation study by remote from the place of its origin. It is argued that displacement of conflict from the place of origin to an unknown and often weaker spot which needs proper release from time to time. Effective teams understand this and allow conflict to be expressed with ease and at the right target while inadequate groups not allowing this to happen routinely transfer the eruption of conflict onto wrong targets. Hence, there is a need to re-examine conflict against a broader canvass within which the antecedents of the conflict are properly identified while the possibility of its origin lying elsewhere in the organisation is to be explored. Kabanoff (1985) has broadened the arena of conflict in organisation by relating it to the structural role theory. He stressed that conflict is aroused at the psychological level as a result of incompatible expectations among people, about their influence, their desire to protect valued roles and to maintain a sense of freedom. De-Dreu (1995) tested hypotheses based upon the finding that people generally tend to evaluate behaviour, contributions and outcomes in terms of whether they are favourable to themselves. The results showed that subjects made self- serving evaluations of conflict behaviour. They viewed their own conflict behaviour as more constructive and as less destructive than those of their opponents. In addition, results revealed that self-serving evaluation of conflict behaviour is associated with increased frustration, with reduced problem-solving and with enhanced likelihood of future conflict.

Berkowitz (1962) noted that individuals can be thought of as having a hierarchy of responses for dealing with conflict situations. At the top of the hierarchy is what Blake and Mouton (1964) called a dominant style of response. This is the behaviour which an individual tends to use habitually and feels most comfortable with. If that behaviour fails to work, the individual may fall back upon the next response in this hierarchy. The individual's response hierarchy can be thought of as being partially shaped by his motives and abilities. For example, problem solving is easier for creative people (Follet, 1941) and also for people who can deal cognitively with complex issues (Schroder, 1967).

Terhune (1970) found that high conflict of interest; anticipated threats from the opponents and actual competition from opponents tend to minimise the effects of personality. Under such circumstances, non coercive responses in an individual's response hierarchy may seem to be effective (Raven, 1970) while coercive tactics and competition orientation are avoided. It has been emphasised that managers with affiliative interaction needs may be more sensitive to other's feelings and may therefore lean towards accommodation (Bass and Dunterman, 1963; Stagner, 1962). Conversely, managers who are task oriented may be more interested in confronting and solving problems (Bass and Dunterman, 1963).Sayeed(1990,1997) has documented that a reciprocal problem solving conflict management style involving confrontation, toning down differences , accommodating and compromising is related with participative, nurturing and task leadership behaviour whereas an authoritative system supported conflict style such as following rules, avoidance etc has a significant relationship with authoritarian and bureaucratic leadership behaviour.

Antonioni (1998) examined the correlations between the "Big Five Personality Factors" (extraversion, openness, conscientiousness, agreeableness, and neuroticism) vis-à-vis five conflict styles (integrating, obliging, dominating, avoiding and compromising). As noted by the author, these styles were defined by Rahim (1983). Interestingly, the author posited that the "contingency approach" (Rahim, 1992) "fails to acknowledge that some individuals may not be flexible enough to use whichever style is best for a particular situation" (1998). Earlier the structure of conflict management behaviour was purported to vary along two dimensions, viz., assertion and co-operation. Dave and Holland (1989) have reported a three dimensional structure of conflict strategies involving openness, distance and control.

Thomas and Walton(1971) in the context of inter departmental relations, found that managers reported using tactics similar to those they saw other party using; forcing was related positively to other's forcing and negatively to other's candour and accommodation. Candour was related positively to other's candour and negatively to other's forcing and avoiding. The upshot is that an individual's orientation towards others has some tendency to be reinforced by generating the predicted behaviour in others regardless of the other's original orientation. If a subordinate avoids confronting his boss because he believes that his boss would not respond to his needs, the boss in his ignorance of his subordinates' needs will not respond to him. In similar fashion Burke(1971) noted that the subordinates perceived conflict to have been handled most constructively when they perceived supervisors as adopting, accommodating or collaborating tactics and least constructively when supervisors adopted competitive or avoiding tactics.

Burke(1971) in an empirical framework investigated the five methods of resolving conflicts proposed by Blake and Mouton(1964) in the context of superior subordinate relations in two major domains, viz.,(a)making constructive use of differences and disagreements and (b) planning job targets and evaluating accomplishments. In that study, managers were asked to describe a time when they felt especially good or bad about the way an interpersonal conflict in which they were also involved and handled actively. These descriptions were then coded into one of the five methods of conflict handling as proscribed by Blake and Mouton (1964) and then categorised into effective or ineffective conflict resolutions. It was found that withdrawal, forcing and compromise were consistently negatively rated while confrontation was positively rated in these two areas. The use of smoothing was however inconsistently related to these areas.

Howat and London (1978) found that perceived conflict frequency is associated with attribution of conflict. Supervisors and subordinates who perceived higher conflict frequency tended to be seen by each other as using force, a strategy indicative of conflict intention. Supervisors who perceived higher conflict frequency were viewed by their subordinates as likely to withdraw from the conflict, whereas subordinates who perceived higher conflict were viewed by their supervisors as likely to avoid confrontation and compromise. Renwick(1975) using more or less the same methods of resolving conflicts as were identified by Blake and Mouton(1964) found that the supervisors relied more on confrontation followed by compromise and smoothing while subordinates were more likely to use compromise, confrontation and forcing in that order. In a slightly different context, London and Howat (1980) attempted to find out the relationship between three measures of employee commitment and use of five strategies of conflict management in the context of interpersonal relations between supervisor and subordinates. The study revealed that confronting was positively related to subordinates' organisational commitment was negatively related to their use of forcing.

Thomas (1976) in his two models of conflict-process and structural models explained the impact of internal dynamics of conflict episodes and environmental constraints and pressures on the behaviour of the individual as he/she tries to resolve conflict in an interpersonal context. Thomas emphasised that understanding of the events involved in an episode may help an individual to adopt functional strategies to resolve the conflict. In other words, an individual can remodify his strategies according to his understanding of the outcome of various episodes and environmental constraints. In a purchase related interdepartmental conflict study, it was observed that a substantial part of such conflict can be accounted for by organisational characteristics such as barriers to communication, the reward system and the ambiguity of departmental responsibilities (Barclay,1991). Between production and sales department conflicting interests of various types often loom large. Konjinendijk (1993) investigated how the production and sales departments of 54 small and medium size industrial companies in the Netherlands coordinate their plans and activities. The problems pointed out by the researcher were of a technical and logistic nature, influencing effective coordination of the two closely linked groups. Philips and Anderson (1992) have shown that in a research and development environment, dual advocacy mediation has shortened workplace conflict resolution time, gained greater commitment from participants and increased long term effectiveness. In this approach, each party to the conflict is assigned a mediator or specialist who functions as a personal advocate during counselling and mediation sessions.

About 500 employee relation cases at the laboratory were analysed by Barclay (1993) to determine the focus of employee and management concerns. Over 45 percent of the cases involved conflict in the area of work relations including such issues as job expectations, employee performance deficiencies, management styles, personality clashes, communication problems and role definition. How effective handling of conflicts influence decision making and smooth implementation was investigated through the analysis of 151 strategic decisions reported by senior executives in 78 multi site hotel companies (Simons, 1996). The results indicated that several types of behaviour affect both decision quality and implementation. Debate, trust, collaboration within the top management groups all improves decision quality, whereas non confrontation undermines it. The open expression of differences in executive groups is crucial to high quality decisions and resolution of differences in a way that fully addresses all concerns central to implementing those decisions. How an egocentric interpretation of fairness in bargaining groups affects the settlement process was investigated by Thompson and Lowenstein (1992). Subjects took part in interactive, dynamic industrial bargaining tasks in which their goal was to reach an agreement with an opponent. Both parties shared the costly burden of a strike if an agreement was not reached. The experiment suggested that people's ego centric interpretation of fairness hinders conflict resolution because people are reluctant to agree to what they perceive to be an equitable settlement. The relationship between organisational conflict and turnover was further investigated in a study of municipal management professionals Cook (1994). It was found that conflict was a frequent cause of turnover among municipal managers who left their positions. Situations involving policy or style disagreements between a manager and the city council were more likely to cause turnover than conflict arising from disagreement among council factions. No significant relationship was found to exist between the role orientation of managers and turnover under conflict circumstances.

Conflict management styles have been studied in diverse settings to predict a variety of organisation related variables. Nicotera (1990) demonstrated the link between ambiguity tolerance, conflict management style, argumentativeness and innovativeness or structural attributes characterised as innovative. The three variables were related to innovativeness in a predicted direction. Ambiguity tolerance, argumentativeness and a solution oriented conflict style were positively correlated. Controlling and non-confrontative conflict styles were negatively related. Weider and Hatfield (1995) in two investigations reported that subordinates using a highly obliging style with supervisors experienced more interpersonal conflict. Supervisors using a highly integrating style with subordinates reported more interpersonal and intra group conflict, low dominating subjects reported greater intra group conflict. In the second investigation highly integrating subordinates reported less interpersonal, intragroup and intergroup conflicts than low integrating subordinates. Integrating was strongly related to all organisational outcomes. Lower job satisfaction and fewer interpersonal rewards were positively related to a highly dominating style. Integrating and compromising were positively related and dominating and avoiding were negatively related to interpersonal outcomes. Morril (1993) investigated the issue of conflict management among top-level executives in two large business organisations. Ethnographic social network and perceptual data were collected on interaction patterns and executive grievance expressions. Results suggest that where executives experienced fragmented and atomised interpersonal networks, they were more likely to manage conflict without confrontation than in a network of strongly and densely connected individuals.

Kozan (1994) investigated the third party roles of Turkish managers and examined hoe these roles were related to conflict management styles used by their subordinates. Subjects' subordinates rated their conflict management styles together with rating typical third party behaviour of their supervisors. Five third party roles were distinguished – restructuring, mediating, laissez faire, autocratic and facilitating. When managers in a third party role were perceived as using mediation and facilitation, subordinates reported increased use of collaboration and compromise towards other parties in conflict situations. Witteman (1991) investigated motivation to work for the group and conflict management styles. It was found that measures were related to solution orientated.

The effect of cultural differences on inter personal conflict management was documented using American and Japanese samples (Ohbuchi and Takahashi, 1994). Japanese subjects were more likely than American subjects to make interpersonal conflict covert and tended to give maintenance of relationship and self- blame as motives for covertness. Japanese subjects also tended to use avoidance and indirect bilateral strategies more than the American subjects and showed a larger difference between desired and engaged strategy. Pinkley (1992) explored disputants' perceptions reflecting a set of dimensions of the conflict frame. Fifty undergraduates and individuals with whom they were having a conflict were asked to describe the conflict they shared. Each subject's conflict description was given a score for each of the dimensions of conflict frame. Secondary results suggest disputants with a relationship perspective were more concerned about procedural issues while those with a task frame focus on distributive goals.

Perceived attribution to superiors of masculine, feminine and androgynous traits was tested along with conflict management behaviour and effectiveness in a group of 30 managers who had been rated by 107 subordinates. Analysis indicated that managers perceived by their subordinates as being androgynous (not dominated with maternalistic and paternalistic management styles) were rated better handlers of conflict than their masculine or feminine peers (Powell, 1994).

2.12 CONFLICT MANAGEMENT STUDIES IN INDIAN CONTEXT

In the Indian context, Sharma and Samantara (1994) examined the relative efficacy of conflict management strategies in terms of their impact on various dimensions of organisational effectiveness like productivity, adaptability and flexibility. The results of the investigation revealed that confrontation or problem-solving was most significantly associated with organisational effectiveness and it was followed by smoothing behaviour. The compromising and withdrawing modes were also positively related to effectiveness, but their effects seemed to be relatively insignificant. In addition, it was noted that the forcing mode of resolving conflicts emerged as the ineffective one. Burka (1969) relied on data obtained at individual level and found that the forcing mode of resolving conflicts was highly unsatisfactory from an individual's standpoint and might have serious dysfunctional consequences. Rather his data suggested that smoothing was an effective backup mode to confrontation whereas forcing was not. These inconsistencies in research findings need to be examined specifically. The conceptualisation of conflict management by Pareek (1982) and others (Bose and Pareek, 1983) emphasised that conflict management strategies require a variable rather than a fixed approach. In order to handle conflicts within the group involving superior-subordinate interfaces or two interdependent groups, such as union and the management, eight conflict handling strategies were proposed under the ' avoidance and approach' conflict management mode(Pareek,1982). The avoidance model includes resignation, withdrawal, appeasement and diffusion, whereas the approach mode encompasses confrontation, arbitration, compromise and negotiation. It was also proposed that choosing a successful combination of conflict management strategies would be different in in-group situations, which vary from low group integration(disorganised) to the high group integration (well organised and cohesive).Application of any of these conflict handling strategies depends upon the criticality of conflict issues and in-group integration. Though the former point is apparent, in-group integration subsumes several key variables, under its fold relating to group structure, communication pattern, feelings for one another and the dynamics state attained by the group in the process of its development.

Sayeed(1990) used the eight conflict management strategies to define two major clusters of conflict- handling methods (or styles) adopted in superior -subordinate to interfaces. These clusters were found to be relatively independent of each other. Within the cluster of strategies overlapped with one another. Taking the two sets of identified strategies separately, it was argued that conflict management styles can be characterised as (a) reciprocal problem-solving style, which consisted of compromising, toning down differences, confronting and accommodating; one and (b) authoritative system supported style i.e. following rules, forcing, consulting(seeking information only or one way consultation with the subordinates) and avoiding. Mathur and Sayeed (1980) found a moderate degree of dissimilarity between the managers' own practices and their perceptions about their immediate superior regarding application of conflict management strategies in the context of job related matters. The strategies preferred by the manager were toning down the differences, confrontation, compromise and following rules. Whereas superiors preferred toning down differences, compromise, confrontation, forcing etc in their respective orders. In another study, Sayeed (1990) further showed that confronting behaviour in conflict management was preferred by the managers compared to a style of forcing or avoidance.

A case study conducted by Sharma and Samantara (1994) on the relative effectiveness of conflict resolution methods as used by Indian managers of a computer manufacturing organisation in resolving differences or disagreements with their subordinates has been quite illuminating. However there is a need to examine the effectiveness of conflict resolution methods across industries in order that the research findings obtained may be viewed as generally applicable in Indian industrial situations. Pareek (1982, 1990) while attempting to conceptualising dimensions of disruptive behaviour in groups has convincingly attempted a summary of conflict behaviour as being a function of concern, goals, resources, power, ideology, norms and relationships. These factors are only potential sources and can either escalate a conflict or dampen it depending on cognitive awareness of the source of potential conflict by the parties to the conflict or perception of cognitive dissonance within themselves. Further the different modes of conflict resolution were also attempted by these guidelines.

2.13 TEXTILE INDUSTRY IN INDIA AND CONFLICT MANAGEMENT

In Indian textile organisations, circumlocutory enquiries were made in the past comprising elements bearing adherence to the effective conflict management. Studies made by Rudrabasavarj (1972) and several textile research organisations on related domains of absenteeism, human resource development and others, shows and confirms the premonition that every individual has his own independent views on any specific issue. When two views do not concur with each other, a conflict situation arises. It may occur in the workplace or in any public place. More often the source of conflict is disagreement. The feelings of anger and frustration worsen a conflict situation. Conflict are necessarily destructive and should be avoided, advocated by many studies in past. This may arouse out of undue residual attention given to the violent conflicts between the organisational components especially to the union-management disputes. Conflicts in the workplace would have severe consequences on the health of both the organisations and the individuals. Yet some argue that conflict is essential in the workplace as it may create a healthy competition among the employees which in turn may facilitate organisational growth. Thus conflict may give rise to new ways of thinking and innovative ideas. Some of the positive effects of conflicts are – strengthening a relationship through better understanding, greater trust that may result out of resolution of the conflict, increased self-esteem for the disputing parties when the conflict is resolved with a positive outcome, enhancing creativity and productivity, etc. Negative effects of conflicts include psychological depression, anger, frustration, insecure feeling, increased stress, etc.

Studies concerning glimpses of role conflict, organisational anomalies including conflicts, improving organisational effectiveness by avoiding conflicts and advocating cooperation etc were attempted in diminutive levels in Indian textile organisations. There is partial evidence that Rudrasamy and Rao advocated an integrative mechanism for managing stress, conflict and absenteeism for the textile mills of southern India as far back as 1973 as part of the professionalisation drive of the organisations. The area of conflict management is consciously/unconsciously ignored and or underrepresented by past researchers for the reasons beyond the purview of the present study. Apart from the modular studies on dispute resolutions, human resource developmental issues and its appraisals, organisational developmental efforts as well as those are available to the general public domains, little scientific extensions were carried out in the past as far as the studies on conflict management is concerned. Though the theoretical sphere of influence of managing the conflicts might have been a topic for several decades, under-representativeness is the one word that applies to this theme more than anything else. This calls for the strengthening of the theoretical framework of facets of managing conflicts in this domicile.

CHAPTER THREE

RESEARCH METHODOLOGY

3.1 RESEARCH QUESTIONS

Conflict seems to be an inevitable aspect of organisational functioning that is frequently apparent to all its human associates. Various studies and reports have shown that there is an urgent need to rephrase and reorganise the conflict managerial practices among the human elements of major organisational/industrial units. Some of them have acquired new capabilities and accustomed to the renewed practices, whereas others (majority) have shown a declining trend on that arena. The successful and distinguishable modes identified concerning management conflicts can be better implemented in those human resource domains of retarded organisations / industries. Those expanded understanding of the issues, perceptions, personality variances, mobilisation of organisational resources and energies, clarification of competing solutions and creative searches for alternatives can very well enhance the ability to work together in the future.

Changes in sociological, economical, political, technical, industrial and other factors in a way or other explain the need to manage the conflicts and its urgent need for review, especially in this era of organisational resurgence. An attempt to study the facets of conflict management in a decent scale, the influence of internal and external forces exercising their options at the managerial measures for conflict handling as well as the manifestation of conflict and conflict management in a focused group of individuals/organisations would be a constant remainder to equip ourselves to the changing needs of our time.

People with divergent personalities, perceptions, attitudes and values occupy the positions in organisations. These positions often have differing or contrasting job charts, different levels of status attached to them and also foster occupational anomalies. An individual experience conflict due to many pressures exerted on him by many groups to which he belongs and demands of various roles he must play in the organisational framework. The higher the organisational interactions, the greater would be the chances for occupational distortions. Managers are usually trying to find ways to get organisational synergy to work and induce people to contribute their efforts to the performance of the task in hand.

A necessary part of learning management therefore is learning about the conditions under which people handle their occupational conflicts and it would be quite natural to start that with the most facilitating, influential and decision making group in the organisation – *managers*. Effectiveness of managers depends on how well they understand the underlying dynamics of the conflict, which may be all together different from its expression, and whether they can identify the crucial tactical points for intervention. This is the challenge of conflict management. An objective assessment to recognise the dynamics of conflict management in the appropriate scale is the theme behind the present study and, it attempts the same with due deliberations concerning the various research schemas and strives to imbibe the spirit of scientific enquiry with the methodological understandings. In the broader framework of the study of conflict management, the present study attempts to address the potential sources of conflict, perceptual relationship of conflict and its management and how the conflict management effectualises organisational goal attainment within the occupational framework of managers.

3.2 ENDEAVOUR OF THE STUDY

The present study aims at to identify, explore, explain, and attempt to modelise the practice of conflict management among the study group.

3.3 PURPOSE OF THE STUDY

In these challenging economic times of "doing more with less", it is imperative that organisations maximise the effectiveness of limited resources. Downturns (which spurred layoffs, hiring moratoriums, and wage freezes) have resulted in more work being allocated to fewer workers. This situation can increase tensions among the remaining staff members. To facilitate completion of the myriad projects facing companies at any one time, team members have to cover multiple assignments. Given the pressures of meeting difficult deadlines, increasing bottom-line orientation and management expectations, it is inevitable that these situational factors trigger conflicts within the workplace. It has been inferred in the past; many organisations had swung their resource to address these issues and produced organisational success. Intertwined with the concept of effective conflict management is the overarching concept of organisational success. In a smooth-running organisation, or during an economic boom, challenges can be readily managed. The true manager, however, is one who can effectively manage during difficult times, and the ability to ameliorate conflict is a key attribute of success.

With increasing advancement through the managerial ranks, it is important to understand the ways in which managers view and handle conflict based on their organisational experiences. One of the intentions of the present study is to identify attitudinal and stylistic differences, if any, in how managers manage organisational conflicts. An organisation's very existence is contingent upon meeting specific objectives; concurrently, a manager's success is predicated on meeting both individual and organisational goals. Using this definition as a benchmark, it is clear that effective conflict management is intrinsic to professional achievement and ofcourse to the respective individual levels too.

Addressing the research questions with the structured research design, the present study attempts to delve deeper into the practice of conflict management among the study group and that too exclusively focusing the occupational conflicts and its subsequent handling. Any major study relative to the attitudinal, integral and stylistic differences about handling conflicts if any, among textile mill managers in India, is yet to be actualised. It is this topic that forms the basis of this academic research. Besides addressing the academic necessities, outcomes of this study can provide some insights to managers/prospective managers with important information regarding various aspects of conflict management to assist them and to arrive at exemplary decisions.

3.4 OBJECTIVES OF THE STUDY

This study makes modest attempts–

- To identify the major source of occupational conflicts and to assess the preferred conflict handling styles and dominant conflict response pattern among the managers in identified textile mills of Coimbatore district (*study group; wide reference 3.7and 3.10*),
- To explore Gandhian and other integrated value systems as an adaptive strategy for managing occupational conflicts,
- To modelise the effectiveness of managing occupational conflicts of the study group.

3.5 STUDY AREA

The Indian Textile Industry is both unique and complex. Its predominant presence in the Indian economy is manifested in terms of its significant contribution to the gross domestic product, employment generation and foreign exchange earnings. It contributes 14 percent of the value addition in the manufacturing sector. Industrial contribution to Gross Domestic Product is 4 percent and export earnings are about 24 % of the total exports of the country (Planning Commission of

India, 2006). The complexity of this sector is on account of its sectoral dispersal matrix with the hand spun and hand woven sectors on one end of the spectrum and the capital intensive sophisticated mill sector on the other, with the decentralised powerloom and knitting sector coming in between. This sector uses a wide range of fibres ranging from natural fibres to synthetic/man-made fibres. For the production of textiles, there is intricate interplay of the processes, which include ginning, reeling, spinning, weaving, processing and garments manufacture.

The textile industry can be broadly classified into two categories, the organised mill sector and the unorganised decentralised sector. Being a controlled sector, the organised mill sector has a complete information base on the organisational set-up, machinery installation, production pattern, employment etc. However, information-base on the decentralised sector on the above parameters are inadequate and policy planning has so far been based on hearsay and rough indirect estimates. The organised sector of the textile industry represents the mills. It could be a spinning mill or a composite mill. Composite mill is one where the spinning, weaving and processing facilities are carried out under one roof. On the other hand, the decentralised sector has been found to be engaged mainly in the weaving activity, which makes it heavily dependent on the organised sector for their yarn requirements. This decentralised sector is comprised of the three major segments viz., powerloom, handloom and hosiery. In addition to the above, there are readymade garments, khadi as well as carpet manufacturing units in the decentralised sector. The Indian textile industry is structurally flawed but perpetuated and, its efficiency and growth depends upon the various corrective measures with their effectiveness. This process of improving the structural aspects of the industry was initiated in the 1985 Textile Policy, which for the first time took a sectoral view of the industry. In order to meet the changed competitive conditions ignited, including those caused by globalisation and liberalisation of the economy, there is an urgent need felt for upgrading the technology levels, human resource development, organisational development, wider componential participation, etc and some of them were addressed in a variety of ways. When compared with other successful contemporary industries, textile industry in India is yet to appreciate and adopt an integrative strategy towards the human developmental issues atleast to satisfactory levels. There seems an urgent need to empower the textile organisations in these regards. The road to success will have a logical beginning with the improvement in the human resource climate of the organised sector. The present research delineations may not advise macro scale operations and it is not at all aimed at this level of research. An inquiry based on the managerial understanding regarding the research questions with an identified population may help to arrive at a decent projection.

Coimbatore, a vibrant industrial centre and district headquarters in Southern India can be expressed as judgmental choice for its concentration of textile mills and generally branded for its managerial adaptability, be it for the autocratic hierarchy in the past or for its latest swing to the professionalistic modern management principles. This study being a genuine quest for a better managerial skill accretion in the aftermath of changed context in the managerial practices, Coimbatore would be one of the ideal locations to explore the potentialities and to better understand the emerging trends in the managerial sector.

3.6 TEXTILE INDUSTRY IN COIMBATORE REGION

Coimbatore is well known today as the textile capital of South India. The district has a geographical area of 7469 sq kms and comprises eight Taluks. The temperature ranges from 22 to 39 degree Celsius. The average rainfall is 800 mm, fairly distributed between the two monsoons. Coimbatore and Tiruppur are the largest commercial centres of the district. The other important towns are Avinashi, Pollachi and Mettupalayam. Based on the Census of 2001, the district has a population of about 6.5 million, with an overall literacy rate of 69.8 %. The work force is 45.7% of the population; 40 % of the work force is dependent on agricultural and allied activities. Employment in the organised sector per hundred thousand of population is 6137 as against the state average of 4115.

Coimbatore is known for its organised textile activities atleast from the later half of nineteenth century. By mid 1888, Sir Robert Stanes founded the Coimbatore Spinning and Weaving Mills (also known as Stanes Mills) in the northern edge of the town after starting a coffee curing factory in Trichy road. Sir Robert Stanes would later assist several others in setting up their ventures. Two more mills (Kalleeswara and Somasundra mills) were established by 1910. Lakshmi Mills Company commenced their operations in 1911 in Papanaickenpalayam. By 1930s a big chunk of textile mills were established around Coimbatore, thanks to the cheap power offered by the Pykara power station. Some of these established mills pave way for new modern variants or metomorphosised into numerous forms.

Today there are over hundred mills in and around Coimbatore region –predominantly/visibly private mills, accounting for over half the textile mills in Tamil Nadu and about 20 percent of the India's organised spinning capacity. With its spinning competence, machinery, skilled labour and good transportation, Coimbatore functions as the counterpart to Mumbai and Ahmedabad of western India. That is, the town cheapens certain resources that the organised sector supplies to the unorganised– yarn, machinery, spares and sometimes, capital for making new investments in the informal sector.

A Textile company in its broader sense can be expressed as "whose business includes yarn spun on spinning systems, weaving, knitting, processing, texturising, made-ups, readymade garmenting and composite milling operations in the organised sector". There exist atleast 192 units in the physical boundary of Coimbatore district alone, if we take the count as defined above (September, 2007). The variance among them may be attributed to organisational setup, functionaries, work process, resources, and priorities regarding their functional units. A framework, well structured with the closer quarters can only provide scope for in-depth study. Considering above facts, predominantly spinning and composite (usually spinning and weaving) mills, those are operational in Coimbatore district is scrutinised. Among them, an urgent need is felt to address the population among comparatively larger mills besides the research requirements for a consistent organisational framework. This does not mean that problems of other strata are not worthy of attention but that they do not come within the purview of the present research considerations.

From the operational feasibility analysis, the research focus was delineated with the large mills in the Coimbatore District which have a spindleage of 25000 installed capacities and in case of rotors and looms 200 and 100 (both shuttle and shuttle less) respectively (arrived at by considering past studies and operational adaptability). A guided approach to this classification was exercised by considering the past studies in textile mills as well as thoughtful reflections from textile practitioners, research groups and Governmental/other officials. A total of forty five (45) units satisfy this criterion. Those mills are sustained by an array of human workforce imbibing a typical organisational typology– top level (executives), middle (a multitudinal human force) and lower (factory workers). Every stratum in the organisation is equally important for the organisational success, atleast in theoretical considerations. A study of the present scale requires an identifiable collection of individual/group at its most potent focus and a subsequent supplementary expansion to other organisational levels. Revisiting the research considerations, there seems to address and focus on the most interactional and influential group/potential group be included. This satisfies the study accentuated on the managerial cadre- officers/managers in the organisational chart – commonly denoted as middle level managers/middle management.

3.7 STUDY GROUP

Historically, in Coimbatore textile mills, when the organisation gets larger and the top executive no longer feels he can cope effectively with all of the management work, he calls on others to help him. This ignites the process of managerial expansion in a variety of ways, including redistributing middle managerial cadres. In its most elementary form, middle management is really an extension of top management. Middle managers exist because top management cannot cope with the workload. When business grows, however, the situation becomes more complex and some significant changes can be identified in the basic role of middle management. There are three aspects of growth in an organisation that affect the role of middle management–sheer numbers, growth related to functions and organisation's physical expansion in product/service range.

Most definitions of middle management identify them as being the managers between the first level of supervision and the top level executives. This is a rough cut but reasonably accurate. The lower and upper limits need to be established to enable a scientific tune to this study. Starting from the basics, middle managers seem to manage other managers and supervisors. In this role, they appear on organisation charts as sub functional heads. In a typical textile mill, the first line supervisor who is supervising primarily exempt employees also should be included in the category of middle manager. First line supervisors who primarily supervise nonexempt employees are excluded. This does not mean that their problems are not worthy of attention but that they do not come within the purview. Thus far an attempt was made to establish the lower limit for inclusion in the middle management. In the same manner, the study needs to set an upper limit for inclusion in the middle management ranks. The following human units were excluded and considered above the upper limit–

- Heads of major functional areas (whether they are vice presidents or not) and heads of staff functions.
- Divisional general managers who have profit and loss responsibility for a segment of products or services.
- Chairman of the board, President, Executive Vice President and Group Vice President.

These people above the upper limit are those who typically have a broader role, more total view of the organisation and its operational objectives. Again it had been excluded from consideration not because they are not worthy of study but because they are beyond the scope of the present academic examination. The operational identification of the organisational functional levels in this present study can be depicted as under.

- *Top level executives*- President/Chairman of the Board and Directors, Managing Director, Vice President, General Manager, Corporate head-staff function and Divisional manager having profit and loss responsibility.
- *Managers*- Middle level- Departmental Managers (HR, Marketing, Finance, Accounts, Systems/IT, Production, etc), Factory Manager, Special Project Officers with managerial responsibility, Spinning /Weaving Master and Assistant Spinning master with managerial responsibilities.
- *General administration*- A collection of supportive, administrative and clerical workforce in each departments/sections.
- *Floor shop*- Process Supervisory workforce, Factory workers and supportive human essentials.

The major surprise of course was the number of levels occupied by middle managers. It may be caused by the factor that the number of middle management levels increased as the size and number of functions in the organisation increased. Apparently, with increased size come an increase in functional and sub functional activities, a greater number of position titles in the entire organisation and a need for the middle management structure to manage and coordinate these activities. It has to be noted that two-thirds to three-fourths of the managerial population in the focused mills are middle managers engaged in a variety of activity spheres in the organisation.

Middle level Managers were operationally identified by the official designation/authority given by the organisation. Proceeding with the organisational charts– Departmental Managers (HR, Marketing, Finance, Accounts, Systems/IT, Production, etc), Factory Manager, and Special Project Officers with managerial responsibility were naturally included. The inclusion of Assistant Spinning (or Weaving in one case) master/Spinning master was necessitated by their managerial roles in the respective organisations as well as their stature as a genuine middle level occupant. In normal cases, 8-12 middle level managers would be associated with every identified textile mill. Multiplying this figure with the number of identified forty five (45) mills, we get the estimated range of middle level managers anywhere between 360 and 540. From the initial scanning and the process-field study, operational feasibility and permission in principle was asserted with a much lesser figure of twenty one (21) mills at the maximum. This follows with the policy to stick to those twenty one mills and the projected range of middle level managers (168-252) in them for the focused approach. The initial feasibility study reflects that a typical middle level manager had atleast sixteen different organisational interactions in a single day– least to say about the conflict dynamics present in all. Considering all the above factors, it would be imperative to imbibe the scientific aspirations with its organisational/social varieties, although they are far from perfect at many times, but reliable in an overall frame. This necessitates the adoption and sustenance of the research mechanism as well as the research appropriations in every sphere of enquiry presented in this study.

3.8 RESEARCH DESIGN

A research design provides a framework for the collection and analysis of data. A choice of research design reflects decisions about the priority being given to a range of dimensions of the research process. Research considerations of the study includes–

- Expressing causal connections between variables,
- Understanding behaviour and the meaning of that behaviour in its specific organisational context,
- Leniency towards generalising to at least to one larger group (study group) of individuals and a potential to find an integrative generalisation than those actually forming part of the investigation,
- Having a temporal appreciation of organisational phenomena, and their interconnections regarding the conceptual and process considerations.

Interactional dynamics among the quantitative and qualitative variables in its synergic construing is the primary and logical pick towards research design. However, interconnections between the different features of quantitative and qualitative research are not as straightforward as theoretical considerations proclaims. Primarily, a qualitative descriptive and partial exploratory element in the study calls for the incorporation of cross-sectional design as a judicious choice. The room for the triangulation within the spheres of cross sectional design was only taken as a secondary constituent and a tributary mechanism /attribution among the componential elements were primarily followed throughout the research process. A cross-sectional design entails the collection of data on more than one case/domain of research (usually quite a lot more than one) and at a single point in time in order to collect a body of quantitative or quantifiable data in connection with two or more variables (usually many more than two), which are then examined to detect patterns of association (Greene, 1994; Alan, 2002).

Research consideration in its manifold– necessitates variation and, variation can be established only when more than one organisation is being examined besides the focus group manifestations. Further the research implies strong control over the data collection period and the required data can only be collected on variables of interest supplied at essentially the same time. A typical experimentative design may not be pragmatically appreciated and the options to strengthen the issues of reliability, replicability and validity can be satisfactorily catered by the necessary appropriation of the research instruments within cross- sectional design, makes the present one a prudently-optimistic choice. Seven componential elements– attitudinal survey research, focus group interviews, supplementary in-depth interviews, behavioural case analysis, semi structured observations, content analysis and expert opinions, constitutes *modus operandi* of the research quest towards the data acquisition strategy(*wide reference 3.12-3.18*). For the inculcation of a genuine cross-sectional approach, these components are not held in water tight compartments; rather they are tributaries to one another in variety of ways towards expanding the horizons of understanding.

3.9 RESEARCH ASSUMPTIONS

- Conflicts are multitudinal and only occupational conflicts come under the study.
- Occupational Conflicts are pre-cursive and part of organisational management.
- Occupational conflicts are essentially organisational derivatives.
- The element of conflict in its multitudinal form is necessary for conflict management.
- Individuals in the organisation have their own identifiable, preferred conflict handling strategies and or dominant conflict response patterns/styles.

3.10 OPERATIONAL DEFINITIONS

Conflict

Conflict is operationally defined as the awareness of the individual/s in the organisation, about differences, discrepancies, disagreements, incompatible wishes, or irreconcilable desires, whilst or aftermath of occupational interactions.

Conflict Management

Conflict management is operationally defined as responsiveness and or the actual execution of a situational decision consciously intended towards handling a conflict in occupational circles normally to promote positivity.

Selected Textile Mill

Textile mills are those large mills in the Coimbatore District which have a spindleage of 25000 installed capacities and in case of rotors and looms, 200 and 100 (shuttle + shuttle less) respectively(arrived at by considering past studies and functional adaptability) are operationally identified for data acquisition, totalling twenty one such units. No individual referential are entertained and camouflaged revelations are followed as permitted throughout academic reporting.

Study Group

Departmental Managers (Human Resource, Marketing, Finance, Accounts, Systems/IT, Production, etc), Factory Manager, Special Project Officers with managerial responsibility, and Assistant Spinning (or Weaving in one case) master/Spinning master of the identified textile mills constitutes the study group.

3.11 STUDY PERIOD

Conscious activation and execution of the research mechanism in terms of time frame is expressed through the phased modules in this study. Preliminary studies including Library research, operational feasibility, economic viability and similar reviews were primarily upto the September 2006. Concurrent field visits and interactive sessions aimed at fine tuning were part of this time frame and it got extended atleast to the month of December 2006. Pilot testing, preparatory analysis, adequate data acquisition, actual execution of mass data acquisition strategies, data tuning and the statistical /other inferential modules were comprehensively carried out upto the month of March 2008.

3.12 ATTITUDINAL SURVEY RESEARCH

Survey research is the method of gathering data from respondents thought to be representative of some population, using an instrument composed of closed structure or open-ended items (questions). Sample frame for the study identifies itself with the middle level managers in the initially asserted twenty one textile mills in the Coimbatore region. Pragmatic and ethical considerations virtually make it extremely difficult to employ an experimental random sample study. During the initial stages of pilot reviews, a simple random sample from a list of managers were ascertained and employed. It revealed a crucial fact that many of those selected as part of sample were unavailable/non-participative for the study due to a variety of reasons; whereas many of their colleagues (members of the study group) were willing to participate, but not selected by the randomised sample list. Sample study with due considerations to the factors enjoying the representativeness of the population seems to be more meaningful data acquisition mechanism that can enhance the statistical research measures. Thus, it became imperative to approach all the elements in the study group and to ascertain comparatively high rate of response.

Considering the numerical constituents, it may not be impossible to approach all the managers *in persona* and to exercise the survey mechanism. In this direction, all the middle level managers of identified textile mills were approached personally by the principal researcher. Out of the 196 managers from the twenty one textile mills, data from115 managers were inculcated for the attitudinal survey. It certainly is the most pragmatic sampling employable keeping the research questions and sounds more logical than the traditional convenience sampling prescribed by sampling theories. The researcher is pleased to describe the present sample as a derivation of situational pragmatism– thus suitable to be called as situational sampling. An aroma of non probability sample to the present study may bring a pragmatic statistical measurability with which inferential assistances can be sought after. This means that the present study may miss some of the probability measures and related statistical verifications. Whereas, the multi track approach to the data acquisition employing triangulations and other qualitative attempts for corroborations through other techniques may enhance or atleast put the standards at its due place concerning reliability, validity, and similar inferential substantiations. An attempt to measure the dynamics of the practice of conflict management among the study group through a sample survey certainly favours and points towards a well structured interview schedule. Considering the fact that the study attempts to explore, explain and infer the behavioural variables that are kinetically intertwined, structured mechanism is the judicious choice to this module.

Rahim's Organisational Conflict Inventory–I & II, Thomas-Kilmann Conflict Mode Instrument, various editions of Conflict Management Inventory, Kraybill's Conflict Resolution Schedule, and psychological tests of conflict management developed by psychological associations among others are widely used to ascertain the conflict management practices of the participants. Most of the inventories seem to be culture specific and predominantly employed for ascertaining the results along the lines of various predetermined conflict styles. In the Indian context- Samantara (1998), Sharma (2000), Saiyaddhin (1989), Sayeed(1996) and others administered some of the standardised tests(usually ROCI or TKI) for evaluating the conflict handling in interpersonal settings.

Most of the above studies exposed the less suitability or disadvantages of the standardised tests in a way or other. Revisiting the research questions, it is certainly a pragmatic decision to employ a tailor made questionnaire with a creative personal intervention in its administration. An exclusive questionnaire cum schedule (Conflict Management Inquest) was prepared to ascertain the personal/attitudinal insights from members of the study group regarding the intentions, dominant style leniency, response preferences, handling actuals, etc regarding conflict management practices along the tidied up variables. The tool consists of eight (8) major components besides that allotted for the demographical entries and employs ranking scales/ seven point scale/checklists and a few open ended questions with a comparatively self instructive guidelines for enumerations. Participants are approached personally by the principal researcher and after the introductory exchanges; actual administration of the tool is requested by the researcher. Adequate time (normally three to seven days) is given for the entry of the responses to every participant. Active intervention through non coercive assistance for clarification is provided if requested by the participants, by the principal researcher through face to face interactions, telephonic conversations and other modes of communication with a conscious effort to minimise the research bias and stimulate reflective responses.

3.13 FOCUS GROUPS

The focus group is a form of group interview in which there are several participants (in addition to the moderator/facilitator); there is an emphasis in the questioning on a particular fairly tightly defined topic; and the accent is upon interaction within the group and the joint construction of meaning. As such, the focus group contains elements of two methods- the group interview, in which several people discuss a number of topics; and what has been called a focused interview, in which interviewees are selected because they " are known to have been involved in a particular situation" (Merton et al. 1956) and are asked about that involvement. The focus group method appends to the focused interview the element of interaction within groups as an area of interest and is more focused than the group interview. Focus group research is based on facilitating an organised discussion with a group of individuals selected because they were believed to be representative of some class/identifiable group. Discussion is used to bring out insights and understandings in ways which simple questionnaire items may not be able to tap. Focus group research has long been prominent in managerial studies (Morgan, 1988), in part because management (especially market) researchers seek to tap emotional and unconscious motivations not amenable to the structured questions of conventional survey research.

The interaction among focus group participants brings out differing perspectives through the language and other non verbal communication that is used by the discussants. People get caught up in the spirit of group discussion and may reveal more than they would in the more formal interview setting. As discussants ask questions of each other, new avenues of exploration are opened. In discussions, multiple meanings are revealed as different discussants interpret topics of discussions in different ways. Interaction is the key to successful focus groups. In an interactive setting, discussants draw each other out, sparking new ideas. The reactions of each person spark ideas in others, and one person may fill in a gap left by others. One may even find a form of collaborative mental work, as discussants build on each other to come to a consensus that no one individual would have articulated on their own.

The present study undertakes the module of focus group within the traditions of qualitative research. This means that they are explicitly concerned to reveal how the group participants vie the issues with which they are confronted; therefore the researcher aim to provide a fairly unstructured setting for the extraction of their views and perspectives. The principal researcher acts as the moderator/facilitator in focus group sessions and guide each session attempting not to be too intrusive. Number of focus group sessions were delineated to the maximum of ten (10) comprising such collections of people as participants from the study group and their organisational co-occupants– top level executives, supervisors, factory workers and others. Prospective participants are approached and those who volunteered for the same were included with a judgemental consideration. Each session got activated for about ninety (90) minutes to the participants ranging between five (5) and nine (9). Every session proceeded adhering to the themes of the research questions with a guided intervention from the part of the facilitator. In view of the practicality and insulating from the supra-voluminous transcription process made out of the interactional recording, documentation in writing prepared by the researcher/facilitator and a supplementary rapport by atleast one participant volunteer for every session were considered as the data for the qualitative analysis.

Focus groups are not a panacea for tapping "true" feelings. People often do not themselves understand their own motivations and preferences and thus cannot articulate them well. People have complex, even conflicting motivations which may come together in unpredictable ways given only slightly varying ways of presenting a stimulus. People may give acceptable or politically correct responses in front of peers, and they may act differently in real situations compared with hypothetical ones. They may be aware of the study and tell the researcher/facilitator and others, what they believe he or she wants to hear. People tend to express views which enhance their own image of themselves, and they also may formulate opinions "on the spot", lacking any real commitment to what they say. And people may lie. Despite these, focus groups may shed some light on the near to real (atleast in theory) discussion on the theme and acts as a pragmatic rejuvenated supplementary module to the present study.

3.14 SUPPLEMENTARY IN-DEPTH INTERVIEWS

There exists a pragmatic assumption that the people who were known to have had a certain experience could be interviewed in a semi structured way about that experience. In-depth interviews provide a platform for them to be open and augment the research purpose. In-depth interview in the present study refers to a context in which interviewer has a series of questions that are in the general form of interview schedule but is able to vary the sequence of questions. The questions are frequently somewhat more general in their frame of reference from that typically found in a structured interview schedule. Also, the interviewer usually has some latitude to ask further questions in response to what are seen as significant replies.

In-depth interview sessions with a judgemental sample of human resource clusters from middle-level managers (study group); supervisors and general workers (subordinates of the study group/assistive workforce); corporate executives (superiors/the reporting authority) are sought out in this regard. Micro- meso projective causative enquiries reflecting the behavioural responses, expectations from various organisational circles; general perceived standards of responses, etc were all major workings in these sessions.

Research considerations delineated the number of sessions to not more than thirty (30) in total and ten (10) each for each identified cluster in particular. The research tool applied in this regard is not aimed to include relative parametric considerations and, certainly lacks the internal validity and /or reliability in statistical sense, but caters to supply the relevant identifiable variance (if any), among the perceived/actual situations of conflict handling; thus acting as a tributary to the research process as well as to other data anthologies.

3.15 BEHAVIOURAL CASE ANALYSIS

Case study research is a time-honored, traditional approach to the study of topics in social science and management. Because only a few instances are normally studied, the case researcher will typically uncover more variables than she or he has data points, making statistical control (ex., through multiple regressions)- an impossibility. This, however, may be considered as strength of case study research; it has the capability of uncovering causal paths and mechanisms, and through richness of detail, identifying causal influences and interaction effects which might not be treated as operationalised variables in a statistical study.

Behavioural case analysis can be expressed as the detailed and intensive analysis of a collection of managerial cases related to the practice of conflict management among the study group. Distinctive situational decisions applied/handled by the representatives of the study group are accrued by employing qualitative tools including the selective appropriation from other modules of the present study. Selective behavioural cases are analysed primarily for explanation building exercises. Under explanation-building, the researcher does not start out with a theory to be investigated. Rather, the researcher attempts to induce theory from behavioural case examples chosen to represent diversity on some dependent variable (e.g., compromising style). A list of possible causes of the dependent variable is constructed through literature review and brainstorming, and information is gathered on each cause for each selected case. The researcher then inventories causal attributes which are common to all cases, common only to cases high on the dependent variable, and common only to cases low on the dependent variable. The researcher comes to a provisional conclusion that the differentiating attributes are the significant causes, while those common to all cases are not. Explanation building process is applied normally to a range of observable instances/behavioural cases in this study. The upper ceiling for analysis fixed to the tune of fifteen (15) behavioural cases acquired through snow ball/judgemental process from the study group/co-organisational workforce, besides the initial input from the other modules of the present study. Case study approaches have difficulty in terms of evaluation of low-probability causal paths in a model as any given case selected for study may fail to display such a path, even when it exists in the larger population of potential cases. Despite these, behavioural cases acquired through triangulation method and an attempt to explanation building analysis/exercise is a judicious choice to uncover the causal effects and the dynamics in the practice of conflict management among the study group.

3.16 SEMI-STRUCTURED OBSERVATIONS

A systematic observation explicitly formulates the rules for the observation and recording of behaviour and calls for the experimental strategies in a way or other. It is not advisable and not required in the present research design and, an attempt to combine some of the good aspects of structured observations in a non-participatory mode can shed some light on the more realistic direct field experience towards finding answers to the research questions. Semi-structured observations are primarily associated with qualitative research and entail the relatively prolonged immersion of the observer in an organisational setting and the observer seeks to observe the behavioural dynamics of that setting and to elicit the meanings they attribute to their environment and behaviour, rarely participating in the happenings. An active attempt to bridge the gap between the theoretical understanding and the real practices followed through this procedure. In the present study, every attempt was taken care to keep the observer being unobtrusive and not observed by those being observed, although it seems to be a difficult task to insulate the observer and the observed in every respect. The research tool is flexible enough and not aiming to a parametrical testing or the likes and applied only during the actual/conscious data collection span. It infuses relatively pragmatic reflections from the real world and carries the multi-mode messages to the analytical responsibilities.

3.17 CONTENT ANALYSIS

Content analysis can be expressed as manual or automated coding of documents, transcripts, newspapers, or even of audio of video media to obtain counts of words, phrases, or word-phrase clusters for purposes of statistical analysis. Typically the researcher creates a dictionary which clusters words and phrases into conceptual categories for purposes of counting. Various constraints may filter the count, such as the constraint that one concept be or not be within so many words of another concept. In the business organisations, content analysis is usually applied to the permitted documents and other various reports. Content analysis module is done exactly in this manner supplemented by the facilitative data from the study group. Permitted organisational documents including reports, diaries /other documentation from the study group and other officials belong to the adorable list of data for content analysis along the lines of research questions. A searching out of underlying themes in the materials being analysed and a recursive and reflexive movement between concept development/enhancement is virtually possible through qualitative interpretation of the content analysis.

3.18 EXPERT OPINIONS/ MANAGERIAL BRAINSTORMING

The guided thoughts from the management consultants, senior managers, textile research staffs, Gandhians, research associates and other distinguished personalities is incorporated through concurrent brainstorming sessions . In addition to the brainstorm sessions, an attempt to incorporate some valuable points from the Delphi method also strengthens this module. The Delphi method is an iterative process for consensus-building among a panel of experts who are anonymous one to another. In its traditional form, extensive questionnaires are distributed to the panel; responses are synthesised and used as feedback to the panel in the next round of questionnaires, for a series of rounds. Experts on the panel do not communicate directly with each other but rather only provide responses to the Delphi administrator. Reservations about the traditional Delphi had resulted in the replacement of structured questionnaire and restrictive rounds, with no upper ceiling for the number of snow balled experts. Face to face interviews with a guided schedule, telephonic conversations, communication involving the latest information technologies including voice chat, video conference etc are explored in this regard. Longitudinal approach enabled an emphasised premeditative sessions with a group of experts and post feedback sessions with others. Selective opinions are put into further analysis, thus supplementing *model-building exercise.*

3.19 RESEARCH HYPOTHESES

Setting up and testing hypotheses is an essential part of statistical inference. In order to formulate such a test, usually some theory has been put forward, either because it is believed to be true or because it is to be used as a basis for argument, but has not been proved. The research design of the study minimises the applicability of parametrical hypothetical tests. Whereas the scope to exercise the options of hypothetical testing applied to the demographical, factorial and situational dimensions enhances the scope of the inferential prospects.

Hypothetico-deductive mechanism is used judiciously in the present research design and study encompassing the representative factorial dimensions. Hypotheses testing enshrine with a relatively creative inclusion rather than aimed at deductive expulsions of the conflict managerial effluent of the study group. It may be a better scheme to address the hypothetical statements as guided ones rather than using those for deductive treatments. Testing of the guided hypotheses and critical analysis of the same is documented in the appropriate section, sticking with the contemporary practices in research reporting.

The guided hypotheses confine the scope and focus the research objectives. Quantifiable verification can be attempted by research hypotheses expressed below. Furthermore the model building exercise is also get enhanced by the inputs received through testing these hypotheses. All the other exploratory factors of this study are attempted by cross sectional verification rather than only by hypotheses testing so as to enable a better philosophising the management of conflicts among the study group.

H1- Multitude of influential and potential factors which acts as sources of conflicts at various levels are perceived differently by the study group and a pattern of ranking preferences operate in organisational life.

H2- Initial approaches towards conflict handling are differentiative among the population along eight indicative approaches- Negotiate, Force, Compromise, Mediational, Arbitrative, Accommodate, Persuade and Avoid.

H3- The effectiveness of various procedural mechanisms to manage conflicts and its components are not equally preferred by the managers.

H4- The multitudinal effects of the preferred styles of conflict results in relational preferences among the various managerial strata

H5- Managerial stratum employ five different modes or styles of behaviour in conflict situations – competing, collaborating, compromising, accommodating, and avoiding and the situational responses along these lines of operations can be summated to identify the preferred modes or the styles as the case may be of the managerial population.

3.20 PILOT TESTING AND FINE TUNING OF DATA ACQUISITION

Concurrent field visits, preludial interactions, understanding organisational mechanism and operational feasibility reviews are all part of the present study's preliminary investigation module. Pilot testing aimed at fine tuning the tools of data acquisition became a logical extension of this to enhance the face validity of the research mechanism. Considerable changes/improvements emerged out of atleast three rounds of phased pilot studies; including those affecting the scaling procedures, data feeding, data mining, tool administration techniques and guiding the facilitative interactions in conversational sessions– among a sizeable testing sample from the study group.

3.21 RESEARCH LIMITATIONS

Multifaceted, unimaginably intertwined and one of the most complex influential organisational factor– practice of occupational conflict management seems to be an interesting thematic exploration enabling an embryonic acquisition of resources relating to it and widening academic understanding. The influential factors related to the management of conflicts and the guided research process followed throughout the present study can only bring a little facet of its multi dimensional capacities for organisational sustenance.

It may require a series of in-depth studies, not in tens or hundreds, perhaps in thousands, that ensure the academic community and practitioners to delve deeper into the less travelled paths of management disciplines like conflict management. The beauty of the research process is that every researcher wants to be as scientific as possible but ends up to select the most pragmatic research design to the field studies. Experimental studies in the field of management research in India are yet a largely unexplored arena. The resources it require, time it consumes, results it generates and inferences it assists are all mimics those scientific experiments in natural science, but still puts the bar little lesser. Perhaps cross sectional design presented in this study may be a stepping stone to experimental managerial research mechanism that can be executed in related cases of managerial research. It is neither possible nor advisable to insulate a managerial research from the managerial ethics.

Uni-disclosure of many communications, maintaining anonymity if requested/required, bureaucratically progressive interactions and a larger scope for conscious or otherwise manipulations are all questions that requires a serious thinking and may act as decelerating forces for the present study. Employing and aiming for partial triangulation with an array of data acquisition methods adding their respective tools as executed by this research design had their own advantages and disadvantages. Research design has its own limitations– limited sample frame, non probability, partially generalising in essence, over dependence on the participants, multitudinal techniques, time frame, resources, etc. Micro to Macro projections and other postulations are certainly not addressed in the research design and not advocatively comprise as a portion in the research questions.

Considering these challenges, present study can be certainly called only as an explorative (may be partially descriptive) managerial academic enquiry in the domain of conflict management in its micro level and an attempt to study the same in the Indian context addressed at this level. Abraham Maslow, who attempted to study and to make patterns concerning the motivational factors of two individuals (1948), accrued a theory of human motivation which revolutionised atleast three major disciplines–Psychology, Management and Organisational studies and had not certainly visualised its full impact while initiating his study. There is always a danger of appreciating or rejecting basic studies in organisational management going through its face value without deeply a rationalised exercise of our understanding.

It depends on multitudinal factors to fully absorb the resultants of the study and its impacts; certainly the present academic enquiry is not an exception. Despite all these reservations concerning identified pros and cons of applicability or rationale of the present study, there emerges several factors that the concerned issue or rather the domain of conflict management among the managerial workforce requires an immediate attention. An enormous organisational energy influenced and or created by conflicts and its management is certainly an area addressed by the present research design, invoking an emerging discipline atleast in Indian managerial-organisational context.

CHAPTER FOUR

CONFLICT MANAGEMENT- A THEORETICAL FRAMEWORK

4.1 CONFLICT BASICS

Conflict has been defined in many ways depending upon the suitability, focus and group interest. Some conflicts are to be characterised as intrapersonal, while others have been described as interpersonal. Some manifestations of conflict have also been recognised in the organisational context. The common element in most of the past definitions of conflict includes-

- Conflict involves opposing interests between parties in a zero sum or negative-sum situation (whatever one player wins, the other loses so that the total benefit of the two players is zero- hence the name. (Micheal Nicholson, 1970)).
- The parties must be aware of the opposing interests between them.
- Each party must believe that the other will thwart or has already thwarted her or his interests.
- Conflict is a process arising from past and current interactions and the context in which they took place.
- There seems to be a hidden message that conflict process can bring changes and a positive frame if applied appropriately.
- Although conflict is normally applied in interpersonal context, conflict process can be initiated and sustained by an individual, interpersonal level, group level or at a system level.

4.2 CHANGING VIEWS OF CONFLICT

Over the years, three distinct philosophies that refer to different managerial attitudes toward conflicts have been identified- the classical, behavioural and the modern interactionist philosophies. The classical approach viewed conflicts as an organisational abnormality, a potentially dangerous process. By this conflict induces mainly negative aspects- anger, resentment, confusion, lack of cooperation, etc. It was regarded as disrupting the smooth functioning of organisational processes and creates chaos and disorder. Conflict is 'bad' and must be avoided at all costs. The organisational structure with its clear policies, elaborated rules and well defined specifications of authority and responsibility should not permit conflicts. Conflicts will not occur if sound management principles are applied. By any chance if conflicts were to develop, the management can easily and quickly resolves them.

Managerial attitude towards conflict was one of fear and disdain. Conflict, by definition was viewed as harmful and was to be avoided as per this philosophy. Behaviouralists also had a similar jaundiced view of conflict. They also believed that conflict, by definition was harmful and should be avoided. Those who generated conflict were troublemakers and were bad for the organisation. This view reflected a "popular preoccupation with morals, human relations and cooperation and the general value that peace is good and conflict bad" (Robbins, 1991). They however accepted the fact that conflict is a natural occurrence in all organisations.

The emerging view of conflict, called as interactionist view, reverses many of the cozy nostrums of human relations management. The interactionist view recognises that the conflict occurs as a process or sequence of events. These events take place in conflict episodes between the parties. Whenever the interactions happen, there exist a wider scope for conflict and its management of the same in organisational context was highly appreciated by this perspective. The process of conflict does not occur in a vacuum. Rather they are shaped by structural parameters of the system, the relatively fixed or slow changing conditions influencing events at the interface between the parties. It recognises that in some cases conflict may be helpful, facilitative and functional. Thus, conflict management traveled its journey through avoidance, acceptance and encouragement and stimulation. The current thought acknowledges the inevitability of conflict and focuses it as a useful tool / vehicle to shake the organisation from stereo type / contention to innovation and creativity.

4.3 ORGANISATIONAL CONFLICT IN MODERN PERSPECTIVE- INTEGRATIVE VIEW

- Conflict is not an organisational abnormality. On the other hand, it is a normal aspect of organisational intercourse. It is a fact of industrial life that must understood rather that fought.
- Conflict is inevitable, sometimes desirable. It is an inherent structural component in the organisational relations.
- Conflict is neither bad nor good for organisations. Perfect organisational health is not free from conflicts.
- Troublemakers do not always cause conflict. It is rather determined by structural factors like the design of a career structure, the physical shape of a building, etc.
- Conflict is integral to the nature of change.

4.4 WAVES OF STYLE AND AMOUNT OF CONFLICT

Studies on the management of organisational conflict have taken two directions. Some researchers have attempted to measure the amount of conflict at various organisational levels and to explore the sources of such conflict. Implicit in these studies is that a moderate amount of conflict may be maintained for increasing organisational effectiveness by altering the sources of conflict. Others had attempted to relate the various styles of handling interpersonal conflict of the organisational participants and their effects on quality of problem solution or attainment of social system objectives. It becomes evident that the distinction between the 'amount of conflict' at various levels and the styles of handling interpersonal conflict is essential for a proper understanding of the nature of conflict management. In recent years, some researchers have used the indices of tension, annoyance, disputes, distrust, disagreement, etc to measure the amount of conflict at various levels. These are measures of the amount of conflict which are quite distinct from the styles of handling conflict (Rahim, 1992).

4.5 BEHAVIOURAL AND STRUCTURAL APPROACH

There are two basic approaches to intervention in conflict- behavioural and structural (Rahim, 1977; Rahim & Bonoma, 1979). The behavioural approach attempts to improve organisational effectiveness by changing members' culture- attitudes, values, norms, beliefs, etc. The behavioural approach is mainly designed to manage conflict by enabling the organisational participants to learn the various styles of handling interpersonal conflict and the situations where they are appropriate. The technique of role analysis may be used to enable organisational members to deal with their intrapersonal conflict functionally. Other behavioural science techniques, such as transactional analysis, team building, and intergroup problem solving may be used to enable the organisational members to deal with interpersonal, intragroup, and intergroup conflicts, respectively.

The structural approach attempts to improve organisational effectiveness by changing the organisation's structural design characteristics– differentiation and integration mechanisms, system of communication, reward structure, etc. This approach mainly attempts to manage conflict by altering the amount of conflict experienced by the organisational members at various levels. The structural interventions, such as job design, provision for ombudsman, analysis of group tasks, and analysis of task interdependence of two or more groups may be used to reduce or generate conflict at intrapersonal, interpersonal, intragroup, and intergroup conflicts, respectively.

4.6 INTERACTIONIST APPROACH

Likert and Likert have extended the concept of participatory management to the areas of conflict management, and have given enough evidence to show that a more participatory style of management improves conflict management. Blake, Shepard and Mouton have suggested different approaches and styles of conflict management. They have proposed that three basic assumptions or orientations are important in relation to conflict management – (a) conflicts are inevitable and agreement is impossible ; (b) conflicts are not inevitable, and yet agreement is not possible; and (c) although there is conflict, agreement is possible. They suggest that these three orientations get combined with three degrees of active-passive attitude (active orientation having high stakes, and passive orientation having low stakes). A combination of three assumption about conflict and three orientations of activeness give nine different modes of conflict handling, they call it as modes of conflict resolution.

Thomas (1976) has suggested two main dimensions of approaching conflicts-cooperativeness (attempting to satisfy other's concerns) and assertiveness (attempting to satisfy one's own concerns). Using a grid model, these two dimensions give five strategies- avoiding (low-low), accommodation (high-low), competition (low-high), collaboration (high-high), and compromise (medium-medium). Filley (1978) has contrasted power-oriented methods with problem-solving methods of conflict management. Thomas Weber (1991) has suggested procedural way of conflict handling and included components of dispute resolution into the conflict resolution or managing the conflicts.

Pruitt (1971) made a distinction between pressure tactics and exchange-oriented tactics. Some of his exchange-oriented tactics includes unilateral concessions, informal conferences/dialogues as well as the inclusion of mediator/third party in facilitating exchanges. Pruitt has further suggested two broad categories of handling (resolving) differences of interest, bargaining and norm following. In bargaining "each party endeavours to coerce or lure its adversary into making maximum concessions while conceding as little as possible itself " (p.134), whereas in norm following " both parties attempt to locate and follow rules that are appropriate to the issue in question " (p.135). He suggests three kind of rules in norm following- content-specific rules, equity rules, and mutual responsiveness, in which each party makes concessions to the extent that the other party makes concessions to the extent that the other party demonstrates its needs for these concessions.

4.7 Approach- Avoidance Modes of Conflict Management

The assumption about conflict will mainly depend upon the perception of the other party/ group (out-group) contrasted with the party of conflict/group (in-group) as concerned. There exist two main dimensions of the perception of the out-group. It may either be perceived as always opposed to the interests of the group and as belligerent (in which case one feels the conflict is seen as inevitable), or as having its own interests, but interested in maintaining good relations (then the conflict will be perceived as a fact of life, but not inevitable). Similarly, the out-group may be perceived as unreasonable (resulting in lack of hope of any solution), or as open to reason (with resultant hope of a solution of the problem). A combination of these two types of perception gives four modes of conflict management- literally paving way for the combinations of Approach and Avoidance modes of conflict management (Pareek, 1981). This comes close to what Blake, Shepard and Mouton suggest as active-passive modes of conflict management.

Approach modes or styles may take aggressive or understanding forms and often equated with the proactive approach to manage the conflicts and attempt to take steps to recognise the problem and find the solution (Pareek, 1992). Confrontation/Competing, Compromise, Mediation, Arbitration and Negotiation are some of the well known tactics in this regard. Avoidance modes or styles of conflict management aim at active/consciously avoiding, rejecting or postponing the conflicts. Withdrawal, Resignation /Ignoring, Defusing and Temporary appeasement are all avoidance modes that are exercised among management circles. Derr (1978) has argued in favour of a contingency approach incorporating some of the major modes explained above along the dual concern model of in-group integration and criticality of the conflict issues. According to Roloff (1987), conflict suppression or avoidance provides necessary stability for individual and coordinated action, even though it may also have negative effects. As Roloff (1987) rightly points out, minimal research has focused this seemingly necessary balance between conflict avoidance and confrontation. A number of researchers also argued for the value and importance of avoidance in effective conflict management (Bergman & Volkma, 1989; Morrill & Thomas, 1992). Researchers, therefore, need to re-conceptualise the notion of conflict, and refine measures of it (Jones, 2000).

4.8 Scanning Major Theories of Conflict Management

Researchers from several academic fields have proposed theories regarding how conflicts are (or should be) managed. Distilling one comprehensive theory that incorporates all elements may not be possible, or necessary. However, opportunities to integrate theories/ models that have been heretofore viewed as parallel or even incompatible were explored, as they contribute to the ongoing scholarly goal of parsimony while simultaneously broadening our thinking about organisational conflict within the congregation of the research framework. Calling conflict an interactive state does not preclude the possibilities of intra-individual conflict, for it is known that a person often interacts with himself or herself. Organisational conflict management may be classified as managerial dynamics pertaining to the levels of intrapersonal, interpersonal, intragroup, and intergroup with its manifold avatars.

The existing theories concerning conflict management approaches in a direct and or circuitous way can be classified as content-dominant and process-dominant for academic expediency. Content-dominant theories deal with what makes conflict management, while process-dominant theories deal with how the *en route* to the conflict managerial dynamics are approached. Historically, content-dominant theories predate process-dominant theories. Content-dominant theories highlight the different aspects of conflict managerial concepts whereas, process-dominant theories refine the cognizant, preferred or imposed choice process of conflict process dynamics. Content-dominant theory only guarantees that the elemental domination of content is very much there and it does not exclude the process or other element although in varying degrees. The above factor is equally applicable to the process-dominant theories as well.

4.9 CONTENT-DOMINANT THEORIES

Major content-dominant theories include the various approach theories of organisational conflict management, realistic conflict theories, relative deprivation theory, and psycho cultural theory besides the inclusion of components of universalistic notations as well as that of normative or contingency approaches.

4.9.1 Organisational approach theories

In his review of the past and present trends in the field of conflict theory and research, Beaumont (1996) distinguished the organisation theory approach to conflict from the industrial relations approach and emphasised the importance of negotiation and networking in non union contexts. He considered the differing perspectives with each. With respect to organisation theory, he argued that before the 1960s, mainstream organisation theory essentially ignored conflict. Classics works such as those of Henri Fayol did not discuss it at all and treated organisations as apolitical systems.

The earliest references to conflict are to be found in the work of Louis Pondy (1967). Although he failed to integrate the topic into mainstream organisation theory, Pondy did make two substantiate points. First, conflict could be naturally occurring phenomenon, that is it was endemic to organisations and second, that it was not necessarily a bad thing. Pondy wrote in the 1960s which were also the high-water mark of contingency theory. The main message of his theory was that there was no one best way to manage the conflicts. This theory focused on fitting one's strategy to one's particular environment and circumstances. Contingency theory did not talk about conflict. It is only fairly recently that main-stream organisation theory has really begun to discuss conflict in an analytical way. The work of Jeffrey Pieffer (1981) was important because it stressed intra-managerial conflict. This is the perspective that holds that an organisation is , in essence a loose grouping of sectional coalition forces that there is a great deal of variance in sub unit power within organisations and that decisions have to be negotiated and bargained over. Martin (1992) distinguished the differentiative and fragmentative perspectives to the subject as standing alongside the currently popular integrationist-unitary one. In order to explain the nature of negotiation and conflict, Pieffer and his colleagues drew heavily on Emerson's (1962) perspective of power dependency. That is, A has power over B because he has control of resources that B cannot obtain from elsewhere.

Pieffer's and Martin's approaches represent a significant move away from the rational, decision making paradigm of organisations and emphasise the importance of the political model of organisations. Alongside the traditional organisational theories, which has moved from the apolitical, rationalist perspective to the sectional conflict-negotiating perspective another perspective has been discerned. This is the unitarist perspective which originated in the 1930s with Elton Mayo and the human relation school of thought. The linear development of that school of research and writing was the organisational change and development literature of the 1960s. The most recent stage of this unitarist school of thinking is represented by William Ouchi's (1981) Theory Z and the work of Peters and Waterman (1982) and their successors. These authors differ from the mainstream organisational theorists mentioned earlier in that, while they recognise conflict, they regard it as neither legitimate nor desirable. Moreover, they propose that it can be solved through increased trust and open communications. Whilst this perspective on conflict is limited, it does nevertheless recognise that conflict exists. These writers advocate an integrationist perspective on corporate culture, recommending that culture should reflect the values of senior management and be embodied in a company value statement. The human resources policy mix within the firm should be designed so as to encourage employees to have these corporate culture values incorporated. The assumption made is that high culture organisations are also high performance organisations partly at least through being conflict free.

The second body of knowledge to be considered in relation to conflict theory is industrial relations. This literature has conflict at its core. There are two perspectives within it. The first is the Marxist perspective which sees conflict as emanating from outside the organisation. It derives from wider ownership control structures within society at large. The second and more mainstream industrial relations literature derives from the pluralist tradition which sees conflict as inevitable and to some extent desirable within an organisation. Such inevitability is the result of the differences in interest between management and workers. Management is committed to change as it relates to dynamic organisational performance. The workers in contrast are more status quo- oriented requiring job security.

The pluralist perspective also makes the point that conflict arises from the superior-subordinate relationship. Once there is a hierarchy, some degree of conflict is inevitable and arguable desirable. A good pluralist will qualify that statement by saying that the conflict, in order to produce positive advantages must be functional in nature. However a pluralist cannot operationalise the notion of functional conflict. There is no empirical way of saying when the conflict is too high or too low. A pluralist talk instead about the need for institutional channels to ensure that conflict does not take an unacceptably destructive form. They traditionally look to collective bargaining and trade unionism to institutionalise and functionalise conflict.

Within the industrial relations paradigm, the pluralists differ from someone like Pieffer in trying to operationalise the determinants of conflict. Pieffer's approach goes back to the sociological perspective of Emerson's power dependency notion of control over resources and the ability to minimise organisational uncertainty. The industrial relations paradigm in contrast draws heavily on Neil Chamberlain's (1951) work, which stresses not so much intra management conflict as employee- management- union conflict. There, the emphasis is on trying to operationalise the notion of bargaining power where the perspective is on the costs of agreement relative to the costs of disagreement. Thus the union or the bargaining group will have increased power in relation to management if it can increase the costs of management disagreeing with the union's demand or lower the costs of management agreeing to the union's demand.

Beamount (1996) argued that developments such as the organisation of the future, globalisation, networking and flatter hierarchy were likely to enhance the importance of both negotiation and conflict resolution practices. This was because the more equally that power was distributed in an organisation; the more likely it was that conflicts of interests and goals would surface as open conflicts. In a sense, organisations were becoming more political. In addition, conflict was likely to become more complex in nature, as negotiation come to involve more parties and not just the union and management with their clearly defined and fixed identities.

These developments have a number of implications. First, an increase of networking by the firms, that is the use of strategic alliances across national boundaries has led to an interest in cross cultural negotiations and conflict resolution practices like that of strategic joint ventures. Weiss (1994) argued that given the diversity of interests in modern organisations, there was a need for flexible, multi-option avenues for resolving differences before they escalated into costly win-lose or lose-lose situations. Second, the increase in the number of non union associations and costs of legal cases has led to the emergence of Alternative Dispute Resolution systems in their organisations.

Alternative Dispute Resolution systems emphasise managerial practices to eliminate the root causes of problems, the use of informal participatory processes to encourage the resolving of problems close to their source and the use of trained mentors, peers, facilitators and ombudsmen to replace expensive outside legal settlements (Rowe, 1993). It is not surprising that the renewed interest in the alternative approaches expanded its horizons by the great industrial management stalwarts like Fisher (1981, 1992), Weiss (1993) among others. All have a strong emphasis on win–win bargaining as opposed to the traditional adversarial approach in their recommendations.

4.9.2 Realistic Conflict Theories

Realistic conflict theory views conflict between groups as generated by an interdependent competition for scarce resources (Bobo, 1983; Hogg & Abrams, 1988). The zero-sum competitive relationship (i.e., only one group can attain a desired goal) between the in-group and out-group is considered to be the source of conflict. The outcome of a zero-sum competition necessarily dictates that one group be higher in status than the other. The possibility of not obtaining the scarce resource thus indicates that the perceived status and value of the in-group is threatened. In an effort to retain value in the face of conflict, a threat to the value of group membership should lead to behaviours that assist the in-group in obtaining the resource. In support of this idea, the presence of realistic conflict has been found to elicit both in-group favouritism and out-group derogation. For example, in-group favouritism was found in laboratory conditions where an interdependent goal was present, compared to a condition where no goal was present (Scheepers, Spears, Doosje, & Manstead, 2002).

Brown, Condor, Mathews, Wade, and Williams (1986) found that perceived realistic conflict predicted employees' intergroup differentiation (the perception of greater differences between the in-group and a relevant out-group), a precursor to in-group favouritism. When explored in racial and ethnic group settings, realistic conflict has been found to predict prejudice towards immigrants (Bizman & Yinon, 2001; Zárate, Garcia, Garza, & Hitlan, 2004).As group members focus on the attempts to retain value by increasing in-group favouritism and out-group derogation, they will be accordingly less likely to perform behaviours that appear to help rather than hinder the out-group in the conflict. In-group members who perceive the out-group to be in competition for scarce resources are unlikely to directly aid the other group in attaining the resource.

4.9.3 Relative Deprivation Theory

Relative deprivation theory considers conflict to arise from perceptions of unequal and unfairly discrepant outcomes between groups. The group-based form of relative deprivation, fraternal relative deprivation, is based on social comparisons between one's own and other groups where one's in-group is disadvantaged by a perceived outcome inequality. Group members believe that their group deserves an outcome, and if they do not receive the outcome yet observe a referent other group unfairly receiving that outcome, they experience relative deprivation (Ellemers, 2002; Hogg & Abrams, 1988). Relative deprivation is dependent upon an outcome with two essential properties- inequality and injustice (or illegitimacy). Tyler and Blader (2003) argue that justice is central to how people construct their social identities, as justice helps maintain a secure and positive identity. Therefore, if an unjust group outcome or process is perceived, it is likely that the previously-secure identity with the group is threatened. Fraternal relative deprivation differs from the individually-based egoistic deprivation, which arises from a comparison between the self and others, not between groups. Fraternal relative deprivation has been studied as a precursor to social collective action (Wright & Tropp, 2002), especially among disadvantaged groups in society (e.g., Tougas & Veilleux, 1988). Low-status group members whose status was due to illegitimate treatment were found to discriminate more in   of the in-group when their disadvantage was seen to be less legitimate (Ellemers, Wilke, & Van Knippenberg, 1993). Resentment on behalf of the group (relative deprivation) was found to mediate the relationship between identification with a group and in-group favouritism (Mummendey, Kessler, Klink, & Mielke, 1999). Theoretical development by Wright and Tropp (2002) posits that when in-group status is illegitimate (indicating the presence of relative deprivation), groups and individuals will engage in action inconsistent with social rules.

4.9.4 Psycho cultural conflict theory

According to Marc Howard Ross (1993), a psycho cultural analysis is based on the understanding that much social action is ambiguous; this approach stresses the importance of the interpretation of words and deeds in explaining why some disputes unleash intense and violent sequences and why others do not. Thus, it is relevant to the intensity of conflicts. Contemporary psychoanalytic ideas are particularly helpful in thinking about the psycho cultural construction of social worlds (Greenberg and Mitchell 1983; Stern 1985; Volkan 1988). Those works emphasised social communication and interaction from the first days of life, placing psychological development squarely in the social realm.

Psycho cultural approach draws our attention to how early relationships create a model, or template, for later ones and provide a set of standards by which groups and individuals evaluate their social worlds. Ross (1989) further states that what individuals share is emphasised both affectively and cognitively, whereas deviations from the norm are selectively ignored or negatively reinforced as incompatible with group membership. He continues by saying that dispositions learned early in life are not only relevant on the perceptual level; they are also implicated in specific behavioural patterns which serve one throughout life, such as how to respond to perceived insults, when to use physical aggression, or whom to trust. The translation of dispositional tendencies into behavioural patterns occurs on the individual level but is fundamentally a social process; where there is social support for certain types of actions they will be learned and maintained; where they are disapproved of they become less common.

4.9.5 Universalistic theories

Universalistic theories have often been referred to as normative within the conflict literature, because they specify a single correct way of doing things and thus internalised, can lead to the formation of a norm (Lewicki, 1985; Thomas, 1982). However, the word normative is often used elsewhere simply as a synonym for prescriptive. Obviously, contingency theories and universalistic theories can be used prescriptively. In conflict literature, the word normative is used in the more restrictive sense, pertaining to norms and norm- related reasoning.

Thus Content-dominated theories may seems to focus on what makes conflict management and try to explain the facets of the constituents of management essentials for handling the conflicts at various levels.

4.10 PROCESS DOMINATED THEORIES

Process-dominant theories include the threshold theory of conflict, attribution theories, arousal and aggression theories, group coalition extension theory, extended group faultline theory, consensus and the struggle for control theory and Distraction-Conflict theories among others.

4.10.1 The threshold theory of conflict

According to Ernest Bormann, groups experience two types of social tension-primary and secondary. Primary tension occurs during the orientation phase when group members feel too restrained by the novelty of the group setting. Secondary tension usually occurs when group's routine patterns of interaction are disrupted by intense disagreement. Although Bormann admits that uncontrolled secondary conflict can destroy the group, he argues that every group has a threshold for tension that represents its optimal level of conflict among the members. Thereby the emphasis was clearly on the positive value of the conflict. Conflict, too below the optimal level; results in group apathy, boredom and lack of involvement. Prolonged conflict above the optimal level on the other hand causes shared disagreement, heightened hostility and a loss of group effectiveness. What is needed then is a balance between too little tension and too much tension. In an ideal situation, group experiences frequent episodes of conflict, these episodes have mostly positive consequences-the clarification of goals, an increased understanding of differences and points of contention, successful discussion, stimulation of interests and the release of hostility. The lively interactions enable a group to apparently manage and develop techniques that limit escalation and thereby to control the magnitude and longevity of the conflict (Tuckman, 1965; Bormann, 1975).

4.10.2 Attribution theories

According to attribution theory, which is a social psychological explanation of how people continually formulate intuitive causes of behaviours and events that transpire in the organisational set up or in the groups(Heider, 1958). During conflict, interactants make attributions about their associates' motives and intentions, and these inferences steer their interpretation of the situation. When group members argue, for example they must determine why they disagree. If members conclude that their disagreement stems merely from the group's attempts to make the right decision, the disagreement will probably not turn into true conflict. However if participants attribute the disagreement to others' incompetence, belligeance or argumentativeness- a simple disagreement can escalate into an impetuous conflict (Horai, 1977).

If the conflicting parties' attributions were always accurate, they would help interactants understand one another better and thereby function as conflict managers. Unfortunately perceptual biases regularly distort individuals' attributional inferences. One bias occurs when attributors assume that other peoples' behaviour is caused by dispositional rather than situational factors. The fundamental attribution error will point out the ill conceived notations against the other persons' personality, beliefs, attitudes, and values for the conflict to rise to alarming levels (Kelley, 1979). The distortion would be minimal when the interpersonal interactions are pleasant or interactants are careful to empathise with one another, but the effect grows stronger during conflict (Regan &Totten, 1975).

Researchers in a series of studies compared the attributions of active observers, those who not only observed others but also interacted with the others – to the attributions of passive observers, individuals who were not actually part of the group. When these two sets of observers later estimated the extent to which the behaviour of the partner was a good indicator of personality, active observers made more dispositional attributions than passive observers, provided the other party had competed. In other words the bias was greatest during conflict situations (Miller & Norman, 1975; Murata, 1982).

These findings and others suggest that people had a tendency to assume the worst about the other members in their organisations. In one study subjects played like that of a Prisoner's Dilemma Game with another whose behaviour was ranging from Competitive to altruistic. When asked to describe their partner's motives, participants were most accurate in interpreting cooperation and altruism. Apparently, the members had difficulty believing that their associates were behaving in an altruistic manner but readily believed the suggestion that their behaviours revealed conflict (Maki, Thorngate, 1979; Prunnet, 1998).

Similarly, Harold Kelley et al (1970, 1989) found that people who tend to compete with others are less accurate in their perceptions than individuals who tend to cooperate. When cooperators play with the other cooperators, their perceptions of their partner's strategy are inaccurate only less than 6% of the time. When competitors play with the cooperators, however they misinterpret their partner's strategy more than 47% of the time, mistakenly believing that the cooperators are competing.

4.10.3 Arousal and aggression Theories

As conflict escalates, anxiety and tension become more dominant (Blascovich, Nash, & Ginsburg, 1978; Van Egeren, 1979). Even when group members begin by discussing their points calmly and dispassionately, as they become locked into their positions; emotional expressions begin to replace logical discussions. Unfortunately, this emotional arousal often exacerbates the conflict. Evidence of this conflict-stimulating effect of emotional arousal comes from the studies of the arousal /aggression hypothesis. This hypothesis is based on early studies of the link between frustration and aggression (Berkowitz, 1989). When group members are unable to attain the goals they desire because of some environmental restraint or personal limitation, they sometimes experience frustration. This frustration, in turn, produces a readiness to respond in an aggressive manner that boils over into hostility if situational cues that serve as releasers are present. Recent research indicates that many unpleasant and noxious conditions, including competition, insults, failures and stress can set the stage for aggressive conflict. These aversive events work by creating a heightened emotional arousal, which is often subjectively labeled anger. This arousal then is the motivation driving the subsequent aggressive actions (Zilmann, 1983, 1996).

John French in an early laboratory study of conflict in groups (1941) demonstrated the link between arousal and aggression by examining the reactions of various groups as they worked on a series of insoluble problems. In groups composed of subjects who had never interacted before the meeting, frustration led to deep divisions in the group. In a similar study Berkowitz et al (1998) found systematic differences among the group members. When the group members knew one another before the actual interaction, the frustration did not produce as much separation between members but interpersonal aggression such as overt hostility, scapegoating and domination was relatively high.

4.10.4 Group coalition extension theory

In many instances conflict in a group occurs because members must compete for the limited organisational resources. Deutsch, a leading researcher in the area, notes that such competition creates contrient interdependence among the group members, whereas cooperation leads to promotive interdependence. Mixed- motive situations, like the prisoner's dilemma and social traps stimulate conflict because they tempt individuals to compete rather than cooperate. Once individuals begin to compete in each situation, cooperation is difficult to establish.

The use of contentious influence strategies, such as threats and punishments also tends to heighten the conflicts, particularly if all the parties in the confrontation have the capacity to threaten one another. Though the relationship between the personal characteristics of members and group behaviour is complicated, people who adopt a competitive interpersonal mode tend to generate more conflict than cooperators. The conflict when becomes visible and felt often intensifies before it begins abate. This conflict spiral is produced by a host of factors, including misperceptions, commitment, entrapment, arousal, reciprocity and coalitions. The attribution theory suggests that conflict is exacerbated by the parties' tendencies to misperceive others and to assume that the other parties' behaviour is caused by personal (dispositional) rather than situational (environmental) factors. This fundamental attribution error is particularly strong during conflict, with the result that people tend to assume the worst about other members.

When individuals defend their viewpoints in groups, attitude elaboration, the need to save face, rationalisation and reactance can all combine to increase their commitment to their position. If this commitment becomes over commitment, entrapment can occur. Further conflict is often arousing. The arousal/ aggression hypothesis predicts that group members will be ready to respond in an aggressive manner. The norm of reciprocity by sanctioning the matching of competition with the competition is partly responsible for the behavioural assimilation seen when a cooperative individual must work with a competitive one.

Although conflict may be confined during the initial stages; when coalition forms, the rest of the group is often drawn into the fracas. Coalitions represent a unique form of intragroup conflict. Forming coalition in most cases a contentious influence strategy that increases competition rather than cooperation among the members of coalition. Through the use of simulation experiments in which subjects form coalitions in order to win points, researchers have found that coalitions tend to include only the minimum number of members necessary exercising the option of cheapest winning solution, be small rather than large, include relatively weak members, exclude powerful new entrants, and differ depending on the issues of gender, race, language, etc. Bargaining theory seems to offer a better explanation of coalition process than either minimum resource theory or minimum power theory the distribution of resources gained through the joint venture be it a real or imaginary because of the coalition formation is often determined by bargaining, concessions, objections, threats and other active interventions from the members.

4.10.5 Extended group faultline theory

Using the coalition theory (Caplow, 1956; Komorita & Kravitz, 1983; Mack & Snyder, 1957; Murnighan,1978) and Schneider's attraction-selection-attrition model of organisational membership (1983), Davidson et al (1991) expanded group faultline theory and propose that if more demographic attributes align in the same way (faultline strength), group members in each subgroup will perceive the similarity within their subgroup. Since similar members are likely to interact with each other more often and find their interactions pleasant and more desirable, they will be likely to form coalitions (Byrne, 1971; Pool, 1976; Roger & Bhowmik, 1971; Stevenson, Pearce, & Porter, 1985). Due to the similarity among group members involved in coalition formation, the conflict within subgroups is apt to decline. However, the existence of coalitions is likely to amplify the salience of in-group/out-group membership causing strain and polarisation between subgroups (Hogg, Turner, & Davidson, 1990).

Once coalitions are formed, the negative effects of stereotyping, in-group favouritism and out-group hostility are likely to sharpen the boundary salience around coalitions and strengthen conflict between them. These group processes are likely to lead to intensification of conflict between subgroups and therefore, promote or activate intergroup conflict. In particular three types of conflict that have been identified in working groups, bicultural teams, and organising entities (Amason, 1996; Jehn, 1997; Jehn and Jageuri, 2001; Jehn, Northcraft, and Neale, 1999; Pelled, 1996; Shah and Jehn, 1993)as well as of inter-subgroup relationships in groups(Hogg et.al 1990) were key constituents of this theory.

4.10.6 Consensus and the struggle for control theory

Conflicts of interest can arise in teams through deliberate design. When team members have to propose as well implement projects, conflicts can reduce cooperation at the implementation stage, and lower incentives to take high effort towards conceiving a strategy. At the same time, since any member desires control at the execution stage only when there are conflicts of interest, increased conflicts can raise the competition for control through creation of superior policy. This trade-off determines whether the principal can gain from the presence of such 'beneficial conflict'. These kinds of conflicts can also be used to understand teamwork, and indeed, fractious teams may prove to be superior platforms for resolving free-rider problems when compared to individual or segregated production. Further, the principal's incentive to choose disputatious teams may be greater when team size is larger.

This theory proposes a perspective on conflict that differs, through its stress on the relation with consensus and the struggle for control, from existing functional theories (see, e.g., Coser,1956 and Simmel,1968), which typically focus on the role of conflict as an 'integrative force' (Simmel , 1955) in society. The results may be useful in comprehending some of the tensions between competition and cooperation in various team or community settings, and the role such strains play in modulating incentive problems. In the context of leadership, the analysis can help understand whether a principal should select a team whose members have well-aligned interests and therefore adopt a cooperative or consensual style of operation, or whether he should encourage 'creative tension' between them. It may also be interesting to investigate the impact of control allocation on the resolution of incentive problems in more general settings, and whether conflicts between vested competitors' influence the distribution of authority-this and many other interrelated factors are conveniently put aside for future enhancers of this theory.

Positional heterogeneity amongst team members is a common feature in many organisations. Members, even while jointly pursuing the common goal of team success, may have differing biases, opinions, interests, divisional objectives, departmental prerogatives, etc. These differences can lead to a diminution of consensus and an exacerbation of conflicts of interest, which can make teamwork difficult and lead to lower team performance. The problem of team conflict has long been recognised in studies of organisational behaviour and structure, and managerial and political leadership (see, e.g., Drucker (1974), George (1980) and Priem (1990)). Team leaders have often been criticised for permitting excessive conflicts, and been commended for adopting a more consensual approach (see, e.g., Katzenbach and Smith (1993), Kakabadse and Smyllie (1994) and Hambrick (1995)). At the same time, it has also been recognised that there may be benefits to encouraging 'productive conflict' (Brown, 1983) or 'constructive conflict' (De Janasz, Dowd and Schneider, 2001) in teams. Conflict in a group can take many forms. Disagreements that arise when one person misinterprets another's position or actions are termed false conflicts (Deutsch, 1973) or autistic conflicts (Holmes & Miller, 1976; Kriesberg, 1973). Other conflicts, sometimes called contingent conflicts, are easily solved by changing some minor situational factors. The group member who arouses the ire of others by consistently arriving for meetings ten minute late can be told to show up on time or be dropped from the group; the discord over who sits where at the rectangular table may be alleviated by moving to a round table. Such disagreements, although of some importance to the group, are easily manageable without any undue increase in group tension (Deutsch, 1973).

Escalating conflict, in contrast, can seriously disrupt the group's internal dynamics. Even when the conflict stems from a minor point of disagreement, such as how to control the flow of communication or when to break for lunch, it can lead to other, more basic points of contentiousness. More issues are brought out into the open, and soon the minor differences extent to many areas. Further members who were reluctant to break the smooth pre conflict interaction now realise that the damage is already done and they join in the fray by expressing the dislikes and disagreements that they had previously suppressed. In spite of the decelerating connotations of the conflict, disagreeing is a natural consequence of joining a group. Observers of all types of groups have documented clashes among the members and have invariably concluded that group conflict is as common as group harmony (Benn's & Shepard, 1956; Fisher, 1980; Tuckman, 1965). The dynamic nature of the group ensures continual change, but along with the change comes stresses and strains that surface in the form of conflict because their actions are perfectly coordinated, but in most groups the push and pull of interpersonal forces inevitably exerts its influence (Dahrendorf, 1958, 1959). Lewis Coser goes as far as to suggest that although conflicts can destroy a group, it can also promote group unity. The idea that conflict creates unification may seem paradoxical, but Coser observed that conflict which serve to sew the social system together by cancelling each other out, thus prevent disintegration along one primary line of cleavage (1956, p.80).

Eminent thinkers on the group philosophy have noted that interdependency among the members and the stability of a group cannot deepen until hostility has surfaced, been confronted, and been resolved (Benn &Shepard, 1956; Deutsch, 1973). Low levels of conflict in a group could be an indication of remarkably positive interpersonal relations, but it is more likely that the group members are simply uninvolved, demotivated and bored. Coser notes that the absence of conflict tells us little about the stability of the group since the more cohesive the group, the more intense is the conflict. Conflict also provides a means of venting personal hostilities but members can reduce this stress by confronting the problem and communicating dissatisfactions honestly and openly. If hostilities are never expresses in the group, they may build up to a point at which the group can no longer continue as a unit and the functioning of the group would be at its stake (Tuckman, 1965).

4.10.7 Line- staff conflict theories

In his classic study, Melville Dalton studied the conflict between line managers, those directly responsible for production, and staff managers, those not directly involved but performing an advisory or staff functions. Line managers are afraid that staff specialists will intrude on their jobs and reduce their authority and power, staff specialists complain that line managers do not make good use of them or provide them with enough authority. Dalton also found that conflict could result because staff specialists consider their knowledge is superior and up to date when compared with the line managers. Whereas the line managers had a hunch that they have the real time exposure and that brings them the real capacity to take pragmatic decisions.

Further staff member's loyalty to the company was also questioned by the line managers as they are relatively new entrants to the organisation and are alien to the customary practices that are essentially basic for their organisation. Loyalty to the discipline rather than to the organisation was also raised by the line managers against the staff specialists. On the other hand the closed mind set of the line managers were questioned by the staff specialists and thus creating every room for an active conflicting interactions within the organisation.

4.10.8 System component conflict theories

Various components in the organisation with its set of policies, procedures and the workflow mechanism are prone to conflicts in a way or other. The functional smooth inflow and organisational workings are often highly depends upon a group of factors or organisational system elements. The interrelatedness among the factors often brings friction and creates the need to reintroduce or creatively redistribute the organisational energy to more positive phases of action.

Formal conflicts within organisation arise when employees do not follow formal procedures and communication channels (Jameson, 1999). Sources of conflict may refer to different ideas, opinions, attitudes (Jehn, 1995; 1997). Managers representing various departments develop attitudes based on different cultures and beliefs (Deshpande & Webster, 1993). On another issue the fact that certain departments gather non formal power leads to high conflict intensity within organisation (Ruekert & Walker, 1987). One department that has negotiating power tries to dominate decisions using non formal power (Lawrence & Lorsch, 1967). Effectiveness of collaboration between departments is influenced by the perception of how much this collaboration is productive and satisfying for different parties (Ruekert & Walker, 1987).

When information flow and joint decision- making is underdeveloped (Kahn, 1996) while managers develop stereotypes each other lacking appreciation and trust (Souder, 1981). Cooperation between managers from different departments (sales, production, R&D, marketing) within cross-functional teams is a critical factor for success. On general joint decision making and information sharing is necessary in order to achieve competitive advantage and meet customer needs (Weinrauch & Anderson 1982). The development of participative management contributes effectively into the integration of procedures and processes (Shaw & Shaw, 1998). Under the above condition managers from different functions integrate their cultures in a higher degree, decreasing intensity of conflict and developing emotions of trust.

4.10.9 Distraction-Conflict theories

Distraction-conflict theories assume that audiences and coactors in conflictual situations increase the parties' arousal and influence in many ways their behaviour (Baron, 1986; Sanders, 1983). In contrast to earlier views, however, distraction- conflict theories suggests that such arousal stems from conflict between two tendencies- (a) the tendency to pay attention to the task being performed, and (b) the tendency to direct attention to an audience or coactors. Such conflict is arousing, and such arousal, in turn, enhances the tendency to perform dominant responses. If these are correct in a given situation, performance is enhanced; if they are incorrect, performance is impaired. While *distraction-conflict theories* may not provide a final answer to the persistent puzzle of psychosocial facilitation, it has certainly added substantially to our understanding of those processes including drive-responses, public-private behaviour, individualistic-participative behaviour and most importantly individuals' belongingness to a team/group/organisation.

4.11 CONFLICT MANAGEMENT MODELS

There exists a plethora of conflict management models. Some of them are directly addressing the conflict and others in circuitous ways. It seems that dual perceptive- explanatory models are popularly followed and widely appreciated by many practitioners and academicians. Individual as a member of the group, in an organisational context is the most addressed managerially acclaimed mechanism for determining the conflict handling strategies/styles explained through many of the models.

4.11.1 Group Identification Model

Inspection of conflict management patterns along this model was based on integration of two widely used models- the Dual Concern Model (Blake & Mouton, 1964; Pruitt & Rubin, 1986; Rahim, 1983) and the *Exit, Voice, Loyalty, Neglect Model* (EVLN Model, Rusbult, 1993), portraying individual reactions to dissatisfaction in relationships. The integrated model comprises five possible patterns of conflict management- Dominance (active-destructive), integration (active-constructive), compromising (active-constructive), obliging (passive-constructive) and avoidance (passive-destructive).The dual concern model, based on motivational dimensions - concern for self and concern for the other - contributed the situational/motivational variable, namely group identification. From the EVLN model concerning with reactions to relationship dissatisfaction, dispositional variable of global and social self-efficacy were drawn to this model by past researchers.

Group identification refers to the perceived relationship of the individual members with the specific group to which he or she belongs. It taps three dimensions- the cognitive that is the member's perception of the group as an element of the self; the affective dimension, namely attraction and positive feelings towards the group; and behavioural dimension encompassing perceived interdependence among the group members required to attain the group goals (Henry, Arrow, & Carini, 1999).

Research has indicated that a person with a higher sense of identification with the group was more likely to select cooperative alternatives, that is cooperate with other group members in contrast with individuals with lower sense of group identification (De-Cremer, 2001). In a similar vein, Rusbult (1993) found that individuals who felt highly committed to their relationships tended to exhibit constructive responses to crisis in interpersonal relationship. Consequently, it was assumed that group identification would be associated with a cooperative motivation, namely a desire to seek constructive ways to deal with intra-group conflict. Obviously the level of identification with the group constitutes a situational variable; it is determined by the particular group to which the individual belongs and her or his perceptions of that collective unit. In addition to learning about the relationship between a factor and conflict management patterns, past researchers were interested to examine the association of dispositional variables to group members' coping modes with intra-group conflict, notably the individuals' self-perceptions of social efficacy.

4.11.2 Multiple sources model

Multiple sources model of conflict proposes three fundamental causes of conflict in organisations-identity-related differences, role incompatibility, and environmental stress.

Identity-related differences- Individuals bring different personal backgrounds, experiences, and cultural values when they enter organisations thus creating their own individual and unique identities. Different socialisation processes, levels of education, and so forth, shape their experiences and values. As a result, their interpretations of events and their expectations about relationships with others in the organisation will vary considerably. Conflicts caused by incongruent personal values *that stem from* these social identities are among the most difficult to resolve because they evoke values we hold deeply.

Role Incompatibility- The complexity inherent in most organisations tends to produce conflict between members whose tasks are interdependent but whose roles are incompatible. This type of conflict is exemplified by the ubiquitous goal conflicts between line and staff, production and sales, marketing, and R and D. Each unit has different responsibilities in the organisation, and as a result each places different priorities on organisational goals (e.g., customer satisfaction, product quality, production efficiency, and compliance with government regulations). It is also typical of firms whose multiple product lines compete for scarce resources. Role incompatibility conflicts may overlap with those arising from identity differences. The personal differences among the members bring to an organisation generally remain dormant until they are triggered by an organisational catalyst, like interdependent task responsibilities. And one reason members often perceive that their assigned roles are incompatible is that they are operating from different bases of information. They communicate with different sets of people, are tied into different reporting systems, and receive instructions from different bosses.

Environmental Stress- Another major source of conflict is environmentally induced stress. Conflicts stemming from identity differences and role incompatibilities are greatly exacerbated by a stressful environment. Uncertainty in the environment also fosters conflict. When individuals find it difficult to predict what is going to happen to them from month to month, they become very anxious and prone to conflict. This type of 'frustration conflict' often stems from rapid, repeated change. If task assignments, management philosophy, accounting procedures, and lines of authority are changed frequently, members find it difficult to cope with the resulting stress, and sharp, bitter conflicts can easily erupt over seemingly trivial problems. This type of conflict is generally intense, but it dissipates quickly once a change becomes routinised, and individuals' stress levels are lowered.

4.11.3 Integrative models

The attempt to study the conflict and ways of dealing with the conflicts were attempted using integrative models by many authors. Latham (1996) modelised conflict management by combining the elements of conflict process, underlying environmental structure and behavioural levels of the parties/players. A combination of short term and long term theories of conflict management was also attempted (Thomas, 1992; Latham, 1996). Alternative approaches to conflict management goals based on the beneficiary and time horizon ventures an exceptional model and was protracted by the empirical studies (Thomas, 1992; Lewicki, 1985). *Co-ordination – conflict model* suggests an active intervention when perceptions and the feelings about a situation got distorted and requires stimulation or even resolution approaches to be exercised (Buchanan & Hucynski, 1997). A combination of personality factors (Thomas, 1992; Rahim, 1986), coordination requirements (Kanter, 1997), organisational effectiveness (Victor, 1989) and better human relationship maintenance were all integrated with the dynamics of conflict management.

4.11.4 Process models

The conflict process refers to the sequence of events that occurs during a conflict and the manner in which earlier events cause later events and outcomes and thus necessitating interventions at various levels. Models of the conflict process necessarily incorporate a number of general assumptions about human behaviour, although these assumptions are often implicit. Causal dynamics of sociopathic, normative considerations, morality and ethical issues are some of the major determinants in these models. Fishbein model (1963) which has been extensively tested in a variety of contexts views behaviour as resulting from intentions and sees intentions as shaped by the additive effects of two forms of reasoning-rational/instrumental reasoning and normative reasoning. Fishbein model is basically cognitive and enhanced by Pondy's conflict episode model (1967) inculcating the value of emotions in a conflict phenomenon. Fishbein and Ajzen (1975) have operationalised an individual's overall normative assessment of an act as the product of the perceived endorsement of the act by a given reference group and the individual's motivation to comply or identification with that group's views, summed across reference groups. Other researchers have commented on the need to add the individual's own normative standards to this equation, as in the original Fishbein formulation. This is equivalent to the common practice in role theory of regarding the focal person as receiving a sent role from the self as well as other members of one's role set affecting wider implications on the conflict management mechanism.

4.11.5 Multi dimensional models

Putnam (1988), Pickering (1989) among others critiqued the two dimensional model of conflict handling from the point of view of communication. Three levels of behavioural constructs were dealt in these models, all of which, in retrospect, involved intentions- orientations, strategic objectives, and tactical intentions. The first two of these are collapsed into strategic intentions and tactical intentions were relabeled as tactical intentions (Thomas, 1992). Orientations were in effect a kind of outcome preference, based on one's valence for his own and the other's concerns in the tradition of the dual concerns model.

Strategic objectives were also based on the perceived feasibility of different outcomes, in essence the instrumentality of attempting to achieve those outcomes. Simpler schemes were derived by Greenhalgh (1987), Masterbroek (1980), and Norem-Habeisen and Johnson (1981) implementing cooperative and confrontational behaviour models. In effect, these schemes appear to collapse or omit some of the strategic intentions in the two- dimensional models. In this connection, Rahim and Van de Vliert's (1989) suggestion that the strategic intentions available to a party may in fact simplify to trichotomies and dichotomies as a conflict escalates. Based on conflict perceived and interaction oriented, an individual opts for a strategy believed to be suitable for a particular situation. This may be called strategy attempted.

Based on the presence and absence of these factors, conflict management strategies were constructed in four possible ways (Fogler and Poole, 1984) or six ways (Barclay, 1991).There appear to be anomalies in the placement of two strategic intentions, however. The most consistent anomaly is that compromising is seen by the parties as more cooperative than its placement in these models. That is, even though compromising withholds something as well as offering something to the other, it is rated as cooperative, as is accommodating or collaborating (Kabanoff, 1987; Ruble and Thomas, 1976).

The other anomaly is restricted to the party's perception of the other's intentions. In ratings of the other's intentions, competing is seen as significantly lower on the cooperativeness continuum than these models suggests (Vliert, 1989). In other words, in ratings of the other's intentions, competing appears not to be perceived as merely uncooperative, but as more actively hostile. This is not the case in perceptions of one's own intentions.

4.11.6 Gandhian models

Thomas Weber, a great contemporary Gandhian scholar who specialises conflict resolution along Gandhian lines propagated the Message focus theory (Weber.T, 2001), a technique, appropriate in cases where personal needs rather than values or beliefs are the focus of the conflict, which allows one to express underlying conflicts, is called the "I-Message". In interpersonal conflict the initial response is often destructive, taking the form of blame which generally obscures the real issues underlying the conflict. Reformulating negative statements of blame into "I-Messages" (which explain the feelings of the speaker as the result of unacceptable behaviour by the other and give the speaker's perception of the consequences of the behaviour to themselves, rather than the more usual blaming of the other for unacceptable behaviour and its consequences), can aid the clarification of the issues and steer the conflict onto a constructive and cooperative path. "You-Messages" that are very often sent, unlike "I-Messages", tend to provoke resistance and rebellion.

Gandhi's distinctiveness lies in his "ends and means" concept. The nature of ends and means must mutually correspond. Modern conflict resolution *modus operandi* disappoints in not taking such practical Gandhian initiatives. Gandhi's conflict resolution is holistic in nature while other prevalent methods prefer to resolve a conflict in a piecemeal fashion. Gandhi aims for the highest and the best while he settles for the second best practicable option. Indeed, such a Gandhian approach is clearly missing in the modern conflict management techniques. Self-encapsulation can also occur through both ideological restraints and tactical approach. If at least one of the parties to the conflict develops an ideology that by its very nature limits the weaponry and violence used in the conflict, it is in an important sense self-encapsulating. Mahatma Gandhi's satyagraha (a word taken from Sanskrit, meaning "insistence on truth") movement in the first half of this century used such techniques, and other movements for social justice and self determination have developed variations on this theme of nonviolent direct action.

Perhaps the most obvious self-limiting aspect of Gandhi's confrontation style was its step-wise rather than spiraling escalation. Each satyagraha campaign involved a series of steps, each more challenging to the opponent than the preceding one. It would begin with negotiation and arbitration. This would be an extremely elaborate and lengthy stage including (1) on-site accumulation and analysis of facts, with opponent participation; (2) identification of interests in common with opponents; (3) formulation of a limited action goal acceptable to all parties and mutual discussion of same; and (4) a search for compromise without ceding on essentials (Naess, 1958). Gandhi did much to avoid further escalation; at this preliminary stage he established the close, cooperative, personal relationships with opponents that would later limit the antagonism normally generated by the escalation process. If in any of these stages, the conflict was resolved, those subsequent would be unnecessary. After each new step, however, there was a built-in period of withdrawal, reflection, and analysis of one's own and one's opponents' positions and tactics. Missing was the escalation of normal conflict, in which a hostile response evokes an even more hostile response in an unbroken upward spiral. This strategy maximised the role of rational and conciliatory action on the part of all concerned, while providing for an intensification of the confrontation as needed to achieve the goals of the movement.

The step-wise approach and the interaction of reflection and action allowed the movement leadership and rank-and-file participants to control, channel, and direct the dynamics of the conflict situations they had created. One might say that the movement's peculiar "self-consciousness" served to gauge the impact of each step in a campaign, to continually reassess its effectiveness and non-hostile intent, and thereby to maximise its self limiting capacity.

The step-wise approach suggests that Gandhi's model of the conflict process is phasic rather than cyclical, with a confrontation proceeding through a series of escalatory steps. In the Gandhian perspective, the conflict should lead the parties to a new level of truth, not back to the point where they began. The internalization of this ideological commitment gave satyagraha a unique form of self-control. No tight command and-control system existed within the satyagraha movement. The leader and participant roles, individual and collective behavior, the influence of norms and peer expectation were all rooted in individual and group self-control. Thus Gandhi can be expressed as both a theoretician and the practitioner of conflict management in every sense.

4.12 ORGANISATIONAL LEVELS AND CONFLICT MANAGEMENT STUDIES

Critical studies were presented by many practitioners and academicians regarding the hierarchical assumptions / organisational roles and the management of conflicts. An attempt is made in this study to critically analyse them and document those closely related ones to the broader objectives of the study for accumulation of guided understanding.

4.12.1 Intra-individualistic conflict handling

Conflicts are not limited to those that take place between individuals. In fact, conflicts those individuals experiences externally often have an internal root. At the core of many disputes between people is conflict within each/both of the protagonists. Disputants feel torn between what they want to do and what they believe they should do (Bazerman, Tenbrunsel, & Wade-Benzoni, 1998). Intrapersonal conflict is not new to psychological aspects of conflict research. Among the earliest conceptualisations is Lewin's (1935; 1951) theoretical analysis of multiple-goal conflicts, which includes the intraindividual tendency to pursue two different goals each with positive valence (approach/approach), to avoid two distinct goals each with negative valence (avoidance/avoidance), and to both pursue and avoid one particular goal having both positive and negative valence simultaneously (approach/avoidance). Higgins' (1987) review articulates a number of different dimensions of the self that create internal conflict. He describes two 'actual' selves-the kind of person an individual believes he actually is and the kind of person an individual believes that others thinks she is (Erikson, 1950/1963; Lecky, 1961; Mead, 1934; Wylie, 1979; Markus & Nurius, 1987).

Similarly, Rogers (1961) distinguishes between what others believe a person should be according to a normative standard and a person's own beliefs about what she would ideally like to be. Elaborating on Freud's (1923/1961) conceptions of the ego and superego, Schafer (1967) and Piers and Singer (1971) differentiate between the moral conscience and the self representing hopes and goals. Coombs and Avrunin (1988) drew a distinction between what they labeled Type 1 conflict-arising "within individuals because they are torn between incompatible goals" (p. 7)—and conflicts between individuals who have to settle for either the same thing (Type II conflict) or different things (Type III conflict). Decision making researchers, too, have begun to investigate how intrapersonal conflict affects behaviour.

Schelling, for example, describes intrapersonal conflict as the multiple self problems (Schelling, 1984, p. 58).At the heart of these problems is the notion that there are two selves desiring different, mutually exclusive outcomes and battling for control over behaviour (Schelling, 1980; 1982; 1984). In other words, two different utility functions exist within an individual. Metaphorically speaking, the selves give different weights to different attributes at different times (Schelling, 1984). Moreover, Schelling's model has a temporal dimension; one of the selves is focused on the present and thus favours a decision that provides immediate benefit. The other self is more future-oriented and prefers an alternative that maximises future benefit. Thus, the far-sighted selves must use a variety of pre-commitment techniques to ensure that their short-sighted selves do not prevail. Although intrapersonal conflicts have been framed as multiple selves' problems, even advocates of the metaphor (Schelling, 1984; Thaler, 1980) "do not believe that there are little selves in people with independent motives, cognitive systems, and so on" (p. 288, Loewenstein, 1996). Rather, they use this description to illustrate the internal inconsistencies that people experience in their preferences. Loewenstein (1996) goes a step further in challenging this metaphor. Specifically, he questions its utility on the grounds that it does not account for what actually takes place during intrapersonal conflict.

As an alternative explanation for what happens when people experience intrapersonal conflict, Loewenstein characterises deviations from rational behaviour as stemming from an internal conflict between a visceral response and a more reasoned cognitive response. He argues that accounting for visceral reactions provides a way of understanding and explaining cleavages between self-interest and behaviour, a problem whose explanation continues to elude decision theorists. Broadly compatible with Loewenstein's (1996) theoretical argument, we posit that people experience intrapersonal conflict as a tension between what they want to do and what they believe they should do (Bazerman et al., 1998). The want self is more impulsive and tries to satisfy short-term interests whereas the other self- *the should self*, is more reasoned and is concerned with longer-term interests. Thus, the want self is likely to be comparatively more powerful at the moment of decision than it would be either well in advance or well after the decision point.

4.12.1.1 *Managing Role conflicts*

In some instances group members may find themselves occupying several roles at the same time, with the requirements of each role making demands on their time and abilities. If the multiple activities required by one mesh with those required by the other, the individuals who adopt these roles experience few problems. If however the expectations that define the appropriate activities associated with these roles are compatible, role conflict may occur (Brief, Schuler, & Van Sell, 1981; Graen, 1976; Kahn, Wolfe, Quinn, Snoek, & Rosenthal, 1964).

Researchers have identified many varieties of role conflict, but two of the more problematic types are interrole conflict and intrarole conflict. Interrole conflict occurs when the person trying to enact two or more roles discovers that behaviours associated with one role are incompatible with those associated with the other roles (Graen, 1976; Katz & Kahn, 1978, Milles, 1996). Intrarole conflicts results from contradictory demands within a single role (Nicholson & Goh, 1983). Researchers have implicated both the role ambiguity and role conflict as potential sources of low employee morale and job stress. In one study of accountants and hospital employees, for example role stress was linked to feelings of tension, decreased job satisfaction and employee turnover (Kemery, Bedeian, Mossholder, & Touliatos, 1985). Similarly, a large scale review of forty two studies of role conflict obtained   indicates that the increases in role ambiguity and conflict were associated with an increased desire to leave the organisation and with the decreases in commitment to the organisation, involvement, satisfaction, and participation in decision making. However it also indicated that the individuals should take care while engaging in behaviours appropriate to the specific roles, because slipping into the wrong role at the wrong time can lead to considerable embarrassment (Gross &Stone, 1964).

4.12.1.2 *Managing Value conflict*

According to Milton Rokeach, a pioneering values researcher, a value is an enduring belief that a specific mode of conduct or end-state of existence is personally or socially preferable to an opposite or converse mode of conduct or end-state existence. An individual's value system is defined as an enduring organisation of beliefs concerning preferable modes of conduct or end-states of existence along a continuum of relative importance. Extensive research supports that differing value systems go a long way toward explaining individual differences in behaviour. Value- behaviour connections have been documented for a wide variety of behaviour including the active aggression. Value conflict can erupt when opposition is based on interpersonal differences in instrumental and terminal values. Instrumental values are alternative behaviour patterns or means by which an individual achieve desired results and includes such dimensions as like that of honesty, independency, and obedience. (Rokeach, 1992)

Highly appreciated terminal values-such as a sense of accomplishment, happiness, pleasure, salvation and wisdom are desired states or life goals. Further there seems to be three distinguishable forms of value conflicts- inner or intrapersonal, interpersonal and individual-organisation. The sources of these conflicts are respectively from inside the person, between people and between the person and organisation.

Inner conflict and resultant stress are usually experienced when highly regarded or preferentially valued by the individuals' instrumental and terminal values pull the individual in different directions. This is somewhat akin to role conflict. The difference lies in the locus of influence. Role conflict involves outside social or organisations' expectations, inner value conflicts involve internal priorities. The interpersonal value conflicts parallels personality conflicts. Just as people have different styles that may or may not mesh, they also embrace unique combinations of instrumental and terminal values that inevitably spark disagreement. When organisation actively pursues to inculcate certain values into their corporate culture, conflicts can occur when values espoused and enacted by the organisation collide with employees' personal values. Value clarification sessions including team building exercises, counselling and other humanistic techniques are used in various degrees by many organisations as a tactical measure to manage the value conflicts among the workforce.

4.12.2 Interpersonal/ Psycho-social conflict management

Extensive research in the fields of organisational behaviour and psychology has addressed the causes, consequences, and management of interpersonal conflict. Much of this work argues that conflicts stem from people's competing preferences for outcomes (De Dreu, Harinck, & Van Vianen, 1999; Klar, Bar-Tal, & Kruglanski, 1988; Thompson, 2001). Dealing with conflict between and among individuals can be one of the most frustrating and uncomfortable experiences for administrators. According to Schmidt and Tannenbaum (1960), when conflict occurs "strong feelings are frequently aroused, objectivity flies out the window, egos are threatened and personal relationships are placed in jeopardy" (p. 107). Robbins (1974) stated that "any attempt by an administrator to alter a specific conflict position requires that he be knowledgeable of its origin. An understanding of the source improves the probability that the proper resolution or stimulation technique will be selected" (p. 29).Individuals are in conflict when they are obstructed or irritated by another individual and inevitably react to it in a beneficial or costly way (Van de Vliert, 1997).

In a similar vein, De Dreu, Harinck and Van Vianen (1999) define conflict as the tension an individual experiences because of perceived differences with others. These definitions clearly show that workplace conflict is inextricably bound up with more or less psychic tension or conflict stress. This solidarity between conflict issues and feelings of tension and stress can be explained from occupational stress theory and research (e.g., Jex, 1998).

Although interpersonal conflict in the workplace has not been studied extensively in the occupational stress literature, there is growing evidence that this may be one of the most important stressors (Keenan & Newton, 1985; Spector & Jex, 1998). Two complementary processes may explain the close bond between conflict and feelings of arousal, tension or stress. Firstly, conflict comes hand in hand with feelings of being obstructed in one's goal-directed actions. This obstruction may trigger feelings of reduced control and increased uncertainty, two conditions that have been considered important prerequisites of a stress response (Sutton & Kahn, 1987; Quick, Quick, Nelson & Hurrell, 1997). Second, conflict threatens one's self esteem (De Dreu et al., 2002), especially when it concerns conflict with another group member.

In general, group membership fulfills a generic need to establish positive and enduring relationships with other people (Baumeister & Leary, 1985). Employees want to be liked by their colleagues because this helps them to maintain a positive social identity (Fiske, 1992). Following this line of reasoning, conflict with coworkers is stressful in itself because it undermines one's sense of self and similarity with others (Frone, 2000).

4.12.2.1 *Culture and Conflict management*

Conflict, as part of interpersonal interactions, occurs in specific cultural settings. Ross (1993) stresses that viewing conflict as cultural behaviour helps explain why disputes over seemingly similar issues can be handled so dissimilarly in different cultures. There has been numerous cross-cultural comparison studies of different conflict management strategies, most studies utilising a 'national culture' approach (e.g., Chua & Gudykunst, 1987; Nomura & Barnlund, 1983; Ting-Toomey, Gao, Trubisky, Yang, Kim, Lin, & Nishida, 1991). The findings reported in the cross-cultural conflict literature point to a picture that collectivists value harmonious interpersonal relationships with others, preferring indirect styles of dealing with conflict, and showing concern for face saving.

While research on cross-cultural styles of handling interpersonal conflict has gained increased attention recently, two major limitations exist. First, an inherent contradiction has existed in much of the work that measures cross-cultural conflict management. Conflict management style, face management, etc. are assessed as individual variables — not cultural norms. Then, researchers aggregate individual level preferences to form cultural measures. The self-construals are measured on the individual level. Hence, it is more logical to link self-construal (as a way people in different cultures conceive of the self), rather than culture level dimensions (e.g., nationality), to conflict management styles of individuals. The second limitation of the past research on cross-cultural conflict management styles stems from confusions regarding conceptualisations of conflict management styles (see Kim & Leung, 2001).

In typical studies of cross-cultural conflict management styles, researchers rely heavily on either three or five-styles of conflict inventories, which were based on two dimensions (variously called "concern for production and concern for people" or "concern for self and concern for others") (Blake & Mouton, 1964; Brown, Yelsma, & Keller, 1981; Thomas, 1976).The conceptualisation of conflict management styles based on these two dimensions may not be generalisable across cultures. For instance, while past literature (e.g., Canary & Spitzberg, 1987; Putnam &Wilson, 1982; Rahim, 1983) in interpersonal and organisational conflict tends to conceptualise the avoidance style as reflective of both low concern for self and other, the use of avoiding style in collectivistic cultures seems to be associated positively with the others-face concern dimension (see Kim & Leung, 2001; Ting Toomey, 1985, 1989). An individual is embedded within a variety of sociocultural contexts or cultures (e.g., country, ethnicity, religion, gender, family, etc). Each of these cultural contexts makes some claim on the person and is associated with a set of ideas and practices (i.e., a cultural framework) about how to be a 'good' person (Markus & Kitayama, 1998). The self, then, is an organised locus of the various, sometimes competing, and understandings of how to be a person. As such, the self functions as an individualised orienting, mediating, interpretive framework, giving shape to what a person notices and thinks about and how she perceives conflict management styles. Triandis (1989), who views the 'self concept' as a mediating variable between culture and individual behaviour, argues that the self can be construed or framed in different ways. Markus and Kitayama (1991) delineated two general 'cultural self-schemata', independent and interdependent. These two images originally were conceptualised as reflecting the emphasis on connectedness and relations often found in 'non-Western' cultures (interdependent self)and the separateness and uniqueness of the individual (independent self) stressed in 'the West'. However, members of any society are likely to vary in the degree to which they internalise these two senses of self.

In the independent construal, most representations of the self (i.e., the ways in which an individual thinks of himself or herself) have as their referent, an individual's abilities, attributes, or goals ('I am friendly' or 'I am ambitious'). These inner characteristics are the primary regulators of behaviour. The normative imperative of such persons is to become independent of others and to discover and express their own unique attributes (Marsella, DeVoss, & Hsu, 1985). This orientation has led to an emphasis on the need to pursue personal 'self actualisation' or 'self-development'. Individual weakness, in this perspective, is to be overly dependent on others or to be unassertive (Bellah, Madsen, Sullivan, Swidler, & Tipton, 1985). By contrast, in the interdependent construal, the self is connected to others; the principal components of the self are one's relationships to others (Markus & Kitayama, 1991). This is not to say that the person with an interdependent view of the self has no conception of internal traits, characteristics, or preferences that are unique to him or her, but rather that these internal, private aspects of the self are not primary forces in directing or guiding behaviour. Instead, behaviour is more significantly regulated by a desire to maintain harmony and appropriateness in relationships. Within such a construal, the self becomes most meaningful and complete when it is cast in the appropriate social relationship. So one's behaviour in a given situation may be a function more of the needs, wishes, and preferences of others than of one's own needs, wishes, or preferences. Weakness in this perspective is to be headstrong, unwilling to accommodate to the needs of others, or self-centered. The distinctions between independent and interdependent construals must be regarded as general tendencies that may emerge when the members of the culture are considered as a whole.

4.12.2.2 *Conflict management Styles*

Conflict management style is defined as the patterned responses or characteristic mode of handling conflict across a variety of communication episodes (Ting-Toomey et al., 1991). The idea that individuals have "preferred" conflict management styles or conflict tendencies has been around since at least the 1970s when Thomas and Kilmann first introduced the Thomas Kilmann Instrument, or TKI (1974; 1977). Individuals have a predominant conflict management style, but it is possible to alter conflict management styles in regards to a specific situation (Cupach & Canary, 1997; Wilmot & Hocker, 2001).Thus, conflict management style is a combination of traits (e.g., cultural background and personality) and states (e.g., situation).

In early 1940's, researchers started using a one-dimensional approach for studying ways of conflict management. In this one dimension, competition and cooperation formed as opposite poles (Deutsch, 1949). Later, Blake and Mouton (1964, 1970) proposed a two-dimensional conflict grid. Popular conflict management scales (e.g., the Rahim Organisational Conflict Inventory, Rahim, 1983; Thomas & Kilmann, 1974) rely heavily on Blake and Mouton's (1964) conceptualisation of conflict management, which yields a five-style configuration based on the two dimensions (self vs. other-concern). The first dimension explains the degree to which a person attempts to satisfy her or his own concern or own face need. The second dimension explains the degree to which a person wants to satisfy the other's face need. Combination of the two dimensions was conceptualised to result in the following styles- (a) dominating style (high self-face need and low other-face need), (b) integrating style (high self-face need and high other-face need), (c) compromising style (a mutual face-need via middle-of-the -road solutions), (d) avoiding style (a low self-face need and low other-face need), and (e) obliging style (a low self-face need and high other-face need).

Thomas (1976) considered the intentions of a party (cooperativeness, i.e., attempting to satisfy the other party's concerns; and assertiveness, i.e., attempting to satisfy one's own concerns) in classifying the modes of handling conflict into five types. Rahim and Bonoma (1979) differentiated the styles of handling conflict on two basic dimensions- concern for self and concern for others. The first dimension explains the degree (high or low) to which a person attempts to satisfy her or his own concern. The second dimension explains the degree (high or low) to which a person wants to satisfy the concern of others. It should be pointed out that these dimensions portray the motivational orientations of a given individual during conflict. The models relying on Blake and Mouton's (1964) work conceptualise avoiding (or withdrawal style) as either negative and/or destructive. According to Rahim (1983), avoiding styles reflect 'low concern for self' and 'low concern for others'. Putnam and Wilson (1982) also consider avoidance or non-confrontation as 'lose-lose' style. Thomas (1976) interprets avoiding as 'unassertive' and 'uncooperative'. Brown et al. (1981) claimed that withdrawing action means 'negative feelings' and 'low task energy'. The flavour of these scales is that confrontation is more desirable than avoidance.

Nicotera (1993) highlights possible logical flaws in existing taxonomic structures of conflict strategies. In the 'three' dimension model (other's view, own view, and emotional/relational valence) *inductively* derived from the data set, Nicotera (1993) for instance distinguishes, 'evasive' style (which is not disruptive to personal relations) from 'estranged' style (which is disruptive to personal relations) (Kim & Leung, 2001). Studies by Ruble and Thomas (1976) and Van de Vliert and Kabanoff (1990) yielded general support for these dimensions. The combination of the above dimensions includes the following conflict modes (styles)-

- **Integrating/Collaborating style** qualifies high concern for self as well as for others. Using integrating style within organisational context encourages open communication, information sharing and problem solving (Hocker &Wilmot, 1998). Integrating style is best used when conflict refers to strategic issues (Rahim, 1985). As a way to handle conflict integration includes two parameters- 1) confrontation, 2) problem solving. Confrontation includes open communication, which leads to creative problem solving (Rahim, Magner & Shapiro, 2000). Lawrence and Lorsch (1967) found this mode (style) to be more effective than others in attaining integration of the activities of different subsystems of an organisation. This style is appropriate for dealing with the strategic issues pertaining to an organisation's objectives and policies, long-range planning, etc (Rahim, Magner & Shapiro, 2000).

- **Obliging /Accommodating style** is associated with low concern for personal goals and high concern for others' goals. Organisational members try to play down differences in order to satisfy the other party's goals (Rahim, 1985). Obliging as a negotiating strategy can be used when one party has the willingness to give something to the other party in order to take something else as an exchange in the future. This style is useful when a party is not familiar with the issues involved in a conflict or the other party is right and the issue is much more important to the other party. Moreover, this style may be appropriate when a party is dealing from a position of weakness or believes that preserving relationship is important. This style involves attempting to play down the differences and emphasising commonalities to satisfy the concern of the other party. An obliging person neglects her or his own concern to satisfy the concern of the other party

- **Dominating/ Competing style** includes high concern for personal goals and low concern for others' goals. Organisational members are oriented towards a 'win-lose' strategy where the other party's goals are ignored (Rahim, Magner & Shapiro, 2000). Dominating style is often used for routine tasks or speedy decisions (Rahim, 1985). This style has been identified with win–lose orientation or with forcing behaviour to win one's position. A dominating or competing person goes all out to win her or his objective and, as a result, often ignores the needs and expectations of the other party. This style is appropriate when the issues involved in a conflict are important to the party or an unfavourable decision by the other party may be harmful to this party. This style is inappropriate when the issues involved in conflict are complex and there is enough time to make a good decision. When both parties are equally powerful, using this style by one or both parties may lead to stalemate. Also, this style is inappropriate when the issues are not important to the party (Rahim, Magner & Shapiro, 2000).

- **Avoiding style** of handling conflict includes low concern for personal goals as wells as for others' goals. Most times avoiding strategy is used for minor conflicts or for making tactical movements within organisation. When cost/ benefit analysis of handling conflict is negative the interested party avoids negotiation and postpone it for future time (Rahim, Magner & Shapiro, 2000). It has been associated with withdrawal, buck-passing, or sidestepping situations. An avoiding person fails to satisfy her or his own concern as well as the concern of the other party. This style may be used to deal with some trivial or minor issues or a cooling off period is needed before a complex problem can be effectively dealt with. Avoiding is inappropriate when the issues are important to a party (Rahim, 1982).

- **Compromising style** is associated with moderate concern for personal goals and also moderate concern for others' goals. Parties try to develop 'give and take' strategies in order to 'split the difference' and to come up with acceptable solutions (Hocker & Wilmot, 1998). Compromising style is used when organisational members have incompatible goals or equal power within business (Rahim, 1985). It involves give-and-take whereby both parties give up something to make a mutually acceptable decision. This style is useful when the goals of the conflicting parties are mutually exclusive or when both parties are equally powerful and have reached an impasse in their negotiation process. This can be used when consensus cannot be reached, the parties need a temporary solution to a complex problem, or other styles have been used and found to be ineffective in dealing with the issues effectively.

Although some behavioural scientists suggest that the integrative or problem-solving style is most appropriate for managing conflict (Blake & Mouton, 1964; Likert & Likert, 1976), it has been indicated by others that, for conflicts to be managed functionally, one style may be more appropriate than another depending upon the situation (Rahim & Bonoma, 1979; Thomas, 1977). In general, integrating and, to some extent compromising, styles are appropriate for dealing with the strategic issues. The remaining styles can be used to deal with tactical or day-to-day problems. (Rahim 1992; Thomas, 1977)

The above discussion on the styles of handling conflict and the situations where they are appropriate is a normative approach to managing conflict. Musser (1982) presented a decisional model to show how a subordinate actually chooses a behavioural style to deal with high-stakes conflict with superior(s). A subordinate selects one of the five styles of handling conflict (strategies) depending on her or his response to each of the variables, such as subordinate's desire to remain in the organisation, subordinate's perceived congruence between the superior's and her or his own attitudes and beliefs, and the subordinate's perceived protection from arbitrary action.

4.12.2.3 *Conflict management style Taxonomies*

A number of taxonomies have been advanced to describe conflict management style (see, for example, Van de Vliert, 1997 for a comprehensive review of various approaches). These have included such early efforts as flight-fight (Cannon, 1929), cooperation-competition (Deutsch, 1973), and moving away, moving toward and moving against framework (Horney, 1945). More recently, Rubin et al. (1994) view conflict management styles in terms of withdrawing, yielding, problem solving or inaction. Perhaps the most common typology used today, based on the work of Blake and Mouton (1964) views conflict management style emerging from an individual's concern for self interests versus concern for the interests of the other. Rahim (1983) categorises and measures, through the ROCI-II instrument, the following five conflict management styles based on the individual's concern for self or other- dominating style (high self/low other concern), obliging style (low self/high other concern), avoiding style (low self/other concern), integrating style (high self/other concern) and compromising style (moderate self/other concern).

Individualistic bias in past inventory of conflict management styles

The models relying on Blake and Mouton's (1964) work conceptualise avoiding (or withdrawal style) as either negative and/or destructive. According to Rahim (1983), avoiding styles reflect 'low concern for self' and 'low concern for others'. Putnam and Wilson (1982) also consider avoidance or nonconfrontation as 'lose-lose' style. Thomas (1976) interprets avoiding as 'unassertive' and 'uncooperative'. Brown et al. (1981) claimed that withdrawing action means 'negative feelings' and 'low task energy'. The flavor of these scales is that confrontation is more desirable than avoidance. Nicotera (1993) highlights possible logical flaws in existing taxonomic structures of conflict strategies. In the 'three' dimension model (other's view, own view, and emotional/relational valence) *inductively* derived from the data set, Nicotera (1993) for instance distinguishes, 'evasive' style (not disruptive to personal relations) from 'estranged'(disruptive) style of handling it .

The work in this area has been biased by the individualistic assumption that confrontation is more desirable than avoidance, which limits a full understanding of the conflict phenomenon. Hsieh, Shybut, and Lotsof (1969) captured the essence of the individualistic ideology in describing mainstream American culture as "a culture that emphasises the uniqueness, independence, and self-reliance of each individual…" It, among other things, places a high value on the ideology of 'openness' in conflict handling. Given the general assumption of the desirability of direct confrontation of conflicts, it is not surprising that researchers have conceptualised the avoidance styles as reflective of low concern for self as well as low concern for the other. This assumption is taken so much for granted in individualistic cultures that it has rarely been stated explicitly. Similarly, some researchers, while considering argument (direct confrontation of matter) as a beneficial and prosocial mode of conflict resolution, view avoidance as less socially acceptable (e.g., Infante, Trebing, Shepherd, & Seeds, 1984; Rancer, Baukus, & Infante, 1985). Because of the individualistic bias, researchers have overlooked the potentially positive attributes of conflict avoidance and suppression. They have ignored the dialectic between conflict avoidance and confrontation and the complexity of avoidance as a conflict management strategy.

Robbins (1978), for instance, found that short-term avoidance may be a very effective way to deal with a conflict situation in order to permit time for one or both of the parties to regain their composure and rationally to think through the issue and circumstances of the conflict situation. The benefits of using avoidance strategies among interdependents comes from being understood without putting one's meaning on record, so that understanding is seen not as the result of putting meaning into words, but rather as the greater understanding of shared perspective, expectations and intimacy.

In a similar vein, studies by Van de Vliert and Kabanoff (1990) and Van de Vliert and Prein (1989) took issue with the two dimensional models and showed how plots of relationships among the five styles do not fit the predicted quadrants in the original Blake and Mouton model. By reanalysing data from six studies of managers, Van de Vliert and Kabanoff (1990) assessed the construct-validity of the two best-known self-report instruments for measuring the five conflict management styles originally defined in Blake and Mouton's (1964) managerial grid (Rahim, 1983; Thomas & Kilmann, 1978). Both instruments (MODE and ROCI) more or less failed to discriminate between avoiding and accommodating. Furthermore, compromising did not occupy a midpoint position. Van de Vliert and Prein (1989) investigated whether people think about conflict management styles in terms of the classic competition-cooperation dichotomy or the five part grid.

The results revealed that the cognitive representations of the four nonforcing types of conflict behaviour have more in common with each other than with the cognitive representation of forcing. That is, dominating or forcing is isolated from the other four styles. The four styles clustered in the same related quadrants.

Conflict management style is also culturally contexted. That is, it is learned during an individual's primary socialisation in a culture/ethnic group (Ting-Toomey et al., 2000a). Members of cultural communities learn from one another the attitudes, knowledge structures, behaviours and strategies for defining and responding to conflict situations. Yet conceptualisations of conflict management style previously discussed have been developed largely within western-based, individualistic cultural contexts (Ting-Toomey et al., 2000a). Further, these taxonomies have not specifically been developed to assess or compare *intercultural* conflict management styles, as the underlying conceptual frameworks are not grounded in culturally based patterns of differences. For example, the model and ROCI-II measure developed by Rahim (1983) of dominating, obliging, avoiding, integrating and compromising styles are suspect in their generalisability to more collectivist, Asian culture systems. Ting-Toomey (1994) posits that an avoiding strategy, viewed in western terms as a strategy that reflects low concern for self interests and low concern for other interests, is employed in collectivist cultures to maintain relational harmony culturally reflects a *high* concern for self and other interests. Previous studies also found that members of the collectivistic culture were found to use a higher level of compromising and integrating styles to handle conflict than members of the individualistic culture (Trubisky, Ting Toomey, & Lin et al., 1991). In Ting-Toomey et al.'s (1991) study, opposite to their predictions, members in collectivistic cultures opted for integrating styles more than members in individualistic cultures.

Overall, the evidence suggests that members of individualistic cultures tend to prefer direct (dominating) conflict communication styles. Conversely, members of collectivistic cultures tend to prefer obliging, compromising, integrating, and conflict-avoidant styles. The latter four styles tend to emphasise the value for passive compliance to a certain degree and for maintaining relational harmony in conflict interactions (see Trubisky et al., 1991). Because of these difficulties with existing conceptualisations of conflict management styles, this study seeks to begin a more adequate explanation of conflict management style use based on cross-cultural differences in the self construal. In the following section we will discuss the relationship between the construals of self and interpersonal communication, including that related to conflict.

The relationship between face-maintenance dimensions and preferences for conflict management styles

Among high interdependents with heightened sense of the other's face concern, there will be efforts to minimise antagonisms that unsettle the groups or that place the individual in confrontation with his group. Overall, the other-face need seems to be expressed through the use of nonforcing strategies (obliging, avoiding, compromising, and integrating styles) of conflict interaction. Obliging and avoiding styles reflect the need for satisfying other-concern and other face-needs. These values are reflective of collectivistic culture communication styles. Regarding integrative style, it emphasises the importance of a mutual face-needs and the creative search for a possible conflict solution that will be acceptable to both parties. Therefore, as the mutual-face maintenance dimension, the integrating style is also more likely to be affected by other-face need.

The compromising style involves give-and-take or sharing to seek a mutually acceptable resolution. Unlike an integrating person, a compromising party may not try to completely satisfy both- her or his own and the other's needs. Even though a compromising person may express issues more directly than an avoiding person, it still has the flavor of cooperation rather than competition. In contrast with dominating style, avoiding, compromising, obliging, and integrating styles may serve to work to dilute antagonisms that might otherwise surface in the immediate situation. The assumption that forcing cognitively takes on an isolated position in relation to the other styles of conflict management, is furthermore based on the (de-) escalation model (Van de Vliert, 1984). A central issue within this model is that avoiding, compromising, negotiating and accommodating all have a short-term de-escalating effect, in which the frustrations of the parties involved do not increase. Forcing, on the other hand, has a short-term escalating effect, in which the frustrations actually do increase.

The fear of shame as a result of damaging or ruffling the social fabric or damaging someone else's face would also lead interdependents to avoid assertive or direct styles of handling conflicts. These arguments all suggest a likely preference among high interdependents for saving the other's face in conflict management by using the cooperative styles conflict management styles, such as avoiding, compromising, problem solving and accommodating. To summarise, we expect those with interdependent selves to be more attentive and sensitive to others' face needs than those with independent selves. In conflict encounters, the concern for the other's face will be more important considerations when individuals have more interdependent views of self.

This, in turn, should result in a relatively greater preference for nonforcing conflict management styles (avoiding, integrating, obliging, and compromising styles). On the other hand, we expect those with independent selves to be more attentive and sensitive to self-face needs than those with interdependent selves. Furthermore, the concern for self-face need may be the immediate antecedent for choosing dominating (forcing) conflict management styles.

4.12.3 Managing Group conflicts

Conflict has been viewed as an inevitable and commonplace phenomenon of social life (Cosier & Ruble, 1981). Members of work groups and teams in organisations experience and manage conflict with their counterparts on everyday basis. Surprisingly, however, research on intra-group dispute management has been relatively scant. Farmer & Roth (1998) argued that this scarcity has stemmed from the fact that conflict within groups intersected with two dominant research areas- decision making in small groups and the general domain of conflict resolution, which focused mainly on interpersonal and intergroup conflict. Yet, in the course of the last decade this shortage of data on intra-group conflict was somewhat rectified. Specifically, a series of studies were launched investigating constructive in comparison to destructive conflict in work teams (Amason, 1996; Jehn, 1994, 1995, 1997, 1999). Intergroup conflict requires actively setting the in-group's interests against the out-group's interests (Tajfel & Turner, 1979). When the presence of an out-group directly challenges the value of belonging to an in-group (as is the case in intergroup conflict), in-group members experience a threat to the value of their group, prompting them to protect their social identity and defend the value of the group (Branscombe, Ellemers, Spears, & Doosje, 1999).

Research demonstrates that when faced with a threat to value, in-group members will engage in more in-group favouritism in order to change the intergroup situation and thus maintain their positive social identities (Ouwerkerk, de Gilder, & de Vries, 2000; Scheepers, Spears, Doosje, & Manstead, 2003). Similar research also demonstrates that threatened in-group members will engage in more out-group derogation (disparaging of the out-group by the in-group) than members facing no threat (Branscombe & Wann, 1994; Esses, Jackson, & Armstrong, 1998). These outcomes are essential when considering the quality of intergroup relations.

Over the years, research on conflict effectiveness has proceeded in two main directions. One has focused on the type of conflict and its associations with conflict outcomes, while stressing the distinction between cognitive (task) disagreement and relationship (affective) dispute. Scholars postulated that task conflict tends to promote effective group performance, whereas relationship conflict interferes with group outcomes (Amason, 1996; Jehn, 1994, 1995, 1997, 1999). Recent meta-analysis of empirical studies on task and relationship conflict and their associations with group performance and members' satisfaction (DeDreu & Weingart, 2002) has cast doubts concerning the differential effects of the two types of conflict. The two dimensions of intragroup conflicts have been interrelated and both were found to exert strong negative impact on group outcomes – team performance and members' satisfaction. The second research path on conflict effectiveness has pertained to conflict management patterns, resting on the assumption that ways of coping with intra-group disagreements affected the outcomes, including the relationships among group members.

4.12.4 Programmed conflict –handling by promoting

Experts in the field define programmed conflict as conflict that raises different opinions regardless of the personal feelings of the managers. The trick is to get contributors to either defend or criticise ideas based on relevant facts rather than on the basis of personal preference or political interests. This requires disciplined role playing. Two programmed conflict techniques with proven track records are devil's advocacy and the dialectic method that stimulates the conflict in the organisational circle.

Devil's advocacy

This technique gets its name from a traditional practice within the Roman Catholic Church. When someone's name came before the College of Cardinals for the elevation to sainthood, it was absolutely essential to ensure that she or he had a spotless record. Consequently, one individual was assigned the role of devil's advocate to uncover and air all possible objections to the person's canonisation.

In accordance with this practice, devil's advocacy in today's organisation involves assigning someone the role of critic. Devil's advocacy alters the usual decision making process in a phased manner. This approach to programmed conflict is intended to generate critical thinking and reality testing. It is a good idea to rotate the job of devil's advocate so that a person does not develop a strictly negative reputation. Moreover, periodic devil's advocacy role-playing is good training for developing analytical and communication skills.

The dialectic method

Like devil's advocacy, the dialectic method is a time-honoured practice towards programmed conflict and traces its origin to the dialectic school of philosophy in ancient Greece. Plato and followers attempted to synthesise truths by exploring opposite positions called thesis and anti thesis. Accordingly today's organisations exercises dialectic method for the managers to foster a structured debate of opposing viewpoints prior to making decisions complementary to the normal decision making process .a major drawback of the dialectic method seems to be a tendency to win the debate that may overshadow the issue at hand. Also, dialectic method requires more skill and hence training than devil's advocacy. Compared with groups that strive to reach a consensus; decision making groups using either devil's advocacy or dialectic method yielded supplementary decisional outputs of elevated quality. But in a more recent laboratory study, group's using devil's advocacy produced more potential solutions and made better recommendations for a case problem than did groups using the dialectic method. In view of this mixed evidence, managers have some latitude in using these two methods to get some creative life back in organisations. Personal preference and the role players' experience may well be deciding factors in choosing one approach over the other. The important thing is to actively stimulate functional conflict when the organisation requires it most.

Creation of conflict in our environment may be beneficial if it induces competition for control and therefore better proposals ex ante. Such conflict is however ex post inefficient as it reduces cooperation at the execution stage. In an analysis of group decision making, a similar point is made by Li (2001), who shows that committees may be able to improve the quality of their decisions by committing ex ante to an ex post inefficient decision standard, as such a commitment can increase the information acquisition incentive of individual committee members. He does not consider conflicts of interest between members, or the ex post moral hazard problem, but rather focuses on the relationship between information acquisition, and the continuation versus rejection of a status quo.

4.12.5 Third party help/interventions

Third-party intervention in workplace conflict has received growing attention from theory (Elangovan, 1995; Kolb, 1986; Sheppard, 1984) and research (Arnold & O'Connor, 1999; Karambayya & Brett, 1989; Pinkley, Neale, Brittain & Northcraft, 1995) as well as the practical field of labour relations, community mediation and international conflict (Kozan & Ilter, 1994). This attention has resulted in the identification and definition of several third-party roles and strategies. That is, third parties that may operate on a neutral basis such as ombudspersons (Arnold & O'Connor, 1999), or may operate primarily as mediators or arbitrators (Conlon & Ross, 1993), such as managers trying to settle a dispute between subordinates (Pinkley et al., 1995). Generally, a distinction is made between third parties with process control, such as a mediator, and more autocratic third parties with decision control, such as an arbiter. In comparing both types, research clearly shows that interventions through process control render more positive outcomes than interventions through decision control. Process control interventions produce better quality outcomes and more satisfied parties; partly because they are considered more procedurally fair (Karambayya & Brett, 1989; Karambayya, Brett & Lytle, 1992). As a consequence, conflict parties also prefer mediation over other forms of third-party intervention (Karambayya & Brett, 1989; Karambayya et al., 1992; Lewicki & Sheppard, 1985).

Conflicting employees can take the initiative to ask a third party to help them to derive structure and meaning in the stressful conflict situation (Volkema, Farquehar & Bergmann, 1996). In line with Ting-Toomey and Oetzel (2001), some authors propose that making use of third-party help may be regarded an additional conflict management style, next to more traditional conflict handling styles such as forcing, problem solving, accommodating, avoiding and other taxonomies. Ting-Toomey and Oetzel (2001) provided theoretical and empirical support for this proposition. The propagators of these concepts defined third-party help in terms of process control as 'involving an outsider to mediate the conflict'. Defined like this, third-party help may be particularly beneficial in promoting accurate information processing by clarifying the real issues at stake and by setting out procedures to go about the conflict. By applying these interventions, a third party cannot issue binding settlements, but rather help stressful conflict parties to recover their control over the process and outcomes of their disputes and to restore their relationship (Arnold & O'Connor, 1999). Consequently, third-party help may buffer the negative consequences of conflict stress, by helping those employees that experience conflict-related stress to break through negative conflict spirals. As such, the conflict management style of third-party help should be theoretically distinguished from social support, a factor that has been previously identified as a buffer to the negative effects of job-stressors (e.g., Cohen & Wills, 1985; Greenglass, Fiksenbaum & Burke, 1994). While social support reflects the general perception of whether one feels surrounded by others who may offer desirable comfort or advice (Quick et al, 1997), third party help refers to the specific conflict management style of actively involving a third party in a dispute.

4.13 THEORETICAL CONTOUR AND RESEARCH CONSIDERATIONS

Through conscious scanning, it is apparent that much has been studied and observed about the broad, overarching concept of conflict and its management. Because it is a richly-textured topic, it has opened the door for hundreds of research projects into the myriad subsets that underpin this subject. Studies abound relative to behavioural styles, personality traits, success/ obstacles for managers and other managerial issues of conflict management. Conflict management as a key component of successful managerial strategy has been researched from many different directions. Many of the studies relate to the differences in the way human resource in an organisation handle conflicts, or the views managers hold as a homogeneous group about this subject. Extensive searching has not unearthed any studies relative to the attitudinal, integral and stylistic differences about handling conflicts if any, among textile mill managers in India. It is this topic that forms the basis of this academic research.

The present study attempts to establish some core values for effective conflict management including fairness, consistency of process and minimum skill standards, matching the approach and the outcomes to the situation/proportionate conflict handling, handling conflicts as close as possible to the source of the conflict, seeking mutually acceptable outcomes where possible, various approaches to conflict management and its appositional dilemmas, adaptable best practices and managerial appraisal of the conflict sources and residual responses towards them.

The appreciation of the individualistic perception and situation handling differences, certainly bring more sensible dimensions to the study. Backdrop research on the psychosocial and organisational theories/models equips the effective appraisal of conflict dynamics including style differences, demographical distinctions and other dissimilarities. It is interesting to view the evolution of the thinking behind behavioural modeling, the changes and refinements that reflect the corresponding evolution of organisational development. But it is not sufficient to merely review the modeling theories, it is necessary to delve deeper into the issues of personality, conflict management vis-à-vis designations, and behaviours. If we accept the premise that effective conflict management is indeed inextricably linked to organisational success, and its entire attendant rewards including – power, privileges, prestige, visibility, and materialistic advancements are operational, besides the process functionaries of individual motives, perceptions, attitudes, preferential and the response dynamics ; then its influence in the organisational arena is a crucial aspect to understand.

This too entitle to attempt to institutionalise the greater synergy attained through the organisational functionaries and the procedural system dynamics to effectively address the conflicts through interactional mechanisms including third party help/interventions. The greater confluence of multi disciplinary notions enhances the wider chances of enquiries and a more hardheaded appraisal of the state of affairs among the study group within the research framework.

4.14 HYPOTHESES

The guided hypotheses confine the scope and focus the research objectives. Quantifiable verification can be attempted by research hypotheses expressed below. Furthermore the model building exercise is also get enhanced by the inputs received through testing these hypotheses. All the other exploratory factors of this study are attempted by cross sectional verification rather than only by hypotheses testing so as to enable a better philosophising the management of conflicts among the study group.

H1- Multitude of influential and potential factors which acts as sources of conflicts at various levels are perceived differently by the study group and a pattern of ranking preferences operate in organisational life.

H2- Initial approaches towards conflict handling are differentiative among the population along eight indicative approaches- Negotiate, Force, Compromise, Mediational, Arbitrative, Accommodate, Persuade and Avoid.

H3- The effectiveness of various procedural mechanisms to manage conflicts and its components are not equally preferred by the managers.

H4- The multitudinal effects of the preferred styles of conflict results in relational preferences among the various managerial strata

H5- Managerial stratum employ five different modes or styles of behaviour in conflict situations – competing, collaborating, compromising, accommodating, and avoiding and the situational responses along these lines of operations can be summated to identify the preferred modes or the styles as the case may be of the managerial population.

CHAPTER FIVE

ANALYSIS OF DATA AND INTERPRETATION

The interactional dynamics of the data accrued through the premeditated phases of research operations extend itself to the analytical processes and its logical interpretations along the lines attempting to answer the research questions. The admixture of quantitative and qualitative components in the data stream necessitated the categorisation of the same in the most representative fashion. Predominantly quantitative data supplied through the questionnaire administered are dealt in the section 5.1. The analytical operations of distinctive variables are enhanced by statistical decision support systems including the interpretative routines like frequency analysis, correlation, multiple regression, factor analysis, various goodness of fit test among others. The adherence to the policies laid down by the objective references of the study, enabled and or required such operations that promote a logical understanding of the variables that are examined.

In the section 5.2, selected behavioural cases accrued through the research specifications are analysed invoking an essay appraisal that is commonly practiced in qualitative data processing. The sectional division constitutes the logical adherence to the policies and frame that is commonly practiced in managerial research at this level. The triangulation attempts are made through these analytical processes and the qualitative data supplied through other data collection mode are synergistically applied to enhance the potentials towards attempting to find a relevant explanation and or exploring the research problems. Modest attempts along these lines are included in the form of essay documentation primarily supplied through the data widely accrued by focus group interviews, supplementary in-depth interviews, behavioural case fundamentals, semi structured observations, content analysis and expert opinions. This exploratory analysis of the data collected in tandem brings a modulating and pragmatic appraisal model to the research dynamics. The flexibility it allows to explore the fundamentals of the research problems through the prism of data thus acquired enhances an in-depth appropriation of the procedural way of analysis. Derivation of situational pragmatism into its fold of operations makes a set of unique responses by this method. In essence it can be equated with an appraisal 'through trial and error exploration', invoking the triangulation methods, rather multiple appreciations of the factors of enquiry. An attempt of quasi-triangulation along these lines can be expressed by the term 'Heuristic appraisal of the conflict management climate' explained through section 5.3.

One of the primary responsibilities of this academic research resembles to attempt to find a pathway that better expresses the management of conflicts in this part of the globe. The rejuvenation of the managerial ideas and practices concerning the handling of conflicts can be explored in its most intrinsic, integral, in-depth and innovative dimensions. The idea of integrative conflict management, certainly not a recent *discovery*- expresses human beings inquest to find the real meaning to various problems perceived in its most inclusive levels of operations. The quintessence of conflict management seems to be inclusively integrative in its core and that was well recognised by the practitioners from wider domains. In this direction– the knowledge, attitude and practices of Mahatma Gandhi; brings 360 degree approach to the domains of conflict management and the exploration of the same along with the guided thoughts and models that are tributary to the domains of integrated conflict management are dealt in section 5.4. Various statistical routines, essentially assisted by the decision support systems incorporating the utilities from information technologies had intertwined the quantitative analysis of the identified variables of this research. For quantitative analysis, social science research software like SPSS16.0, Systat 12.0, and Minitab 15 are utilised appropriately, besides the specific routines invoking the usage of R for Linux. The cross reference was made possible by more than one routines supplied by various software solution providers. In case of qualitative analysis, the decelerators of barriers from the areas of language encoding/decoding, non-experimental setup, resource and other constraints had restrictive influence on the usage of computerised routines. Besides the common word processing packages, a limited utilisation of CAQDAS packages, IS World, N6 and Nvivo are all attempted.

5.1 QUANTITATIVE ANALYSIS AND INTERPRETATION

Sample survey research was carried out as the method of gathering quantitative/quantifiable data from respondents thought to be the representative of study population, using Conflict Management Inquest (CMI)-an exclusive questionnaire-cum-schedule (*Refer Appendix*) composed of an array of various structured and open-ended items. In this direction, all the middle level managers of identified textile mills were approached personally by the principal researcher. Out of the 196 managers from the twenty one textile mills, 118 managers were participated in this sample survey. The rest were not willing/ unapproachable because of the reasons that better known to them. The responses from the three respondents were incomplete/highly lenient towards neutrality and not included in the final set of responses. Thus 115 completed responses were included for the final analysis.

Frequency analyses are appropriately used to convey logical dimensions to the analytical operations. Descriptive statistics are widely put to the structural analysis and interpreted as applicable. In cases constituting correlation analysis, majority of them are approached through Kendall's tau. Kendall tau is defined as, T = (# agreements – # disagreements) / total number of pairs. Kendall's tau is equivalent to the Spearman R statistic with regard to the underlying assumptions. It is also comparable in terms of its statistical power. However, Spearman R and Kendall tau are usually not identical in magnitude because their underlying logic, as well as their computational formulas are very different. Siegel and Castellan (1988) express the relationship of the two measures in terms of the inequality--1 $\leq$ 3 * Kendall tau - 2 * Spearman R $\leq$ 1.

More importantly, Kendall tau and Spearman R imply different interpretations. While Spearman R can be thought of as the regular Pearson product-moment correlation coefficient as computed from ranks, Kendall tau rather represents a probability. Specifically, it is the difference between the probabilities that the observed data are in the same order for the two variables versus the probability that the observed data are in different orders for the two variables. Kendall (1948, 1975), Everitt (1977), and Siegel and Castellan (1988) discuss Kendall tau in greater detail. Two different variants of tau are computed, usually called tau_b and tau_c. These measures differ only with regard as to how tied ranks are handled. Kendall's tau_b is applied to the necessary operations in this quantitative analysis where it seems to suit well.

The general purpose of multiple regressions used in the appropriate analyses attempted to express the relationship between several independent or predictor variables and a dependent or criterion variables as such. The main application of factor analysis techniques in this analytical process includes that to reduce the number of variables and to detect structure in the relationships between variables that is to classify variables. Therefore, factor analysis is applied as a data reduction or exploratory structure detection method throughout the process of analysis.

The adoption of guided factor dimensions combined with the cut off procedural specifications, the adoption of principal components method with varimax rotation are all unidirectional towards the above specified links. Besides these measures, the appropriate statistical tests were applied in the structured fashion. The logical clustering of the variables thus analysed are documented fittingly under the classified sections.

5.1.1 Profile of the respondents

Considering the facts that demographic variables plays an important part in the academic study, factors such as age, education level, gender, organisational position, work experience etc were ascertained through the administered tool exposited to the sample studied group (N=115).

The average age of the study group was ascertained as 47.92 years and range being 28-58 years. Median of the group can be expressed as 50 years and standard deviation was 6.71. Complete absence of the female strata was another interesting emergent. In case of determining the education level, the highest degree obtained was taken. Forty two (36.52%) respondents possessed professional degrees that better represent their field of specialisation. This includes predominantly in the fields of Business administration, Social Work, Textile and other related Engineering/Technology and a few from Information technology. One doctoral qualified manager in his capacity as special project officer participated in the study. Thirty (26.08%) respondents indicated that they possess post graduate degrees, other than the professional streams mentioned above. The rest of the groups, forty two (36.52%) respondents are graduates.

In the departmental stratification exercise, thirty one (26.96%) managers can be expressed as representatives from finance department. Thirty managers (26.09%) belong to human resource department and half of the amount from marketing and sales (13.05%). Twenty eight (24.35%) respondents represented production department, four (3.48%) participants from systems division in their capacity among others offered the profound outreach of the present study. Six factory managers and one special Project officer (6.09%) are representatives of their respective operations and influence in this academic study. In the case of work experience, average years at present position/designation of the respondents can be ascertained as 9.63 years, range being 1-24 in years and standard deviation to the tune of 6.55 years. The experience in managerial related routines seems to be important to the present study and it was asserted along with the other technical related experience. The average managerial years of experience of the respondents is 18.57 in years and average years in other related exposure seem to be 4.94 in years. Average work experience accruing the above dimensions seems to be 23.51 in years. The median of the same is 24 in years and the standard deviation being 5.99. These data when translated into a working understanding, reveals that the study group belongs to a highly educated and professionally qualified, managerial cadre personnel with influential understanding about their working know- how generated and or resulted through a high/very high degree of work related experience and exposure.

Table 5.1: Job Demographics of managerial respondents*

Age		Education		Department[#]		Sector		Total Years of Experience	
Year	*%*	*Level*	*%*	*Principal Dept.*	*%*	*Item*	*%*	*Managerial including Tech/Gen*	*%*
25-30	1.74	Professional	36.52	FIN	26.96	Public	32.17	Less than 5	0.87
31-35	3.48	PG-Gen	26.09	FSP	6.09	Private	67.83	6-10	2.61
36-40	8.70	Graduate	36.52	HR	26.09			11-15	7.83
41-45	22.61	Doctoral	0.87	MKG	13.04			16-20	10.43
46-50	13.91			PRD	24.35			21-25	36.52
51-55	41.74			SYS	3.48			26-30	33.04
55-59	7.83							31-35	8.70
Avg. 47.92*yrs*								**Avg. 23.51*yrs***	

*N=115

[#] FIN-Finance & Accounts; FSP- Factory Manager and Special Officials; HR- Human Resource; MKG- Marketing including Sales; PRD- Production; SYS- Systems -including EDP.

5.1.2 Potential Sources of Conflict

The potential for the conflicts to occur in every organisational level is alarmingly high. The historical importance attached to the conflicts at the interpersonal levels/individual levels alone may not bring the desired results in these days. The better we understand the potentials for the conflict in influential organisational levels, the better we can frame a decent mechanism to cope up with those situations.

Furthermore it has been widely acclaimed and assumed by this research frame that a conflict arises at one level can spawn or moves to another or other level/s and vice versa. Part C of the CMI (refer appendix) attempts to identify the major elements that were responsible to inculcate the conflict potentials among the respondents. The scales of operation recognise as well as infuse the wider scope for analysis and an attempt was made to identify the major elements that cause conflicts among the respondents in their respective organisations, in the statistical sense.

Considering the fact that there exists a multitude of influential and potential factors which acts as sources of conflicts at various levels, it was attempted to experimentally explore some of the major potential sources of conflicts through logical clustering various organisational levels presented in exhibit 5.1.

Exhibit 5.1 Potential sources of conflict

Item No.	Variable/ Potential source of Conflict	Categorisation levels*
5	Managerial Supervision, direction and control (too less or too much of freedom, participation in decision making, etc).	Interactional
13	Personal habits or mannerisms (including dress, way of conversation, etc).	Interactional
14	Personality differences (such as cultural background, education, social patterns etc).	Interactional
15	Differences in basic values, beliefs or opinions.	Interactional
16	Personal dislike.	Interactional
17	Barriers to interpersonal communication.	Interactional
21	Need for tension release.	Interactional
22	Drive for autonomy.	Interactional
1	Conflict over job objectives.	Issue
3	Work standards to be accomplished (volume of work expected, time limits, etc).	Issue
9	Amount of time spent on the job (not meeting deadlines, arriving late, leaving early, etc).	Issue
10	Errors, misinterpretation of orders, carelessness etc.	Issue
18	Differences in knowledge or expertise.	Issue
2	Planning of activities (what should be done, how it should be done, who should do it, etc).	Procedural
4	The question as to how the resources and facilities are to be used or other technical issues are to be dealt with.	Procedural
6	Performance appraisal (evaluation of task execution, goal attainment, etc).	Procedural
7	Organisational policies and procedures.	Organisational
8	Administration of wages, salaries, promotions, sanction of leave etc.	Organisational
11	Physical working environment (including noise, space, office temperature, ventilation etc).	Organisational
12	General market trends and other economic fluctuations.	Organisational
19	Compensation for a particular position, power or recognition.	Organisational
20	Hierarchical differences in status power and rewards.	Organisational

✄ *Independent Ranking Scale: Least (1)–Highest (10)*

These 22 items indicated in Table 5.2 represented the major sources of conflicts perceived by the managerial strata and recorded a range between 4.25 and 5.09 at its average on the scale. Majority of the items was scored between 1 and 8, except a few that recorded scores between 3 and 8. The standard deviation among these variables can be adjudged as less contrasting and the functional distribution is less approaching to the normal distribution at its clustered level. Whereas in its totality, the sampled population identified diversified and scattered potential sources of conflicts. This indeed seems to be an indicator of the effectiveness of the ranking scale and the reflection it brought to the spectrum of analysis can be operationally enhancing. Interestingly, all the variables recorded the scores that can be regarded as significant and this situation explains the need for further treatment of the statistical data.

The chi square values for the individual variables were explored, seeing that this can be considered as a common routine among the standard non parametric testing methods at these levels. The elemental approach to the chi square analysis is essentially assumed randomisation which in this case, can act only as a rule of thumb. The comparative chi square values as well as the goodness of fit analysis can shed some light on the dependency dimensions prevailing among the variables. Minimum expected cell frequencies are calculated for each cell and are grouped as presented in the table 5.2. These 22 variables can be grouped into three categories according to their *df* values of 5, 6 or 7 as the case may be. Majority of the variables (1-3, 6-12, 14-18, 20) recorded a minimum expected cell frequency of 14.4 and indicated as group 'a'. In group 'b', expected cell frequency accrued was 19.2 and variables being 4, 5, 13, 19 and 22 items. Variable 22 recorded an expected cell frequency of 16.4. Dependency/equal preference of ranking elements can be ascertained through the appropriation of the chi square values as an exploratory method in this distribution.

Hypothesis Testing -The research hypothesis (H1) - *Multitude of influential and potential factors which acts as sources of conflicts at various levels are perceived differently by the study group* can be put into test. H_0 is assumed and can be expressed as there was an equal preference of ranking scales/frequencies and they are independent. H_a negates both the independency and equal preference strategy. In case of group a, the chi square table value for *df*= 7, probability of error-alpha at 0.01 can be expressed as 18.475 and all those calculated chi square values in this group are much higher than the table value. In that sense, the equal preference of ranking scales/ frequencies are questioned and it is clearly evident that there seems to be a wider distributed and or selectively preferred score values expressed by the managers.

In addition, the preferred frequencies are visibly more along the middle level values of the scale. The much higher chi square values indirectly indicates the heightened squared observed values which in turn was a resultant of the variables' importance to act as a perceived potential source of conflict. Interestingly almost all the variables in this group 'a' act exactly as described and a few variables like item-7, 8, 15 etc are crucial factors to be considered in this direction, keeping the observed recordings it got as well as the heightened chi square values of them. It can be explained that apart from these measures to determine the preferential recordings and its variations, chi square tests may not be experimentative for ascertaining other determinants to this group.

In case of group b and c, the H_0 is assumed and can be expressed as there was an equal preference of ranking scales/frequencies and they are independent. H_1 negates both the independency and equal preference strategy. For group b, the chi square table value for $df=$ 5, probability of error-alpha at 0.01 can be expressed as 15.086 and all those calculated chi square values in this group are much higher than the table value.

In that sense, the equal preference of ranking scales/ frequencies are questioned and it is clearly evident that there seems to be a wider distributed and or selectively preferred score values expressed by the managers. For group c, the chi square table value for $df=$ 6, probability of error-alpha at 0.01 can be expressed as 16.812 and all those calculated chi square values in this group are much higher than the table value. The denominations of group a equally applies to these two groups b and c. Interestingly, the differential value difference is not considerably heightened as was evident in a selected few variables of group a. The chi square analyses pretend that the three groups negate the H_0 and accept H_a. This can be attributed to the factors that are indicative of the preferred set of values and scoring pattern that was exercised by the managers. Further it indicates the need for necessary processing to ascertain various dimensions of the data structure. Both Friedman's chi square value for the scale and variances are expressive in this direction. The standard deviations are indicative of the wider preferences of the managers towards the ranking patterns. A moderate level of reliability of the scale can be regarded as a satisfactory measure considering the fact that there exists multitude of variables and a flexible yet impulsive ranking scale was adopted. The scale mean and variable means are all pinpointing vividly a preferential pattern that can be adjudged through the correlations and other methods of analysis.

Table 5.2: Descriptive statistics-Potential sources of conflict

Item No.	Variable/ Potential source of Conflict	Categorization levels*	Min	Max	Mean	Standard Deviation	Variance	Chi-Square	df	Mean if deleted	Var. if deleted	St.Dev. if deleted	Item Total. Corre lated.	Alpha if. deleted
1	Conflict over job objectives.	Issue	1	8	4.54	1.92	3.67	32.13[a]	7	100.10	95.60	9.78	0.21	0.47
2	Planning of activities (what should be done, how it should be done, who should do it, etc).	Procedural	1	8	4.82	1.77	3.12	46.88[a]	7	99.82	96.17	9.81	0.23	0.47
3	Work standards to be accomplished (volume of work expected, time limits, etc).	Issue	1	8	5.09	1.65	2.71	50.50[a]	7	99.55	100.73	10.04	0.12	0.49
4	The question as to how the resources and facilities are to be used or other technical issues are to be dealt with.	Procedural	3	8	4.86	1.49	2.23	38.13[b]	5	99.77	104.64	10.23	0.01	0.51
5	Managerial Supervision, direction and control (too less or too much of freedom, participation in decision making, etc).	Interactional	3	8	4.80	1.40	1.95	34.79[b]	5	99.83	99.44	9.97	0.21	0.48
6	Performance appraisal (evaluation of task execution, goal attainment, etc).	Procedural	3	8	4.82	1.48	2.19	39.49[b]	5	99.82	103.87	10.19	0.04	0.50
7	Organisational policies and procedures.	Organisational	1	8	4.70	1.38	1.91	105.5[a]	7	99.93	103.75	10.19	0.06	0.50
8	Administration of wages, salaries, promotions, sanction of leave etc.	Organisational	1	8	4.70	1.51	2.28	87.78[a]	7	99.93	97.23	9.86	0.26	0.47
9	Amount of time spent on the job (not meeting deadlines, arriving late, leaving early, etc).	Issue	1	8	4.25	1.90	3.63	32.69[a]	7	100.38	101.66	10.08	0.05	0.51
10	Errors, misinterpretation of orders, carelessness etc.	Issue	1	8	4.08	1.79	3.21	40.06[a]	7	100.56	96.66	9.83	0.21	0.47
11	Physical working environment (including noise, space, office temperature, ventilation etc).	Organisational	1	8	4.95	1.63	2.65	51.33[a]	7	99.69	100.46	10.02	0.13	0.49
12	General market trends and other economic fluctuations.	Organisational	1	8	4.84	1.70	2.91	47.43[a]	7	99.79	98.15	9.91	0.19	0.48
13	Personal habits or mannerisms (including dress, way of conversation, etc).	Interactional	3	8	4.86	1.46	2.12	34.17[b]	5	99.77	100.49	10.02	0.16	0.48
14	Personality differences (such as cultural background, education, social patterns etc).	Interactional	1	8	4.83	1.68	2.82	52.44[a]	7	99.80	98.91	9.95	0.17	0.48

15	Differences in basic values, beliefs or opinions.	Interactional	1	8	4.70	1.52	2.32	82.91[a]	7	99.93	103.32	10.16	0.05	0.50
16	Personal dislike.	Interactional	1	8	4.80	1.77	3.13	37.56[a]	7	99.83	94.90	9.74	0.27	0.46
17	Barriers to interpersonal communication.	Interactional	1	8	4.75	1.58	2.51	61.35[a]	7	99.89	102.01	10.10	0.09	0.50
18	Differences in knowledge or expertise.	Issue	1	8	4.95	1.73	2.98	43.68[a]	7	99.69	94.91	9.74	0.28	0.46
19	Compensation for a particular position, power or recognition.	Organisational	3	8	4.90	1.51	2.29	29.89[b]	5	99.74	101.38	10.07	0.12	0.49
20	Hierarchical differences in status power and rewards.	Organisational	1	8	4.77	1.50	2.25	67.19[a]	7	99.86	101.72	10.09	0.11	0.49
21	Need for tension release.	Interactional	1	8	4.81	1.52	2.30	61.58[c]	6	99.83	101.73	10.09	0.11	0.49
22	Drive for autonomy.	Interactional	3	8	4.81	1.27	1.61	57.85[b]	5	99.83	103.69	10.18	0.08	0.50

*These categorisations enable the positional analysis. Further the variables are multidependent and can span all these levels in many actuals.

[a] 0 cells (.0%) have expected frequencies less than 5. The minimum expected cell frequency is **14.4**.

[b] 0 cells (.0%) have expected frequencies less than 5. The minimum expected cell frequency is **19.2**.

[c] 0 cells (.0%) have expected frequencies less than 5. The minimum expected cell frequency is **16.4**.

NPar *Test*			**Reliability Statistics**	
Model assumption:			Common Mean	4.75
Friedman's Chi-Square Value	**47.181**		Common Variance	2.62
df	**21**		True Variance	0.13
Sig	**0.001**		Error Variance	2.49
Log of Determinant of-			Common inter-item Variance	0.04
Unconstrained Matrix	**17.69**		Reliability of Scale	0.48
Constrained Matrix	**20.98**		Reliability of Scale (Unbiased)	0.50

Summary statistics for scale

Mean: **104.63478261**	Sum: **12033.000000**	Average Inter-Item Correlation: **0.042407581**
Standard Deviation: **10.401864235**	Variance: **108.19877956**	Cronbach's alpha: **0.498037915**
Minimum: **85.000000000**	Maximum: **133.00000000**	Standardized alpha: **0 .6219844467**
Skewness: **0.339822200**	Kurtosis: **-0.339719218**	

Table 5.3: Kendall's Tau Correlations- Potential sources of conflict*

Item/Variable	1	2	3	4	5	6	7	8	9	10	11	12	13	14	15	16	17	18	19	20	21	22
1	1.00	0.02	-0.07	-0.12	0.00	**0.15**	0.09	**0.15**	0.04	**0.21**	0.06	0.05	-0.01	0.04	0.00	**0.19**	0.02	0.11	-0.11	-0.05	0.04	0.06
2	0.02	1.00	0.05	-0.06	0.10	**-0.16**	**0.14**	**0.16**	0.12	0.07	**0.33**	0.12	0.01	**-0.13**	-0.02	0.07	0.12	**0.16**	0.03	0.02	-0.01	0.02
3	-0.07	0.06	1.00	0.05	0.03	-0.09	-0.08	0.09	0.09	0.12	-0.04	**0.15**	0.00	0.09	-0.11	0.09	0.00	**0.12**	0.08	-0.04	0.03	**-0.16**
4	-0.12	-0.06	0.05	1.00	0.07	**0.13**	-0.03	-0.06	-0.07	-0.04	-0.06	0.02	0.04	0.11	0.01	-0.08	**0.14**	0.01	0.10	0.10	0.02	-0.10
5	0.00	0.10	0.03	0.07	1.00	-0.06	0.05	-0.01	-0.02	0.05	0.04	0.03	0.04	**0.23**	0.00	0.07	0.05	**0.17**	0.00	**0.16**	0.05	-0.01
6	**0.15**	**-0.16**	-0.09	**0.13**	-0.06	1.00	-0.03	-0.12	-0.07	-0.03	-0.06	-0.09	0.10	0.06	0.04	0.07	0.01	0.00	0.08	0.04	0.02	0.07
7	0.09	**0.14**	-0.08	-0.03	0.05	-0.03	1.00	0.08	0.04	-0.09	-0.09	-0.01	-0.04	0.02	-0.04	**0.14**	0.04	-0.01	-0.02	0.09	-0.01	**0.16**
8	**0.15**	**0.16**	0.07	-0.06	-0.01	-0.12	0.08	1.00	0.09	0.11	0.08	0.07	0.09	**0.14**	-0.09	**0.15**	-0.11	0.11	0.04	0.04	**0.15**	0.02
9	0.04	0.12	0.07	-0.07	-0.02	-0.07	0.04	0.09	1.00	**0.15**	0.04	-0.07	-0.03	0.03	0.02	-0.03	0.00	0.08	-0.06	-0.02	-0.05	0.00
10	**0.21**	0.07	0.12	-0.04	0.05	-0.03	-0.09	0.11	**0.15**	1.00	-0.01	0.01	0.04	0.03	-0.01	**0.16**	-0.04	0.01	0.00	-0.06	0.08	-0.04
11	0.06	**0.33**	-0.04	-0.06	0.04	-0.06	-0.09	0.08	0.04	-0.01	1.00	0.08	0.03	-0.03	-0.07	-0.01	0.05	0.05	-0.01	0.03	0.11	0.10
12	0.05	0.12	**0.15**	0.02	0.03	-0.09	-0.01	0.07	-0.07	0.01	0.08	1.00	0.01	0.08	-0.03	-0.01	0.09	**0.26**	0.06	0.10	-0.03	0.03
13	-0.01	0.01	0.00	0.04	0.04	0.10	-0.04	0.09	-0.03	0.04	0.03	0.01	1.00	0.05	0.01	0.05	0.00	0.10	**0.34**	0.06	0.00	0.03
14	0.04	**-0.13**	0.05	0.11	**0.23**	0.06	0.02	**0.14**	0.03	0.03	-0.03	0.08	0.05	1.00	0.01	0.08	0.00	0.09	-0.05	0.00	-0.01	-0.04
15	0.00	-0.02	-0.11	0.01	0.00	0.04	-0.04	-0.09	0.02	-0.01	-0.07	-0.03	0.01	0.01	1.00	0.10	0.11	0.02	0.06	-0.01	-0.03	0.11
16	**0.19**	0.07	0.05	-0.08	0.07	0.07	**0.14**	**0.15**	-0.03	**0.16**	-0.01	-0.01	0.05	0.08	0.10	1.00	-0.06	0.02	0.00	-0.03	**0.16**	0.10
17	0.02	0.12	0.00	**0.14**	0.05	0.01	0.04	-0.11	0.00	-0.04	0.05	0.09	0.00	0.00	0.11	-0.06	1.00	0.09	-0.03	**0.13**	-0.10	0.07
18	0.11	**0.16**	**0.12**	0.01	**0.17**	0.00	-0.01	0.11	0.08	0.01	0.05	**0.26**	0.10	0.09	0.02	0.02	0.09	1.00	0.00	0.05	**-0.13**	-0.11
19	-0.11	0.03	0.08	0.10	0.00	0.08	-0.02	0.04	-0.06	0.00	-0.01	0.06	**0.34**	-0.05	0.06	0.00	-0.03	0.00	1.00	**0.17**	0.10	0.09
20	-0.05	0.02	-0.04	0.10	**0.16**	0.04	0.09	0.04	-0.02	-0.06	0.03	0.10	0.06	0.00	-0.01	-0.03	**0.13**	0.05	**0.17**	1.00	-0.03	0.03
21	0.04	-0.01	0.03	0.02	0.05	0.02	-0.01	**0.15**	-0.05	0.08	0.11	-0.03	0.00	-0.01	-0.03	**0.16**	-0.10	**-0.13**	0.10	-0.03	1.00	0.09
22	0.06	0.02	**-0.16**	-0.10	-0.01	0.07	**0.16**	0.02	0.00	-0.04	0.10	0.03	0.03	-0.04	0.11	0.10	0.07	-0.11	0.09	0.03	0.09	1.00

*Correlations highlighted by bolded are significant at p <0.05000

NB: Other major non parametric correlation analyses including Gamma Correlations as well as the Spearman's Rank order   correlation signifies more or less the same bivariate correlation commonalities with indicative figures.

Correlations- There exist atleast three major factors that pave ways for the operational enhancements through correlations–the simplicity, applicability and the relational adaptability that it infuses to the studied data. Kendall tau seems to be the most applicable correlation method and is defined as, T = (# agreements – # disagreements) / total number of pairs. The probability value of +/- 0.05 was applied to determine the significant correlations among these variables. Table 5.3 shows that majority of the positive correlations and a few negative correlations (tau_b) have considerably lesser values. This can be a resultant of either that of the highly independent or multidependent characteristics of the potential source of conflict (22 items).

Variables 13 and 19 taken together recorded a positive and moderately high *(0.34)* correlation/agreeability, so does between variables 2 and 11*(0.33)*. The cases are similar between variables 5 and 14*(0.23)*, between variables 1 and 10*(0.21)*. A positive correlation was recorded between the variable 1 and 16*(0.19)*. Few paired variables registered positive correlations that are less than 0.18 (19 pairs).Interestingly four moderately very low negative paired correlations were also recorded. Kendall's tau_b reestablishes the fact that some of the variables are far from approaching the correlation spectrum though a few variables seems to be influenced by others. Statistically speaking the very low level of correlation exists and partially establishes H_0 that there is no significant correlation among all variables. This further establishes the importance of all the sources of conflict indicated in the scale as operational and influential as perceived by the managerial workforce. Other major non parametric correlation analyses including Gamma Correlations as well as the Spearman's Rank order correlation signifies more or less the same bivariate correlation commonalities with indicative figures and perfectly resonate the indicative pattern explained above.

Group analysis- In table 5.4, Group analysis and rank differentials were projected through the average score operations for each potential source of conflict. The indicative differentials if any can be ascertained among the sample strata. The departmental dimensions can play a major role in this regard and the same was taken for the analysis of projective rank differentials. The group analysis was carried out assuming the multiple dependent characteristics of the potential sources of conflicts. The range of average rank (8.98–12.30) reestablishes the close knit operational potentials and the multitudinal effects of the potential sources of conflict.

Table 5.4: Rank Analysis–potential sources of conflict

Item No.	Variable/Potential source of Conflict	Group Analysis*		Mean Rank[1]	Managerial Strata**					
		Average Rank	Sum of Ranks		HR[2]	PRD[3]	MKG[4]	FIN[5]	SYS[6]	FSP[7]
1	Conflict over job objectives.	10.348	1190.0	20	18	20	8	19	7	2
2	Planning of activities (what should be done, how it should be done, who should do it, etc).	11.391	1310.0	10	8	12	14	12	12	14
3	Work standards to be accomplished (volume of work expected, time limits, etc).	12.304	1415.0	1	3	9	2	4	2	7
4	The question as to how the resources and facilities are to be used or other technical issues are to be dealt with.	11.796	1356.5	5	2	16	18	8	17	10
5	Managerial Supervision, direction and control (too less or too much of freedom, participation in decision making, etc).	11.970	1376.5	14	12	6	12	10	13	15
6	Performance appraisal (evaluation of task execution, goal attainment, etc).	11.752	1351.5	9	10	11	19	2	18	5
7	Organisational policies and procedures.	11.770	1353.5	18	15	15	7	13	6	19
8	Administration of wages, salaries, promotions, sanction of leave etc.	11.535	1326.5	17	13	3	11	21	3	16
9	Amount of time spent on the job (not meeting deadlines, arriving late, leaving early, etc).	9.404	1081.5	21	20	21	22	22	1	4
10	Errors, misinterpretation of orders, carelessness etc.	8.983	1033.0	22	22	22	21	20	4	22
11	Physical working environment (including noise, space, office temperature, ventilation etc).	12.135	1395.5	2	9	4	15	7	8	11
12	General market trends and other economic fluctuations.	11.591	1333.0	7	5	19	1	5	14	21
13	Personal habits or mannerisms (including dress, way of conversation, etc).	11.896	1368.0	6	6	1	16	15	22	8
14	Personality differences (such as cultural background, education, social patterns etc).	11.917	1370.5	8	16	14	10	1	9	17
15	Differences in basic values, beliefs or opinions.	11.052	1271.0	19	14	17	13	14	20	1
16	Personal dislike.	11.700	1345.5	13	21	5	5	6	10	6
17	Barriers to interpersonal communication.	11.530	1326.0	16	1	18	20	18	16	13
18	Differences in knowledge or expertise.	12.052	1386.0	3	4	13	9	3	11	9
19	Compensation for a particular position, power or recognition.	11.957	1375.0	4	11	7	6	9	21	3
20	Hierarchical differences in status power and rewards.	11.878	1366.0	15	7	8	17	16	19	20
21	Need for tension release.	11.861	1364.0	11	19	2	3	17	5	18
22	Drive for autonomy.	12.178	1400.5	12	17	10	4	11	15	12

*(Multiple dependent variables)   **HR- Human Resource; PRD- Production; MKG- Marketing &Sales; FIN-Finance & Accounts; SYS- Systems & EDP; FSP- Factory Manager and Special Officials

Table Contd…

[1]ANOVA Chi Sqr. (N=115, df=21) = 45.025   p= 0.00172   Coefficient of concordance= 0.01864   Aver. rank r = 0.01004
[2]ANOVA Chi Sqr. (N = 30, df = 21) = 27.03   p= 0.16985   Coefficient of concordance= 0.04291   Aver. rank r = 0.00990
[3]ANOVA Chi Sqr. (N = 28, df = 21) = 30.873 p= 0.07581   Coefficient of concordance= 0.05251   Aver. rank r = 0.01741
[4]ANOVA Chi Sqr. (N = 15, df = 21) = 25.820 p= 0.21340   Coefficient of concordance= 0.08197   Aver. rank r = 0.01640
[5]ANOVA Chi Sqr. (N = 31, df = 21) = 28.621 p= 0.12340   Coefficient of concordance= 0.04397   Aver. rank r = 0.01210
[6]ANOVA Chi Sqr. (N = 4, df = 21) = 20.0072 p= 0.52081   Coefficient of concordance= 0.23818   Aver. rank r = -0.0158
[7]ANOVA Chi Sqr. (N = 7, df = 21) = 15.817   p= 0.77981   Coefficient of concordance= 0.10760   Aver. rank r = -0.0411

Table 5.5: Concordance Analysis of Managerial Strata–potential sources of conflict

| Group | MANAGERIAL STRATA | | | | | | | | | | | | | | | | | |
| | HR | | | PRD | | | MKG | | | FIN | | | SYS | | | FSP | | |
	Chi Sqr	Aver. rank r	(W)	Chi Sqr	Aver. rank r	(W)	Chi Sqr	Aver. rank r	(W)	Chi Sqr	Aver. rank r	(W)	Chi Sqr	Aver. rank r	(W)	Chi Sqr	Aver. rank r	(W)
Study Group	33.866	0.613	**0.806**	30.308	0.443	**0.722**	27.889	0.328	**0.664**	36.854	0.755	**0.877**	15.557	-0.259	**0.37**	23.454	0.117	**0.558**
HR		******		22.672	0.079	**0.539**	19.138	0.576	**0.456**	28.387	0.351	**0.675**	11.691	-0.443	**0.278**	20.964	-0.001	**0.499**
PRD	22.671	0.079	**0.539**		******		26.917	0.281	**0.640**	24.284	0.156	**0.578**	18.024	-0.142	**0.429**	20.798	-0.009	**0.495**
MKG	19.138	-0.088	**0.455**	26.917	0.281	**0.641**		******		28.743	0.368	**0.684**	24.142	0.149	**0.575**	20.016	-0.047	**0.477**
FIN	28.387	0.352	**0.676**	24.284	0.156	**0.578**	28.743	0.368	**0.684**		******		16.008	-0.238	**0.381**	23.146	0.102	**0.551**
SYS	11.691	-0.443	**0.278**	18.023	-0.141	**0.429**	24.142	0.149	**0.575**	16.007	-0.237	**0.381**		******		16.411	-0.218	**0.391**
FSP	20.964	-0.001	**0.499**	20.798	-0.009	**0.495**	20.016	-0.047	**0.477**	23.146	0.102	**0.551**	16.411	-0.218	**0.391**		******	

- *(W)*= Kendall's Coefficient of Concordance.
- ANOVA according to Friedman.   Aver. rank r is calculated according to Spearman's

Strata Analysis: ANOVA Chi Sqr. (N = 6, df = 21) = **23.115**   p= **0.18345**   Coefficient of concordance= **0.10760**   Aver. rank r = **0.02014**

Rank Analysis- Projective rank analysis assess the differential rankings obtained through the incorporations of mean scores for each potential source of conflict among the sampled population with that of the sub groups-departmental classification. H_0 explains that there is no difference of ranking preferences among the groups and to assess this, deductive treatment of the ranks and concordance analysis attempt were made. The logical categorisation of the sample was attempted along the lines of departments as this can be the appropriate and situational reliant factor for such an operation. Further the aforesaid categorisation can be regarded as an attempt to exercise reflective projections. This departmental categorisation can act only as an indicative variant as the sampled data may not allow an establishment of the variant resultants to those particular departmental strata. Further the sample frame of the study had not inductively construed these categorisations.

Work standards to be accomplished, an issue level source of conflict had got the top rank among the studied population, followed by physical working environment, differences in knowledge or expertise, and others. Interestingly, the ranks obtained by the substratum concerning these factors were different, though these three variables find a higher place as a potential source of conflict among others. Among the human resource officials–barriers to interpersonal communication, resource allocation and technical issues and work standards to be accomplished, find their respective top slots. This was in tune with their operations and the potential distortion that can arise in their work related environment. In case of production department officials–personal habits or mannerisms need for tension release and administration of wages, salaries, promotions, sanction of leave etc, indicated their potentials to emulate conflicts.

Surprisingly, some of the factors like administration of wages, etc-a function deemed to be of that of human resource department, among others were recorded higher ranks by them. This can be attributed to interdepartmental interactions, particularly of overdependence, procedural flaws, administrative metabolism, or a combination of these among others. The marketing group, the perceived bread winners indicated that general market trends and other economic fluctuations, work standards to be accomplished and need for tension release acts as major sources of conflicts. This perfectly reflects an admixture of organisational, interactional and issue level sources that can commonly attributed to this group. Personality differences, performance appraisal and differences in knowledge or expertise spelt top sources of conflict for the finance professionals as these are indicative of their professional characteristics.

The two least represented sampled population– system professionals and the factory general administration inculcated the depth that was required for the analysis. System professionals, though technical personalities indicated higher ranks to those issue level sources of conflict as such as amount of time spent, work standards etc. Interestingly, they conceded higher ranks to the administration of wages as this can be attributed to the higher market consciousness/awareness about the profession among them. One of the most influential group–factory general administrations had indicated that differences in values, beliefs etc can be most influential in this regard. This seems to be a resultant of generalisation of their primal professional workflow. Interestingly, job objectives and the compensation package were also indicated as major potential source of conflicts by them among other sources ranked accordingly. The intra-indicative factors that acts as potential source of conflict was significantly similar among all subgroups but the concordance of assigning the scores was not as similar as such among all them. The calculated anova chi square values for the subgroups were all below the chi square table values for respective degrees of freedom and only moderated concordance were obtained for all groups. Thus H_0, which can be expressed as the subgroups have same intra ranking patterns, can only be partially acceptable. H_a– that the subgroups had different ranking patterns can also be partially rejected. The ranking patterns of all subgroups were indicating the *primal variables-source of conflicts* and the intra ranking scores were departed even among the intragroup levels.

The similarity of ranking pattern among various subgroups and with the total population can be tested with Kendall's coefficient of concordance, *W*. Overall pattern of the studied population was more concordant with that of finance and human resource professionals, followed by other groups. This can be attributed to the dominance of these two groups among the sample population. Human resource professionals scored are more concordant with finance officers (0.675) among others. *W* of production and marketing officials (0.640); marketing and finance (0.684); system and marketing (0.575); factory generalists and finance (0.551) were all indicative of their higher concordance with each others. Interestingly, most of the *W*'s indicated high concordance with others (totaling 23 out of 30 pairs), except 7 pairs of analysis including that of all subgroups and the total sampled population. H_0 which may be expressed as there are differences among the concordance stratum, can be accepted since the table value for *df*=21, (38.938) is higher than the anova chi square value obtained-23.115.

Group Tables 5.6- 5.10 Factor Analysis of Potential sources of conflict

Table 5.6: Issue Level*[#]

	Factor Loadings		Communality		
Variable	F1[@]	F2	From F1	From F2	Multiple R^2
1	**0.837**	-0.088	0.701	0.708	0.111
3	-0.140	**0.785**	0.020	0.635	0.060
9	0.246	**0.529**	0.061	0.340	0.069
10	**0.718**	**0.306**	0.516	0.610	0.157
18	0.105	**0.542**	0.011	0.305	0.051
Expl.Var	1.307	1.290	*Prin.Components extraction		
Prp.Totl	0.261	0.258	Rotation: Varimax		

Table 5.7: Organisational Level*[#]

	Factor Loadings			Communality			
Variable	F3	F4	F5	From F3	From F4	From F5	Multiple R^2
7	-0.038	**-0.835**	-0.142	0.001	0.699	0.719	0.043
8	0.029	**-0.466**	**0.569**	0.001	0.218	0.542	0.023
11	-0.052	0.224	**0.787**	0.003	0.053	0.673	0.035
12	**0.485**	0.042	**0.404**	0.235	0.237	0.400	0.032
19	**0.789**	0.166	-0.137	0.622	0.650	0.668	0.044
20	**0.609**	-0.391	0.043	0.371	0.524	0.525	0.057
Expl.Var	1.233	1.148	1.148	*Principal Components extraction			
Prp.Totl	0.205	0.191	0.191	Rotation: Varimax			

Table 5.8: Procedural Level*[#]

	Factor Loadings	Communality	
Variable	F6	From F6	Multiple R^2
2	**0.624**	0.389	0.029
4	**-0.596**	0.355	0.025
6	**-0.719**	0.518	0.044
Expl.Var	1.262	*Prin.Components	
Prp.Totl	0.421	Unrotated	

bold marked are >0.30 cut-off point
@ F1-F10 Factor Derivatives

Table 5.9: Interactional Level*[#]

	Factor Loadings				Communality				
Variable	F7	F8	F9	F10	From F7	From F8	From F9	From F10	Multiple R^2
5	**0.755**	0.062	0.108	0.004	0.571	0.575	0.586	0.586	0.096
13	0.110	-0.030	-0.049	**-0.947**	0.012	0.013	0.015	0.912	0.012
14	**0.779**	-0.017	0.019	-0.091	0.607	0.607	0.608	0.616	0.097
15	0.066	**0.759**	0.047	0.056	0.004	0.580	0.582	0.586	0.057
16	0.219	0.239	**0.627**	0.048	0.048	0.105	0.499	0.501	0.064
17	0.123	**0.553**	**-0.451**	0.076	0.015	0.321	0.524	0.530	0.036
21	0.008	-0.105	**0.753**	0.004	0.000	0.011	0.578	0.578	0.060
22	-0.282	**0.548**	**0.308**	**-0.332**	0.080	0.379	0.474	0.585	0.048
Expl.Var	1.337	1.255	1.274	1.027	*Principal Components extraction				
Prp.Totl	0.167	0.157	0.159	0.128	Rotation: Varimax				

Table 5.10: *Supplementary Cells*

[C1]Categorisation	F	Eigen value	%Total Variance	Cumulative Eigen value	Cumulative %	[C2]Categorisation	F	Eigen value	%Total Variance	Cumulative Eigen value	Cumulative %
Issue Level	F1	1.523	30.451	1.523	30.451	Procedural Level	F6	1.262	42.051	1.262	42.051
Issue Level	F2	1.075	21.506	2.598	51.957	Interactional Level	F7	1.446	18.074	1.446	18.074
Organisational Level	F3	1.318	21.969	1.318	21.969	Interactional Level	F8	1.239	15.484	2.685	33.558
Organisational Level	F4	1.155	19.250	2.473	41.219	Interactional Level	F9	1.206	15.071	3.890	48.629
Organisational Level	F5	1.055	17.584	3.528	58.803	Interactional Level	F10	1.003	12.536	4.893	61.165

Factor score exploration and analysis- The main application of factor analysis techniques in this analytical process of potential source of conflict under logical clustering of factors, assumes to reduce the number of variables and to detect structure in the relationships between variables that is to classify variables. Therefore, factor analysis was applied as a data reduction or exploratory structure detection method throughout the process of analysis. To maximise the variation among the components, the Varimax rotation technique was adopted with principal components extraction of factor analysis. The potential sources of conflicts grouped under four levels accordingly acted as four factors with all their clustered variables. A *cut off strategy* integrated with equaling one or more of eigenvalues and greater than 0.30 factor loadings indicate the necessary appropriation of the factor analysis to suit the needs of the present study *(wide reference Item variables - 5.4; factor analysis-tables 5.6 through 5.10).*

<u>Factor- Issue level</u>

Issue level conflicts are those which are necessarily occurred out of a single/multiple cause/s of incidental issues of work related concerns and the focus here usually on the topic and on the task to be performed. Under this factor, five variables are dealt with (1, 3,9,10 and 18) in this study *(table 5.6).* The exploratory factors-F1 and F2 and their respective loadings, combined with the communality and variance assessment shed some light on the combination of the variables' potentialities to act as sources of conflict. In the case of F1, variables 1 and 10 indicated much higher factor loadings, compared with all other possible combinations (0.837 and 0.718, respectively). The combined variables of *conflict over job objectives, errors, misinterpretation of orders, carelessness, etc* can be indicative of the asymmetrical application of functional understanding regarding work related routines. This may be initiated from the sides of the employees or can be a resultant of the organisational structural mislays. This particular combination-factor derivative (F1) may explain the variance regarding the sources identification, up to 30.451 %. Structural flaw in determining job objectives combined with the judgemental misinterpretations plays vital roles as potential sources of conflict.

In case of F2, variables 3,9,10 and 18 arrive at significant loadings. Further this combination prevents a significant role to variable 1; rather that variable was negative loaded. Communality from F2 was visibly more and significant than that from F1. A combination of work standards to be accomplished, amount of time spent, errors and misinterpretations of orders, differences in basic values, beliefs or opinions etc plays a significant role in effectuating the potentiality of conflicts.

These variables can be logically clustered into the broader fold indicating the effectiveness of applied technical knowhow– necessarily a resultant factor at issue level. Obviously, the work standards to be accomplished was loaded with much higher score followed by other variables like differences in knowledge or expertise, amount of time spent on a particular job as well as errors, misinterpretations of orders ,carelessness, etc. Interestingly, the absence of variable 1- conflict over job objectives can stimulate conflicts at these levels. That indicates the negative relationship operating between these clustered factor and conflict over job objectives, though less significant. F1 and F2 can explain the variance among the managerial understanding of potential sources of conflicts up to 51.957 %. Further the multiple R^2 was mostly influenced by variables 10 and 1 among others and they are unavoidable for any combination of deterministic analysis regarding potential sources of conflicts.

Factor- Organisational Level

Organisational variables are broader in their approach and techniques of problem solving in a team-such as analytic methods, decision methods, creativity techniques, formal internal rules for the team, the use of auxiliary means, besides the way in which information and contacts are cultivated with the rest of the organisation, including the rules regarding delegation of work, etc are all dealt at these levels. In this study, six variables (7, 8, 11, 12, 19 and 20) are explored in this regard with three factor derivatives-F3, F4 and F5 (58.803% variance explained). 21.969% variance can be explained with F3, which has significantly higher factor loadings of variables 19, 20 and 12 respectively. Compensation for particular position, hierarchical power differences and general market trends are all indicating the impact of external relations that being enjoyed by the studied population and its effective influence on them.

Negative loadings derived by variables 7 and 8 for F4 indicates that they are pragmatically adjusted with the situation and organisational policies, administration of wages, promotions, etc are no less significant in combination with others. Whereas this indicates that F3 can play a significant role if underrepresented and have the necessary potentialities to emulate conflicts. Variables 8, 11 and 12 are also strengthening in this regard and acts as a corollary to the above two factors explained. The extrageneous influence on the organisational matters, particularly the administration of wages and related matters combined with the market trends and the internal physical working environment infuses conflicts.

Factor- Procedural Level

The variants concerning the planning of activities, resource allocation, appraisal methods are all indicative of the procedural flow among the workforce at snapshot views. Three variables–2, 4 and 6 were explored with a single factor derivative (F6) in this regard. Significant positive factor loading and respective communality for variable 2 enables to explain its basic relationship with that of negatively loaded significant variables 6 and 4. Flaws/constraints of planning operations combined with less effective performance appraisal mechanism and the technical issues concerning resource allocation are all indicative of the clustered influence of operational deficiency essentially accrued through resource limitation and or methodological misappropriations. 42.051% variance can be explained with this factor derivative and certainly it indicates a delimited procedural productiveness infused by organisational constraints.

Factor- Interactional Level

Interactional dynamics among the human workforce at various levels are always potent to act as the source of conflicts. Four factor derivatives (F7-F10), explored with eight variables (5, 13, 14, 15, 16, 17, 21, 22) in combinations, expressing cumulative variance up to 61.165% are dealt in this study. In case of F7, variables 14 and 5 are loaded with positive loadings explain personality differences combined with the inappropriate/ineffective managerial supervision, direction control, etc can be a potential source of conflict and these variables are similar to each. This combination brings a higher communality and the variance. In F8, variables 15, 17 and 22 the intrapersonal dimensions like differences in basic values, beliefs or opinions combined with interpersonal communication barriers and a higher drive for autonomy are all indicative of a relative intrapersonal influential; particularly the drives and approaches can play a vital role in stimulating conflicts.

A combination of variables, 21, 16 and 22 which are positively loaded, and a negatively loaded variable-17 intermittently influence the potentials of conflict, which are all indicative of the effect of individualistic dominance among the organisational communication and workflows. Surprisingly variables 22 and 13 of F10 recorded negative loadings and explain the combined effect. It was further indicated that drive for autonomy– essentially an intrapersonal variable was expressed through the personal habits and mannerisms, which can if negatively perceived becomes potential source of conflicts. F4, with the largest eigenvalues can be regarded as the most influential source of conflict in the interactional level, followed by others.

5.1.3 Past approaches, satisfaction, feelings and emotions of handling conflicts

Approaches- The research hypothesis H2 explains that *Initial approaches towards conflict handling are differentiative among the population along eight indicative approaches- Negotiate, Force, Compromise, Mediational, Arbitrative, Accommodate, Persuade and Avoid.* Eight indicative approaches are put into analysis that spelt mean scores and the differential ranking of the same was carried out *(table 5.11 and 5.12).* The factorial analysis can shed some light on the combinations of variables through factor derivatives *(table 5.13).* The mean values for the variables range between 5.817 to 4.374, and this explain the close knit operational influence of each and every variable/approaches. Compromise, avoidance and arbitrative approaches occupied top three slots followed by others, whereas the differential treatment were only indicative since the mean differences are shrinking in nature. Kendall's tau revealed a positive correlation/agreeability of moderately significant for force and compromise, seeking mediation and accommodative, as well as avoidance and force approaches. Negative tau was recorded between accommodate and force approaches. These dimensions reveal the interrelationship dimensions existing among the eight approaches.

Hypothesis Testing -Projective rank analyses assess the differential rankings obtained through the incorporations of mean scores for each potential source of conflict among the sampled population with that of the *sub groups-departmental* classification. H_0 explains that there is no difference of ranking preferences among the groups in the identified eight approaches and to assess this, deductive treatment of the ranks and concordance analysis attempt were made. The logical categorisation of the sample was attempted along the lines of departments as this can be the appropriate and situational reliant factor for such an operation and the aforesaid categorisation can be regarded as an attempt to exercise reflective projections. The intra-indicative factors that acts as approaches to handle conflict was significantly similar among all subgroups but the concordance of assigning the scores was not as similar as such among all them. The calculated anova chi square values for the subgroups were all below the chi square table values for respective degrees of freedom and only moderated concordance were obtained for all groups. Thus H_0, which can be expressed as the subgroups have same intra ranking patterns to approach and handle conflicts, can only be partially acceptable. H_a- that the subgroups had different ranking patterns of approach mechanism can also be partially rejected. The ranking patterns of all subgroups were indicating the primal variables-approaches of handling conflicts and the intra ranking scores were deviant even among the intragroup levels.

Table 5.11: Conflict and Initial approach

Item/Variable	Avg. Rank	Sum of Ranks	Mean	Std. Dev	Mean Rank	Kendall's Tau Correlations*							
						Negotiate	Force	Compromise	Seek Mediation	Seek Arbitration	Accommodate	Persuade	Avoid
1.Negotiate	4.222	485.500	5.000	1.816	6	1.000	-0.094	0.027	0.000	0.108	-0.040	-0.073	-0.028
2.Force	4.557	524.000	5.148	1.728	4	-0.094	1.000	**0.163**	-0.005	0.049	**-0.165**	0.104	**0.181**
3.Compromise	4.909	564.500	5.374	1.603	1	0.027	**0.163**	1.000	-0.039	0.004	-0.094	0.063	0.038
4. Mediational	4.152	477.500	4.817	1.770	8	0.000	-0.005	-0.039	1.000	0.029	**0.139**	0.105	-0.108
5.Arbitrative	4.787	550.500	5.191	1.747	3	0.108	0.049	0.004	0.029	1.000	-0.124	0.053	-0.094
6.Accomodate	4.517	519.500	5.078	1.738	5	-0.040	**-0.165**	-0.094	**0.139**	-0.124	1.000	-0.106	-0.077
7.Persuade	4.200	483.000	4.817	1.725	7	-0.073	0.104	0.063	0.105	0.053	-0.106	1.000	0.014
8.Avoid	4.657	535.500	5.270	1.506	2	-0.028	**0.181**	0.038	-0.108	-0.094	-0.077	0.014	1.000

(*Correlations highlighted by **bolded** are significant at $p < 0.05000$)

Table 5.12: Rank Analysis– Conflict and Initial approach

Item/Variable	Mean Rank-Managerial Strata**												N=115	
	FIN[1]		FSP[2]		HR[3]		MKG[4]		PRD[5]		SYS[6]		Mean	Mean Rank
	Mean	Rank		Rank	Mean	Rank	Mean	Rank	Mean	Rank	Mean	Rank		
1.Negotiate	5.161	2	5.429	2	4.667	6	5.533	1	4.786	8	5.000	3	5.000	6
2.Force	5.032	6	5.143	4	5.267	5	5.333	3	5.071	6	5.000	4	5.148	4
3.Compromise	5.516	1	5.429	3	5.433	2	5.000	5	5.393	2	5.000	5	5.374	1
4. Mediational	4.516	8	5.143	5	4.467	7	4.533	7	5.250	3	7.250	1	4.817	8
5.Arbitrative	5.065	5	6.000	1	5.467	1	4.867	6	5.107	5	4.500	6	5.191	3
6.Accomodate	5.161	3	4.857	8	5.333	4	4.467	8	4.893	7	6.500	2	5.078	5
7.Persuade	4.871	7	5.000	7	4.233	8	5.133	4	5.250	4	4.250	8	4.817	7
8.Avoid	5.097	4	5.143	6	5.333	3	5.467	2	5.429	1	4.500	7	5.270	2

[1] ANOVA Chi Sqr. (N = 31, df = 7) = 6.335462 $p = 0.50117$ Coeff. of Concordance = 0. 02920 Aver. rank r = -0.0032
[2] ANOVA Chi Sqr. (N = 7, df = 7) = 2.925573 $p = 0.89180$ Coeff. of Concordance = 0. 05971 Aver. rank r = -0.0970
[3] ANOVA Chi Sqr. (N = 30, df = 7) = 17.78444 $p = 0.01298$ Coeff. of Concordance = 0. 08469 Aver. rank r = 0.05313
[4] ANOVA Chi Sqr. (N = 15, df = 7) = 4.210660 $p = 0.75522$ Coeff. of Concordance = 0. 04010 Aver. rank r = -0.0285
[5] ANOVA Chi Sqr. (N = 28, df = 7) = 4.937044 $p = 0.66765$ Coeff. of Concordance = 0. 02519 Aver. rank r = -0.0109
[6] ANOVA Chi Sqr. (N = 4, df = 7) = 9.681818 $p = 0.20734$ Coeff. of Concordance = 0. 34578 Aver. rank r = -0.12771
Scale: ANOVA Chi Sqr. (N = 115, df = 7) = 11.82870 $p = 0.10634$ Coeff. of Concordance = 0. 01469 Aver. rank r = 0.00605

Table 5.13: Factor Analysis– Conflict and initial approach

Factor Analysis Conflict initial approach *[#]						
Factor Loadings			*Communality*			
Item/ Variable	F1[@]	F2	F3	From F1	From F2	From F3	Multiple R^2
1.Negotiate	-0.147	**-0.682**	-0.197	0.021	0.486	0.525	0.098
2.Force	**0.726**	0.209	0.004	0.527	0.571	0.571	0.177
3.Compromise	**0.490**	-0.023	-0.008	0.240	0.240	0.240	0.062
4. Mediational	-0.179	0.070	**0.718**	0.032	0.037	0.552	0.089
5.Arbitrative	0.270	**-0.751**	0.123	0.073	0.637	0.652	0.116
6.Accomodate	**-0.678**	0.284	0.143	0.460	0.541	0.561	0.171
7.Persuade	**0.414**	0.117	**0.641**	0.171	0.185	0.596	0.088
8.Avoid	**0.303**	**0.397**	**-0.497**	0.092	0.249	0.497	0.083
Expl.Var	1.617	1.329	1.248	*Principal Components extraction			
Prp.Totl	0.202	0.166	0.156	Rotation: Varimax			

Bold marked are >0.30 cut-off point
@ F1, F2 and F3 are Factor Derivatives

F	Eigen value	%Total Variance	Cumulative Eigen value	Cumulative %
F1	1.624	20.296	1.624	20.296
F2	1.330	16.629	2.954	36.925
F3	1.240	15.496	4.194	52.421

Figure 5.1: Box and Whiskers Plot–Conflict and initial approach

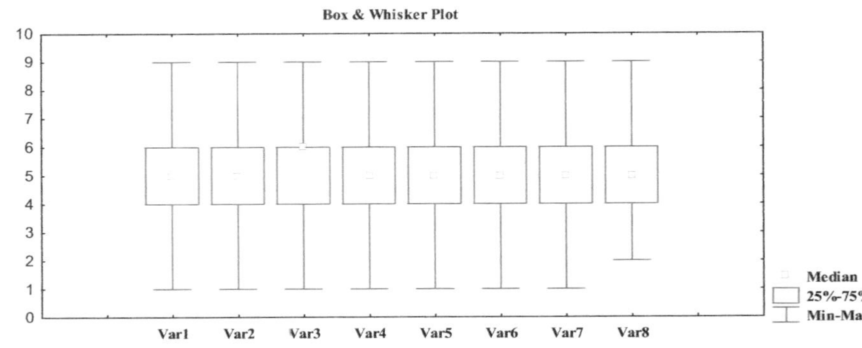

Factorial exploration of handling conflicts- An exploratory analysis along the lines of factorial determination was carried out *(table 5.13)*. Eight variables/approaches were grouped under three factor derivatives considering the factorial notations and cut-off values. In F1, variables-force, compromise, persuade and avoid, obtained positive factor loadings along with a negative loading for accommodate approach. The combination of these five approaches brings a unique derivative which can be attributed to the more self-centric approaches prevailing among the managers. Combinations of approaches are usually perceived to be operative at all these plains. Further a much higher loading obtained by force approach indicates attempts of quick fix solutions to the conflicts by the managers. The gap between avoidance and the other variables shows a shrinking sign and a leniency to avoid rather than compromise, or persuade are tempting to their minds, besides a deep frozen thoughts to accommodate.F2 explains a mutually exclusive approach rendered towards handling conflicts-one being to avoid and the other being a combination of arbitration and negotiation. This vividly points and act as a corollary to the F1 explaining the leniency to avoid. Interestingly, mediation and persuasion find much positive loadings in F3, when the managers detach themselves from the avoidance approach. 52.421% variance of the sampled population can be explained through these three derivatives which concurrently apply through their factorial influence as well as the communality values. Box and whiskers plot *(figure 5.1)* expresses the differential variations of eight approaches for handling conflicts at its most basic levels.

<u>*Satisfaction and managing conflicts in past-*</u>

An exploratory analysis was carried out using a forced checklist to ascertain the perceived satisfaction of the managerial group in case of handling past conflicts *(table 5.14)*. 39.130% managers indicated low level of satisfaction pertaining to the handling of conflicts in past and 19.130% indicated very low level of the same. A cumulative percentage of 29.656 were obtained for the high and very high satisfaction levels. Mean score of 2.678 was ascertained on a conversion (1-5) scale of the satisfaction levels. All the standard test values rendered significant and rejected normality of the function, indicating the true raw analysis.

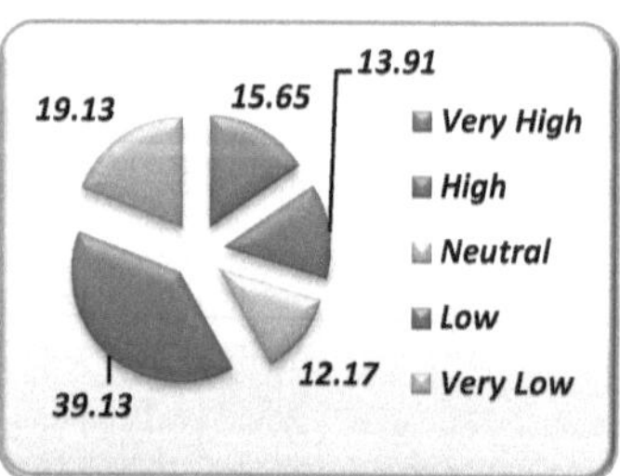

Figure 5.2
Satisfaction and past conflict handling

Table 5.14: Frequency Analysis– Satisfaction and managing past conflict

Item	Count	Cumulative Count	% of cases	Cumulative %	% Rank	
Very High	18	18	15.652	15.652	3	**Mean**=2.678
High	16	34	13.913	29.565	4	**Total**=308.000
Neutral	14	48	12.174	41.739	5	*Min*=1
Low	45	93	39.130	80.870	1	*Max*=5
Very Low	22	115	19.130	100.000	2	**Variance**=1.834
						Std.Dev.=1.354
						Std.Error=0.126

Tests for Normality

- Max D= 0.274358
- **Kolmogorov-Smirnov test:** p is $p < .01$
- **Lilliefors test, mean/std. dev unknown:** p is $p < .01$
- **Shapiro-Wilk's W test**: W= 0.856350
- p= 3.512E-9

(Test values are Significant and rejects Normality of the Function)

Table 5.15: Frequency Analysis– Conflict and Feelings

Item	Count	% of cases*	% Rank
Strong	41	35.652	4
Happy	8	6.957	8
Stressed	56	57.391	3
Preventable	25	21.739	6
Worried	59	60.000	2
Blissful	21	18.261	7
Unavoidable	32	27.826	5
Not unusual	31	70.435	1
Terrible	1	0.870	9
Unwanted	1	0.870	10
Total	**345**	* N=115	

Table 5.16: Frequency Analysis– Conflict and Immediate Emotion

Item	Count	% of cases*	% Rank
Anger	92	80.000	1
Confusion	23	20.000	4
Calm	19	16.522	5
Disturbed	14	12.174	6
Tension	84	73.043	2
Anxiety	55	47.826	3
Indecisiveness	1	0.870	8
Withdrawal	1	0.870	9
Sad	2	1.739	7
Enmity	1	0.870	10
Outburst	1	0.870	11
Total	**293**	* N=115	

Table 5.17: Frequency Analysis– Conflict aftermath

Item	Count	% of cases*	% Rank	Item	Count	% of cases*	% Rank
Angry	24	20.870	11	Stressed	28	24.348	8
Betrayed	80	69.565	3	Strong	100	86.957	2
Competent	28	24.348	7	Satisfied	26	22.609	10
Desperate	49	42.609	5	Relieved	103	89.565	1
Guilty	45	39.130	6	Vengeance	1	0.870	13
Powerful	78	67.826	4	Job's part	2	1.739	12
Sad	27	23.478	9	Frustration	1	0.870	14

Total Count=592
*N=115

Feelings, emotions and conflict aftermath- The immediate emotions and feelings expressed when a conflict occurred in past as well the immediate conflict responses are ascertained by suitable checklists that allows to not only record the expressed responses but also other responses, if the managers wishes so. Frequency analysis was carried out and the resultants showed predominant factor/s in each category. The data was less suitable for testing and the research frame intends only an exploration in these regards. In case of feelings, conflict as not unusual, worried about the conflicts and the stress it produces were occupied in the top three slots *(table 5.15)*. Positive feelings like strengthening tendencies, etc was recorded by a considerable percentage, though the negative and or indifferent feelings about the past conflicts were visibly dominating among the studied population. Immediate emotions expressed by the conflict situation were assessed through the checklist method, with an open slot to record other option/s *(table 5.16)*. Interestingly anger was recorded as the top emotion expressed by the group, followed by tension and anxiety. Other disturbing emotions are also recorded and ranked accordingly.

The immediate response following the conflict aftermath was also ascertained through checklist method, with open slots *(table 5.17)*. It seems that the higher pattern allocation to the relieved stature and a strengthening of the position are all indicative of the positive outfit that follows after an *end* of conflict situations. It seems that the feelings, emotions and immediate aftermath of conflict situations are all indicative of the heightened negativity of the conflict that was prevail among the sampled population.

5.1.4 Comparing managerial styles and the other party in picture

The identified conflict management styles and their adoption, when the other party being hierarchically superior, subordinate or peer etc was accrued through a forced rank list method. Rank frequencies for each group/other party were calculated and the same can shed some on the differences, if any in these regards *(table 5.18)*. Cumulative rank frequencies were calculated keeping the rank denominations and utilising the differential point allocation. Three points were allotted to rank 1, two to rank 2 and one to rank 3 in this regard. The other party being superior, subordinate, peer, friend, woman/man, elder/younger were all explored through these scales which requires the recording of ranking of top three slots that are most appropriately perceived as applicable by the managers.

Table 5.18: Rank Frequency Analysis- Other Party and Style

Style Set	Rank Frequency																	
	Boss/Superiors						Peers/Colleagues						Subordinates					
	1st	%	2nd	%	3rd	%	1st	%	2nd	%	3rd	%	1st	%	2nd	%	3rd	%
Accommodate	56	48.70			38	33.04											3	2.61
Avoid							30	26.09					29	25.22	3	2.61		
Yield	54	46.96	56	48.70			59	51.30							56	48.70		
Compete							26	22.61							30	26.09		
Compromise	2	1.74	59	51.30	36	31.30			89	77.39	5	4.35	45	39.13			30	26.09
Collaborate	3	2.61			41	35.65			26	22.61	56	48.70	8	6.96	26	22.61	52	45.22
Ignore											54	46.96	33	28.70			30	26.09
Force																		
Total	115	100	115	100	115	100	115	100	115	100	115	100	115	100	115	100	115	100

Style Set	Rank Frequency																	
	Friend						Woman/Man						Elder/Younger					
	1st	%	2nd	%	3rd	%	1st	%	2nd	%	3rd	%	1st	%	2nd	%	3rd	%
Accommodate	32	27.83					8	6.96	6	5.22	5	4.35	32	27.83	23	20.00	3	2.61
Avoid	11	9.57			5	4.35	2	1.74	5	4.35	26	22.61	36	31.30	12	10.43	23	20.00
Yield			1	0.87			4	3.48	4	3.48	12	10.43	2	1.74	2	1.74	3	2.61
Compete					27	23.48	25	21.74	56	48.70	33	28.70	3	2.61	3	2.61	25	21.74
Compromise	32	27.83	83	72.17			41	35.65	15	13.04	37	32.17	36	31.30	38	33.04	22	19.13
Collaborate	34	29.57	29	25.22	29	25.22	35	30.43	21	18.26			5	4.35	22	19.13	33	28.70
Ignore	5	4.35	2	1.74	54	46.96			2	1.74			1	0.87	14	12.17	4	3.48
Force	1	0.87							6	5.22	2	1.74			1	0.87	2	1.74
Total	115	100	115	100	115	100	115	100	115	100	115	100	115	100	115	100	115	100

Table 5.19: Cumulative Rank Frequency Analysis (weighted) - Other Party and Style

Style Set	Boss/Superior		Peers/Colleagues		Subordinates		Friend		Woman/Man		Elder/Younger	
	Wgtd.	Rank	Wgtd.	Rank	Wgtd.	Rank	Wgtd.	Rank	Wgtd.	Rank	Wgtd.	Rank
Accommodate	59.71	2	0.00	7	0.87	7	27.83	3	11.88	5	42.03	3
Avoid	0.00	5	26.09	4	26.96	5	11.01	5	12.17	4	44.93	2
Yield	79.42	1	51.30	2	32.46	4	0.58	8	9.28	6	3.77	7
Compete	0.00	6	22.61	5	17.39	6	7.83	6	63.77	1	11.59	5
Compromise	46.33	3	53.04	1	47.83	1	75.94	1	55.07	2	59.71	1
Collaborate	14.49	4	31.30	3	37.10	3	54.78	2	42.61	3	26.67	4
Ignore	0.00	7	15.65	6	37.39	2	21.16	4	1.16	8	10.14	6
Force	0.00	8	0.00	8	0.00	8	0.87	7	4.06	7	1.16	8

In case of boss/superior, being the other party to the conflict, managers recorded a preferred and or dominant conflict styles. 79.42 points were recorded for the yield style, which occupies the top slot in this category followed by accommodate (59.71 points), compromise (46.38 points) among others up to the eight rankings indicated in *table 5.19*. When the other party seems to be peers– managers preferred compromise (53.04 points), yield (32.46 points), collaborate (31.30 points) in top slots among others. When it was their subordinates; compromise (47.83 points), ignore (37.39 points), and collaborate (37.10 points) were recorded in top slots followed by other options. If the party was a friend, the top slots were lenient towards compromise (75.94 points), collaborate (54.78 points), and accommodate (27.83 points), followed through others. The gender differentials were recorded vividly in this regard as indicated by higher points given to 3C-approaches (compete, compromise and collaborate). Compromise, avoid and accommodate approaches among others were recorded higher points to those when the other party was younger/elder-presenting the age differentials. It was clearly evident by the points obtained by each stratum that there exists a predominant approach or approaches that highly depend on the other party, hierarchically speaking.

5.1.5 Conflict and Conflict Management basics

There exists a multitude of factors that impulsively responsible for perceived differentials concerning conflicts and its management. The fundamental assumptions regarding conflicts that are necessarily different from the prejudiced positions among the managers and the related organisational characteristics are all explored and assessed through a seven point scale set exhibited in part b of CMI (*refer appendix*). Twenty one items are logically grouped into five exploratory factorial dimensions *(table 5.22-5.26)* alongside the basic statistical operations expressed through *table 5.20*. Kendall's tau correlations are calculated to compare the agreeability or disagreeability among these variables *(table 5.21)*.

Majority of the mean scores were indicating a higher agreeability towards the statements and only five variables (6, 9, 10, 13 and 15) had expressed lesser mean score-pointing the disagreeability about the stated variables. The standard deviation was also corollary to these and a box and whiskers plot was expressive of the relative importance attached to those twenty one statements expressed.

Table 5.20: Frequency Analysis–Conflict basics
(Nature, Initial Responses, Gender, Age, Hierarchical levels, etc.)

Item. No.	Description	SD		D		DS		N		AS		A		SA		Mean	Std. Dev.
		Count	%	Count	%	Count	%	Count	%	Count	%	Count	%	Count	%		
1	Unavoidability		*		*	1	0.87	4	3.48	49	42.61	32	27.83	29	25.22	4.635	1.209
2	Positive Force		*		*		*	1	0.87	62	53.91	19	16.52	33	28.70	4.704	0.982
3	Age -Younger		*		*	1	0.87	1	0.87	63	54.78	11	9.56	39	33.91	4.730	1.037
4	Leaders' Trait		*		*		*		*	67	58.26	24	20.87	24	20.87	4.626	0.811
5	Time factor		*		*		*		*	63	54.78	15	13.04	37	32.17	4.774	0.909
6	Gender-1	8	6.95		*	54	46.96	25	21.74	26	22.61	1	0.87	1	0.87	2.478	1.524
7	Age –Elder-1		*		*		*		*	71	61.74	20	17.39	24	20.87	4.591	0.815
8	Hierarchy-1	4	3.48		*	31	26.96	16	13.91	43	37.39	8	6.95	13	11.30	3.365	1.718
9	Destructivity		*		*	49	42.61	22	19.13	33	28.70	5	4.35	6	5.22	2.957	1.635
10	Punished in	9	7.83		*	47	40.87	22	19.13	28	24.35	4	3.48	5	4.35	2.713	1.658
11	Humor		*		*		*		*	74	64.35	17	14.78	24	20.87	4.565	0.818
12	Style different		*		*		*		*	69	60	18	15.65	28	24.35	4.643	0.850
13	Gender-2	28	24.35		*	41	35.65	19	16.52	10	8.69		*	17	14.78	2.548	1.925
14	Age –Elder-2		*		*		*		*	68	59.21	19	16.52	28	24.35	4.652	0.849
15	Comfortability	28	24.35		*	40	34.78	18	15.65	11	9.57		*	18	15.65	2.609	1.941
16	Time factor		*		*		*		*	75	65.21	17	14.78	23	20	4.548	0.808
17	Gender-3		*		*		*		*	72	62.61	15	13.04	28	24.35	4.617	0.854
18	Hierarchy-2		*	28	24.35	45	39.13	10	8.69	19	19.52		*	13	11.30	3.000	1.493
19	Anger		*		*		*		*	73	63.48	15	13.04	27	23.48	4.600	0.846
20	Aggressiveness		*		*		*	6	5.21	57	50.89	18	15.65	34	29.57	4.539	1.378
21	Hierarchy-3		*		*		*		*	72	62.61	14	12.17	29	25.21	4.626	0.863

Item wise- *1) Conversion Scale 1-6*   *2) Mean substituted for neutral values*   *3) N=115*

Figure 5.3: Box and Whiskers Plot– conflict basics

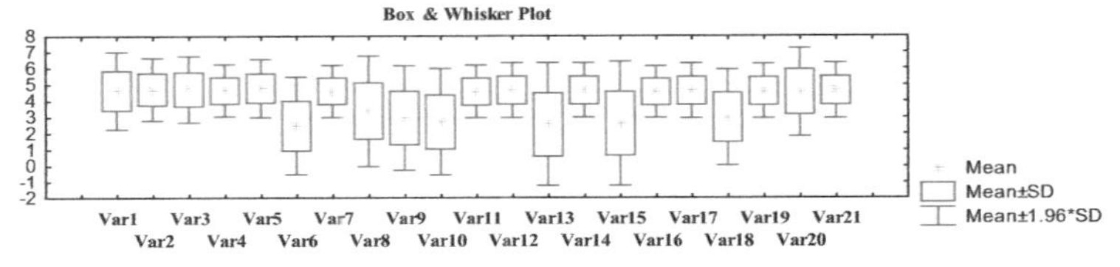

Kendall's tau correlation matrix shows a moderate positive correlations operating among the variables/statements between 4 and 16 (0.37), 6 and 9 (0.25), 12 and 14 (0.25), 9 and 14 (0.24), 3 and 16 (0.22). Ten pairs show a leniency towards positive correlations with tau less than 0.19 and seven pairs show leniency towards negative correlation, though significant but very low within the spheres adjacent to -0.20.This was not unexpected as the statements were only explorative in these regards. The factorial grouping and the supplementary negation operations exercised among the variables brings few factor clusters that was essentially derivative, keeping these dimensions.

Tables 5.22-5.26 explore these variables alongside with a logical clustering of them through five identifiable dimensions-factors conflict nature, age dimensions, gender dimensions, conflict management-initial responses and managerial hierarchy. Factor analysis of conflict nature establishes two factor derivatives-F1 and F2 clustering variables/statements 1, 2, 4 and 9. In F1, moderately higher positive factor loadings were obtained to variables 2 and 1. Concurrently moderately higher negative factor loadings were obtained to variables 4 and 9. Conflict as a positive force for change and growth was appreciated in this regard by the managers and a higher positive loading towards it as an unavoidable factor also establishes a new added dimension to the nature of conflict. Further, negative loadings to variables 4 and 9 reveal a diametrically opposite dimension regarding conflict as an important leadership trait and its destructive nature. In F2, variables 9 and 1 obtained higher positive factor loadings, indicating that the destructive nature of conflicts was perfectly correlated with its unavoidability. In essence, conflict as a positive force and unavoidable in workplaces was negatively attributed towards it being a leadership trait or as a destructive one. Interestingly, if it is regarded as a leadership trait then it projects a destructive picture to the organisational understanding. 56.825% variance can be explained with these two factor derivates shows the importance it rendered to this factor- perceived nature of conflict.

Gender differentials were explored through factor derivatives F3 and F4 (statements 6, 13 and 17). F3 reveals higher positive and negative loadings to 13 and 6 respectively, establishing a fact that managers are highly comfortable managing parties being woman, though they seems to agree to disagree about the fact that women can be managed more easily than men. Gender differentials are highly influential for managing conflicts, revealed by very high positive loading in F2 to 17.

Table 5.21: Kendall's tau correlations*- Conflict Basics

Item	1	2	3	4	5	6	7	8	9	10	11	12	13	14	15	16	17	18	19	20	21
1	1.00	0.06	0.01	-0.03	-0.02	**-0.16**	0.04	-0.05	0.09	-0.11	0.07	0.00	0.02	0.03	-0.02	0.02	-0.06	-0.01	0.03	**-0.13**	0.02
2	0.06	1.00	-0.10	-0.07	**-0.13**	-0.10	0.01	**-0.13**	-0.07	0.01	0.10	-0.10	-0.07	-0.04	**0.16**	0.02	0.06	-0.02	-0.02	-0.03	**0.17**
3	0.01	-0.10	1.00	-0.02	-0.09	0.01	0.07	**0.14**	0.04	0.06	**0.16**	0.02	0.06	-0.12	0.08	**0.22**	-0.05	-0.08	**0.17**	-0.02	0.01
4	-0.03	-0.07	-0.02	1.00	**-0.15**	0.10	**-0.18**	0.01	0.09	-0.05	-0.11	**0.18**	0.03	0.06	-0.01	**0.37**	-0.04	0.06	0.08	-0.09	0.02
5	-0.02	**-0.13**	-0.09	**-0.15**	1.00	0.07	**0.17**	-0.04	0.04	0.11	-0.03	0.05	-0.03	0.01	0.02	**-0.13**	-0.01	-0.03	-0.20	0.06	-0.01
6	**-0.16**	-0.10	0.01	0.10	0.07	1.00	0.04	-0.01	**0.25**	-0.05	0.00	0.06	0.00	0.01	0.03	0.07	0.00	-0.10	**-0.02**	**0.13**	0.07
7	0.04	0.01	0.07	**-0.18**	**0.17**	0.04	1.00	0.01	0.03	-0.02	**0.15**	0.11	0.05	**0.12**	**-0.17**	-0.07	-0.01	**-0.14**	-0.07	**0.14**	**0.17**
8	-0.05	**-0.13**	**0.14**	0.01	-0.04	-0.01	0.01	1.00	-0.09	**-0.15**	0.08	0.06	-0.02	0.02	0.00	-0.02	-0.01	0.11	0.02	-0.08	-0.04
9	0.09	-0.07	0.04	0.09	0.04	**0.25**	0.03	-0.09	1.00	0.02	-0.06	0.06	-0.05	**0.24**	0.01	0.04	-0.04	-0.02	**0.12**	0.01	-0.11
10	-0.11	0.01	0.05	-0.05	0.11	-0.05	-0.02	**-0.15**	0.02	1.00	-0.03	-0.07	-0.05	0.00	0.09	0.00	-0.07	-0.06	-0.01	-0.10	-0.06
11	0.07	0.10	**0.16**	-0.11	-0.03	0.00	**0.15**	0.08	-0.06	-0.03	1.00	**-0.18**	-0.10	-0.11	-0.04	0.05	-0.04	0.05	**0.20**	0.07	**-0.13**
12	0.00	-0.10	0.02	**0.18**	0.05	0.06	0.11	0.06	0.06	-0.07	**-0.18**	1.00	0.01	**0.25**	-0.01	**0.13**	0.01	-0.09	-0.06	**-0.13**	-0.03
13	0.02	-0.07	0.06	0.03	-0.03	0.00	0.05	-0.02	-0.05	-0.05	-0.10	0.01	1.00	-0.01	-0.03	0.02	-0.01	-0.02	0.04	0.03	0.03
14	0.03	-0.04	-0.12	0.06	0.01	0.01	**0.12**	0.02	**0.24**	0.00	-0.11	**0.25**	-0.01	1.00	-0.01	**-0.15**	-0.08	-0.02	-0.08	-0.03	-0.02
15	-0.02	**0.16**	0.08	-0.01	0.02	0.03	**-0.17**	0.00	0.01	0.09	-0.04	-0.01	-0.03	-0.01	1.00	0.09	0.10	-0.02	0.00	0.10	0.09
16	0.02	0.02	**0.22**	**0.37**	**-0.13**	0.07	-0.07	-0.02	0.04	0.00	0.05	**0.13**	0.02	**-0.15**	0.09	1.00	0.04	-0.02	0.07	-0.11	0.00
17	-0.06	0.06	-0.05	-0.04	-0.01	0.00	-0.01	-0.01	-0.04	-0.07	-0.04	0.01	-0.01	-0.08	0.10	0.04	1.00	0.06	**-0.15**	0.01	-0.12
18	-0.01	-0.02	-0.08	0.06	-0.03	-0.10	**-0.14**	0.11	-0.02	-0.06	0.05	-0.09	-0.02	-0.02	-0.02	-0.02	0.06	1.00	0.11	-0.11	0.00
19	0.03	-0.02	**0.17**	0.08	**-0.20**	-0.02	-0.07	0.02	**0.12**	-0.01	**0.20**	-0.06	0.04	-0.08	0.00	0.07	**-0.15**	0.11	1.00	**0.13**	-0.06
20	**-0.13**	-0.03	-0.02	-0.09	0.06	**0.13**	**0.14**	-0.08	0.01	-0.10	0.07	**-0.13**	0.03	-0.03	0.10	-0.11	0.01	-0.11	**0.13**	1.00	0.02
21	0.02	**0.17**	0.01	0.02	-0.01	0.07	**0.17**	-0.04	-0.11	-0.06	**-0.13**	-0.03	0.03	-0.02	0.09	0.00	-0.12	0.00	-0.06	0.02	1.00

*Correlations highlighted by bolded are significant at p <0.05000

Table 5.22: Factor Analysis Conflict-Nature

Conflict Nature*[#]					
Factor Loadings			**Communality**		
Item	F1[@]	F2	From F1	From F2	Multiple R^2
1	**0.409**	**0.732**	0.167	0.702	0.029
2	**0.678**	0.087	0.460	0.467	0.022
4	**-0.617**	0.084	0.381	0.388	0.015
9	**-0.400**	**0.745**	0.160	0.715	0.026
Expl.Var	1.168	1.105	*Prin. Components extraction		
Prp.Totl	0.292	0.276	Rotation: Varimax		

Bold marked are >0.30 cut-off point
@ F1 and F2 are Factor Derivatives

F	Eigen value	%Total Variance	Cumulative Eigen value	Cumulative %
F1	1.169	29.222	1.169	29.222
F2	1.104	27.602	2.273	56.825

Table 5.23: Factor Analysis Gender-Dimension

Gender Dimension*[#]					
Factor Loadings			**Communality**		
Item	F3[@]	F4	From F3	From F4	Multiple R^2
6	**-0.711**	0.045	0.505	0.507	0.000
13	**0.710**	0.045	0.504	0.506	0.000
17	0.000	**0.998**	0.000	0.996	0.000
Expl.Var	1.009	1.000	*Prin. Components extraction		
Prp.Totl	0.336	0.333	Rotation: Varimax		

Bold marked are >0.30 cut-off point
@ F3 and F4 are Factor Derivatives

F	Eigen value	%Total Variance	Cumulative Eigen value	Cumulative %
F3	1.009	33.645	1.009	33.645
F4	1.000	33.334	2.009	66.980

Table 5.24: Factor Analysis Age-Dimension

Age Dimension*[#]					
Factor Loadings			**Communality**		
Item	F5[@]	F6	From F5	From F6	Multiple R^2
3	0.001	**-0.909**	0.000	0.826	0.014
7	**0.759**	**-0.338**	0.576	0.691	0.030
14	**0.756**	**0.342**	0.571	0.689	0.030
Expl.Var	1.148	1.057	*Prin. Components extraction		
Prp.Totl	0.383	0.352	Rotation: Varimax		

Bold marked are >0.30 cut-off point
@ F5 and F6 are Factor Derivatives

F	Eigen value	%Total Variance	Cumulative Eigen value	Cumulative %
F5	1.148	38.258	1.148	38.258
F6	1.057	35.249	2.205	73.507

Table 5.25: Factor Analysis Conflict Management-Initial Responses

	Conflict Management Initial Responses								
	Factor Loadings				Communality				
Item No.	F7[@]	F8	F9	F10	From F7	From F8	From F9	From F10	Multiple R^2
5	0.067	**-0.629**	0.127	0.094	0.005	0.401	0.417	0.426	0.089
10	**0.580**	**-0.368**	**0.413**	-0.276	0.337	0.472	0.643	0.719	0.058
11	**0.546**	**0.424**	-0.023	0.034	0.299	0.479	0.479	0.480	0.086
12	**-0.732**	0.007	0.172	-0.180	0.536	0.536	0.565	0.598	0.096
15	-0.086	-0.048	**0.822**	0.194	0.007	0.010	0.685	0.722	0.032
16	-0.147	**0.483**	**0.427**	**-0.447**	0.021	0.255	0.438	0.638	0.053
19	0.200	**0.662**	0.092	0.258	0.040	0.478	0.487	0.554	0.122
20	0.073	0.074	0.178	**0.849**	0.005	0.011	0.042	0.764	0.077
Expl.Var	1.250	1.392	1.114	1.144	* Principal Components extraction, Varimax Rotated				
Prp.Totl	0.156	0.174	0.139	0.143	[@] F7-F10- Factor Derivatives, **bold** marked are >0.30 cut-off point				

F	Eigen value	%Total Variance	Cumulative Eigen value	Cumulative %
F7	1.452	18.151	1.452	18.151
F8	1.307	16.342	2.759	34.493
F9	1.114	13.924	3.873	48.417
F10	1.027	12.840	4.901	61.257

Table 5.26: Factor Analysis- Managerial Hierarchy

Managerial Hierarchy*[#]				
Factor Loadings		Communality		
Item	F11[@]	F12	From F11	From F12	Multiple R^2
8	**0.613**	**0.459**	0.375	0.586	0.013
18	**0.833**	-0.206	0.694	0.737	0.008
21	0.074	**-0.889**	0.005	0.796	0.006
Expl.Var	1.075	1.044	*Prin. Components extraction		
Prp.Totl	0.358	0.348	Rotation: Varimax		

Bold marked are >0.30 cut-off point
@ F11 and F12 are Factor Derivatives

F	Eigen value	%Total Variance	Cumulative Eigen value	Cumulative %
F11	1.106	36.858	1.106	36.858
F12	1.013	33.781	2.119	70.639

Age differentials were explored through F5 and F6 with variables-3, 7 and 14 *(table 5.24)*. F5 revealed the respect enjoyed by the older persons and the effectiveness established by age through higher positive loadings to 7 and 14. In F6, negative loadings for 3 and 7 and a positive loading for the variable 14, seems to be disturbed the spectrum with an admixture of old and young parties to the conflict. The rationalisation if compared with that of the effectiveness of conflict handling between aged and young managers indicate a leniency towards an indifferent approach with younger parties and an assuming effectiveness of handling conflicts by the older persons. 73.507% of variance can be explained through these two factor derivatives regarding the age dimensions.

An array of initial responses towards conflict handling, particularly related to the skills, applicability, methods, techniques were all dealt through four factor derivatives comprising statements–5, 10,11,12 15,16,19 and 20 in this regard *(table.5.25)*. F7 recorded moderately higher positive loadings 10 and 11, concurrently enabling a higher negative loading to statement 12.This can be attributed that displaying emotions, humorist attitudes definitely affects the different styles in managing conflicts or in other words, emotional and humorist tendencies are more appreciated than using different styles by this factor derivative. In F8, negative loadings to 5 and 10 combined with positive loadings to 19, 16 and 11 reveals that anger management, changed conflict styles and a humourist attitude certainly affects the perceived skill denominations and its related excessive emotional expressions. Inverse proportional dimensions rendered to these two set of skills/methods reestablishes their relative importance and the skill applicability/adaptability in conflict situations.

In F9, higher positive loading to 15 and moderate positive loadings to 16 and 10 reveal that the handling of conflicts and the comfortability have highly related to changed conflict style/usually improved over time and the controlled expression of excessive emotions. F10 had a negative loading on 16 and a higher positive loading on 20. This necessarily reveals the preference/applicability of the lesser display of aggressive styles over the time in a managerial career.

Hierarchical differentials are accrued through F11 and F12, variables 8, 18 and 21. F11 vividly prefers effectiveness in handling conflicts improves through ladders (higher designations) and F12 indicate the differential assumptions about the hierarchical levels of operations. 70.639% variance can be expressed through these two factor derivatives.

5.1.6 Predominant conflict responses

The idea behind a hypothetical exploration of predominant conflict responses during and or immediate conflict aftermath was systematically followed through the seventy five item measure that was designed to discover the different styles and feelings about conflict that individuals have when handling conflict *(part d of CMI)*. It contains five subscales (15 questions in each) exploring, all within the context of workplace conflicts, regarding the respondents'– feelings and beliefs regarding confrontation, emotional expression, public/private behaviour, conflict avoidance, and self-disclosure. (*Wide reference part d of CMI for itemised scales*)

Participants were asked to rate the degree to which a statement reflects their approach to conflict resolution, using a scale from 1 (strongly disagree) to 6 (strongly agree). To control for something known as *response bias*, items for each subscale (i.e., the themes identified by each of the five subscales outlined above) were balanced- for half the questions a rating of '1' reflects a 'higher" score on the subscale while for the other half a higher score is associated with a rating of '6'. Thus, when analysing the questionnaire data, half of the response ratings to each subscale must be reversed so that all scores end up going in the same direction (i.e., so that a rating of '6' has a parallel meaning for all subscale questions). This is a fairly common practice in survey design and analysis. Neutral responses logically yielded with the mean values for computational necessities. For scoring purposes the questions fall into the following subscales, the * denotes reverse scoring.

Exhibit 5.2 Predominant conflict responses' subscales

Conflict Approach/Avoidance Subscale- (4*, 6*, 15*, 18, 23*, 33, 40, 46, 52, 55, 66, 69, 71, 73*, 75*)

Confrontation Subscale- (1, 8*, 12*, 20*, 22*, 25*, 29*, 31*, 38*, 43, 48, 53, 57*, 61*, 67*)

Public/Private Behaviour Subscale- (2*, 11*, 16, 21, 24, 26*, 30*, 35*, 45, 49, 51*, 59, 63, 70, 74)

Emotional Expression Subscale- (5*, 9*, 14*, 19*, 27*, 37*, 42*, 47, 50*, 54, 58, 62, 64*, 68, 72)

Self-Disclosure Subscale- (3*, 7*, 10*, 13*, 17*, 28*, 32*, 34, 36, 39, 41, 44, 56*, 60, 65)

Factor analyses were explored with these subscales along the lines of the variables/statements expressed through the items–totalling seventy five, besides the basic statistical analysis. Factor derivatives with an eigenvalues of one or more was considered for further analysis along with the varimax rotation on the principal components method of factor operations.

<u>Conflict approach/avoidance</u> One of the most influential and expressive responses in managerial conflict situations seems to be that of the approach with which the parties follow and the tendencies to avoid the conflict intentionally.

Seven factor derivatives explained through the factorial influential shed some light on these dimensions *(table 5.28)* appropriately rendered through the basic statistical operations explained in *table 5.27*. In F1, moderately higher positive loadings were obtained by variables-55 and 66, followed by positively loaded 4 and 71. Statement 15 got a moderately higher negative loading too. Conflicts are not perceived to be exciting by the respondents and certainly the arguments do bother them. They are lenient toward waiting to see if the dispute/dissonance resolves itself, rather than to argue with others. They certainly not much appreciate the challenges raised by others against them. Interestingly, the arguments with the *friends* are negatively loaded with these dimensions, indicating their preference to act opposite of what was explained above. F2 reveals strong negative loading to variables 40 and 23, combined with a slight negative loading to 55 and a positive one to the variable 66. Arguments do bother the respondents in normal cases. When others pick arguments with them, managers seems to argue and can find conflicts a little bit exciting comparatively, which can be ascertained by a positive loading to variable 66 and a slight negative to 55.

F3 reveals that when managers do not enjoy the challenging the opinion of the others they feel being drawn into conflicts and or dislike the arguments and vice versa. F4 describes that the arguments pretended to be not to be fun; they do not find conflicts exciting and will never start arguments, when they feel conflicts will never make interesting relationships. Majority of the respondents expressed that they will wait to see if the dispute/dissonance settles itself with time, when they feel others will not challenge their opinions, revealed by F5. Surprisingly, this seems to be an overt reaction through the avoidance approach.

Due to the distress that may occur after the arguments that are necessarily seems to be drawn unnecessarily as perceived by the managers, they will opt out from arguments that leads to conflicts, inferred by F6. From F7, it can be ascertained that there seems to be strong tendency to avoid conflicts at its face value and most of them feel that they are drawn into the conflicts. When they do not avoid, it may be a resultant of the above factor derivatives. In essence the managerial preferences to approach a conflict or to avoid a conflict are greatly influenced by various dimensions like argumentative nature, challenged stature, personal relationships, etc.

Table 5.27: Conflict approach/avoidance subscale—basic statistics

Item No.	Mean	Sum	Min.	Max.	Variance	Std. Dev	Std. Error
4	2.634	295	1	5	1.081	1.040	0.098
6	2.369	263	1	3	0.671	0.819	0.078
15	3.136	323	1	5	1.746	1.321	0.130
18	3.740	389	2	6	1.747	1.322	0.130
23	2.432	270	1	3	0.593	0.770	0.073
33	4.559	506	4	6	0.558	0.747	0.071
40	2.867	324	2	3	0.116	0.341	0.032
46	2.878	331	2	3	0.108	0.328	0.031
52	1.461	168	1	3	0.373	0.611	0.057
55	1.661	191	1	3	0.366	0.605	0.056
66	1.817	209	1	3	0.431	0.657	0.061
69	4.577	508	4	6	0.555	0.745	0.071
71	1.757	202	1	3	0.361	0.601	0.056
73	2.420	271	1	3	0.552	0.743	0.070
75	2.454	276	1	3	0.539	0.734	0.069

Figure 5.4: Conflict approach/avoidance subscale

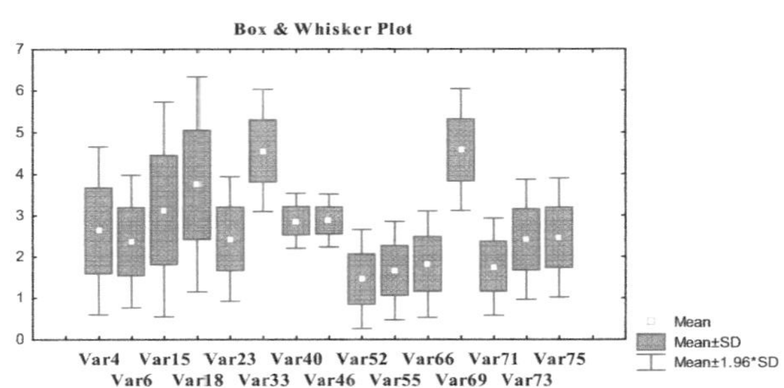

Table 5.28: Predominant conflict responses-Conflict approach/avoidance

Factor Analysis **Conflict Approach/Avoidance Subscale ***														
	Factor Loadings							*Communality*						
Item No.	F1[@]	F2	F3	F4	F5	F6	F7	From F1	From F2	From F3	From F4	From F5	From F6	From F7	Multiple R²
4	**0.324**	0.082	0.105	0.290	**0.691**	0.098	-0.070	0.105	0.111	0.123	0.207	0.685	0.694	0.699	0.114
6	0.022	0.136	**-0.769**	0.062	0.139	-0.055	0.059	0.000	0.019	0.610	0.614	0.634	0.637	0.640	0.128
15	**-0.592**	0.146	0.202	-0.102	0.004	0.190	0.282	0.350	0.372	0.412	0.423	0.423	0.459	0.538	0.103
18	-0.071	-0.022	0.165	**-0.716**	0.117	-0.101	-0.069	0.005	0.006	0.033	0.546	0.560	0.570	0.575	0.120
23	0.099	**-0.769**	0.047	-0.082	0.029	0.016	-0.014	0.010	0.601	0.603	0.610	0.611	0.611	0.611	0.165
33	-0.020	0.001	**-0.320**	0.004	0.113	**-0.393**	**0.676**	0.000	0.000	0.103	0.103	0.116	0.270	0.726	0.223
40	-0.049	**-0.778**	-0.068	0.152	-0.083	0.060	-0.001	0.002	0.608	0.613	0.636	0.643	0.647	0.647	0.170
46	-0.031	0.184	**0.704**	0.014	0.194	-0.130	0.053	0.001	0.035	0.530	0.530	0.568	0.585	0.588	0.127
52	0.067	-0.255	0.007	**-0.331**	0.089	**0.534**	0.104	0.005	0.070	0.070	0.180	0.188	0.472	0.483	0.072
55	**0.671**	**-0.076**	-0.003	**-0.383**	0.045	0.058	0.017	0.450	0.456	0.456	0.603	0.605	0.608	0.608	0.093
66	**0.559**	**0.352**	0.182	0.279	-0.259	0.118	0.183	0.313	0.437	0.470	0.548	0.615	0.629	0.662	0.239
69	0.164	0.158	-0.150	**-0.502**	-0.244	0.111	-0.039	0.027	0.052	0.075	0.326	0.386	0.398	0.400	0.049
71	**0.307**	0.005	0.065	0.230	**-0.785**	0.017	-0.135	0.094	0.094	0.099	0.152	0.768	0.768	0.786	0.299
73	-0.062	0.010	0.116	0.082	-0.007	0.108	**0.813**	0.004	0.004	0.017	0.024	0.024	0.036	0.697	0.112
75	0.066	-0.054	0.082	-0.167	0.007	**-0.834**	0.088	0.004	0.007	0.014	0.042	0.042	0.738	0.746	0.142
Expl.Var	1.371	1.501	1.355	1.316	1.322	1.257	1.285	* Principal Components extraction, Varimax Rotated							
Prp.Totl	0.091	0.100	0.090	0.088	0.088	0.084	0.086	[@] F1-F7 Factor Derivatives, **bold** marked are >0.30 cut-off point							

...

Factor[#]	Eigen value	%Total Variance	Cumulative Eigen value	Cumulative %
1	1.689	11.261	1.689	11.261
2	1.630	10.865	3.319	22.125
3	1.435	9.565	4.754	31.690
4	1.280	8.535	6.034	40.225
5	1.168	7.789	7.202	48.014
6	1.132	7.549	8.334	55.563
7	1.072	7.146	9.406	62.709

\# Extraction: Principal components

<u>Confrontation-leniency subscale</u>   Most of the conflict situations occurred out of confrontational approach or attitude among the managerial forces. An attempt was made to ascertain the influence it communicate and the immediate circumstantial responses expressed by the managerial preferences. Basic statistical measures reveal considerable amount of preferential responses and the factorial analysis arrived at seven factor derivatives for this subscale.

Factor derivative F1, loaded with high negative factor loadings to variable 57 and 67, with a moderately low negative one to variable 31 reveals that this factor was negatively affected by the above mentioned variables. Managers may not expect their co-workers to know what was in their mind and they may not feel uncomfortable after a dispute, especially to face the parties of conflict and they agree that they prefer to guess the reason that upset the relationships with others. These dimensions lessen the confrontational expressions exercised by the managerial strata, as shown by the negative loadings rendered to them. In F2, variables 1 and 25 got high negative loadings, indicating their combined influence to this factor derivative. It shows that managers feel more comfortable having an argument over other modes like telephonic talk rather than face to face confrontation and this can be certainly influenced by the fact that majority of them dislike about the eye contact during an argument, visibly a projected protective sign. This combined preferential may bring down the direct confrontational approach in the conflict situations. F3 shows the lessening of the confrontations influenced by the preferences regarding toning down their differences with the co-workers and not letting it to climb hierarchy or in cases regarding maintaining/covering up of certain facts, especially past mistakes.

The tendency to express disagreements through writing positively relates with F4, which was also influenced negatively by variables 22 and 53, expressing managerial assumptions that physical confrontations may occur in cases regarding sharp disagreements and their toning down strategies for conflicts with co-workers. F5 reveals that any serious disagreements may initiate a confrontational approach and managers may feel uncomfortable when personal thoughts or believes are questioned by others during dispute. Managers may prefer to wait for the right time to solve issues and in cases express their desire for face to face discussions, bringing down the confrontational leniency, inferred through F6. F7 indicates their naturalistic tendencies for face to face discussions that may not give concessions to others at all and are intended towards lesser confrontations, profited through the goodwill generated by giving a passionate hearing to others.

Table 5.29: Confrontation subscale—basic statistics

Item No.	Mean	Sum	Min.	Max.	Variance	Std. Dev	Std. Error
1	3.841	411	2	6	1.569	1.253	0.121
8	2.454	265	1	4	0.792	0.890	0.086
12	3.490	363	1	5	1.650	1.285	0.126
20	3.123	331	1	5	1.975	1.405	0.137
22	4.148	448	4	5	0.127	0.357	0.034
25	2.436	268	1	3	0.634	0.796	0.076
29	4.079	465	4	5	0.073	0.271	0.025
31	3.467	371	1	5	0.629	0.793	0.077
38	2.615	285	1	4	0.776	0.881	0.084
43	2.929	328	2	4	0.085	0.291	0.028
48	4.591	505	4	6	0.593	0.770	0.073
53	4.564	502	4	6	0.560	0.748	0.071
57	2.450	272	1	3	0.559	0.748	0.071
61	4.019	434	3	6	0.878	0.937	0.090
67	2.441	271	1	3	0.558	0.747	0.071

Figure 5.5: Confrontation subscale

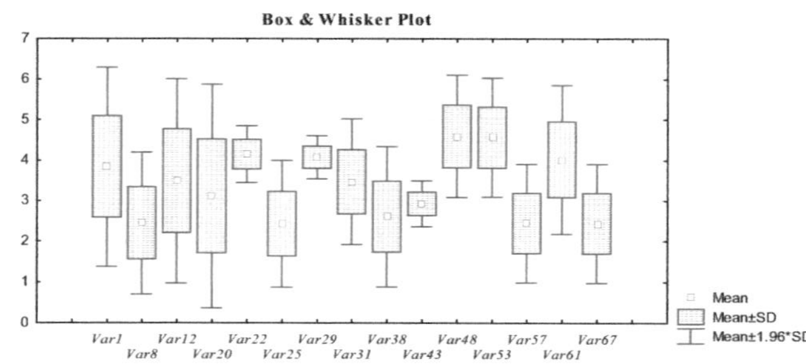

Table 5.30: Predominant conflict responses-Confrontation

| Item No. | Factor Analysis **Confrontation Subscale** * | | | | | | | | | | | | | |
| | *Factor Loadings* | | | | | | | *Communality* | | | | | | | Multiple R^2 |
	F1[@]	F2	F3	F4	F5	F6	F7	From F1	From F2	From F3	From F4	From F5	From F6	From F7	
1	0.049	**-0.815**	0.083	0.044	0.029	0.030	0.074	0.002	0.666	0.673	0.675	0.676	0.677	0.682	0.227
8	0.046	0.060	0.056	0.033	0.027	-0.131	**-0.775**	0.002	0.006	0.009	0.010	0.011	0.028	0.629	0.085
12	0.045	-0.288	-0.240	0.056	**-0.741**	-0.128	0.029	0.002	0.085	0.143	0.146	0.695	0.711	0.712	0.228
20	-0.164	-0.026	-0.029	**0.677**	0.254	-0.183	0.197	0.027	0.028	0.029	0.487	0.551	0.585	0.623	0.077
22	-0.038	-0.168	-0.071	**-0.659**	0.233	-0.270	0.136	0.001	0.030	0.035	0.470	0.524	0.597	0.615	0.094
25	0.017	**-0.810**	0.040	-0.134	-0.084	-0.068	0.026	0.000	0.657	0.658	0.676	0.683	0.688	0.689	0.254
29	-0.014	0.119	0.134	-0.050	**-0.788**	0.037	0.065	0.000	0.014	0.032	0.035	0.656	0.657	0.662	0.104
31	**-0.301**	-0.086	0.107	0.121	0.138	0.264	-0.263	0.091	0.098	0.109	0.124	0.143	0.213	0.282	0.054
38	0.011	-0.219	-0.126	0.148	-0.086	**-0.801**	-0.163	0.000	0.048	0.064	0.086	0.093	0.735	0.762	0.136
43	0.015	0.041	0.012	-0.068	0.029	0.083	**-0.678**	0.000	0.002	0.002	0.007	0.008	0.014	0.474	0.044
48	0.055	0.248	0.241	-0.290	0.070	**-0.593**	0.156	0.003	0.064	0.122	0.206	0.211	0.563	0.588	0.067
53	-0.005	0.065	**-0.774**	**-0.307**	0.031	0.114	0.043	0.000	0.004	0.603	0.698	0.699	0.712	0.714	0.135
57	**-0.842**	0.038	0.009	0.030	0.002	0.011	0.038	0.709	0.710	0.710	0.711	0.711	0.711	0.713	0.245
61	0.076	0.075	**-0.774**	0.231	-0.051	-0.114	0.062	0.006	0.011	0.611	0.664	0.667	0.680	0.684	0.159
67	**-0.840**	0.050	0.027	0.031	-0.007	0.013	0.045	0.705	0.707	0.708	0.709	0.709	0.709	0.711	0.246
Expl.Var	1.549	1.582	1.378	1.195	1.333	1.244	1.258	* Principal Components extraction, Varimax Rotated							
Prp.Totl	0.103	0.105	0.092	0.080	0.089	0.083	0.084	[@] F1-F7 Factor Derivatives, **bold** marked are >0.30 cut-off point							

Factor[#]	Eigen value	%Total Variance	Cumulative Eigen value	Cumulative %
1	1.846	12.306	1.846	12.306
2	1.552	10.344	3.398	22.650
3	1.454	9.693	4.851	32.343
4	1.296	8.640	6.147	40.983
5	1.173	7.818	7.320	48.801
6	1.147	7.645	8.467	56.446
7	1.072	7.145	9.539	63.590

Extraction: Principal components

<u>Public/Private Behaviour subscale-</u> The differential treatment rendered towards the public or private behavioural pattern among the managerial strata was explored through these dimensions. Seven exploratory factor derivatives were identified alongside the basic statistical operations. In F1, variables 11, 51 and 49 are negatively loaded, combined with a positive loading to variable 21. In a public place, managers expressed their hesitation to argue and it can be perfectly correlated with the facts that they feel uncomfortable seeing others argue in public or even with a friend, when others are there. Surprisingly, this factor shows a disturbance experienced by managers when others refuse to discuss a disagreement and this negatively affects F1. In F2, variables 26, 35 and 24 are negatively loaded. This can be interpreted as corollary to F1, that the managers avoid arguments in public and feel uncomfortable when others argue. Interestingly, the leniency towards neutrality in cases regarding not paying attention to the others, when they argue are pointing towards other influentials in this regards.

F3 reveals that the managers avoid arguments in public, even that involving strangers in most of the cases and this factor shows negative relationship existing between these and not such uncomfortability with those arguments involving their friends. F4 reveals interesting dimensions regarding the preference of maintaining the secrecy of arguments that occurred in past by managers, with co-workers and a clear cut distinction regarding arguments– both in public or private. Positive loadings express their related influence on this factor. In F5, variables 30, 49 and 21 are positively loaded. This clearly indicates that managers prefer not to have the arguments to get the attention from others and they are equally annoyed by the nondisclosure of facts by other parties of conflict. Interestingly, they do mind being involved in arguments in a public place with their fellow workers.

In F6, variable 16 was high negatively loaded combined with a low positively loaded variable 21, indicating a inverse relationship existing between them. This clearly indicates the managerial attitude towards arguing in a public place and a preference, not to do so in cases involving their fellow workers. F7 reveals the intra-personal interpretation regarding arguments. When managers do not bother about the others when they argue, their public behaviour would show visible signs of arguments even with fellow workers and vice versa of this dimension may also happen. In total, 63.516 % of the variance can be explained by these seven factors and mean score obtained by fifteen variables of this subscale.

Table 5.31: Public/Private Behaviour subscale—basic statistics

Item No.	Mean	Sum	Min.	Max.	Variance	Std. Dev	Std. Error
2	2.916	312	1	5	1.417	1.191	0.115
11	2.387	265	1	3	0.621	0.788	0.075
16	3.777	389	2	6	1.724	1.313	0.129
21	2.858	303	2	3	0.123	0.350	0.034
24	2.861	309	2	3	0.121	0.347	0.033
26	2.450	272	1	3	0.595	0.772	0.073
30	2.955	331	1	5	1.016	1.008	0.095
35	2.405	267	1	3	0.571	0.755	0.072
45	2.887	332	2	3	0.101	0.318	0.030
49	4.598	515	4	6	0.603	0.776	0.073
51	5.400	621	4	6	0.347	0.589	0.055
59	1.678	193	1	3	0.360	0.600	0.056
63	1.765	203	1	3	0.374	0.612	0.057
70	4.568	507	4	6	0.502	0.709	0.067
74	1.791	206	1	3	0.377	0.614	0.057

Figure 5.6: Public/Private Behaviour subscale

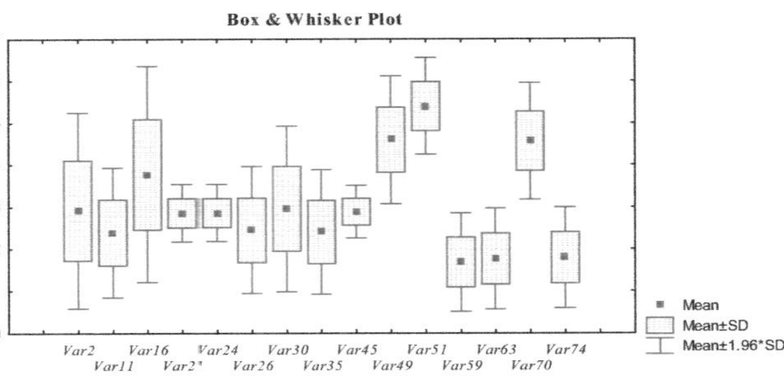

Table 5.32: Predominant conflict responses- Public/Private Behaviour

| Factor Analysis Public/Private Behaviour Subscale * | | | | | | | | | | | | | |
| Factor Loadings | | | | | | | Communality | | | | | | |
Item No.	F1[@]	F2	F3	F4	F5	F6	F7	From F1	From F2	From F3	From F4	From F5	From F6	From F7	Multiple R^2
2	0.109	0.047	0.101	-0.099	-0.031	0.094	**-0.601**	0.012	0.014	0.024	0.034	0.035	0.044	0.405	0.064
11	**-0.748**	0.091	0.272	-0.006	0.116	0.149	0.021	0.560	0.568	0.642	0.642	0.656	0.678	0.678	0.208
16	0.106	0.000	0.067	0.007	0.068	**-0.854**	0.124	0.011	0.011	0.016	0.016	0.020	0.749	0.764	0.113
21	**0.363**	0.271	0.079	0.035	**0.406**	**0.399**	**0.368**	0.132	0.205	0.211	0.213	0.378	0.537	0.672	0.125
24	0.189	**-0.363**	0.078	**0.526**	-0.069	0.286	0.267	0.036	0.168	0.174	0.450	0.455	0.537	0.608	0.105
26	-0.054	**-0.733**	0.116	0.074	-0.094	-0.091	0.082	0.003	0.540	0.553	0.559	0.568	0.576	0.583	0.173
30	0.046	-0.201	-0.092	-0.117	**0.791**	0.067	-0.017	0.002	0.043	0.051	0.065	0.690	0.694	0.694	0.244
35	0.095	**-0.724**	-0.166	-0.130	0.240	0.081	-0.002	0.009	0.533	0.561	0.578	0.635	0.642	0.642	0.191
45	-0.041	-0.050	0.104	-0.149	0.009	0.002	**0.748**	0.002	0.004	0.015	0.037	0.037	0.037	0.597	0.096
49	**-0.307**	0.120	0.112	0.089	**0.716**	-0.190	0.075	0.094	0.108	0.121	0.129	0.642	0.678	0.684	0.243
51	**-0.631**	-0.043	**-0.340**	0.085	0.058	-0.052	0.298	0.399	0.401	0.516	0.524	0.527	0.530	0.619	0.126
59	0.020	0.054	0.146	**0.677**	-0.207	-0.284	0.022	0.000	0.003	0.024	0.483	0.526	0.607	0.607	0.141
63	-0.169	0.078	-0.209	**0.685**	0.181	0.147	-0.170	0.029	0.035	0.078	0.547	0.580	0.602	0.631	0.135
70	-0.297	-0.229	**0.682**	-0.233	-0.143	0.152	0.019	0.088	0.140	0.605	0.660	0.680	0.703	0.703	0.226
74	0.103	0.135	**0.744**	0.138	0.092	-0.176	-0.006	0.011	0.029	0.582	0.601	0.610	0.641	0.641	0.140
Expl.Var	1.386	1.416	1.372	1.363	1.501	1.215	1.274	* Principal Components extraction, Varimax Rotated							
Prp.Totl	0.092	0.094	0.091	0.091	0.100	0.081	0.085	[@] F1-F7 Factor Derivatives, **bold** marked are >0.30 cut-off point							

...

Factor[#]	Eigen value	%Total Variance	Cumulative Eigen value	Cumulative %
1	1.713	11.417	1.713	11.417
2	1.515	10.097	3.227	21.514
3	1.471	9.808	4.698	31.323
4	1.394	9.292	6.092	40.614
5	1.227	8.178	7.319	48.793
6	1.147	7.649	8.466	56.442
7	1.061	7.073	9.527	63.516

Extraction: Principal components

Emotional Expression subscale- Expression of various emotions and responsive or proactive feelings are all seems to be influencing the conflict response pattern. Fifteen variables were explored with this factor generating eight factor derivatives through this subscale along with the input ensued by mean scores of this subscale. F1 of this factor shows high negative factor loading to the variables 54 and 58, clearly showing managers preference to be open enough in all cases and their expressed controlled emotional behaviour. Cautious optimism was advocated by the managers, regarding the emotional expression was at the core of operations in this regard as evident through F1. In F2, variables 50 and 72 are positively loaded, clearly indicating that they may not avoid those who show their emotions easily during conflicts. Further they feel not uncomfortable when emotions are shown during conflicts.

F3 shows negatively loaded variable 37 and 9. This indicates that the negation of emotional expressions and its recognition may worsen conflicts and they are against to do so. F4 contains negatively loaded variables 64 and 68 combined with a positively loaded variable 19. This shows that when managers perceive that showing the signs of emotions may weaken their respective positions, they prefer neither to express emotions nor they argue. But when they feel showing emotions are not problematic, they feel frustrated when others discourage their emotions and feel issues can be resolved more easily when people show their emotions. F5, negatively loaded with variables 47 and 14 combined with a positively loaded 19 reveals that when managers feel that showing their emotions as sign of weakness, they may view being angry too as such and or refrain from displaying emotions. When they feel displaying emotions are not as signs of weakness, then this factor may advocate expressing the emotions. In any case, displaying anger was presumably taken as an emotional display at all, though there seems to be a spectrum of emotions that are identified as such.

F6 favours a negatively loaded 27 and 42 clearly indicating that managers may not prefer a non-display of emotions at all, though they have their own reservations regarding the same. F7 favours an expression of emotions– positively loaded, whereas the element of anger may disturb the emotional pattern and sometimes regarded as wastage of time. F8 clearly shows the relationship existing among the perceived factors of emotional expression and negatively favours the expression of emotions. This can be attributed to the facts that emotions are generally perceived to be disturbing in cases dealing with conflicts, though they are not excluded at all.

Table 5.33: Emotional Expression subscale—basic statistics

Item No.	Mean	Sum	Min.	Max.	Variance	Std. Dev	Std. Error
5	2.514	274	1	5	0.845	0.919	0.088
9	2.405	267	1	3	0.607	0.779	0.074
14	2.360	262	1	3	0.596	0.772	0.073
19	2.396	266	1	3	0.587	0.766	0.073
27	2.450	272	1	3	0.595	0.772	0.073
37	2.464	271	1	3	0.581	0.762	0.073
42	2.423	269	1	3	0.610	0.781	0.074
47	4.578	499	4	6	0.598	0.773	0.074
50	2.404	274	1	3	0.508	0.713	0.067
54	1.623	185	1	3	0.343	0.586	0.055
58	1.649	188	1	3	0.354	0.595	0.056
62	4.573	503	4	6	0.559	0.748	0.071
64	2.436	268	1	3	0.542	0.736	0.070
68	4.577	508	4	6	0.555	0.745	0.071
72	4.635	533	4	6	0.392	0.626	0.058

Figure 5.7: Emotional Expression subscale

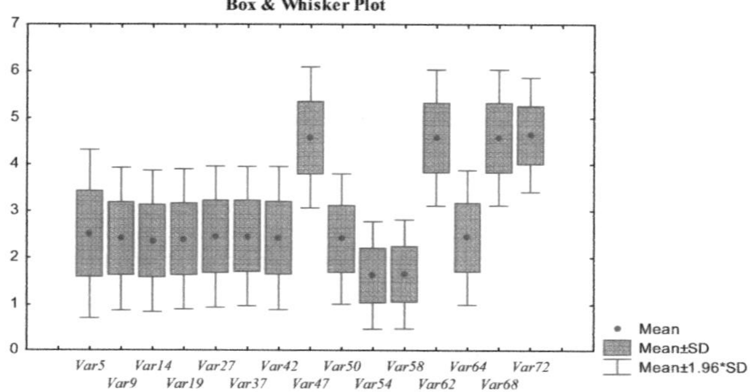

Table 5.34: Predominant conflict responses- Emotional Expression

Factor Analysis **Emotional Expression Subscale** *

Item No.				*Factor Loadings*								*Communality*					
	F1[@]	F2	F3	F4	F5	F6	F7	F8	From F1	From F2	From F3	From F4	From F5	From F6	From F7	From F8	Multiple R^2
5	0.015	-0.075	0.085	0.057	-0.071	0.089	-0.877	0.077	0.000	0.006	0.013	0.016	0.021	0.029	0.799	0.805	0.081
9	0.013	-0.180	**-0.727**	-0.011	0.035	-0.224	-0.006	0.097	0.000	0.032	0.560	0.560	0.562	0.612	0.612	0.621	0.120
14	0.019	0.029	0.028	0.102	**-0.677**	0.082	**-0.310**	-0.059	0.000	0.001	0.002	0.012	0.471	0.478	0.574	0.578	0.095
19	0.059	-0.207	0.215	**0.412**	**0.421**	0.291	0.215	0.097	0.004	0.047	0.093	0.263	0.440	0.525	0.571	0.580	0.066
27	0.000	-0.066	-0.188	0.023	0.033	**-0.747**	0.010	0.017	0.000	0.004	0.040	0.040	0.041	0.600	0.600	0.600	0.125
37	0.023	0.134	**-0.740**	0.082	0.038	0.216	0.086	-0.031	0.001	0.018	0.566	0.573	0.574	0.621	0.628	0.629	0.112
42	0.022	0.030	0.195	0.077	0.051	**-0.699**	0.080	0.023	0.000	0.001	0.039	0.045	0.048	0.537	0.543	0.544	0.104
47	0.033	-0.155	0.127	0.058	**-0.729**	0.084	**0.398**	0.158	0.001	0.025	0.041	0.044	0.575	0.582	0.741	0.766	0.085
50	0.034	**0.831**	0.089	-0.013	0.078	-0.054	0.007	0.129	0.001	0.691	0.699	0.699	0.705	0.708	0.708	0.725	0.069
54	**-0.998**	0.005	0.013	0.009	0.016	0.010	-0.001	0.011	0.996	0.996	0.997	0.997	0.997	0.997	0.997	0.997	0.995
58	**-0.997**	-0.009	0.020	0.010	0.012	0.012	0.014	0.004	0.995	0.995	0.995	0.995	0.995	0.996	0.996	0.996	0.995
62	0.024	-0.008	0.054	0.042	0.023	-0.013	0.022	**-0.866**	0.001	0.001	0.004	0.005	0.006	0.006	0.007	0.757	0.145
64	0.024	0.019	0.055	**-0.811**	0.086	0.110	0.072	0.162	0.001	0.001	0.004	0.662	0.669	0.681	0.686	0.712	0.060
68	0.011	-0.148	0.086	**-0.569**	0.071	0.052	0.035	**-0.471**	0.000	0.022	0.029	0.353	0.358	0.361	0.362	0.584	0.094
72	-0.071	**0.602**	-0.135	0.083	-0.110	0.245	0.125	**-0.468**	0.005	0.368	0.386	0.393	0.405	0.465	0.481	0.700	0.231
Expl.Var	2.005	1.204	1.259	1.191	1.209	.329	1.108	1.289				* Principal Components extraction, Varimax Rotated					
Prp.Totl	0.134	0.080	0.084	0.079	0.081	0.089	0.074	0.086				[@] F1-F8 Factor Derivatives, **bold** marked are >0.30 cut-off point					

Factor[#]	Eigen value	%Total Variance	Cumulative Eigen value	Cumulative %
1	2.010	13.400	2.010	13.400
2	1.572	10.479	3.582	23.879
3	1.376	9.174	4.958	33.053
4	1.292	8.611	6.250	41.664
5	1.139	7.591	7.388	49.255
6	1.125	7.499	8.513	56.754
7	1.057	7.048	9.570	63.802
8	1.023	6.819	10.593	70.622

Extraction: Principal components

<u>Self-disclosure subscale-</u> Openly embracing the possible responses that are taken when dealing with similar situations and or hypothetical preferences was dealt with in this section inducting fifteen, relatively and presumably independent variables. Statistical mean scores were obtained and factorial exploration was also concurrently exercised to identify possible combinations of significant factor derivatives that are acting at these levels of operations.

F1 derivates negatively loaded variables 17, 39 and 34. Open discussions from all quarters are preferred by the managers, though they are less happening, indicated by negative loadings. F2 indicates that managers may become silent when others pressurise them or force them to display the emotions during the conflicts. The exact opposite to this may also happen when managers may not become silent and certainly that seems to be a resultant of not pressured situations or compulsions for emotional display, necessarily initiated by other parties of the conflicts. F3 reveals combinations of facts that may annoy managers when they do not want to let the others know what they are thinking and their needs and preferences are not being expressed. Further this may become inversely increase when someone compels them to talk about the conflict. F4, negatively loaded with variables 41, 32 and 34 indicates that when managers may not be glad when they are asked to disclose openly the facts and or not asked to discuss the same regarding conflicts.

In F5, variables 7,10,3 and 13 are negatively loaded. This indicates that managers, though not prefer to hide their feelings, they may not let it to know others too. They are comfortable with most of the parties expressing disagreements but they may certainly feel annoyed when they are asked to state their feelings which they do not want to share/express at all. This combination negatively relates with the self disclosure assumptions. F6 was loaded with variables 44, 60 and 3. Managers opine that though they may prefer not to let the other person/s know what they are thinking, they feel annoyed and disturbed by the fact that the other person/s got upset with them and not expressing it openly. This may also affects the expression of the facts by the managers with them and furthering the dialogues. F7 reveals that the tendency to become silent by managers were taken by this factor derivative, when the other parties expressed the thoughts and personal feelings in a conflictual situation- visibly a sign of inverse relationship operating between these two. 61.185% variance can be explained through these seven factor derivatives and comparatively equally distributive variance allows all the factor derivatives to be significant.

Table 5.35: Self-disclosure subscale—basic statistics

Item No.	Mean	Sum	Min.	Max.	Variance	Std. Dev	Std. Error
3	3.439	368	1	5	1.720	1.312	0.127
7	2.402	269	1	3	0.621	0.788	0.074
10	2.394	261	1	4	0.667	0.817	0.078
13	3.206	327	1	5	1.729	1.315	0.130
17	2.387	265	1	3	0.585	0.765	0.073
28	2.368	270	1	3	0.571	0.756	0.071
32	2.436	268	1	3	0.597	0.773	0.074
34	4.573	503	4	6	0.577	0.760	0.072
36	2.862	312	2	4	0.138	0.372	0.036
39	4.577	508	4	6	0.592	0.769	0.073
41	4.568	507	4	6	0.593	0.770	0.073
44	4.657	503	4	6	0.639	0.799	0.077
56	2.336	257	1	3	0.666	0.816	0.078
60	4.554	510	4	6	0.574	0.757	0.072
65	1.817	209	1	3	0.396	0.629	0.059

Figure 5.8: Self disclosure subscale

Box & Whisker Plot

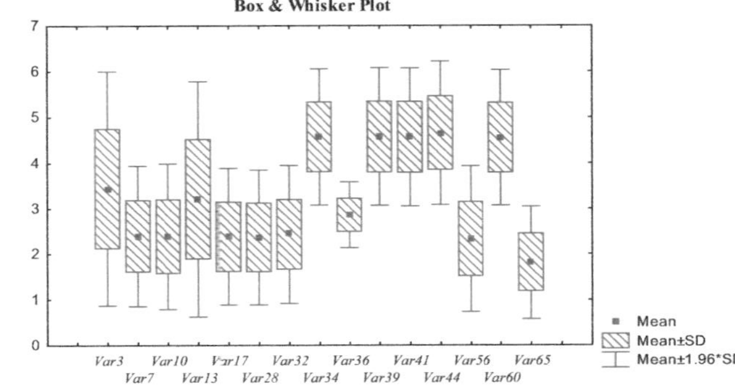

Table 5.36: Predominant conflict responses- Self-Disclosure

Item No.		Factor Loadings							Communality						
	F1[@]	F2	F3	F4	F5	F6	F7	From F1	From F2	From F3	From F4	From F5	From F6	From F7	Multiple R^2
3	0.066	0.038	**-0.667**	-0.122	**-0.335**	**-0.309**	0.103	0.004	0.006	0.451	0.466	0.578	0.674	0.685	0.194
7	-0.018	-0.143	-0.057	0.035	**-0.759**	0.008	-0.058	0.000	0.021	0.024	0.025	0.601	0.601	0.605	0.137
10	0.075	0.281	0.050	0.085	**-0.665**	0.130	0.036	0.006	0.085	0.087	0.095	0.536	0.553	0.555	0.086
13	0.154	**-0.433**	**0.344**	-0.116	**-0.330**	0.128	0.183	0.024	0.211	0.329	0.343	0.452	0.468	0.502	0.078
17	**-0.740**	-0.060	0.001	0.032	0.020	0.035	-0.014	0.548	0.552	0.552	0.553	0.553	0.554	0.554	0.128
28	0.058	0.006	0.073	0.020	-0.007	0.035	**-0.904**	0.003	0.003	0.009	0.009	0.009	0.010	0.828	0.031
32	0.147	0.282	0.089	**-0.644**	0.169	0.152	-0.039	0.022	0.101	0.109	0.524	0.552	0.575	0.577	0.094
34	**-0.464**	0.072	0.130	**-0.536**	0.024	0.064	0.130	0.215	0.220	0.237	0.524	0.525	0.529	0.546	0.143
36	0.063	-0.030	**-0.810**	0.092	0.140	0.219	0.020	0.004	0.005	0.661	0.669	0.689	0.737	0.737	0.144
39	**-0.726**	0.037	0.034	0.036	0.029	0.026	0.015	0.527	0.528	0.529	0.530	0.531	0.532	0.532	0.104
41	0.046	-0.286	-0.110	**-0.774**	-0.045	-0.070	-0.019	0.002	0.084	0.096	0.695	0.697	0.702	0.703	0.218
44	0.029	-0.059	0.041	0.075	0.091	**-0.741**	-0.073	0.001	0.004	0.006	0.012	0.020	0.569	0.574	0.085
56	0.155	**-0.550**	0.139	0.166	0.199	0.108	0.222	0.024	0.327	0.346	0.374	0.414	0.425	0.475	0.057
60	0.048	0.148	-0.022	-0.002	0.024	**-0.717**	0.097	0.002	0.024	0.025	0.025	0.025	0.539	0.548	0.089
65	0.238	**0.728**	0.204	0.130	0.022	-0.010	**0.335**	0.057	0.586	0.628	0.645	0.646	0.646	0.758	0.251
Expl.Var	1.439	1.318	1.332	1.399	1.341	1.286	1.063	* Principal Components extraction, Varimax Rotated							
Prp.Totl	0.096	0.088	0.089	0.093	0.089	0.086	0.071	[@] F1-F7 Factor Derivatives, **bold** marked are >0.30 cut-off point							

The header row spans: Factor Analysis **Self-disclosure** Subscale *

...

Factor[#]	Eigen value	%Total Variance	Cumulative Eigen value	Cumulative %
1	1.653	11.018	1.653	11.018
2	1.408	9.387	3.061	20.406
3	1.376	9.175	4.437	29.581
4	1.309	8.730	5.747	38.311
5	1.264	8.427	7.011	46.737
6	1.137	7.577	8.147	54.314
7	1.031	6.871	9.178	61.185

Extraction: Principal components

5.1.7 Procedural way of handling conflicts and its effectiveness

Guided methods influence the handling of conflicts and subsequently enforce its preferential treatment in cases exhibiting conflicts. This includes not only the advocacy of procedural mechanism but also the usage of same in its entirety or a combination derived from them. Negotiation, mediation, counselling, arbitration, other legalistic interventions, etc or a combination of any two or more of these with other approaches may guide the way of handling conflicts into certain directions. The tendencies to adopt/adapt these procedural ways, their perceived importance expressed by the studied population and or effectiveness were explored using *part H and E* of CMI respectively. Basic statistics revealed the usage of the procedural ways and indicated their relative importance with the help of mean scores *(table 5.37)*. Reliability tests indicated a significantly moderate level of scale and item reliability – not a decelerating trend, considering that the study consists of primarily exploratory phenomenon. Variance expressed through the analysis also indicates a pattern that seems to be preferential, while handling the conflicts which was essentially procedural in its most dynamical state of affairs. Factorial denominations were explored and the highly relevant factors were thus explained, utilising a combination of study results generated through statistical decision-support systems.

Moderately higher concordance was recorded among the sampled population regarding procedural ways of handling conflicts. Most of the responses to the statements presented in the part H were revealing that a combination of approaches may be suitable for indicating the pattern. The concept of hybrid methods in the theoretical sense needs to be extended as these in its most dynamic perceptions, may need a revised stature or modulations. Factorial expressions provide the necessary scope and depth to analyse these dimensions. Further the sets of exploratory combinations may bring those critical dimensions with which the hybrid methods are operating and or their effect in an indirect way. This may well suited as a comparative mechanism can be operative at these levels with the perceived importance measured through part E of CMI. The incidental importance will always plays a major role in procedural ways of handling conflicts. It will be interesting to note that the attitudes, approaches and actual rendered importance given to these factors from a population that seems to be large enough for analysis brings a pattern that have satisfactory inter-item correlations expressed through the tables succeeding this paragraph, reserving its statistical rights regarding alpha coefficients and variances, though expressing moderately higher concordance.

Table 5.37: Procedural conflict handling–Basic statistics

Item No.	Mean*	Sum	Variance	Std. Dev.	Std. Error	Average Rank	Sum of Ranks	Mean if deleted	Var. if deleted	St.Dev. if deleted	Item Total. Correlated.	Alpha if. deleted
1	4.557	524	0.652	0.808	0.075	25.878	2976.000	119.800	65.360	8.085	0.159	0.400
2	4.513	519	0.620	0.788	0.073	25.709	2956.500	119.844	65.245	8.077	0.175	0.399
3	2.965	341	1.999	1.414	0.132	12.939	1488.000	121.391	62.499	7.906	0.161	0.394
4	4.443	511	0.565	0.752	0.070	25.087	2885.000	119.913	66.740	8.169	0.063	0.412
5	4.313	496	0.427	0.654	0.061	24.370	2802.500	120.044	67.955	8.243	-0.028	0.421
6	2.991	344	1.903	1.380	0.129	12.748	1466.000	121.365	63.414	7.963	0.127	0.401
7	3.000	345	1.912	1.383	0.129	13.091	1505.500	121.357	62.803	7.925	0.155	0.395
8	4.583	527	0.596	0.772	0.072	26.304	3025.000	119.774	66.853	8.176	0.050	0.414
9	4.487	516	0.498	0.705	0.066	25.817	2969.000	119.870	65.731	8.107	0.162	0.402
10	2.974	342	1.815	1.347	0.126	12.691	1459.500	121.383	62.688	7.918	0.169	0.393
11	4.530	521	0.550	0.741	0.069	26.139	3006.000	119.826	65.344	8.084	0.183	0.399
12	4.426	509	0.422	0.650	0.061	25.409	2922.000	119.930	65.873	8.116	0.170	0.402
13	2.817	324	1.589	1.261	0.118	11.713	1347.000	121.539	65.188	8.074	0.065	0.413
14	4.565	525	0.546	0.739	0.069	26.265	3020.500	119.791	66.530	8.157	0.083	0.410
15	4.322	497	0.431	0.656	0.061	24.404	2806.500	120.035	67.512	8.217	0.012	0.417
16	2.783	320	1.523	1.234	0.115	11.487	1321.000	121.574	65.392	8.087	0.059	0.414
17	4.261	490	0.352	0.594	0.055	24.091	2770.500	120.096	65.252	8.078	0.259	0.395
18	2.809	323	1.717	1.311	0.122	11.878	1366.000	121.548	60.804	7.798	0.274	0.371
19	2.817	324	1.677	1.295	0.121	11.796	1356.500	121.539	66.840	8.176	-0.020	0.430
20	2.843	327	1.730	1.315	0.123	12.183	1401.000	121.513	64.250	8.016	0.100	0.407
21	4.261	490	0.370	0.608	0.057	24.143	2776.500	120.096	65.026	8.064	0.274	0.393
22	2.730	314	1.988	1.410	0.131	11.704	1346.000	121.626	63.417	7.963	0.120	0.403
23	4.261	490	0.633	0.796	0.074	24.013	2761.500	120.096	65.669	8.104	0.138	0.403
24	2.713	312	1.891	1.375	0.128	11.313	1301.000	121.644	66.316	8.143	-0.005	0.429
25	2.704	311	1.596	1.263	0.118	11.078	1274.000	121.652	67.079	8.190	-0.029	0.431
26	2.687	309	1.603	1.266	0.118	10.970	1261.500	121.670	63.908	7.994	0.128	0.401
27	2.783	320	1.733	1.316	0.123	11.704	1346.000	121.574	68.784	8.294	-0.112	0.448
28	2.765	318	1.672	1.293	0.121	11.378	1308.500	121.591	64.763	8.048	0.080	0.411
29	4.313	496	0.427	0.654	0.061	24.404	2806.500	120.044	67.346	8.206	0.028	0.416
30	4.313	496	0.427	0.654	0.061	24.348	2800.000	120.044	67.381	8.209	0.025	0.416
31	2.774	319	1.685	1.298	0.121	11.674	1342.500	121.583	64.487	8.030	0.092	0.408
32	2.861	329	1.700	1.304	0.122	12.391	1425.000	121.496	65.554	8.097	0.040	0.419
33	2.730	314	1.707	1.307	0.122	11.400	1311.000	121.626	62.843	7.927	0.172	0.392
34	4.287	493	0.399	0.632	0.059	24.239	2787.500	120.070	65.543	8.096	0.209	0.398
35	3.174	365	1.601	1.265	0.118	15.239	1752.500	121.183	66.619	8.162	-0.006	0.427

...contd   *Scale 1-6, neutral values encoded with mean values.

ANOVA Chi Sqr. (N = 115, d² = 34) = 1827.995   p =0.00001   Coeff. of Concordance = 0.46752   Aver. rank r = 0.46285

Summary statistics for the Scale

Mean: 124.356   Sum: 14301
Standard Deviation: 3.2867   Variance: 68.6700
Skewness: 0 .09652–635   Kurtosis: 1.517178445
Minimum: 97   Maximum: 153
Cronbach's alpha: 0.415406   Standardized alpha: 0 .477359
Average Inter-Item Correlation: 0.026826009

Analysis of Variance

Effect	Sum of Squares	df	Mean Squares	F	p
Between Subjects	223.668	114.000	1.962		
Within Subjects	6949.257	3910.000	1.777		
Between Items	2503.586	34.000	73.635	64.199	0.000
Residual	4445.671	3876.000	1.147		
Total	7172.925	4024.000			

Figure 5.9: Procedural conflict handling

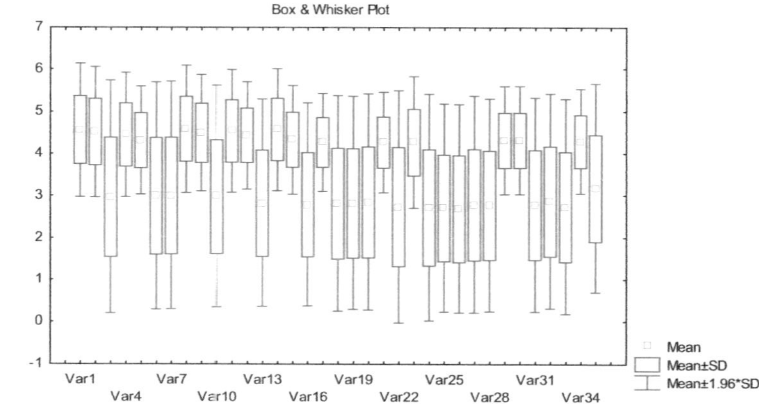

Table 5.38: Factor Analysis **Negotiation**

	Factor Analysis **Negotiation***										
	Factor Loadings					*Communality*					
Item No.	F1[@]	F2	F3	F4	F5	From F1	From F2	From F3	From F4	From F5	Multiple R^2
1	0.096	0.080	0.016	-0.069	**0.912**	0.009	0.016	0.016	0.021	0.852	0.056
3	0.066	-0.060	**0.811**	0.231	0.176	0.004	0.008	0.666	0.719	0.750	0.074
7	**0.612**	-0.156	0.058	0.063	0.127	0.375	0.399	0.402	0.406	0.422	0.103
16	-0.207	**0.825**	0.076	-0.059	0.062	0.043	0.724	0.730	0.733	0.737	0.124
20	-0.107	**-0.348**	0.184	**0.747**	0.078	0.011	0.132	0.166	0.724	0.731	0.132
21	**0.698**	**0.378**	-0.058	0.116	0.073	0.487	0.630	0.633	0.646	0.652	0.141
22	0.273	**0.344**	-0.107	0.749	-0.194	0.074	0.193	0.204	0.766	0.804	0.163
23	**0.696**	**-0.302**	0.050	-0.068	-0.090	0.485	0.576	0.578	0.583	0.591	0.124
35	0.002	0.208	**0.669**	**-0.304**	**-0.383**	0.000	0.043	0.490	0.582	0.729	0.093
Expl.Var	1.489	1.231	1.166	1.296	1.087	* Principal Components extraction, Varimax Rotated					
Prp.Totl	0.165	0.137	0.130	0.144	0.121	[@] F1-F5- Factor Derivatives, **bold** marked are >0.30 cut-off point					

F	Eigen value	%Total Variance	Cumulative Eigen value	Cumulative %
F1	1.673	18.584	1.673	18.584
F2	1.216	13.514	2.889	32.099
F3	1.208	13.427	4.097	45.525
F4	1.136	12.621	5.233	58.146
F5	1.036	11.508	6.269	69.654

Table 5.39: Kendall's Tau Correlations* and Group Analysis- **Negotiation**

Item	1	3	7	16	20	21	22	23	35	Group Analysis					
										Average Rank	Sum of Ranks	Mean	Std. Dev	Mean Rank	X^2 =349.498
1	1.000	-0.022	-0.001	0.032	0.012	0.091	-0.091	0.003	**-0.128**	7.317	841.500	4.557	0.808	1	
3	-0.022	1.000	0.090	-0.024	**0.147**	-0.043	0.100	-0.073	0.065	3.961	455.500	2.965	1.414	6	W=0.379
7	-0.001	0.090	1.000	**-0.138**	0.000	**0.148**	0.109	**0.195**	-0.096	3.978	457.500	3.000	1.383	5	
16	0.032	-0.024	**-0.138**	1.000	**-0.142**	-0.003	0.030	**-0.233**	0.118	3.717	427.500	2.783	1.234	8	r =0.374
20	0.012	**0.147**	0.000	**-0.142**	1.000	-0.003	**0.198**	0.056	-0.105	3.870	445.000	2.843	1.315	7	
21	0.091	-0.043	**0.148**	-0.003	-0.003	1.000	**0.155**	**0.214**	-0.073	6.935	797.500	4.261	0.608	2	*(p<0.05)
22	-0.091	0.100	0.109	0.030	**0.198**	**0.155**	1.000	0.020	-0.089	3.665	421.500	2.730	1.410	9	
23	0.003	-0.073	**0.195**	**-0.233**	0.056	**0.214**	0.020	1.000	0.000	6.900	793.500	4.261	0.796	3	
35	**-0.128**	0.065	-0.096	0.118	-0.105	-0.073	-0.089	0.000	1.000	4.657	535.500	3.174	1.265	4	

Factor- Negotiation The process of discussing something with someone in order to reach an agreement with them, or the discussions themselves–commonly denoted by the terminology – *negotiations* are explored in multitude through nine variables (1,3,7,16,20,21,22,23,35) expressed in *table 5.38*. From F1, it can be inferred that the managers seems to disagree that the common interests are seized in a negotiation process, though they agree that there are no hard and fast rules in every negotiation process and this flexibility helps the negotiations to get succeed. The positive loaded variables indicate a continuation of the trend with these dimensions. In F2– variables 16, 21 and 22 are positively loaded along with negative loaded variables 20 and 23. These combinations clearly indicate that the negotiation process would become different when there are no hard and fast rules. In case of negotiation process, there are solid principles and the gender preferential (preferably men rather than women as managers) that are agreed as influentials indicated by the managerial population. Managers prefer to discuss both positive and other implications of the issue concerned with the parties involved and it strengthens when principled on demand negotiations are not adhered by the organisation policies as indicated through the components of F4. The components of F5 indicates that the negotiation as a leadership trait was positively loaded while negatively loaded variable 35 influence this factor very much. Openly discussing both positive and other implications of the issue concerned with the parties involved may affect the above perceptions negatively.

Moderate level of concordance expressed through the analysis indicate managerial preferences and the non parametric chi square test reinforces the same as the table value was less than the computed value of X^2 *(table 5.39)*. The indicative correlations are all moderately influencing the relationships among the variables studied. This further rejuvenates the above inferences and operationally identifies the explorative factor derivatives as more appropriate for pattern finding rather than the individual results generated through the statement frequencies.

Factor- Counselling To give advice– especially on organisational problems, which are essentially psycho-social determinants are most sought by managerial population. Variables 2,4,14 and 17; combined with their constituents shed some light on these dimensions *(table 5.40)*. F6 indicates and strengthens that counselling as an approach got full appreciation and aged managers seems to be perceived to be effective and preferred in this regard.

Table 5.40: Factor Analysis **Counselling**

Factor Analysis **Counselling***					
Factor Loadings			*Communality*		
Item No.	F6[@]	F7	From F6	From F7	Multiple R^2
2	**-0.473**	**0.621**	0.224	0.609	0.078
4	**0.730**	-0.099	0.533	0.543	0.061
14	**0.680**	0.113	0.463	0.476	0.029
17	0.197	**0.859**	0.039	0.776	0.030
Expl.Var	1.258	1.145	*Prin. Components extraction		
Prp.Totl	0.315	0.286	Rotation: Varimax		

F	Eigen value	%Total Variance	Cumulative Eigen value	Cumulative %
F6	1.335	33.365	1.335	33.365
F7	1.069	26.731	2.404	60.096

[@] F6 and F7 are Factor Derivatives, **bold** marked are >0.30 cut-off point

Table 5.41: Kendall's Tau Correlations- **Counseling**

Item*	2	4	14	17	Group Analysis				
					Average Rank	Sum of Ranks	Mean	Std. Dev	Mean Rank
2	1.000	**-0.199**	-0.072	**0.197**	2.587	297.500	4.513	0.788	2
4	**-0.199**	1.000	**0.138**	0.029	2.452	282.000	4.443	0.752	3
14	-0.072	**0.138**	1.000	0.001	2.683	308.500	4.565	0.739	1
17	**0.197**	0.029	0.001	1.000	2.278	262.000	4.261	0.594	4

(*Correlations highlighted by **bolded** are significant at p <0.05000)

ANOVA Chi Sqr. (N = 115, df = 3) = 11.85922   p =0.00788   Coeff. of Concordance = 0. 03437   Aver. rank r = 0. 02590

Figure 5.10: Procedural conflict handling–Counseling

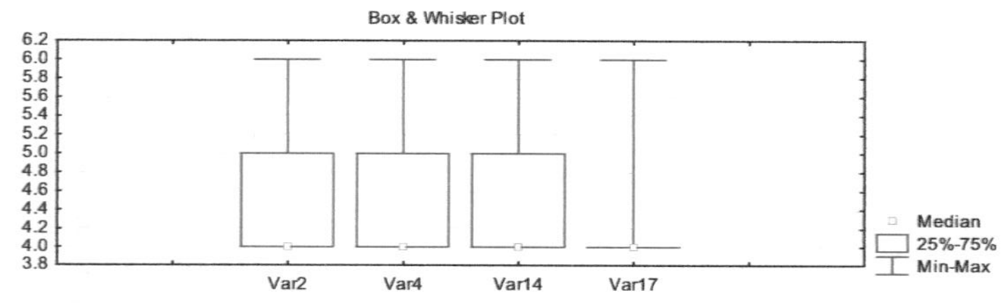

Whereas the negative loading of variable 2 in F6 indicates that the hesitation or the indirect restriction of counselling process consciously ignited by the managers are affecting this factor though managers prefer to counsel their subordinates/colleagues. This was strengthened by F7 that if managerial workforce make every effort to counsel others directly, subordinates/colleagues may approach them as indicated by positive factor loadings rendered to them. Moderate level of concordance expressed through the analysis indicate managerial preferences and the non parametric chi square test reinforces the same as the table value was less than the computed value of chi square *(table 5.41)*. The indicative correlations are all lenient towards influencing the relationships, though in a very least way among the variables studied. This further rejuvenates the above inferences and operationally identifies the explorative factor derivatives as more appropriate for pattern finding rather than the individual results generated through the statement frequencies.

Factor- Mediation Mediation represents to talk to two separate people or groups involved in a disagreement to try to help them to agree or find a solution to their problems. Organisational mediation not only includes responsive ones but also of proactive too. Variables 9, 13, 15 and 25 explored various facets of mediation through factorial and other analysis *(table 5.42 and 5.43)*. F8 with its projective components indicate that managers may be lenient towards accepting a mediatory role that may bring necessary solutions to the dissonance. In an interesting way, they are in no uncertain terms indicated their preference for avoiding the third party mediators from outside the organisation. This may be contra influencing in many ways, though the effectiveness analysis of procedural way of conflict handling in general and that of mediatory roles in particular seems to be beyond the scope of the present study. The constituents of F9 also reinforce these dimensions when the managers are indicative of their uncomfortability when outsiders are approached for mediation and a leniency towards maintaining insider initiated mediation. Moderate level of concordance expressed through the analysis indicate managerial preferences and the non parametric chi square test reinforces the same as the table value was less than the computed value of chi square *(table 5.43)*. The only one indicative correlation between variables 13 and 25 seems to be lenient towards influencing the relationships, though in a very least way among the variables studied. This further rejuvenates the above inferences and operationally identifies the explorative factor derivatives as more appropriate for pattern finding rather than the individual results generated through the statement frequencies.

Table 5.42: Factor Analysis **Mediation**

Factor Analysis Mediation*					
Factor Loadings			*Communality*		
Item No.	F8[@]	F9	From F8	From F9	Multiple R^2
9	-0.123	**0.790**	0.015	0.639	0.020
13	**0.826**	-0.182	0.682	0.715	0.042
15	0.155	**0.588**	0.024	0.370	0.014
25	**0.685**	**0.352**	0.469	0.593	0.056
Expl.Var	1.190	1.126	*Prin. Components extraction		
Prp.Totl	0.298	0.282	Rotation: Varimax		

F	Eigen value	%Total Variance	Cumulative Eigen value	Cumulative %
F8	1.249	31.232	1.249	31.232
F9	1.067	26.684	2.317	57.916

[@] F8 and F9 are Factor Derivatives, **bold** marked are >0.30 cut-off point

Table 5.43: Kendall's Tau Correlations- **Mediation**

Item*	9	13	15	25	Group Analysis				
					Average Rank	Sum of Ranks	Mean	Std. Dev	Mean Rank
9	1.000	-0.021	0.100	0.070	3.396	390.500	4.487	0.705	1
13	-0.021	1.000	-0.038	**0.150**	1.726	198.500	2.817	1.261	3
15	0.100	-0.038	1.000	0.019	3.187	366.500	4.322	0.656	2
25	0.070	**0.150**	0.019	1.000	1.691	194.500	2.704	1.263	4

(*Correlations highlighted by **bolded** are significant at $p < 0.05000$)

ANOVA Chi Sqr. (N = 115, df = 3) = 209.0928   p =0.00001   Coeff. of Concordance = 0. 60607   Aver. rank r = 0. 60261

Figure 5.11: Procedural conflict handling- Mediation

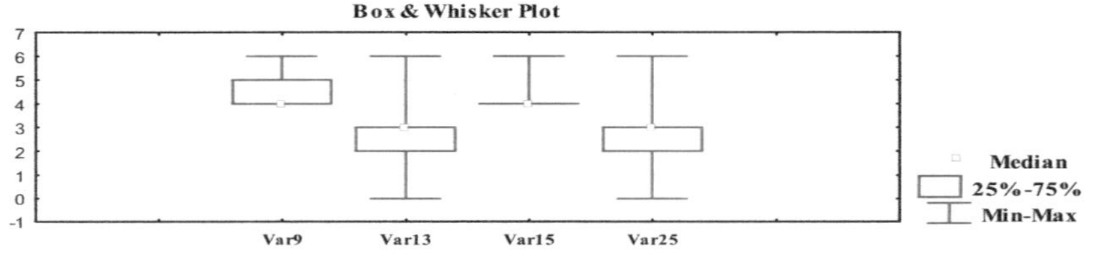

Table 5.44: Factor Analysis **Interventions**

Factor Analysis Interventions *					
Factor Loadings			*Communality*		
Item No.	F10[@]	F11	From F10	From F11	Multiple R^2
6	**0.952**	0.030	0.907	0.908	0.733
8	0.178	**0.754**	0.032	0.600	0.130
10	**0.947**	0.013	0.896	0.896	0.730
12	-0.003	**0.810**	0.000	0.657	0.130
24	-0.275	**0.392**	0.075	0.229	0.036
Expl.Var	1.910	1.380	*Prin. Components extraction		
Prp.Totl	0.382	0.276	Rotation: Varimax		

F	Eigen value	%Total Variance	Cumulative Eigen value	Cumulative %
F10	1.918	38.356	1.918	38.356
F11	1.372	27.434	3.290	65.790

[@] F10 and F11 are Factor Derivatives, **bold** marked are >0.30 cut-off point

Table 5.45: Kendall's Tau Correlations- **Interventions**

Item*	6	8	10	12	24	Group Analysis				
						Average Rank	Sum of Ranks	Mean	Std. Dev	Mean Rank
6	1.000	0.093	**0.842**	0.050	-0.115	2.339	269.000	2.991	1.380	3
8	0.093	1.000	0.055	**0.377**	-0.009	4.183	481.000	4.583	0.772	1
10	**0.842**	0.055	1.000	0.009	-0.072	2.317	266.500	2.974	1.347	4
12	0.050	**0.377**	0.009	1.000	0.068	4.026	463.000	4.426	0.650	2
24	-0.115	-0.009	-0.072	0.068	1.000	2.135	245.500	2.713	1.375	5

(*Correlations highlighted by **bolded** are significant at p <0.05000)

ANOVA Chi Sqr. (N = 115, df = 4) = 224.7892   p =0.00001   Coeff. of Concordance = 0. 48867   Aver. rank r = 0. 48419

Figure 5.12: Procedural conflict handling- Interventions

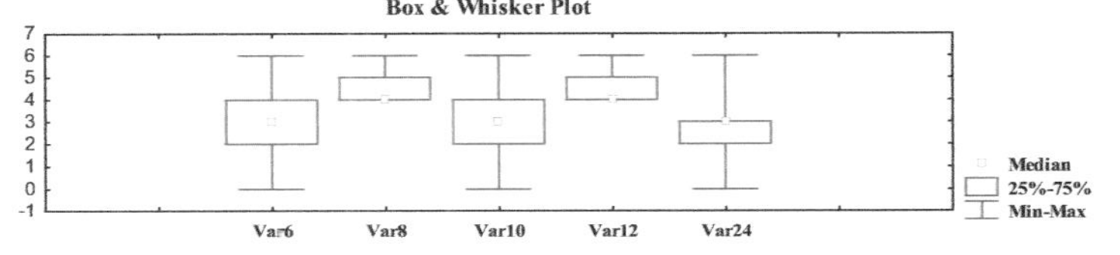

Box & Whisker Plot

Factor- Interventions. Managerial tendencies to intentionally become involved in a difficult situation in order to improve it or prevent it from getting worse were explored through variables–6, 8, 10, 12 and 24. F10 reveals that managers have very highly preferred tendencies to operate and or exercise authoritative organisational interventions including legalistic options.F11 indicates that this factor got influenced by positive loadings from 12, 8 and 24. This reflects that the legalistic interventions are usually succeeded by a perceived disturbance from managerial population, whereas they accept that forced organisational interventions are part of organisational workflow. Neutral tendencies to take actions on behalf of others also influence this factor derivative with its positive loading. Moderate level of concordance expressed through the analysis indicates managerial preferences and the non parametric chi square test reinforces the same as the table value was less than the computed value of chi square. The indicative correlations among variables 6 and 10 and 8 and12, seems to be lenient towards influencing the relationships, though in a very least way among the variables studied. This further rejuvenates the above inferences and operationally identifies the explorative factor derivatives as more appropriate for pattern finding rather than the individual results generated through the statement frequencies. Forced organisational interventions are part of managerial life seems to be one of the most influencing facts that make every interventions exercised by the managerial population as consciously done.

Factor- Social exchanges/predispositions Psycho-social interactions fundamentally operating along with the factors mentioned above are all indicative of the procedural operations. Though they are assumed to be independent for factorial evaluation the expressed variance and the indicative patterns are to be evaluated with the adoption of broader spectrum of variables. The indicative patterns expressed through this factorial analysis and all the above helps only to identify the operational variances at its most micro level of system dependable *(table 5.46)*.

F12, positively loaded with variables 31, 32 and 33 along with negatively loaded variable-29 indicates that these variables are operating under this banner. The componential analysis shows that when appropriate words and physical responses during organisational dialogues were not exercised by managers, then that seems to be influenced by an array of assumptions by them. It includes, a feeling that no real solution was possible to the conflict, predominant thinking about a physical fight or victimised by physical assault from other parties. Further F12 indicates that these *assumptions* may also be resultants of not using appropriate behavioural pattern.

Table 5.46: Factor Analysis **Social Exchanges / Predispositions**

Factor Analysis –**Social Exchanges / Predispositions***

Item No.			*Factor Loadings*						*Communality*				
	F12[@]	F13	F14	F15	F16	F17	From F12	From F13	From F14	From F15	From F16	From F17	Multiple R^2
5	-0.150	-0.141	0.016	0.173	**0.787**	0.011	0.022	0.042	0.043	0.072	0.692	0.693	0.107
11	0.150	0.284	-0.066	-0.225	**0.676**	-0.103	0.022	0.103	0.107	0.158	0.615	0.625	0.127
18	0.033	0.037	**0.507**	**-0.504**	0.214	-0.200	0.001	0.002	0.260	0.514	0.560	0.600	0.129
19	-0.092	**0.501**	0.079	0.002	0.161	0.236	0.008	0.259	0.265	0.265	0.291	0.347	0.090
26	-0.021	0.039	**0.880**	0.090	-0.097	0.034	0.000	0.002	0.776	0.784	0.793	0.794	0.116
27	0.001	**-0.843**	0.020	-0.012	0.070	0.107	0.000	0.710	0.711	0.711	0.716	0.727	0.187
28	-0.087	0.207	0.158	0.231	0.035	**-0.749**	0.008	0.050	0.075	0.129	0.130	0.691	0.130
29	**-0.307**	**0.305**	0.142	**0.361**	0.072	**0.599**	0.094	0.188	0.208	0.338	0.343	0.702	0.308
30	0.064	0.020	0.071	**0.850**	0.056	-0.086	0.004	0.004	0.010	0.733	0.736	0.743	0.156
31	**0.771**	0.006	0.031	0.035	0.016	-0.116	0.595	0.595	0.596	0.597	0.597	0.611	0.261
32	**0.739**	0.084	-0.197	-0.157	-0.154	0.126	0.545	0.552	0.591	0.616	0.640	0.655	0.317
33	**0.707**	-0.300	0.193	0.216	0.124	0.201	0.500	0.589	0.627	0.673	0.689	0.729	0.337
34	0.261	**0.349**	0.066	0.104	-0.156	**0.557**	0.068	0.190	0.194	0.205	0.229	0.540	0.259
Expl.Var	1.869	1.419	1.174	1.333	1.236	1.428	* Principal Components extraction, Varimax Rotated						
Prp.Totl	0.144	0.109	0.090	0.103	0.095	0.110	[@] F12-F17- Factor Derivatives, **bold** marked are >0.30 cut-off point						

F	Eigen value	%Total Variance	Cumulative Eigen value	Cumulative %
F12	1.957	15.050	1.957	15.050
F13	1.682	12.937	3.638	27.988
F14	1.347	10.362	4.985	38.349
F15	1.294	9.954	6.279	48.303
F16	1.121	8.621	7.400	56.924
F17	1.059	8.144	8.459	65.068

Figure 5.13: Procedural conflict handling- Social Exchanges / Predispositions

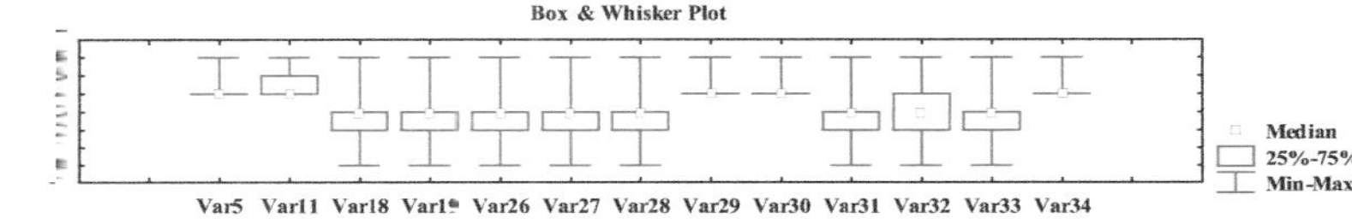

In F13, positively loaded variables 19, 34 and 29 and highly negative loaded 27 with their projective components indicates that the reconciliatory efforts/measures are neutralised with the combination of factors. The tendency to ignore some frictional relationships among the workforce, sidelining ethical issues in an argumentative bargaining and related physical responses may negatively influence the reconciliatory efforts. Whereas the combination of leniency explained may not be operative when reconciliatory efforts are perceived as important on a particular issue. F14 reinforces that managers may not be lenient towards physical measures while making every efforts towards reconciliation steps. F15, positively loaded with variables 30 and 29 along with negatively loaded variable 18 indicate that they may feel uncomfortable after heavy dosed verbal exchanges, though they make every effort in their physical responses and they are averse to adhere to make physical assault on others. F16 reveals the managerial perceptions that there seems to be more than one procedural way of conflict handling in use by them and in their respective organisations. F17 indicates openness in the communication. Negative inter-item responses indicate that the managerial leniencies towards making every effort to use appropriate words and physical responses during organisational dialogues are checked by their tendency to hide facts during the same.

Moderate level of concordance expressed by a majority of variables and a slightly higher tau correlation among the variables 31 and 32, 29 and 34, 31 and 33, 32 and 33- through the analysis indicate their respective managerial preferences *(table 5.47)*. Non parametric chi-square test reinforces the same as the table value was less than the computed value of chi square *(table 5.48)*. The indicative correlation among variables expressed above and other significant correlations seem to be lenient towards influencing the relationships, though in a very least way among the variables studied. This further rejuvenates the above inferences and operationally identifies the explorative factor derivatives as more appropriate for pattern finding rather than the individual results generated through the statement frequencies. The indicative pattern necessarily incorporates the multitudinal ways of resolving the conflicts and the fact that the managers are not averse towards using more than one way of procedural conflict handling method. They seem to be more concerned about the usage of psycho-social interactions as a major element in conflict handling process. The factor derivatives from F1 to F17 were indicative of the elements, usage and the fundamental approaches towards procedural way of conflict handling that are necessarily perceived as such by the managerial population.

Table 5.47: Kendall's Tau Correlations*- **Social Exchanges / Predispositions**

Item*	5	11	18	19	26	27	28	29	30	31	32	33	34
5	1.000	**0.183**	**0.138**	0.083	-0.025	0.097	0.007	0.048	**0.149**	-0.039	**-0.169**	-0.007	-0.080
11	**0.183**	1.000	0.059	0.026	-0.017	-0.060	0.109	0.041	**-0.140**	0.071	-0.019	0.045	-0.038
18	**0.138**	0.059	1.000	0.027	0.076	0.064	0.061	**-0.184**	**-0.196**	-0.018	-0.027	-0.048	-0.033
19	0.083	0.026	0.027	1.000	0.073	**-0.180**	-0.034	**0.148**	0.030	-0.093	0.042	-0.047	0.055
26	-0.025	-0.017	0.076	0.073	1.000	-0.054	0.081	0.094	0.065	0.074	-0.024	**0.184**	0.019
27	0.097	-0.060	0.064	**-0.180**	-0.054	1.000	-0.083	-0.091	0.012	-0.064	-0.010	**0.161**	**-0.140**
28	0.007	0.109	0.061	-0.034	0.081	-0.083	1.000	**-0.147**	0.073	0.026	-0.088	-0.071	-0.106
29	0.048	0.041	**-0.184**	**0.148**	0.094	-0.091	**-0.147**	1.000	**0.152**	**-0.197**	**-0.128**	0.090	**0.288**
30	**0.149**	**-0.140**	**-0.196**	0.030	0.065	0.012	0.073	**0.152**	1.000	0.088	-0.028	0.082	0.075
31	-0.039	0.071	-0.018	-0.093	0.074	-0.064	0.026	**-0.197**	0.088	1.000	**0.301**	**0.283**	0.036
32	**-0.169**	-0.019	-0.027	0.042	-0.024	-0.010	-0.088	**-0.128**	-0.028	**0.301**	1.000	**0.280**	0.212
33	-0.007	0.045	-0.048	-0.047	**0.184**	**0.161**	-0.071	0.090	0.082	**0.283**	**0.280**	1.000	0.167
34	-0.080	-0.038	-0.033	0.055	0.019	**-0.140**	-0.106	**0.288**	0.075	0.036	0.212	**0.167**	1.000

(*Correlations highlighted by **bolded** are significant at p <0.05000)

Table 5.48: Group Analysis- **Social Exchanges / Predispositions**

Item	**Group Analysis**						
	Average Rank	Sum of Ranks	Mean	Std. Dev	Mean Rank
5	9.957	1145.000	4.313	0.654	2
11	10.522	1210.000	4.530	0.741	1
18	5.204	598.500	2.809	1.311	8
19	5.165	594.000	2.817	1.295	7
26	4.830	555.500	2.687	1.266	13
27	5.074	583.500	2.783	1.316	9
28	4.996	574.500	2.765	1.293	11
29	9.930	1142.000	4.313	0.654	3
30	9.974	1147.000	4.313	0.654	4
31	5.087	585.000	2.774	1.298	10
32	5.448	626.500	2.861	1.304	6
33	4.965	571.000	2.730	1.307	12
34	9.848	1132.500	4.287	0.632	5

$X^2 = 649.4953$ (N = 115, df = 12; p =0.0001)

$W = 0.47065$

$r = 0.46601$

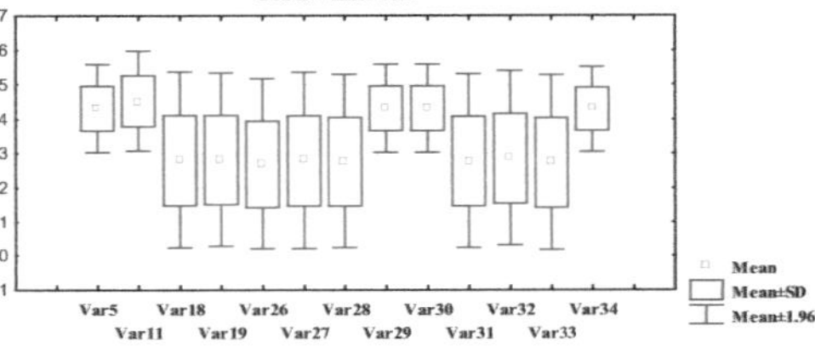

Figure 5.14: Group Analysis- **Social Exchanges / Predispositions**

Procedural conflict handling and effectiveness–attitudinal analysis- The research hypothesis H3 states that *the effectiveness of various procedural mechanisms to manage conflicts and its components are not equally preferred by the managers.* This is tested through attitudinal scale incorporated in part E of CMI. Twelve major components were taken for the analysis and the preferred combined efforts are also explored with the corollary data supplied through this measure. For the analysis, 1-6 transforming/replacement values were utilised in places of *not applicable* to *very effective* scale values *(table 5.49).* The chi square values for the individual variables were explored, seeing that this can be considered as a common routine among the standard non parametric testing methods at these levels. The elemental approach to the chi square analysis is essentially assumed randomisation which in this case, can act only as a rule of thumb. The comparative chi square values as well as the goodness of fit analysis can shed some light on the dependency dimensions prevailing among the variables.

Hypothesis Testing- Minimum expected cell frequencies are calculated for each cell and are grouped as presented in the table 5.49. These 12 variables can be grouped into four categories according to their *df* values of 5, 4, 3 or 2 as the case may be. Majority of the variables (all except 1, 2, 11 and 12) recorded a minimum expected cell frequency of 23 and indicated as group 'a'. In group 'b', expected cell frequency accrued was 19.2 and variables being 1 and 2. Variable 11 and12 recorded an expected cell frequency of 28.8 and 38.3 respectively. Dependency/equal preference of ranking elements can be ascertained through the appropriation of the chi square values as an exploratory method in this distribution. H_0 was assumed and can be expressed as there was an equal preference of ranking scales/frequencies and they are independent. H_a negates both the independency and equal preference strategy. In case of group a, the chi square table value for *df*= 5, probability of error-alpha at 0.01 can be expressed as 15.086 and all those calculated chi square values in this group are much higher than the table value. In that sense, the equal preference of ranking scales/ frequencies are questioned and it is clearly evident that there seems to be a wider distributed and or selectively preferred score values expressed by the managers. In addition, the preferred frequencies are visibly more along the middle level values of the scale. The much higher chi square values indirectly indicates the heightened squared observed values which in turn was a resultant of the variables' importance to act as a perceived potential source of conflict. Interestingly almost all the variables in this group 'a' act exactly as described and a few variables like item-5, 8, 10 etc are crucial factors to be considered in this direction, keeping the observed recordings it got as well as the heightened chi square values of them.

It can be explained that apart from these measures to determine the preferential recordings and its variations, chi square tests may not be experimentative for ascertaining other determinants to this group. In case of group b and c, the H_0 is assumed and can be expressed as there was an equal preference of ranking scales/frequencies and they are independent. H_a negates both the independency and equal preference strategy. For group b, the chi square table value for $df= 4$, probability of error-alpha at 0.01 can be expressed as 13.277 and all those calculated chi square values in this group are much higher than the table value. In that sense, the equal preference of ranking scales/ frequencies are questioned and it is clearly evident that there seems to be a wider distributed and or selectively preferred score values expressed by the managers. For group c (variable 11), the chi square table value for $df= 3$, probability of error-alpha at 0.01 can be expressed as 11.645 and all those calculated chi square values in this group are very much higher than the table value. For variable 12 with $df=2$, table value being 9.210; calculated value seems to be slightly higher-9.617. The denominations of group a equally applies to these three groups b, c and d. Interestingly, the differential value difference is not considerably heightened as was evident in a selected few variables of group *a* and a variable in *b*.

The chi square analyses pretend that the four groups negate the H_0 and accept H_a. This can be attributed to the factors that are indicative of the preferred set of values and scoring pattern that was exercised by the managers. Further it indicates the need for necessary processing to ascertain various dimensions of the data structure. Both Friedman's chi square value for the scale and variances are expressive in this direction. The standard deviations are indicative of the wider preferences of the managers towards the ranking patterns.

A moderate level of reliability of the scale can be regarded as a satisfactory measure considering the fact that there exists multitude of variables and a flexible yet impulsive ranking scale was adopted. The scale mean and variable means are all pinpointing vividly a preferential pattern that can be adjudged through the moderate positive correlations operating among variables 4 and 10, 3 and 9, 1 and 2, 9 and 10, 2 and10, 4 and 7,3 and 7 as well as a moderately negative correlation between variables 6 and 7*(table 5.50)*.Interestingly the relative independency and moderate interdependency operating among these variables are indicative of the relational importance as perceived by the managerial population.

Table 5.49: Procedural way of dealing conflicts- perceived denominations

Item No.	Variable/ Procedural way of dealing conflicts	Chi-Square	df	Average Rank	Sum of Ranks	Percent Mean[#]	Variance	Std. Dev	Std. Error	Combined approaches preferred Rank 1[@]	Rank 2	Rank 3	Mean Rank
1	Open Negotiation/Bargaining	18.957[a]	4	7.122	819.000	3.130	1.623	1.274	0.119	6.957	******	******	4
2	Participative Discussions/Dialogues	62.000[a]	4	7.622	876.500	3.322	1.132	1.064	0.099	34.783	6.087	******	2
3	Third party intervention by Mutual Consent	17.574[b]	5	6.070	698.000	2.713	2.031	1.425	0.133	******	******	******	11
4	Mediation by a Consultant/Others	17.574[b]	5	6.370	732.500	2.826	2.005	1.416	0.132	6.087	******	******	8
5	Exercising Organisational Power/Rules	37.713[b]	5	7.000	805.000	3.078	1.880	1.371	0.128	******	******	******	5
6	Collective Bargaining	22.478[b]	5	6.317	726.500	2.800	2.056	1.434	0.134	******	******	******	10
7	Industrial Mediations	17.574[b]	5	6.287	723.000	2.817	1.993	1.412	0.132	24.348	******	******	9
8	Intra Organisational Counseling	35.522[b]	5	7.348	845.000	3.243	1.589	1.261	0.118	27.826	66.087	******	3
9	Authoritative Organisational Interventions	20.809[b]	5	6.543	752.500	2.922	1.915	1.384	0.129	******	******	******	7
10	Legalistic Interventions	34.165[b]	5	6.683	768.500	2.957	1.796	1.340	0.125	******	******	******	6
11	Mutually Volunteered Agreements	96.930[c]	3	8.296	954.000	3.643	0.845	0.919	0.086	******	27.826	54.783	1
12	Collaborative Efforts and Work Execution	9.617[d]	2	2.343	269.500	1.139	0.542	0.736	0.069	******	******	45.217	12

Percent mean value. Correctional error assumed to be less significant for current analysis.
@ Rank indicated by the percentage of the sampled unit. Case wise deletion attributed for a few non indicative frames.
a. 0 cells (.0%) have expected frequencies less than 5. The minimum expected cell frequency is 23.0.
b. 0 cells (.0%) have expected frequencies less than 5. The minimum expected cell frequency is 19.2.
c. 0 cells (.0%) have expected frequencies less than 5. The minimum expected cell frequency is 28.8.
d. 0 cells (.0%) have expected frequencies less than 5. The minimum expected cell frequency is 38.3.

ANOVA Chi Sqr. (N = 115, df = 11) = 229.1047   p =0.00001   Coeff. of Concordance = 0.18111   Aver. rank r = 0.17393

Figure 5.15: Box and Whiskers Plot- Procedural Conflict Handling

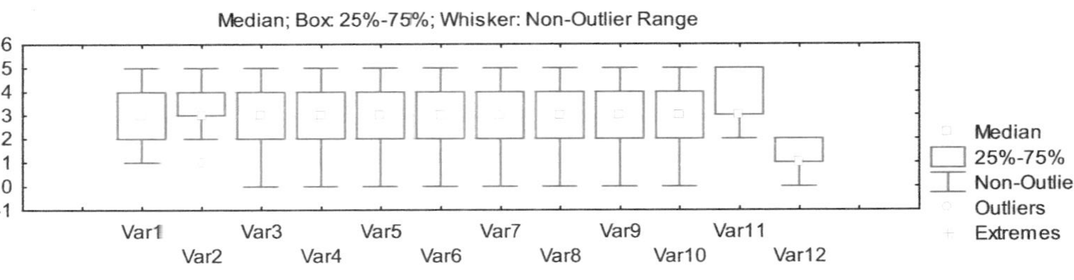

Table 5.50: Correlation(r) among the variables of procedural way of handling conflicts*

Item/ Variable	1	2	3	4	5	6	7	8	9	10	11	12
1	1.00	**0.28**	0.12	0.08	-0.03	0.04	-0.00	-0.19	0.00	0.09	0.04	-0.04
2	**0.28**	1.00	-0.04	0.14	**0.22**	0.01	0.10	-0.03	0.14	**0.26**	-0.03	0.03
3	0.12	-0.04	1.00	0.10	0.06	-0.02	**0.23**	0.04	**0.30**	0.00	0.05	-0.10
4	0.08	0.14	0.10	1.00	-0.11	-0.13	**0.24**	0.00	0.07	**0.32**	-0.03	-0.05
5	-0.03	**0.22**	0.06	-0.11	1.00	-0.06	0.05	-0.03	0.01	0.01	-0.09	-0.00
6	0.04	0.01	-0.02	-0.13	-0.06	1.00	**-0.21**	0.07	**0.24**	0.10	-0.13	0.06
7	-0.00	0.10	**0.23**	**0.24**	0.05	**-0.21**	1.00	-0.01	-0.03	0.03	0.17	0.02
8	**-0.19**	-0.03	0.04	0.00	-0.03	0.07	-0.01	1.00	0.02	0.09	0.10	-0.02
9	0.00	0.14	**0.30**	0.07	0.01	**0.24**	-0.03	0.02	1.00	**0.27**	-0.05	0.11
10	0.09	**0.26**	0.00	**0.32**	0.01	0.10	0.03	0.09	**0.27**	1.00	-0.04	0.08
11	0.04	-0.03	0.05	-0.03	-0.09	-0.13	0.17	0.10	-0.05	-0.04	1.00	0.04
12	-0.04	0.03	-0.10	-0.05	-0.00	0.06	0.02	-0.02	0.11	0.08	0.04	1.00

* N=115; **Bold** Marked correlations are significant at p <0.05000

5.1.8 Predominant conflict management styles

Conflict management style can be defined as the patterned responses and characteristic mode of handling conflict across a variety of communication episodes. The idea that individuals have *preferred* conflict styles or conflict tendencies has been around since at least the 1970s when Thomas and Kilmann first introduced the Thomas Kilmann Instrument. Along those lines, an attempt was made in this study to assess the style dimensions– control, collaborate, compromise, accommodate and avoid encompassing the personality dimensions. All five styles and their variations are equally available responses to conflict. The fact that a manager prefers a given style does not mean he or she will not use other styles. Indeed, this model assumes that they use each style at one point or another. Nevertheless, managerial dominant style reflects their particular beliefs about conflict, preferences and comfort zone. Secondary choices constitute backups preferences when they find it necessary to abandon their preferences, creating a response pattern or a response hierarchy, as the case may be. Preferential data was collected through part F of CMI, consisting twelve hypothetical situations and five possible states of responses reflecting each possible conflict styles explained above. All the style-responses were grouped accordingly and the representative scores were taken as style quotients described in *table 5.51*.

Majority of the style quotients recorded the values in the range 4–6.5, except three situational-response quotients. Interestingly the midrange values obtained through this analysis indicates the managerial presumed acceptance of the situational flows. This further strengthens the assumed model through above dimensions that manager use each style at one point or another and the operational efficiency in using preferential style may always be acceptable to them. The mean operatives and the variance propelled by the variables are all indicative of the multitudinal mechanism that may be exercised by the managerial population in *table 5.52*. The tau correlations are calculated to determine the inter-item dynamics that are operating among them. Moderately positive correlations were obtained among variables controller and compromiser (0.285), controller and collaborator (0.233), accommodator and avoider (0.184), avoider and controller (0.167), compromiser and collaborator (0.124). These positive correlations reveal the inter-relational dynamism existing among the various dimensions. Identifying the relationship incorporating each situational response also indicates more or less the same factorial relationship existing among the individual options.

Table 5.51: Style quotient

Item/ Option	1	2	3	4	5	6	7	8	9	10	11	12
A	5 [2]	5.1 [2]	4.9 [2]	4.6 [5]	5 [1]	5.1 [2]	5 [1]	5.1 [1]	4.9 [2]	4.8 [1]	5 [4]	6.6 [4]
B	5.2 [1]	4.8 [1]	5 [3]	4.9 [2]	5.1 [2]	4.7 [1]	5.2 [2]	5.2 [2]	5.2 [3]	5.1 [2]	5 [1]	6.5 [1]
C	5.2 [3]	5.1 [5]	5.3 [5]	5 [3]	5.5 [3]	5.4 [5]	5.3 [3]	4.7 [5]	4.9 [4]	4.7 [3]	5.1 [2]	6.4 [5]
D	5 [5]	4.3 [3]	4.9 [4]	4.2 [1]	4.8 [4]	2.6 [3]	4.9 [4]	4.9 [3]	5 [1]	5.2 [4]	5.1 [5]	6.4 [2]
E	5.2 [4]	3.6 [4]	4.7 [1]	3.4 [4]	5 [5]	2.3 [4]	4.9 [5]	4.9 [4]	5 [5]	5.2 [5]	4.8 [3]	6.3 [3]

Rounded to two decimals-(average score, out of 10)

[1] *Controller*   [2] *Compromiser*   [3] *Collaborator*   [4] *Accommodator*   [5] *Avoider*

Table 5.52: Style quotient- Basic statistics and Kendall's Tau

Style Denominator	Mean*	Sum	Min*	Max*	Variance	Std. Dev.	Std. Error	Kendall Tau Correlations[#]				
								Controller	*Compromiser*	*Collaborator*	*Accommodator*	*Avoider*
Controller	59.896	6888	46	77	39.270	6.267	0.584	1.000	**0.285**	**0.233**	0.109	**0.167**
Compromiser	62.113	7143	45	78	47.154	6.867	0.640	**0.285**	1.000	**0.124**	0.068	-0.001
Collaborator	59.009	6786	47	72	29.026	5.388	0.502	**0.233**	**0.124**	1.000	0.105	0.069
Accommodator	55.748	6411	40	72	36.278	6.023	0.562	0.109	0.068	0.105	1.000	**0.184**
Avoider	61.748	7101	49	74	34.822	5.901	0.550	**0.167**	-0.001	0.069	**0.184**	1.000

* Out of 120 (10*12 items)   #**Bold** Marked correlations are significant at p <0.05000

Style quotient and managerial strata- The research hypothesis (H4) states that *the multitudinal effects of the preferred styles of conflict results in relational preferences among the various managerial strata.* An explorative analysis was carried out to find the relational preferences existing among the various managerial strata. The indicative differentials if any can be ascertained among the sample strata. The departmental dimensions can play a major role in this regard and the same was taken for the analysis of projective rank differentials. The group analysis was carried out assuming the multiple dependent characteristics of the styles. The mid range of average rank differentials reestablishes the close knit operational potentials and the multitudinal effects of the preferred styles of conflict.

Hypothesis Testing- H_0 explains that there is no difference of *ranking* preferences among the groups and to assess this, deductive treatment of the ranks and concordance analysis attempt were made. The logical categorisation of the sample was attempted along the lines of departments as this can be the appropriate and situational reliant factor for such an operation. Interestingly, the aforesaid categorisation can be regarded as an attempt to exercise reflective projections. This departmental categorisation can act only as an indicative variant as the sampled data may not allow an establishment of the variant resultants to those particular departmental strata. Further the sample frame of the study had not inductively construed these categorisations. The intra-indicative factor that acts as styles was significantly similar among all subgroups. The concordance of quotient *rankings* was also as similar or more as such among all them. The calculated anova chi square values for the subgroups were all above the chi square table values for respective degrees of freedom though moderated concordance were obtained for all groups. Thus H_0, which can be expressed as the subgroups have same intra ranking patterns, can only be partially acceptable. H_a- that the subgroups had different ranking patterns can also be partially rejected. The ranking patterns of all subgroups were indicating the primal variables-style quotients and the intra ranking scores were departed even among the intragroup levels. It can be ascertained that though there seems to be a little managerial style difference operating among the subgroups, they are certainly not significant. This may be a resultant of less adequate number of populations.

Factor–Style quotient F1 reveals a relational operation among the 3C styles– compromiser, controller and collaborator. F2 explains the relational strength operating among the three styles-avoider, accommodator and collaborator. It can be ascertained that these two factor derivatives operationalise themselves at two levels assuming merging at collaborations.

Table 5.53: Rank analysis of style quotients

Style Denominator	Group Analysis*				MANAGERIAL STRATA**												
	Average Rank	Sum of ranks	Mean[@]	Mean Rank[1]	FIN[2]		FSP[3]		HR[4]		MKG[5]		PRD[6]		SYS[7]	
					Mean	Rank	Mean	Rank	Mean	Rank	Mean	Rank	Mean	Rank	Mean	Rank
Controller	3.004	346	59.896	3	59.290	3	58.714	4	60.600	3	60.333	2	60.179	3	57.750	4
Compromiser	3.548	408	62.113	1	62.871	1	63.429	2	61.433	2	60.000	3	62.607	1	63.500	1
Collaborator	2.813	324	59.009	4	58.097	4	58.000	5	60.033	4	58.400	4	59.571	4	58.500	3
Accommodator	2.035	234	55.748	5	56.839	5	58.857	3	54.167	5	54.400	5	55.929	5	57.500	5
Avoider	3.600	414	61.748	2	61.742	2	63.571	1	61.967	1	61.600	1	61.500	2	59.250	2

*(Multiple dependent variables) ** FIN-Finance & Accounts; FSP- Factory Manager and Special Officials; HR- Human Resource; MKG- Marketing & Sales; PRD- Production; SYS- Systems & EDP; [@] Out of 120 (10*12 items)

ANOVA Chi Sqr. (N = 115, df = 4) = 76.42451   p =0.00001   Coeff. of Concordance = 0.16614   Aver. rank r = 0.15883
ANOVA Chi Sqr. (N = 31, df = 4) = 20.00657   p =0.00050   Coeff. of Concordance = 0.16134   Aver. rank r = 0.13339
ANOVA Chi Sqr. (N = 7, df = 4) = 6.072993   p =0.19377   Coeff. of Concordance = 0.21689   Aver. rank r = 0.08637
ANOVA Chi Sqr. (N = 30, df = 4) = 29.79898   p =0.00001   Coeff. of Concordance = 0.24832   Aver. rank r = 0.22240
ANOVA Chi Sqr. (N = 15, df = 4) = 12.31186   p =0.01518   Coeff. of Concordance = 0.20520   Aver. rank r = 0.14843
ANOVA Chi Sqr. (N = 28, df = 4) = 18.36330   p =0.00105   Coeff. of Concordance = 0.16396   Aver. rank r = 0.13299
ANOVA Chi Sqr. (N = 4, df = 4) = 0. 9620253   p =0.91550   Coeff. of Concordance = 0.06013   Aver. rank r = -0.2532

Table 5.54: Factor analysis- Style quotient

Style Quotient*#						F	Eigen value	%Total Variance	Cumulative Eigen value	Cumulative %
Factor Loadings		Communality								
Style Denominator	F1[@]	F2	From F1	From F2	Multiple R[2]	F1	1.807	36.134	1.807	36.134
Controller	**0.777**	0.218	0.603	0.651	0.251	F2	1.118	22.352	2.924	58.486
Compromiser	**0.810**	-0.166	0.655	0.683	0.160					
Collaborator	**0.537**	**0.301**	0.289	0.379	0.119					
Accommodator	0.103	**0.763**	0.011	0.592	0.114					
Avoider	0.070	**0.784**	0.005	0.619	0.130					
Expl.Var	.563	1.361	*Prin. Components extraction							
Prp.Totl	0.313	0.272	Rotation: Varimax							

Bold marked are >0.30 cut-off point
@ F1 and F2 are Factor Derivatives

Figure 5.16 Style Quotient–Box and Whiskers plot

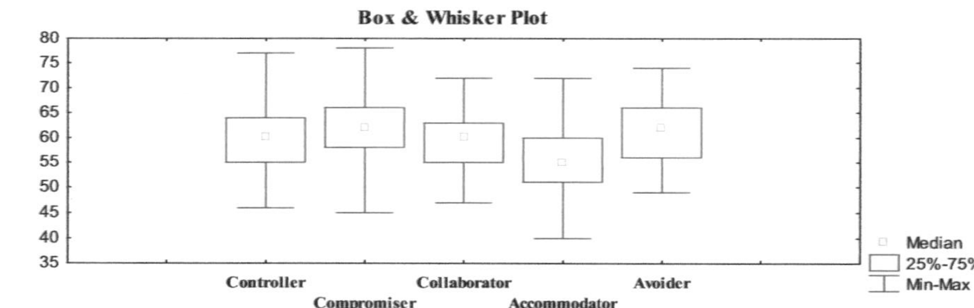

Table 5.55: Reliability analysis-Style Quotient

Style Denominator	Mean if deleted	Var. if deleted	St.Dev. if deleted	Item Total. Correlated.	Squared Multiple R	Alpha if. deleted
Controller	238.617	207.001	14.388	0.460	0.251	0.393
Compromiser	236.400	228.744	15.124	0.257	0.160	0.528
Collaborator	239.504	246.563	15.702	0.316	0.119	0.489
Accommodator	242.765	241.571	15.543	0.274	0.114	0.511
Avoider	236.765	246.788	15.710	0.256	0.130	0.521

Summary for scale:

Mean= 298.513   St.Dev. =18.2061

Cronbach's alpha: 0.546491   Standardized alpha: 0.549523

Average inter-item correlation.: 0.198542

5.1.9 Preferred conflict modes and Dominant conflict responses

There seems to be a general agreement in the conflict literature that managerial stratum employ five different modes or styles of behaviour in conflict situations - competing, collaborating, compromising, accommodating, and avoiding. Though there are functional differences when these modes are theoretically transplanted – it may contravene to five, six, eight or more predominant mode of operations. The situational responses along these lines of operations can be summated to identify the preferred modes or the styles as the case may be of the managerial population. The previous section attempted to spot out the style preferences exclusively with the projective situations, whereas part G of CMI intended to find out the response pattern in much broader situations.   The research hypothesis-H5 states that *Managerial stratum employ five different modes or styles of behaviour in conflict situations – competing, collaborating, compromising, accommodating, and avoiding and the situational responses along these lines of operations can be summated to identify the preferred modes or the styles as the case may be of the managerial population. Table 5.56* articulate basic statistical operations, regarding the possible 125 combinations of the twenty five statements, which were put into the structure of analysis. Majority of the preferential modes were within the range of 2-9. The mean score of each possible response along with the variances were also explored. Interestingly, the operational preferences through this analysis substantiate that singular or a combination of mode of responses are recorded as preferred over and above others, by the respondents. Internal rankings of the mode of responses are also indicative in these grounds. Projective rank analyses assess the differential rankings obtained through the incorporations of mean scores for each mode of responses.

Hypothesis Testing-H_0 explains that there is no difference of ranking preferences among the groups in the identified five modes/styles and to assess this, deductive treatment of the ranks, anova chi-square and concordance analysis attempts were made. The logical categorisation of the sample was attempted along the lines of each statements (totaling twenty five such) as this can be the appropriate and situational reliant factor for such an operation and the aforesaid categorisation can be regarded as an attempt to exercise reflective projections. The intra-indicative factors that acts as modes/styles to handle conflict was significantly similar among population as a whole and the concordance of assigning the scores was also as similar or higher as such among all them. The calculated anova chi square values for individual statements were all above the chi square table values for respective degrees of freedom and high/very high concordance were obtained for all statements.

Thus H_0, which can be expressed, as the group as a whole has same intra ranking patterns/preferential modes of responses to approach and handle conflicts, seems to be acceptable. H_a– that the group as a whole had different ranking patterns of approach mechanism/preferred mode of responses can be naturally rejected, though the preferential modes were dissimilar among the individual statements, ranking patterns of group as a whole were indicating the primal variables-preferred modes of responses as well as approaches of handling conflicts. Further the intra ranking scores were not at all deviant even among the group levels, indicating the preferential adoption of these preferred modes with their respective magnitude. The departmental and other stratifications were also explored, returning a less momentous and or with that of minimal significance. Kendall's tau correlations revealed an array of statistically significant relationships operating at various levels. Most of the *taus* are less correlated, except a few high correlations as the cases indicate.

Factor score exploration and analysis- The main application of factor analysis techniques in these analytical process of preferred mode of responses in conflict situations under logical clustering of factors, assumes to reduce the number of variables/ major modes of responses (both singular/combined) and to detect structure in the relationships between variables that enables to classify variables. Therefore, factor analysis was applied as a data reduction or exploratory structure detection method throughout the process of analysis concerning all twenty- five situations/statements. To maximise the variation among the components, the Varimax rotation technique was adopted with principal components extraction of factor analysis. The potential sources of conflicts grouped under four levels accordingly acted as four factors with all their clustered variables. A *cut off strategy* integrated with equaling one or more of eigenvalues and greater than 0.30 factor loadings indicate the necessary appropriation of the factor analysis to suit the needs of the present study and the summated factor preferential were recorded in *tables 5.83.*

Ranked preferences are expressed with the tabular expressions and the guided combination of factorial exploration concerning all the twenty five situations/ statements were attempted to reveal the significance it bears in the process of conflict handling. A comparative analysis of these responses with that of the standard / indicative modes of responses, highlighted by previous studies was attempted as expressed in table 5.82. The generative analyses with these denominations present *projective* preferential modes of responses.

Table 5.56: Preferred conflict mode- Basic Statistics and Kendall's Tau

Item	Mean*	Sum	Min	Max	Variance	Std. Dev.	Std. Error	Average Rank	Sum of Ranks	Internal Rank[§]	Kendall's Tau b[#]				
											CF	AO	CI	AV	CP
1 CF	2.965	341	2	4	0.490	0.700	0.065	1.970	226.5	5	1.000	0.120	**-0.348**	-0.002	-0.077
1 AO	6.757	777	6	8	0.730	0.854	0.080	4.487	516.0	2	0.120	1.000	0.000	0.011	-0.007
1 CI	6.783	780	6	8	0.698	0.835	0.078	4.513	519.0	1	**-0.348**	0.000	1.000	**-0.145**	0.116
1 AV	2.991	344	2	4	0.482	0.695	0.065	1.996	229.5	4	-0.002	0.011	**-0.145**	1.000	**0.224**
1 CP	3.026	348	2	4	0.482	0.694	0.065	2.035	234.0	3	-0.077	-0.007	0.116	**0.224**	1.000
2 CF	6.757	777	6	8	0.659	0.812	0.076	4.009	461.0	2	1.000	**0.192**	**-0.029**	0.054	**-0.203**
2 AO	3.061	352	2	4	0.479	0.692	0.065	1.504	173.0	4	**0.192**	1.000	0.089	**0.501**	0.021
2 CI	6.791	781	6	9	0.710	0.843	0.079	4.048	465.5	1	-0.029	0.089	1.000	**0.175**	**0.287**
2 AV	3.061	352	2	4	0.479	0.692	0.065	1.496	172.0	5	0.054	**0.501**	**0.175**	1.000	0.095
2 CP	6.757	777	6	8	0.659	0.812	0.076	3.943	453.5	3	**-0.203**	0.021	**0.287**	0.095	1.000
3 CF	3.052	351	2	4	0.453	0.673	0.063	2.017	232.0	3.5	1.000	**0.134**	-0.060	**0.167**	**0.130**
3 AO	6.774	779	6	8	0.668	0.817	0.076	4.504	518.0	1	**0.134**	1.000	-0.102	**0.151**	**-0.140**
3 CI	6.765	778	6	8	0.655	0.809	0.075	4.496	517.0	2	-0.060	-0.102	1.000	0.054	**0.161**
3 AV	3.017	347	2	4	0.456	0.675	0.063	1.965	226.0	5	**0.167**	**0.151**	0.054	1.000	**-0.151**
3 CP	3.052	351	2	4	0.453	0.673	0.063	2.017	232.0	3.5	**0.130**	**-0.140**	**0.161**	**-0.151**	1.000
4 CF	6.817	784	6	8	0.677	0.823	0.077	4.048	465.5	1	1.000	0.064	**0.263**	-0.017	**0.350**
4 AO	6.817	784	6	9	0.712	0.844	0.079	4.035	464.0	2	0.064	1.000	-0.119	-0.080	0.012
4 CI	6.757	777	6	8	0.659	0.812	0.076	3.917	450.5	3	**0.263**	-0.119	1.000	0.068	**0.191**
4 AV	3.052	351	2	4	0.453	0.673	0.063	1.491	171.5	5	-0.017	-0.080	0.068	1.000	-0.009
4 CP	3.061	352	2	4	0.444	0.666	0.062	1.509	173.5	4	**0.350**	0.012	**0.191**	-0.009	1.000
5 CF	3.061	352	2	4	0.444	0.666	0.062	2.504	288.0	2.5	1.000	0.007	**0.333**	-0.111	0.327
5 AO	3.061	352	2	4	0.444	0.666	0.062	2.500	287.5	4	0.007	1.000	**0.418**	-0.049	0.397
5 CI	3.052	351	2	4	0.453	0.673	0.063	2.491	286.5	5	**0.333**	**0.418**	1.000	-0.117	0.854
5 AV	7.000	805	6	9	0.825	0.908	0.085	5.000	575.0	1	-0.111	-0.049	-0.117	1.000	-0.195
5 CP	3.061	352	2	4	0.444	0.666	0.062	2.504	288.0	2.5	0.327	0.397	0.854	-0.195	1.000
6 CF	7.061	812	6	9	0.847	0.920	0.086	5.000	575.0	1	1.000	**-0.150**	-0.032	**-0.146**	0.056
6 AO	3.052	351	2	4	0.453	0.673	0.063	2.491	286.5	4.5	**-0.150**	1.000	**0.379**	**-0.168**	**0.262**
6 CI	3.061	352	2	4	0.444	0.666	0.062	2.509	288.5	2.5	-0.032	**0.379**	1.000	**-0.614**	**0.842**
6 AV	3.078	354	2	4	0.441	0.664	0.062	2.491	286.5	4.5	**-0.146**	**-0.168**	**-0.614**	1.000	**-0.723**
6 CP	3.061	352	2	4	0.444	0.666	0.062	2.509	288.5	2.5	0.056	**0.262**	**0.842**	**-0.723**	1.000
7 CF	3.070	353	2	4	0.451	0.672	0.063	2.226	256.0	4	1.000	**0.160**	0.104	**0.653**	0.036
7 AO	5.304	610	2	9	4.933	2.221	0.207	3.583	412.0	2	**0.160**	1.000	**0.157**	**0.141**	-0.069
7 CI	3.070	353	2	4	0.451	0.672	0.063	2.243	258.0	3	0.104	**0.157**	1.000	0.107	-0.121
7 AV	3.052	351	2	4	0.453	0.673	0.063	2.209	254.0	5	**0.653**	**0.141**	0.107	1.000	0.113
7 CP	7.183	826	5	9	1.115	1.056	0.098	4.739	545.0	1	0.036	-0.069	-0.121	0.113	1.000
8 CF	3.052	351	2	4	0.453	0.673	0.063	1.722	198.0	5	1.000	0.117	-0.003	**0.422**	-0.011
8 AO	7.191	827	5	9	1.191	1.091	0.102	4.213	484.5	2	0.117	1.000	**-0.128**	**0.251**	-0.042
8 CI	7.148	822	5	9	1.180	1.086	0.101	4.261	490.0	1	-0.003	**-0.128**	1.000	**-0.231**	-0.065

Item	Mean*	Sum	Min	Max	Variance	Std. Dev.	Std. Error	Average Rank	Sum of Ranks	Internal Rank[§]	Kendall's Tau b[#]				
											CF	AO	CI	AV	CP
8 AV	3.052	351	2	4	0.453	0.673	0.063	1.726	198.5	4	**0.422**	**0.251**	**-0.231**	1.000	**0.159**
8 CP	5.226	601	2	9	4.773	2.185	0.204	3.078	354.0	3	-0.011	-0.042	-0.065	**0.159**	1.000
9 CF	3.122	359	2	4	0.511	0.715	0.067	1.974	227.0	5	1.000	-0.022	**0.982**	0.075	0.104
9 AO	7.183	826	5	9	1.203	1.097	0.102	4.496	517.0	2	-0.022	1.000	-0.026	**-0.173**	**0.141**
9 CI	3.139	361	2	4	0.489	0.699	0.065	2.000	230.0	4	**0.982**	-0.026	1.000	0.062	0.101
9 AV	7.200	828	5	9	1.179	1.086	0.101	4.504	518.0	1	0.075	**-0.173**	0.062	1.000	**-0.241**
9 CP	3.157	363	2	4	0.484	0.696	0.065	2.026	233.0	3	0.104	**0.141**	0.101	**-0.241**	1.000
10 CF	7.191	827	5	9	1.156	1.075	0.100	4.491	516.5	2	1.000	0.034	0.072	-0.104	**0.228**
10 AO	3.139	361	2	4	0.489	0.699	0.065	2.000	230.0	4	0.034	1.000	**0.358**	0.064	0.078
10 CI	3.139	361	2	4	0.489	0.699	0.065	1.996	229.5	5	0.072	**0.358**	1.000	**0.454**	**-0.125**
10 AV	3.148	362	2	4	0.478	0.691	0.064	2.004	230.5	3	-0.104	0.064	**0.454**	1.000	-0.009
10 CP	7.235	832	6	9	1.023	1.012	0.094	4.509	518.5	1	**0.228**	0.078	**-0.125**	-0.009	1.000
11 CF	3.122	359	2	4	0.494	0.703	0.066	1.983	228.0	5	1.000	0.048	-0.029	**0.453**	-0.103
11 AO	7.200	828	6	9	1.074	1.036	0.097	4.530	521.0	1	0.048	1.000	**-0.134**	-0.027	-0.026
11 CI	7.191	827	6	9	1.033	1.016	0.095	4.470	514.0	2	-0.029	**-0.134**	1.000	0.110	-0.080
11 AV	3.130	360	2	4	0.500	0.707	0.066	1.987	228.5	4	**0.453**	-0.027	0.110	1.000	**-0.274**
11 CP	3.148	362	2	4	0.495	0.704	0.066	2.030	233.5	3	-0.103	-0.026	-0.080	**-0.274**	1.000
12 CF	3.139	361	2	4	0.489	0.699	0.065	2.087	240.0	3	1.000	**-0.335**	0.103	0.100	**0.228**
12 AO	7.174	825	6	9	1.057	1.028	0.096	4.496	517.0	2	**-0.335**	1.000	-0.044	**-0.160**	**-0.367**
12 CI	3.009	346	2	4	0.447	0.669	0.062	1.922	221.0	5	0.103	-0.044	1.000	**0.299**	0.037
12 AV	3.052	351	2	4	0.453	0.673	0.063	1.991	229.0	4	0.100	**-0.160**	**0.299**	1.000	-0.078
12 CP	7.183	826	6	9	1.045	1.022	0.095	4.504	518.0	1	**0.228**	**-0.367**	0.037	-0.078	1.000
13 CF	7.113	818	5	9	1.031	1.015	0.095	4.522	520.0	1	1.000	0.118	-0.097	0.091	**-0.184**
13 AO	3.078	354	2	4	0.441	0.664	0.062	2.000	230.0	5	0.118	1.000	**-0.316**	-0.086	-0.010
13 CI	3.078	354	2	4	0.459	0.677	0.063	2.004	230.5	3.5	-0.097	**-0.316**	1.000	**-0.174**	-0.045
13 AV	3.096	356	2	4	0.438	0.662	0.062	2.004	230.5	3.5	0.091	-0.086	**-0.174**	1.000	**-0.159**
13 CP	7.113	818	4	9	1.206	1.098	0.102	4.470	514.0	2	**-0.184**	-0.010	-0.045	**-0.159**	1.000
14 CF	3.061	352	2	4	0.461	0.679	0.063	1.983	228.0	5	1.000	**0.358**	**0.897**	**0.405**	-0.001
14 AO	7.174	825	6	9	1.040	1.020	0.095	4.561	524.5	1	**0.358**	1.000	**0.308**	0.043	0.102
14 CI	3.078	354	2	4	0.459	0.677	0.063	2.004	230.5	4	**0.897**	**0.308**	1.000	**0.418**	-0.073
14 AV	3.087	355	2	4	0.466	0.683	0.064	2.013	231.5	3	**0.405**	0.043	**0.418**	1.000	-0.017
14 CP	7.174	825	6	9	1.040	1.020	0.095	4.439	510.5	2	-0.001	0.102	-0.073	-0.017	1.000
15 CF	3.087	355	2	4	0.466	0.683	0.064	2.483	285.5	5	1.000	**0.155**	**0.530**	0.020	**0.423**
15 AO	3.087	355	2	4	0.466	0.683	0.064	2.513	289.0	2	**0.155**	1.000	**0.320**	0.112	**0.480**
15 CI	3.078	354	2	4	0.494	0.703	0.066	2.500	287.5	4	**0.530**	**0.320**	1.000	0.087	**0.518**
15 AV	7.157	823	6	9	1.028	1.014	0.095	5.000	575.0	1	0.020	0.112	0.087	1.000	0.042
15 CP	3.070	353	2	4	0.504	0.710	0.066	2.504	288.0	3	**0.423**	**0.480**	**0.518**	0.042	1.000
16 CF	3.087	355	2	4	0.501	0.708	0.066	2.017	232.0	3	1.000	0.080	-0.059	**-0.198**	0.027
16 AO	7.122	819	6	9	1.003	1.001	0.093	4.509	518.5	1	0.080	1.000	**0.143**	**-0.230**	**0.393**
16 CI	3.052	351	2	4	0.471	0.686	0.064	1.974	227.0	5	-0.059	**0.143**	1.000	**0.289**	**0.151**

Item	Mean*	Sum	Min	Max	Variance	Std. Dev.	Std. Error	Average Rank	Sum of Ranks	Internal Rank§	Kendall's Tau b#				
											CF	AO	CI	AV	CP
16 AV	3.070	353	2	4	0.469	0.685	0.064	2.009	231.0	4	-0.198	-0.230	0.289	1.000	-0.143
16 CP	7.130	820	6	9	1.027	1.013	0.094	4.491	516.5	2	0.027	0.393	0.151	-0.143	1.000
17 CF	7.183	826	6	9	1.045	1.022	0.095	5.000	575.0	1	1.000	-0.241	0.220	0.292	0.385
17 AO	3.070	353	2	4	0.469	0.685	0.064	2.500	287.5	3.5	-0.241	1.000	-0.446	0.001	-0.014
17 CI	3.061	352	2	4	0.461	0.679	0.063	2.500	287.5	3.5	0.220	-0.446	1.000	0.252	0.276
17 AV	3.070	353	2	4	0.469	0.685	0.064	2.513	289.0	2	0.292	0.001	0.252	1.000	0.386
17 CP	3.061	352	2	4	0.461	0.679	0.063	2.487	286.0	5	0.385	-0.014	0.276	0.386	1.000
18 CF	3.061	352	2	4	0.461	0.679	0.063	2.487	286.0	5	1.000	-0.050	0.123	-0.207	-0.211
18 AO	7.165	824	6	9	1.016	1.008	0.094	5.000	575.0	1	-0.050	1.000	-0.014	0.139	0.043
18 CI	3.078	354	2	4	0.459	0.677	0.063	2.496	287.0	4	0.123	-0.014	1.000	-0.416	-0.146
18 AV	3.070	353	2	4	0.469	0.685	0.064	2.504	288.0	3	-0.207	0.139	-0.416	1.000	0.034
18 CP	3.087	355	2	4	0.466	0.683	0.064	2.513	289.0	2	-0.211	0.043	-0.146	0.034	1.000
19 CF	7.174	825	6	9	1.040	1.020	0.095	4.457	512.5	2	1.000	-0.249	-0.139	-0.190	0.071
19 AO	3.061	352	2	4	0.479	0.692	0.065	1.991	229.0	4.5	-0.249	1.000	0.604	-0.140	-0.202
19 CI	3.061	352	2	4	0.461	0.679	0.063	1.991	229.0	4.5	-0.139	0.604	1.000	-0.260	0.100
19 AV	7.174	825	6	9	1.040	1.020	0.095	4.543	522.5	1	-0.190	-0.140	-0.260	1.000	-0.037
19 CP	3.070	353	2	4	0.469	0.685	0.064	2.017	232.0	3	0.071	-0.202	0.100	-0.037	1.000
20 CF	3.052	351	2	4	0.471	0.686	0.064	1.996	229.5	4	1.000	0.287	-0.274	0.064	-0.214
20 AO	3.052	351	2	4	0.471	0.686	0.064	1.991	229.0	5	0.287	1.000	-0.021	0.081	-0.115
20 CI	7.157	823	6	9	1.028	1.014	0.095	4.470	514.0	2	-0.274	-0.021	1.000	0.086	0.056
20 AV	3.061	352	2	4	0.479	0.692	0.065	2.013	231.5	3	0.064	0.081	0.086	1.000	0.224
20 CP	7.139	821	6	9	1.033	1.016	0.095	4.530	521.0	1	-0.214	-0.115	0.056	0.224	1.000
21 CF	7.148	822	6	9	1.022	1.011	0.094	4.370	502.5	1	1.000	-0.020	0.007	0.046	-0.141
21 AO	4.104	472	2	6	1.971	1.404	0.131	2.113	243.0	4	-0.020	1.000	0.533	0.428	0.063
21 CI	4.070	468	2	6	1.907	1.381	0.129	2.074	238.5	5	0.007	0.533	1.000	0.184	-0.014
21 AV	4.096	471	2	6	1.912	1.383	0.129	2.122	244.0	3	0.046	0.428	0.184	1.000	0.052
21 CP	7.183	826	6	9	1.045	1.022	0.095	4.322	497.0	2	-0.141	0.063	-0.014	0.052	1.000
22 CF	4.035	464	1	6	2.192	1.480	0.138	2.443	281.0	3	1.000	-0.047	-0.029	0.637	0.102
22 AO	7.165	824	6	9	1.016	1.008	0.094	4.435	510.0	1	-0.047	1.000	-0.384	-0.085	-0.043
22 CI	7.009	806	5	9	1.535	1.239	0.116	4.357	501.0	2	-0.029	-0.384	1.000	0.070	-0.017
22 AV	3.843	442	2	6	1.203	1.097	0.102	2.130	245.0	4	0.637	-0.085	0.070	1.000	-0.072
22 CP	3.070	353	2	4	0.469	0.685	0.064	1.635	188.0	5	0.102	-0.043	-0.017	-0.072	1.000
23 CF	3.043	350	2	4	0.463	0.680	0.063	2.504	288.0	3	1.000	0.071	0.100	-0.002	-0.073
23 AO	3.043	350	2	4	0.463	0.680	0.063	2.517	289.5	2	0.071	1.000	-0.200	0.031	-0.125
23 CI	7.009	806	5	9	1.500	1.225	0.114	5.000	575.0	1	0.100	-0.200	1.000	0.129	-0.319
23 AV	3.026	348	2	4	0.447	0.668	0.062	2.491	286.5	4	-0.002	0.031	0.129	1.000	0.034
23 CP	3.026	348	2	4	0.429	0.655	0.061	2.487	286.0	5	-0.073	-0.125	-0.319	0.034	1.000
24 CF	3.017	347	2	4	0.421	0.649	0.060	1.961	225.5	5	1.000	-0.048	-0.367	-0.084	-0.270
24 AO	6.991	804	5	9	1.517	1.232	0.115	4.483	515.5	2	-0.048	1.000	0.088	0.513	0.039
24 CI	3.078	354	2	6	0.546	0.739	0.069	2.035	234.0	3	-0.367	0.088	1.000	0.162	0.392

Item	Mean*	Sum	Min	Max	Variance	Std. Dev.	Std. Error	Average Rank	Sum of Ranks	Internal Rank[§]	Kendall's Tau b[#]				
											CF	AO	CI	AV	CP
24 AV	7.009	806	5	9	1.553	1.246	0.116	4.513	519.0	1	-0.084	**0.513**	**0.162**	1.000	0.120
24 CP	3.026	348	2	4	0.429	0.655	0.061	2.009	231.0	4	**-0.270**	0.039	**0.392**	0.120	1.000
25 CF	2.991	344	1	4	0.482	0.695	0.065	1.996	229.5	4	1.000	0.000	**-0.145**	**0.131**	**0.309**
25 AO	3.000	345	2	4	0.421	0.649	0.061	2.013	231.5	3	0.000	1.000	**-0.129**	**-0.377**	-0.048
25 CI	7.183	826	6	9	1.045	1.022	0.095	4.500	517.5	1	**-0.145**	**-0.129**	1.000	-0.092	-0.075
25 AV	3.009	346	2	4	0.430	0.656	0.061	1.991	229.0	5	**0.131**	**-0.377**	-0.092	1.000	**-0.173**
25 CP	7.174	825	6	9	1.040	1.020	0.095	4.500	517.5	2	**0.309**	-0.048	-0.075	**-0.173**	1.000

CF –Competing/Forcing   **AO- Accommodation/Obliging**   **CI- Collaboration/Integrating**   **AV- Avoiding**   **CP- Compromise/Problem-solving**   *Average score, out of **10**   [#] Item wise Correlations highlighted by **bolded** are significant at $p < 0.05000$
[§] Internal ranks credited through itemised preferred mode

NB: Other major non parametric correlation analyses including Gamma Correlations as well as the Spearman's Rank order correlation signifies more or less the same bivariate correlation commonalities with indicative figures.

Item Concordance and Chi Square values

[1] ANOVA Chi Sqr. (N = 115, df = 4) = 379.0659   p =0.00001   Coeff. of Concordance = 0.82406   Aver. rank r = 0.82251
[2] ANOVA Chi Sqr. (N = 115, df = 4) = 384.1761   p =0.00001   Coeff. of Concordance = 0.83517   Aver. rank r = 0.83372
[3] ANOVA Chi Sqr. (N = 115, df = 4) = 382.3198   p =0.00001   Coeff. of Concordance = 0.83113   Aver. rank r = 0.82965
[4] ANOVA Chi Sqr. (N = 115, df = 4) = 375.5236   p =0.00001   Coeff. of Concordance = 0.81636   Aver. rank r = 0.81474
[5] ANOVA Chi Sqr. (N = 115, df = 4) = 293.2439   p =0.00001   Coeff. of Concordance = 0.63749   Aver. rank r = 0.63431
[6] ANOVA Chi Sqr. (N = 115, df = 4) = 302.6499   p =0.00001   Coeff. of Concordance = 0.65793   Aver. rank r = 0.65493
[7] ANOVA Chi Sqr. (N = 115, df = 4) = 327.7791   p =0.00001   Coeff. of Concordance = 0.71256   Aver. rank r = 0.71004
[8] ANOVA Chi Sqr. (N = 115, df = 4) = 316.5090   p =0.00001   Coeff. of Concordance = 0.68806   Aver. rank r = 0.68533
[9] ANOVA Chi Sqr. (N = 115, df = 4) = 377.9276   p =0.00001   Coeff. of Concordance = 0.82158   Aver. rank r = 0.82002
[10] ANOVA Chi Sqr. (N = 115, df = 4) = 383.3430   p =0.00001   Coeff. of Concordance = 0.83335   Aver. rank r = 0.83189
[11] ANOVA Chi Sqr. (N = 115, df = 4) = 385.5483   p =0.00001   Coeff. of Concordance = 0.83815   Aver. rank r = 0.83673
[12] ANOVA Chi Sqr. (N = 115, df = 4) = 384.7822   p =0.00001   Coeff. of Concordance = 0.83648   Aver. rank r = 0.83505
[13] ANOVA Chi Sqr. (N = 115, df = 4) = 378.8056   p =0.00001   Coeff. of Concordance = 0.82349   Aver. rank r = 0.82194
[14] ANOVA Chi Sqr. (N = 115, df = 4) = 402.3992   p =0.00001   Coeff. of Concordance = 0.87478   Aver. rank r = 0.87368
[15] ANOVA Chi Sqr. (N = 115, df = 4) = 331.6940   p =0.00001   Coeff. of Concordance = 0.72107   Aver. rank r = 0.71863
[16] ANOVA Chi Sqr. (N = 115, df = 4) = 383.2100   p =0.00001   Coeff. of Concordance = 0.83307   Aver. rank r = 0.83160
[17] ANOVA Chi Sqr. (N = 115, df = 4) = 264.6503   p =0.00001   Coeff. of Concordance = 0.57533   Aver. rank r = 0.57160
[18] ANOVA Chi Sqr. (N = 115, df = 4) = 262.9423   p =0.00001   Coeff. of Concordance = 0.57161   Aver. rank r = 0.56786
[19] ANOVA Chi Sqr. (N = 115, df = 4) = 380.0613   p =0.00001   Coeff. of Concordance = 0.82622   Aver. rank r = 0.82470
[20] ANOVA Chi Sqr. (N = 115, df = 4) = 385.8649   p =0.00001   Coeff. of Concordance = 0.83884   Aver. rank r = 0.83742
[21] ANOVA Chi Sqr. (N = 115, df = 4) = 331.3589   p =0.00001   Coeff. of Concordance = 0.72035   Aver. rank r = 0.71789
[22] ANOVA Chi Sqr. (N = 115, df = 4) = 333.5402   p =0.00001   Coeff. of Concordance = 0.72509   Aver. rank r = 0.72268
[23] ANOVA Chi Sqr. (N = 115, df = 4) = 272.5708   p =0.00001   Coeff. of Concordance = 0.59255   Aver. rank r = 0.58897
[24] ANOVA Chi Sqr. (N = 115, df = 4) = 387.6337   p =0.00001   Coeff. of Concordance = 0.84268   Aver. rank r = 0.84130
[25] ANOVA Chi Sqr. (N = 115, df = 4) = 380.4065   p =0.00001   Coeff. of Concordance = 0.82697   Aver. rank r = 0.82545

Group tables 5.57 - 5.81: Factor Analysis of Preferred conflict modes

Table 5.57: Item1*[#]

Preferred Mode	Factor Loadings			Communality			
	F1[@]	F2	F3	From F1	From F2	From F3	Multiple R^2
1 CF	**0.742**	0.080	**0.324**	0.550	0.557	0.662	0.176
1 AO	0.047	-0.012	**0.956**	0.002	0.002	0.916	0.039
1 CI	**-0.864**	0.053	0.155	0.746	0.749	0.773	0.189
1 AV	0.236	**-0.804**	-0.073	0.056	0.702	0.707	0.095
1 CP	-0.265	**-0.766**	0.076	0.070	0.657	0.662	0.086
Expl.Var	1.424	1.242	1.054	*Principal Components extraction			
Prp.Totl	0.285	0.248	0.211	Rotation: Varimax			

 # Bold marked are >0.30 cut-off point
@ F1, F2, F3 are Factor Derivatives

F	Eigen value	%Total Variance	Cumulative Eigen value	Cumulative %
F1	1.461	29.221	1.461	29.221
F2	1.238	24.768	2.699	53.989
F3	1.021	20.412	3.720	74.401

Table 5.58: Item2*[#]

Preferred Mode	Factor Loadings		Communality		
	F4[@]	F5	From F4	From F5	Multiple R^2
2 CF	**0.421**	**0.543**	0.177	0.472	0.090
2 AO	**0.851**	0.052	0.724	0.727	0.305
2 CI	0.287	**-0.659**	0.082	0.517	0.119
2 AV	**0.811**	-0.188	0.658	0.694	0.300
2 CP	0.007	**-0.800**	0.000	0.640	0.130
Expl.Var	1.642	1.408	*Prin. Components extraction		
Prp.Totl	0.328	0.282	Rotation: Varimax		

 # Bold marked are >0.30 cut-off point
@ F4 and F5 are Factor Derivatives

F	Eigen value	%Total Variance	Cumulative Eigen value	Cumulative %
F3	1.664	33.286	1.664	33.286
F5	1.386	27.714	3.050	61.000

Table 5.59: Item3*[#]

Preferred Mode	Factor Loadings		Communality		
	F6[@]	F7	From F6	From F7	Multiple R^2
3 CF	-0.249	**0.787**	0.062	0.681	0.095
3 AO	**0.482**	**0.464**	0.233	0.448	0.066
2 CI	**-0.566**	-0.041	0.321	0.322	0.061
3 AV	0.176	**0.665**	0.031	0.473	0.090
3 CP	**-0.818**	0.068	0.669	0.674	0.120
Expl.Var	1.315	1.283	*Prin. Components extraction		
Prp.Totl	0.263	0.257	Rotation: Varimax		

 # Bold marked are >0.30 cut-off point
@ F6 and F7 are Factor Derivatives

F	Eigen value	%Total Variance	Cumulative Eigen value	Cumulative %
F6	1.413	28.261	1.413	28.261
F7	1.185	23.701	2.598	51.962

Table 5.60: Item4*#

Factor Loadings			Communality		
Preferred Mode	F8@	F9	From F8	From F9	Multiple R^2
4 CF	**0.812**	0.088	0.659	0.667	0.203
4 AO	0.119	**0.732**	0.014	0.550	0.036
4 CI	**0.576**	**-0.460**	0.331	0.543	0.112
4 AV	0.021	**-0.643**	0.000	0.414	0.018
4 CP	**0.755**	0.091	0.569	0.578	0.159
Expl.Var	1.575	1.177	*Prin. Components extraction		
Prp.Totl	0.315	0.235	Rotation: Varimax		

\# **Bold** marked are >0.30 cut-off point
@ F8 and F9 are Factor Derivatives

F	Eigen value	%Total Variance	Cumulative Eigen value	Cumulative %
F8	1.581	31.618	1.581	31.618
F9	1.171	23.412	2.751	55.030

Table 5.61: Item5*#

Factor Loadings			Communality		
Preferred Mode	F10@	F11	From F10	From F11	Multiple R^2
5 CF	0.208	**-0.726**	0.043	0.571	0.178
5 AO	**0.794**	0.261	0.630	0.698	0.247
5 CI	**0.874**	**-0.319**	0.765	0.867	0.780
5 AV	0.012	**0.673**	0.000	0.454	0.066
5 CP	**0.839**	**-0.396**	0.705	0.861	0.777
Expl.Var	2.143	1.307	*Prin. Components extraction		
Prp.Totl	0.429	0.261	Rotation: Varimax		

\# **Bold** marked are >0.30 cut-off point
@ F10 and F11 are Factor Derivatives

F	Eigen value	%Total Variance	Cumulative Eigen value	Cumulative %
F10	2.413	48.263	2.413	48.263
F11	1.037	20.737	3.450	69.000

Table 5.62: Item6*#

Factor Loadings			Communality		
Preferred Mode	F12@	F13	From F12	From F13	Multiple R^2
6 CF	0.179	**-0.845**	0.032	0.746	0.083
6 AO	**0.375**	**0.656**	0.141	0.571	0.220
6 CI	**0.899**	0.244	0.808	0.868	0.780
6 AV	**-0.870**	0.129	0.757	0.774	0.568
6 CP	**0.939**	0.062	0.883	0.886	0.807
Expl.Var	2.621	1.225	*Prin. Components extraction		
Prp.Totl	0.524	0.245	Rotation: Varimax		

\# **Bold** marked are >0.30 cut-off point
@ F12 and F13 are Factor Derivatives

F	Eigen value	%Total Variance	Cumulative Eigen value	Cumulative %
F12	2.668	53.359	2.668	53.359
F13	1.177	23.549	3.845	76.908

Table 5.63: Item7*#

Factor Loadings			Communality		
Preferred Mode	**F14@**	**F15**	**From F14**	**From F15**	**Multiple R²**
7 CF	**0.879**	0.104	0.772	0.783	0.430
7 AO	0.190	**0.558**	0.036	0.347	0.038
7 CI	0.133	**0.680**	0.018	0.480	0.051
7 AV	**0.897**	0.025	0.805	0.806	0.437
7 CP	0.291	**-0.689**	0.084	0.559	0.055
Expl.Var	1.715	1.259	*Prin. Components extraction		
Prp.Totl	0.343	0.252	Rotation: Varimax		

\# **Bold** marked are >0.30 cut-off point
@ F14 and F15 are Factor Derivatives

F	**Eigen value**	**%Total Variance**	**Cumulative Eigen value**	**Cumulative %**
F14	1.740	34.810	1.740	34.810
F15	1.234	24.678	2.974	59.487

Table 5.64: Item8*#

Factor Loadings			Communality		
Preferred Mode	**F16@**	**F17**	**From F16**	**From F17**	**Multiple R²**
8 CF	**-0.719**	0.013	0.517	0.517	0.228
8 AO	**-0.626**	-0.087	0.391	0.399	0.095
8 CI	0.254	**-0.573**	0.064	0.393	0.096
8 AV	**-0.768**	**0.386**	0.590	0.739	0.336
8 CP	0.206	**0.828**	0.042	0.728	0.034
Expl.Var	1.604	1.172	*Prin. Components extraction		
Prp.Totl	0.321	0.234	Rotation: Varimax		

\# **Bold** marked are >0.30 cut-off point
@ F16 and F17 are Factor Derivatives

F	**Eigen value**	**%Total Variance**	**Cumulative Eigen value**	**Cumulative %**
F16	1.702	34.030	1.702	34.030
F17	1.075	21.491	2.776	55.521

Table 5.55: Item9*#

Factor Loadings			Communality		
Preferred Mode	**F18@**	**F19**	**From F18**	**From F19**	**Multiple R²**
9 CF	**0.992**	-0.008	0.984	0.984	0.967
9 AO	-0.054	**0.603**	0.003	0.367	0.052
9 CI	**0.991**	-0.004	0.982	0.982	0.967
9 AV	0.108	**-0.741**	0.012	0.561	0.119
9 CP	0.186	**0.720**	0.035	0.553	0.117
Expl.Var	2.015	1.431	*Prin. Components extraction		
Prp.Totl	0.403	0.286	Rotation: Varimax		

\# **Bold** marked are >0.30 cut-off point
@ F18 and F19 are Factor Derivatives

F	**Eigen value**	**%Total Variance**	**Cumulative Eigen value**	**Cumulative %**
F18	2.015	40.305	2.015	40.305
F19	1.431	28.623	3.446	68.928

Table 5.66: Item10*[#]

Factor Loadings			Communality		
Preferred Mode	$F20^{@}$	F21	From F20	From F21	Multiple R^2
10 CF	0.041	**0.759**	0.002	0.577	0.129
10 AO	**0.590**	**0.301**	0.348	0.438	0.186
10 CI	**0.889**	-0.035	0.791	0.792	0.426
10 AV	**0.725**	-0.212	0.525	0.570	0.305
10 CP	-0.069	**0.768**	0.005	0.594	0.144
Expl.Var	1.670	1.301	*Prin. Components extraction		
Prp.Totl	0.334	0.260	Rotation: Varimax		

Bold marked are >0.30 cut-off point
@ F20 and F21 are Factor Derivatives

F	Eigen value	%Total Variance	Cumulative Eigen value	Cumulative %
F20	1.672	33.445	1.672	33.445
F21	1.299	25.980	2.971	59.425

Table 5.67: Item11*[#]

Factor Loadings			Communality		
Preferred Mode	$F22^{@}$	F23	From F22	From F23	Multiple R^2
11 CF	**0.744**	0.275	0.554	0.630	0.259
11 AO	0.009	**0.746**	0.000	0.556	0.033
11 CI	0.226	**-0.738**	0.051	0.595	0.054
11 AV	**0.861**	-0.008	0.741	0.741	0.323
11 CP	**-0.564**	0.066	0.318	0.323	0.097
Expl.Var	1.664	1.181	*Prin. Components extraction		
Prp.Totl	0.333	0.236	Rotation: Varimax		

Bold marked are >0.30 cut-off point
@ F22 and F23 are Factor Derivatives

F	Eigen value	%Total Variance	Cumulative Eigen value	Cumulative %
F22	1.664	33.286	1.664	33.286
F23	1.181	23.611	2.845	56.896

Table 5.68: Item12*[#]

Factor Loadings			Communality		
Preferred Mode	$F24^{@}$	F25	From F24	From F25	Multiple R^2
12 CF	**0.683**	-0.183	0.467	0.501	0.170
12 AO	**-0.811**	0.137	0.658	0.677	0.307
12 CI	0.046	**-0.770**	0.002	0.596	0.121
12 AV	0.053	**-0.831**	0.003	0.693	0.179
12 CP	**0.769**	0.191	0.592	0.628	0.232
Expl.Var	1.722	1.373	*Prin. Components extraction		
Prp.Totl	0.344	0.275	Rotation: Varimax		

Bold marked are >0.30 cut-off point
@ F24 and F25 are Factor Derivatives

F	Eigen value	%Total Variance	Cumulative Eigen value	Cumulative %
F24	1.791	35.812	1.791	35.812
F25	1.304	26.084	3.095	61.896

Table 5.69: Item13*[#]

Factor Loadings			Communality		
Preferred Mode	F26[@]	F27	From F26	From F27	Multiple R^2
13 CF	0.273	-0.585	0.075	0.418	0.071
13 AO	**0.805**	0.06	0.648	0.652	0.161
13 CI	**-0.802**	0.115	0.643	0.656	0.190
13 AV	0.022	**-0.655**	0.000	0.430	0.113
13 CP	0.157	**0.740**	0.025	0.572	0.089
Expl.Var	1.390	1.338	*Prin. Components extraction		
Prp.Totl	0.278	0.268	Rotation: Varimax		

Bold marked are >0.30 cut-off point
@ F26 and F27 are Factor Derivatives

F	Eigen value	%Total Variance	Cumulative Eigen value	Cumulative %
F26	1.469	29.382	1.469	29.382
F27	1.259	25.178	2.728	54.560

Table 5.70: Item14*[#]

Factor Loadings			Communality		
Preferred Mode	F28[@]	F29	From F28	From F29	Multiple R^2
14 CF	**0.919**	0.203	0.845	0.885	0.833
14 AO	**0.398**	**0.641**	0.159	0.569	0.194
14 CI	**0.934**	0.099	0.871	0.881	0.830
14 AV	**0.667**	-0.168	0.445	0.473	0.233
14 CP	-0.193	**0.811**	0.037	0.695	0.051
Expl.Var	2.358	1.146	*Prin. Components extraction		
Prp.Totl	0.472	0.229	Rotation: Varimax		

Bold marked are >0.30 cut-off point
@ F28 and F29 are Factor Derivatives

F	Eigen value	%Total Variance	Cumulative Eigen value	Cumulative %
F28	2.412	48.245	2.412	48.245
F29	1.092	21.839	3.504	70.085

Table 5.71: Item15*[#]

Factor Loadings			Communality		
Preferred Mode	F30[@]	F31	From F30	From F31	Multiple R^2
15 CF	**0.772**	-0.146	0.596	0.618	0.354
15 AO	**0.532**	**0.474**	0.283	0.507	0.291
15 CI	**0.826**	0.087	0.682	0.690	0.431
15 AV	-0.044	**0.904**	0.002	0.819	0.024
15 CP	**0.825**	0.173	0.680	0.710	0.466
Expl.Var	2.243	1.101	*Prin. Components extraction		
Prp.Totl	0.449	0.220	Rotation: Varimax		

Bold marked are >0.30 cut-off point
@ F30 and F31 are Factor Derivatives

F	Eigen value	%Total Variance	Cumulative Eigen value	Cumulative %
F30	2.324	46.475	2.324	46.475
F31	1.020	20.405	3.344	66.879

Table 5.72: Item16*#

Factor Loadings			Communality		
Preferred Mode	F32@	F33	From F32	From F33	Multiple R^2
16 CF	0.116	**-0.497**	0.013	0.260	0.046
16 AO	**0.823**	-0.165	0.677	0.704	0.266
16 CI	**0.428**	**0.710**	0.183	0.688	0.188
16 AV	-0.243	**0.815**	0.059	0.722	0.245
16 CP	**0.808**	-0.023	0.653	0.654	0.212
Expl.Var	1.586	1.443	*Prin. Components extraction		
Prp.Totl	0.317	0.289	Rotation: Varimax		

Bold marked are >0.30 cut-off point
@ F32 and F33 are Factor Derivatives

F	Eigen value	%Total Variance	Cumulative Eigen value	Cumulative %
F32	1.642	32.830	1.642	32.830
F33	1.387	27.746	3.029	60.576

Table 5.73: Item17*#

Factor Loadings			Communality		
Preferred Mode	F34@	F35	From F34	From F35	Multiple R^2
17 CF	**0.648**	**0.321**	0.420	0.524	0.292
17 AO	0.078	**-0.924**	0.006	0.860	0.334
17 CI	**0.339**	**0.749**	0.115	0.676	0.369
17 AV	**0.778**	0.002	0.605	0.605	0.238
17 CP	**0.815**	0.054	0.664	0.667	0.311
Expl.Var	1.810	1.521	*Prin. Components extraction		
Prp.Totl	0.362	0.304	Rotation: Varimax		

Bold marked are >0.30 cut-off point
@ F34 and F35 are Factor Derivatives

F	Eigen value	%Total Variance	Cumulative Eigen value	Cumulative %
F34	2.124	42.473	2.124	42.473
F35	1.207	24.144	3.331	66.616

Table 5.74: Item18*#

Factor Loadings			Communality		
Preferred Mode	F36@	F37	From F36	From F37	Multiple R^2
18 CF	-0.195	**-0.696**	0.038	0.523	0.108
18 AO	**0.461**	-0.144	0.213	0.234	0.031
18 CI	**-0.680**	-0.288	0.462	0.545	0.208
18 AV	**0.844**	0.138	0.712	0.731	0.240
18 CP	-0.089	**0.827**	0.008	0.692	0.082
Expl.Var	1.433	1.292	*Prin. Components extraction		
Prp.Totl	0.287	0.258	Rotation: Varimax		

Bold marked are >0.30 cut-off point
@ F36 and F37 are Factor Derivatives

F	Eigen value	%Total Variance	Cumulative Eigen value	Cumulative %
F36	1.678	33.557	1.678	33.557
F37	1.047	20.930	2.724	54.487

Table 5.75: Item19*[#]

Factor Loadings			Communality			
Preferred Mode	F38[@]	F39	F40	From F38	From F39	From F40	Multiple R^2
19 CF	**0.362**	**0.788**	0.034	0.131	0.752	0.754	0.162
19 AO	**-0.868**	-0.102	-0.264	0.753	0.764	0.833	0.533
19 CI	**-0.895**	0.091	0.176	0.801	0.809	0.841	0.517
19 AV	**0.377**	**-0.778**	-0.028	0.142	0.748	0.749	0.166
19 CP	0.028	0.034	**0.987**	0.001	0.002	0.977	0.163
Expl.Var	1.829	1.247	1.077	*Principal Components extraction			
Prp.Totl	0.366	0.249	0.215	Rotation: Varimax			

\# **Bold** marked are >0.30 cut-off point
@ F38, F39 and F40 are Factor Derivatives

F	Eigen value	%Total Variance	Cumulative Eigen value	Cumulative %
F38	1.843	36.853	1.843	36.853
F39	1.309	26.178	3.152	63.031
F40	1.002	20.031	4.153	83.061

Table 5.76: Item20*[#]

Factor Loadings		Communality		
Preferred Mode	F41[@]	F42	From F41	From F42	Multiple R^2
20 CF	**-0.838**	-0.112	**0.702**	0.715	0.250
20 AO	**-0.697**	0.147	**0.486**	0.508	0.122
20 CI	**0.443**	**0.313**	0.196	0.294	0.121
20 AV	-0.224	**0.834**	0.050	0.746	0.108
20 CP	0.295	**0.685**	0.087	0.557	0.140
Expl.Var	1.522	1.298	*Prin. Components extraction		
Prp.Totl	0.304	0.260	Rotation: Varimax		

\# **Bold** marked are >0.30 cut-off point
@ F41 and F42 are Factor Derivatives

F	Eigen value	%Total Variance	Cumulative Eigen value	Cumulative %
F41	1.594	31.886	1.594	31.886
F42	1.226	24.512	2.820	56.399

Table 5.77: Item21*[#]

Factor Loadings		Communality		
Preferred Mode	F43[@]	F44	From F43	From F44	Multiple R^2
21 CF	0.053	**0.769**	0.003	0.594	0.040
21 AO	**0.925**	-0.074	0.856	0.861	0.646
21 CI	**0.663**	0.023	0.440	0.441	0.239
21 AV	**0.860**	0.014	0.739	0.740	0.580
21 CP	0.067	**-0.760**	0.004	0.582	0.037
Expl.Var	2.043	1.176	*Prin. Components extraction		
Prp.Totl	0.409	0.235	Rotation: Varimax		

\# **Bold** marked are >0.30 cut-off point
@ F43 and F44 are Factor Derivatives

F	Eigen value	%Total Variance	Cumulative Eigen value	Cumulative %
F43	2.046	40.911	2.046	40.911
F44	1.172	23.450	3.218	64.361

Table 5.78: Item22*[#]

Preferred Mode	Factor Loadings			Communality			
	F45[@]	F46	F47	From F45	From F46	From F47	Multiple R^2
22 CF	**-0.944**	0.025	0.116	0.891	0.892	0.905	0.644
22 AO	0.067	**0.851**	-0.085	0.004	0.729	0.736	0.225
22 CI	0.029	**-0.859**	-0.081	0.001	0.739	0.746	0.240
22 AV	**-0.942**	-0.067	-0.101	0.888	0.892	0.902	0.641
22 CP	-0.008	-0.005	**0.994**	0.000	0.000	0.987	0.068
Expl.Var	1.784	1.468	1.025	*Principal Components extraction			
Prp.Totl	0.357	0.294	0.205	Rotation: Varimax			

Bold marked are >0.30 cut-off point
@ F45, F46 and F47 are Factor Derivatives

F	Eigen value	%Total Variance	Cumulative Eigen value	Cumulative %
F45	1.801	36.014	1.801	36.014
F46	1.453	29.064	3.254	65.078
F47	1.023	20.467	4.277	85.546

Table 5.79: Item23*[#]

Preferred Mode	Factor Loadings			Communality			
	F48[@]	F49	F50	From F48	From F49	From F50	Multiple R^2
23 CF	0.170	**0.493**	0.000	0.029	0.272	0.272	0.022
23 AO	**0.882**	0.262	0.097	0.777	0.846	0.855	0.142
23 CI	**-0.648**	**0.564**	0.268	0.419	0.738	0.809	0.260
23 AV	0.007	-0.041	**0.984**	0.000	0.002	0.970	0.048
23 CP	0.056	**-0.836**	0.065	0.003	0.702	0.706	0.192
Expl.Var	1.229	1.330	1.054	*Principal Components extraction			
Prp.Totl	0.246	0.266	0.211	Rotation: Varimax			

Bold marked are >0.30 cut-off point
@ F48, F49 and F50 are Factor Derivatives

F	Eigen value	%Total Variance	Cumulative Eigen value	Cumulative %
F48	1.422	28.450	1.422	28.450
F49	1.172	23.447	2.595	51.897
F50	1.017	20.349	3.612	72.246

Table 5.80: Item24*[#]

Preferred Mode	Factor Loadings		Communality		
	F51[@]	F52	From F51	From F52	Multiple R^2
24 CF	**-0.743**	-0.013	0.551	0.552	0.185
24 AO	0.001	**0.900**	0.000	0.810	0.361
24 CI	**0.796**	0.114	0.633	0.646	0.260
24 AV	0.142	**0.882**	0.020	0.799	0.383
24 CP	**0.728**	0.057	0.530	0.534	0.182
Expl.Var	1.735	1.605	*Prin. Components extraction		
Prp.Totl	0.347	0.321	Rotation: Varimax		

Bold marked are >0.30 cut-off point
@ F51 and F52 are Factor Derivatives

F	Eigen value	%Total Variance	Cumulative Eigen value	Cumulative %
F51	1.946	38.928	1.946	38.928
F52	1.393	27.859	3.339	66.788

Table 5.81: Item25*#

Preferred Mode	Factor Loadings			Communality			
	F53[@]	F54	F55	From F53	From F54	From F55	Multiple R^2
25 CF	**-0.721**	-0.184	**-0.359**	0.520	0.554	0.683	0.200
25 AO	0.132	**0.792**	**-0.374**	0.017	0.645	0.785	0.222
25 CI	0.092	-0.018	**0.886**	0.008	0.009	0.794	0.083
25 AV	0.126	**-0.860**	-0.276	0.016	0.755	0.832	0.285
25 CP	**-0.886**	0.147	0.112	0.786	0.807	0.820	0.221
Expl.Var	1.348	1.423	1.142	*Principal Components extraction			
Prp.Totl	0.270	0.285	0.228	Rotation: Varimax			

F	Eigen value	%Total Variance	Cumulative Eigen value	Cumulative %
F53	1.433	28.659	1.433	28.659
F54	1.423	28.462	2.856	57.121
F55	1.057	21.144	3.913	78.265

 # Bold marked are >0.30 cut-off point

@ F53, F4 and F55 are Factor Derivatives

Table 5.82: Rank analysis of preferred conflict modes   *n=115*

Item No.	Theoretical Dominant mode	Calculated Mean Rank*				
		CF	AO	CI	AV	CP
1	Accommodating/Obliging	5	2	1	4	3
2	Competing/Forcing	2	4	1	5	3
3	Collaboration/Integrating	4	1	2	5	3
4	Competing/Forcing	1	2	3	4	4
5	Compromise/ Problem-solving	3	4	5	1	2
6	Competing/Forcing	1	4	2	5	3
7	Avoiding	4	2	3	5	1
8	Collaboration/Integrating	5	2	1	4	3
9	Avoiding	5	2	4	1	3
10	Compromise/ Problem-solving	2	4	5	3	1
11	Collaboration/Integrating	5	1	2	4	3
12	Accommodating/Obliging	3	2	5	4	1
13	Competing/Forcing	1	5	3	4	2
14	Avoiding	5	1	4	3	2
15	Avoiding	5	2	4	1	3
16	Accommodating/Obliging	3	1	5	4	2
17	Compromise/ Problem-solving	1	3	4	2	5
18	Avoiding	5	1	4	3	2
19	Accommodating/Obliging	2	4	5	1	3
20	Collaboration/Integrating	4	5	2	3	1
21	Compromise/ Problem-solving	1	4	5	3	2
22	Avoiding	3	1	2	4	5
23	Collaboration/Integrating	3	2	1	4	5
24	Compromise/ Problem-solving	5	2	3	1	4
25	Accommodating/Obliging	4	3	1	5	2

CF -Competing/Forcing   AO- Accommodation/Obliging   CI- Collaboration/Integrating   AV- Avoiding   CP- Compromise/Problem-solving

Table 5.83: Factorial preferences of conflict modes *

Item No.	Theoretical Dominant mode	Factorial preferences 1					Factorial preferences 2					Factorial preferences 3				
		CF	AO	CI	AV	CP	CF	AO	CI	AV	CP	CF	AO	CI	AV	CP
1	Accommodating/Obliging	++		—						—	—	+	++			
2	Competing/Forcing	+	++		++		+		–		—					
3	Collaboration/Integrating		+	–		—	++	+		++						
4	Competing/Forcing	++		+		++		++	–	–						
5	Compromise/ Problem-solving		++	++		++	—		–	+	–					
6	Competing/Forcing		+	++	—	++	—	++								
7	Avoiding	++			++			+	++		—					
8	Collaboration/Integrating	—	–		—			–	+	++						
9	Avoiding	++		++				+		—	++					
10	Compromise/ Problem-solving		+	++	++		++	+			++					
11	Collaboration/Integrating	++			++	–		++	—							
12	Accommodating/Obliging	++	—			++			—	—						
13	Competing/Forcing		++	—			–			–	+					
14	Avoiding	++	+	++	+			+			++					
15	Avoiding	++	+	++		++		+		++						
16	Accommodating/Obliging		++	+		++	–		++	++						
17	Compromise/ Problem-solving	+		+	++	++	+	—	++							
18	Avoiding		+	—	++		—				++					
19	Accommodating/Obliging	+	—	—	+		++			—						++
20	Collaboration/Integrating	—	—	+					+	++	++					
21	Compromise/ Problem-solving		++	+	++		++				—					
22	Avoiding	—			—			++	—							++
23	Collaboration/Integrating		++	—			+		+		—				++	
24	Compromise/ Problem-solving	—		++		++	++			++						
25	Accommodating/Obliging	—				—		++		—		–	–	++		

*n=115

+ Positive degree of factorial influence   ++ High positive degree of factorial influence   – Negative degree of factorial influence

— High negative degree of factorial influence

CF –Competing/Forcing   AO- Accommodation/Obliging   CI- Collaboration/Integrating   AV- Avoiding   CP- Compromise/Problem-solving

5.1.10 Global Analysis

Cross tabulation of the global variables of the survey research enables the process verification and an exploration along these lines may indicate potential relationship existing among them. Categorical appropriation of the scales and the respective variables acted as global variables, besides the conflict styles' battery. In that respect the job demographics, conflict response subscales, potential sources of conflicts at their respective levels, selected procedural way of handling conflicts as well as conflict styles, including its transcending dimensions deemed to be fit for an exploratory global analysis. The dimensional variants presented by the CMI and the data obtained through it reflectively used for these measures.

Exhibit 5.3

-    *Conflict handling styles*................Conflict modes (Part G) and Style quotients (Part F).
-    *Job Demographics*......................Part Basic (Intro) excluding personal references.
-    *Conflict Responses*.....................Five interrelated Subscales (Part D).
-    *Potential Sources of Conflict*..........22 Factorial variables of 4 broad categories (Part C).
-    *Procedural Way of- Handling Conflicts*............. Selected 5 Factorial variables (Part H).

Multiple regression analysis comprising these identified global variables reflects the significant and other relationship existing among them. The general purpose of *multiple regressions* (the term was first used by Pearson, 1908) seems to analyse the relationship between several independent or predictor variables and a dependent or criterion variable. The computational problem that needs to be solved in *multiple regression* analysis is to fit a straight line (or plane in an n-dimensional space, where n is the number of independent variables) to a number of points. In the simplest case - one dependent and one independent variable - one can visualise this in a scatter plot (scatter plots are two-dimensional plots of the scores on a pair of variables). In the present analysis, multiple linear regression procedures along with its various dimensions are used as an exploratory method for assessing the relationship existing among the global variables. The logical adherence for fixing dependency and independency among the variables, naturally indicate the interactional dependability of the conflict styles with other global variables.

Along with the normal multiple regression coefficients, beta coefficients, partial correlation, redundancy check as well the Durbin Watson d was explored. The *beta coefficients* are the regression coefficients obtained when the operation first standardised all of the variables to a mean of 0 and a standard deviation of 1. Thus, the advantage of *beta coefficients* (as compared to B Coefficients that are not standardised) is that the magnitude of these *beta coefficients* allows the analysis to compare the relative contribution of each independent variable in the prediction of the dependent variable. Intercepts which formed as part of the regression equations are rendered through its significance (p<0.010) and the proportional global variables with significant and other relations are all constituents of the multiple regression equations and analysis. Multiple linear regression analyses are shown through the *tables 5.84 – 5.88* along with the significant statistical tests. Conflict styles with its five categorical approaches acts as dependent variables and the other global variables function themselves as independent ones.

Methodical Result- In case of multiple regression analysis of dependent variable-Controller, with the other global variables; *conflict approach/avoidance* subscale had shown a significant negative regression coefficient and the F, *d* as well as redundancy tests also confirm the same. Other positive and negative relationship between global variables (dependent being controller) and multiple correlation are all indicating the importance of the intercepts while analysing the regression equations. For the dependent variable-Compromiser, only *emotional expression* subscale had shown a significant negative B. Whereas, for the dependent variable-Collaborator; two subscale from the conflict responses global– *conflict approach/avoidance* and *confrontation* had indicated significant B and the tests also confirm their relative importance to the regression equations. Interestingly, dependent variable produced little *B*-significances with the other global variables. Dependent variable-Avoider produced three significant B with the job demographics. Managerial experience and exposure to other organisational positions negatively influence this variable. Positive multiple correlation and regression obtained to *work experience* indicate that when managers are experienced, the tendencies to adopt these styles are indicative.

Intercepts obtained through regression analysis for the representative global variables seems to be important while assessing the regression equations. The goodness of fit tests and the Durbin Watson statistic also promotes the global variables' approach towards the normality. The exploratory analysis along these lines may only be taken as representative by the study and various combinations of the variables mentioned in the subscales of the CMI can be indicative in this regard. Further the residual analysis and graphical plots were all strengthening the essence of relationships existing among the global variables pointed out by regression analysis.

Table 5.84: Global Analysis – Multiple Regression Analysis among Scale-Controller and Competing/Forcing and identified global variables/subscales

Global Variable/ Subscale		Regression Summary for Dependent Variable: Controller						Variables currently in the Equation				
		Beta	Std.Error. of Beta	B	Std.Error. of B	t	p-level	Beta in	Partial Cor.	Semi Part Cor.	Tolerance	R-square
Job Demographic	Intercept			168.459	6.905	24.396	0.001					
	Age	-0.031	0.170	-0.041	0.227	-0.180	0.858	-0.031	-0.017	-0.017	0.313	0.687
	Years in Present Pos.	-0.085	0.106	-0.116	0.145	-0.801	0.425	-0.085	-0.077	-0.076	0.808	0.192
	Years Managerial Pos.	3.183	3.630	4.845	5.525	0.877	0.382	3.183	0.084	0.083	0.001	0.999
	Years Other Positions	2.855	3.325	4.745	5.526	0.859	0.392	2.855	0.082	0.082	0.001	0.999
	Work Experience	-3.114	3.683	-4.660	5.511	-0.846	0.400	-3.114	-0.081	-0.080	0.001	0.999
Conflict Response Subscales	Intercept			171.976	21.262	8.088	0.001					
	Conflict app/ avoidance	**-0.245**	**0.094**	**-7.942**	**3.048**	**-2.605**	**0.010**	**-0.245**	**-0.242**	**-0.238**	**0.943**	**0.057**
	Confrontation	-0.103	0.094	-2.054	1.875	-1.096	0.276	-0.103	-0.104	-0.100	0.939	0.061
	Public/priv behaviour	0.097	0.092	3.460	3.281	1.054	0.294	0.097	0.100	0.096	0.993	0.007
	Emotional expression	0.133	0.092	5.468	3.759	1.455	0.149	0.133	0.138	0.133	0.995	0.005
	Self-disclosure	-0.006	0.092	-0.216	3.241	-0.067	0.947	-0.006	-0.006	-0.006	0.987	0.013
Potential Sources and Levels	Intercept			174.986	8.679	20.161	0.001					
	Procedural level	-0.147	0.097	-1.500	0.991	-1.513	0.133	-0.147	-0.143	-0.142	0.938	0.062
	Issue level	-0.098	0.095	-0.893	0.868	-1.028	0.306	-0.098	-0.098	-0.096	0.966	0.034
	Interactional level	0.073	0.098	1.036	1.387	0.747	0.456	0.073	0.071	0.070	0.921	0.079
	Organisational level	0.012	0.098	0.154	1.243	0.124	0.902	0.012	0.012	0.012	0.915	0.085
Procedural Way of Handling Conflicts	Intercept			177.413	13.721	12.930	0.001					
	Negotation	-0.128	0.098	-2.652	2.023	-1.311	0.193	-0.128	-0.125	-0.124	0.927	0.073
	Counselling	-0.026	0.098	-0.652	2.452	-0.266	0.791	-0.026	-0.025	-0.025	0.929	0.071
	Mediation	0.095	0.096	1.510	1.518	0.995	0.322	0.095	0.095	0.094	0.973	0.027
	Legal Intervention	0.044	0.095	0.526	1.142	0.461	0.646	0.044	0.044	0.043	0.978	0.022
	Reconciliation	-0.054	0.096	-0.975	1.719	-0.567	0.572	-0.054	-0.054	-0.053	0.966	0.034

Global Variable/ Subscale	Dependent Variable: Controller Summary Statistics						Durbin Watson d	Serial Corr.
	Multiple R	Multiple R²	Adjusted R²	F	p-level	Std.Error. of Estimate		
Job Demographic	0.120	0.014	-0.031	0.319	0.901	9.106	1.812	0.082
Conflict Response Subscales	0.299	0.089	0.048	2.141	0.066	8.753	1.754	0.111
Potential Sources and Levels	0.178	0.032	-0.004	0.899	0.467	8.985	1.821	0.078
Procedural Way of Handling Conflicts	0.175	0.031	-0.014	0.691	0.632	9.030	1.846	0.065

● Intercept highly Significant, p< 0.010

● Bold coefficients are Significant at p<0.05

Table 5.85: Global Analysis – Multiple Regression Analysis among Scale-Compromiser and compromising/problem-solving and identified global variables/subscales

Global Variable/ Subscale		Regression Summary for Dependent Variable: Compromiser						Variables currently in the Equation				
		Beta	Std.Error. of Beta	B	Std.Error. of B	t	p-level	Beta in	Partial Cor.	Semi Part Cor.	Tolerance	R-square
Job Demographic	Intercept			182.524	6.239	29.256	0.001					
	Age	0.073	0.170	0.089	0.205	0.433	0.666	0.073	0.041	0.041	0.313	0.687
	Years in Present Pos.	-0.078	0.105	-0.097	0.131	-0.743	0.459	-0.078	-0.071	-0.070	0.808	0.192
	Years Managerial Pos.	2.388	3.620	3.293	4.992	0.660	0.511	2.388	0.063	0.063	0.001	0.999
	Years Other Positions	2.180	3.316	3.283	4.993	0.657	0.512	2.180	0.063	0.062	0.001	0.999
	Work Experience	-2.563	3.673	-3.476	4.980	-0.698	0.487	-2.563	-0.067	-0.066	0.001	0.999
Conflict Response Subscales	Intercept			215.267	19.312	11.147	0.001					
	Conflict app/ avoidance	-0.063	0.094	-1.862	2.769	-0.672	0.503	-0.063	-0.064	-0.062	0.943	0.057
	Confrontation	0.033	0.095	0.598	1.703	0.351	0.726	0.033	0.034	0.032	0.939	0.061
	Public/priv. behaviour	0.073	0.092	2.373	2.980	0.796	0.428	0.073	0.076	0.073	0.993	0.007
	Emotional expression	**-0.246**	**0.092**	**-9.150**	**3.414**	**-2.680**	**0.009**	**-0.246**	**-0.249**	**-0.246**	**0.995**	**0.005**
	Self-disclosure	-0.121	0.092	-3.860	2.944	-1.311	0.193	-0.121	-0.125	-0.120	0.987	0.013
Potential Sources and Levels	Intercept			186.812	7.910	23.617	0.001					
	Procedural level	-0.119	0.097	-1.104	0.903	-1.222	0.224	-0.119	-0.116	-0.115	0.938	0.062
	Issue level	-0.081	0.096	-0.663	0.791	-0.839	0.404	-0.081	-0.080	-0.079	0.966	0.034
	Interactional level	0.040	0.098	0.516	1.264	0.408	0.684	0.040	0.039	0.039	0.921	0.079
	Organisational level	0.012	0.099	0.139	1.133	0.123	0.903	0.012	0.012	0.012	0.915	0.085
Procedural Way of Handling Conflicts	Intercept			171.783	12.360	13.898	0.001					
	Negotiation	-0.013	0.097	-0.247	1.823	-0.135	0.893	-0.013	-0.013	-0.013	0.927	0.073
	Counselling	0.132	0.097	2.987	2.209	1.352	0.179	0.132	0.128	0.127	0.929	0.071
	Mediation	0.105	0.095	1.518	1.368	1.110	0.270	0.105	0.106	0.104	0.973	0.027
	Legal Intervention	-0.040	0.095	-0.440	1.029	-0.427	0.670	-0.040	-0.041	-0.040	0.978	0.022
	Reconciliation	-0.111	0.095	-1.803	1.549	-1.164	0.247	-0.111	-0.111	-0.109	0.966	0.034

Global Variable/ Subscale	Dependent Variable: Compromiser Summary Statistics						Durbin-Watson d	Serial Corr.
	Multiple R	Multiple R²	Adjusted R²	F	p-level	Std.Error. of Estimate		
Job Demographic	0.141	0.020	-0.025	0.442	0.819	8.228	1.744	0.128
Conflict Response Subscales	0.291	0.085	0.043	2.023	0.081	7.950	1.664	0.168
Potential Sources and Levels	0.142	0.020	-0.015	0.567	0.687	8.189	1.691	0.153
Procedural Way of Handling Conflicts	0.205	0.042	-0.002	0.952	0.451	8.135	1.685	0.157

- Intercept highly Significant, p< 0.010
- Bold coefficients are Significant at p<0.05

203

Table 5.86: Global Analysis – Multiple Regression Analysis among Scale-Collaborator and Collaboration/integrating and identified global variables/subscales

Global Variable/ Subscale		Regression Summary for Dependent Variable: Collaborator						Variables currently in the Equation				
		Beta	Std.Error. of Beta	B	Std.Error. of B	t	p-level	Beta in	Partial Cor.	Semi Part Cor.	Tolerance	R-square
Job Demographic	Intercept			178.935	5.024	35.619	0.001					
	Age	-0.070	0.167	-0.070	0.165	-0.422	0.674	-0.070	-0.040	-0.039	0.313	0.687
	Years in Present Pos.	-0.203	0.104	-0.206	0.105	-1.956	0.053	-0.203	-0.184	-0.182	0.808	0.192
	Years Managerial Pos.	-4.264	3.554	-4.822	4.019	-1.200	0.233	-4.264	-0.114	-0.112	0.001	0.999
	Years Other Positions	-3.972	3.256	-4.905	4.021	-1.220	0.225	-3.972	-0.116	-0.114	0.001	0.999
	Work Experience	4.446	3.606	4.943	4.010	1.233	0.220	4.446	0.117	0.115	0.001	0.999
Conflict Response Subscales	Intercept			209.873	15.568	13.481	0.001					
	Conflict app./ avoidance	**-0.260**	**0.093**	**-6.268**	**2.232**	**-2.808**	**0.006**	**-0.260**	**-0.260**	**-0.253**	**0.943**	**0.057**
	Confrontation	**-0.196**	**0.093**	**-2.889**	**1.373**	**-2.105**	**0.038**	**-0.196**	**-0.198**	**-0.190**	**0.939**	**0.061**
	Public/priv. behaviour	0.082	0.090	2.184	2.403	0.909	0.365	0.082	0.087	0.082	0.993	0.007
	Emotional expression	-0.027	0.090	-0.832	2.752	-0.302	0.763	-0.027	-0.029	-0.027	0.995	0.005
	Self-disclosure	-0.153	0.091	-3.996	2.373	-1.684	0.095	-0.153	-0.159	-0.152	0.987	0.013
Potential Sources and Levels	Intercept			180.444	6.491	27.799	0.001					
	Procedural level	-0.111	0.098	-0.844	0.741	-1.138	0.258	-0.111	-0.108	-0.107	0.938	0.062
	Issue level	-0.084	0.096	-0.571	0.649	-0.879	0.381	-0.084	-0.084	-0.083	0.966	0.034
	Interactional level	0.023	0.098	0.246	1.037	0.237	0.813	0.023	0.023	0.022	0.921	0.079
	Organisational level	0.021	0.099	0.202	0.929	0.217	0.828	0.021	0.021	0.021	0.915	0.085
Procedural Way of Handling Conflicts	Intercept			182.334	10.147	17.969	0.001					
	Negotiation	0.056	0.097	0.858	1.496	0.573	0.568	0.056	0.055	0.054	0.927	0.073
	Counselling	-0.067	0.097	-1.249	1.814	-0.689	0.493	-0.067	-0.066	-0.065	0.929	0.071
	Mediation	0.112	0.095	1.316	1.123	1.172	0.244	0.112	0.112	0.110	0.973	0.027
	Legal Intervention	-0.017	0.095	-0.151	0.845	-0.179	0.858	-0.017	-0.017	-0.017	0.978	0.022
	Reconciliation	-0.167	0.095	-2.223	1.271	-1.748	0.083	-0.167	-0.165	-0.164	0.966	0.034

Global Variable/ Subscale	Dependent Variable: Collaborator Summary Statistics						Durbin-Watson d	Serial Corr.
	Multiple R	Multiple R²	Adjusted R²	F	p-level	Std.Error. of Estimate		
Job Demographic	0.234	0.055	0.012	1.267	0.283	6.625	1.923	0.038
Conflict Response Subscales	0.340	0.116	0.075	2.850	0.019	6.409	1.871	0.064
Potential Sources and Levels	0.137	0.019	-0.017	0.527	0.716	6.720	1.968	0.016
Procedural Way of Handling Conflicts	0.199	0.040	-0.004	0.900	0.484	6.678	2.025	-0.012

- Intercept highly Significant, p< 0.010
- Bold coefficients are Significant at p<0.05

Table 5.87: Global Analysis – Multiple Regression Analysis among Scale-Accommodator and Accommodating/Obliging and identified global variables/subscales

Global Variable/ Subscale		Regression Summary for Dependent Variable: Accommodator						Variables currently in the Equation				
		Beta	Std.Error. of Beta	B	Std.Error. of B	t	p-level	Beta in	Partial Cor.	Semi Part Cor.	Tolerance	R-square
Job Demographic	Intercept			186.505	6.074	30.707	0.001					
	Age	-0.015	0.170	-0.018	0.200	-0.089	0.929	-0.015	-0.009	-0.008	0.313	0.687
	Years in Present Pos.	-0.100	0.106	-0.121	0.127	-0.951	0.344	-0.100	-0.091	-0.090	0.808	0.192
	Years Managerial Pos.	-2.547	3.620	-3.418	4.860	-0.703	0.483	-2.547	-0.067	-0.067	0.001	0.999
	Years Other Positions	-2.305	3.316	-3.378	4.861	-0.695	0.489	-2.305	-0.066	-0.066	0.001	0.999
	Work Experience	2.557	3.673	3.375	4.848	0.696	0.488	2.557	0.067	0.066	0.001	0.999
Conflict Response Subscales	Intercept			171.427	19.516	8.784	0.001					
	Conflict app./ avoidance	-0.009	0.098	-0.256	2.798	-0.091	0.927	-0.009	-0.009	-0.009	0.943	0.057
	Confrontation	0.024	0.098	0.414	1.721	0.240	0.810	0.024	0.023	0.023	0.939	0.061
	Public/priv. behaviour	0.040	0.095	1.263	3.012	0.419	0.676	0.040	0.040	0.040	0.993	0.007
	Emotional expression	0.104	0.095	3.776	3.450	1.094	0.276	0.104	0.104	0.104	0.995	0.005
	Self-disclosure	-0.029	0.096	-0.895	2.975	-0.301	0.764	-0.029	-0.029	-0.029	0.987	0.013
Potential Sources and Levels	Intercept			182.752	7.739	23.615	0.001					
	Procedural level	0.005	0.098	0.043	0.884	0.049	0.961	0.005	0.005	0.005	0.938	0.062
	Issue level	0.100	0.097	0.799	0.774	1.033	0.304	0.100	0.098	0.098	0.966	0.034
	Interactional level	-0.031	0.099	-0.390	1.236	-0.315	0.753	-0.031	-0.030	-0.030	0.921	0.079
	Organisational level	-0.022	0.099	-0.245	1.108	-0.221	0.826	-0.022	-0.021	-0.021	0.915	0.085
Procedural Way of Handling Conflicts	Intercept			177.318	12.042	14.725	0.001					
	Negotiation	-0.143	0.097	-2.606	1.776	-1.468	0.145	-0.143	-0.139	-0.138	0.927	0.073
	Counselling	0.024	0.097	0.530	2.152	0.246	0.806	0.024	0.024	0.023	0.929	0.071
	Mediation	0.115	0.095	1.605	1.333	1.205	0.231	0.115	0.115	0.113	0.973	0.027
	Legal Intervention	0.102	0.095	1.079	1.002	1.077	0.284	0.102	0.103	0.101	0.978	0.022
	Reconciliation	0.053	0.095	0.845	1.509	0.560	0.577	0.053	0.054	0.053	0.966	0.034

Global Variable/ Subscale	Dependent Variable: Accommodator Summary Statistics						Durbin-Watson d	Serial Corr.
	Multiple R	Multiple R²	Adjusted R²	F	p-level	Std.Error. of Estimate		
Job Demographic	0.140	0.020	-0.025	0.435	0.824	8.010	1.418	0.280
Conflict Response Subscales	0.117	0.014	-0.032	0.301	0.911	8.034	1.377	0.303
Potential Sources and Levels	0.101	0.010	-0.026	0.281	0.889	8.011	1.429	0.277
Procedural Way of Handling Conflicts	0.200	0.040	-0.004	0.911	0.477	7.925	1.327	0.327

- Intercept highly Significant, p< 0.010

- **Bold coefficients are Significant at p<0.05**

Table 5.88: Global Analysis – Multiple Regression Analysis among Scale–Avoider as well as Avoiding and identified global variables/subscales

Global Variable/ Subscale		Regression Summary for Dependent Variable: Avoider						Variables currently in the Equation				
		Beta	Std.Error. of Beta	B	Std.Error. of B	t	p-level	Beta in	Partial Cor.	Semi Part Cor.	Tolerance	R-square
Job Demographic	Intercept			164.984	5.237	31.501	0.001					
	Age	-0.145	0.165	-0.151	0.172	-0.875	0.384	-0.145	-0.083	-0.081	0.313	0.687
	Years in Present Pos.	0.144	0.103	0.154	0.110	1.397	0.165	0.144	0.133	0.129	0.808	0.192
	Years Managerial Pos.	**-7.413**	**3.530**	**-8.800**	**4.190**	**-2.100**	**0.038**	**-7.413**	**-0.197**	**-0.194**	**0.001**	**0.999**
	Years Other Positions	**-6.890**	**3.234**	**-8.930**	**4.192**	**-2.131**	**0.035**	**-6.890**	**-0.200**	**-0.197**	**0.001**	**0.999**
	Work Experience	**7.612**	**3.582**	**8.885**	**4.180**	**2.125**	**0.036**	**7.612**	**0.199**	**0.197**	**0.001**	**0.999**
Conflict Response Subscales	Intercept			148.024	17.205	8.604	0.001					
	Conflict app./ avoidance	0.090	0.098	2.268	2.467	0.920	0.360	0.090	0.088	0.087	0.943	0.057
	Confrontation	0.042	0.098	0.655	1.517	0.432	0.667	0.042	0.041	0.041	0.939	0.061
	Public/priv. behaviour	-0.071	0.095	-1.969	2.655	-0.742	0.460	-0.071	-0.071	-0.070	0.993	0.007
	Emotional expression	0.068	0.095	2.163	3.042	0.711	0.478	0.068	0.068	0.067	0.995	0.005
	Self-disclosure	0.047	0.095	1.279	2.622	0.488	0.627	0.047	0.047	0.046	0.987	0.013
Potential Sources and Levels	Intercept			156.640	6.766	23.152	0.001					
	Procedural level	-0.052	0.097	-0.412	0.773	-0.533	0.595	-0.052	-0.051	-0.050	0.938	0.062
	Issue level	0.168	0.095	1.191	0.677	1.760	0.081	0.168	0.165	0.165	0.966	0.034
	Interactional level	0.039	0.098	0.429	1.081	0.397	0.692	0.039	0.038	0.037	0.921	0.079
	Organisational level	-0.038	0.098	-0.377	0.969	-0.389	0.698	-0.038	-0.037	-0.037	0.915	0.085
Procedural Way of Handling Conflicts	Intercept			152.929	10.730	14.253	0.001					
	Negotiation	-0.018	0.098	-0.294	1.582	-0.186	0.853	-0.018	-0.018	-0.018	0.927	0.073
	Counselling	-0.022	0.098	-0.434	1.918	-0.226	0.822	-0.022	-0.022	-0.021	0.929	0.071
	Mediation	0.099	0.096	1.222	1.187	1.029	0.306	0.099	0.098	0.097	0.973	0.027
	Legal Intervention	0.001	0.096	0.007	0.893	0.008	0.993	0.001	0.001	0.001	0.978	0.022
	Reconciliation	0.119	0.096	1.661	1.344	1.235	0.219	0.119	0.118	0.117	0.966	0.034

Global Variable/ Subscale	Dependent Variable: Avoider Summary Statistics						Durbin-Watson d	Serial Corr.
	Multiple R	Multiple R^2	Adjusted R^2	F	p-level	Std.Error. of Estimate		
Job Demographic	0.260	0.068	0.025	1.586	0.170	6.907	1.851	0.064
Conflict Response Subscales	0.141	0.020	-0.025	0.442	0.818	7.082	1.978	0.001
Potential Sources and Levels	0.181	0.033	-0.003	0.926	0.452	7.004	2.012	-0.015
Procedural Way of Handling Conflicts	0.160	0.026	-0.019	0.572	0.722	7.062	1.955	0.011

◁ **Intercept highly Significant, p< 0.010**

◁ **Bold coefficients are Significant at p<0.05**

5.1.11 Canonical Analysis-Global variables

Canonical correlation is an additional procedure for assessing the relationship between variables. Specifically, this module allows investigating the relationship between two sets of global variables of this study. The tests of significance of the canonical correlations are based on the assumption that the distributions of the variables in the population (from which the sample was drawn) are multivariate normal. However, with a sufficiently large sample size in this study, the results from canonical correlation analysis are usually quite robust. Canonical R reported in *table 5.89* pertains to the first and most significant canonical root. Thus, this value can be interpreted as the simple correlation between the weighted sum scores in each set, with the weights pertaining to the first (and most significant) canonical root. The values in the *variance extracted* row indicate the average amount of variance extracted from the variables in the respective set by all canonical roots. Thus, all the roots extract 100% of the variance from the left set, and the respective variance from right set. Chi square and p values are calculated along these sets. Interestingly, the absence of significant canonical correlations was noted and contributes to those global variables which seem to approach significance.

Five global variables identified through the appropriate mechanism as indicated in exhibit 5.3 were put into the canonical analysis. The combinations among them are explored and the canonical R, chi square as well as redundancy variations were calculated using canonical analysis routines. The variance extracted is computed by summing up the squared canonical factor loadings across variables in a set for a particular canonical root, and then dividing that sum by the number of variables in the set. The resulting proportion can be interpreted as the average proportion of variance accounted for in the respective variables by the respective root. The total proportion of variance extracted that is reported at the top of the results dialog can be interpreted as the average proportion of variance accounted for by all canonical roots.

Methodical result- Among the ten possible bivariate combinations concerning the global variables none qualified for the significant level. Interestingly, three bivariate canonical R are approaching the significance level as indicated in *table 5.89*. The individual factorial scores of subscales seem to be more redeemable when compared with the canonical root analysis. The exploratory significance well establish and or strengthens the above fact. Eigenvalues, canonical roots, factor procedures, canonical weights as well as redundancy analyses positively follows these lines.

Table 5.89: Canonical analysis–Global variables

Global Variable/ Subscale		Job Demographic		Conflict Response Subscales		Potential Sources and Levels		Procedural Way of Handling Conflicts		Conflict Styles	
		Left Set	Right Set	Left Set	Right Set	Left Set	Right Set	Left Set	Right Set	Left Set	Right Set
Job Demographic	No. of variables			8	5	8	4	8	5	8	5
	Variance extracted (%)			59.99	100.00	56.59	100.00	64.28	100.00	61.68	100.00
	Total redundancy (%)			3.42	4.72	3.08	6.04	5.34	8.16	4.25	7.45
	Canonical R			**0.29717**		**0.31630**		**0.45536**		**0.36764**	
	Chi²			26.338		25.620		49.510		42.664	
	p			0.95249		0.78010		0.14426		0.35741	
Conflict Response Subscales	No. of variables	5	8			5	4	5	5	5	5
	Variance extracted (%)	100.00	59.99			80.93	100.00	100.00	100.00	100.00	100.00
	Total redundancy (%)	4.72	3.42			3.50	4.23	3.03	3.12	6.69	6.47
	Canonical R	**0.29717**				**0.37175**		**0.26621**		**0.44983**	
	Chi²	26.338				22.468		16.649		41.832	
	p	0.95249				0.31573		0.89406		0.01879	
Potential Sources and Levels	No. of variables	4	8	4	5			4	5	4	5
	Variance extracted (%)	100.00	56.59	100.00	80.93			100.00	78.02	100.00	87.25
	Total redundancy (%)	6.04	3.08	4.23	3.50			4.87	3.73	2.05	2.27
	Canonical R	**0.31630**		**0.37175**				**0.33400**		**0.24130**	
	Chi²	25.620		22.468				20.233		9.5806	
	p	0.78010		0.31573				0.44349		0.97514	
Procedural Way of Handling Conflicts	No. of variables	5	8	5	5	5	4			5	5
	Variance extracted (%)	100.00	64.28	100.00	100.00	78.02	100.00			100.00	100.00
	Total redundancy (%)	8.16	5.34	3.12	3.03	3.73	4.87			3.31	3.56
	Canonical R	**0.45536**		**0.26621**		**0.33400**				**0.25716**	
	Chi²	49.510		16.649		20.233				18.952	
	p	0.14426		0.89406		0.44349				0.79934	
Conflict Styles	No. of variables	5	8	5	5	5	4	5	5		
	Variance extracted (%)	100.00	61.68	100.00	100.00	87.25	100.00	100.00	100.00		
	Total redundancy (%)	7.45	4.25	6.47	6.69	2.27	2.05	3.56	3.31		
	Canonical R	**0.36764**		**0.44983**		**0.24130**		**0.25716**			
	Chi²	42.664		41.832		9.5806		18.952			
	p	0.35741		0.01879		0.97514		0.79934			

5.1.12 Reliability Testing

Reliability refers to the extent to which a quantified scale produces consistent results, if the measurements are repeated a number of times. Reliability analysis is determined by obtaining the proportion of systematic variation from CMI battery, which can be done by determining the association between the scores obtained from different administrations of the scale. Thus, if the association in reliability analysis is high, the scale yields consistent results and is therefore reliable. Internal consistency is usually measured with Cronbach's alpha, a statistic calculated from the pair wise correlations between items. Internal consistency ranges between zero and one. A commonly-accepted rule of thumb is that an alpha (α)-coefficient of 0.6-0.7 indicates acceptable reliability, and 0.8 or higher indicates good reliability. High reliabilities (0.95 or higher) are not necessarily desirable, as this indicates that the items may be entirely redundant. The goal in designing a reliable instrument is for scores on similar items to be related (internally consistent), but for each to contribute some unique information as well.

Validity is the strength of research conclusions, inferences or propositions. More formally, Cook and Campbell (1979) define it as the best available approximation to the truth or falsity of a given inference, proposition or conclusion. Conclusion validity verifies the relationship among the dimensions included and the hypothetical ramifications of this research study are expressions of this statement.

Internal validity attempts to measure the causal relationships and the same got enriched by the incorporation of factor testing and other causal testing procedures. Construct validity is put into test by emancipating cross sectional research design and inducting accepted conflict management facets. Construct validity is the degree to which inferences out of this be generalised to the concepts underlying the conflict management and within the confined boundaries specified in the research design.

The structural factoring of all the sets of items and indices, it was considered necessary to perform scale analysis on the factorially defined sub scales with its various dimensions. The reliability analyses were, therefore systematically performed and reported in *table 5.90*. These scale analyses were defined and retained by the dimensional structures and had explicitly shown greater unidimensionality within the sub scales.

Departmental stratification was also attempted to reassess the reliability dimensions to its various stratums. In case of departmental classifications, the asymmetrical size may act upon as a potential limitation. It was further assumed that the expressive stratification is of educative in character and not to be equated to the standardised domains of closed and diverging stratums.

In case of potential sources of conflict, the subscales-procedural and interactional levels show comparatively acceptable alpha coefficients, 0.727 and 0.713 respectively. Issue and Organisational levels are not far behind and approaching a higher reliability. Further this global module is having 0.498 as coefficient of alpha as a scale. Conflict approaches in the initial phase is considered to be an important scale and its reliability of 0.596 reveals interesting denominations. The subscale- initial approaches scores to be of highly reliable-0.813 and all the other dimensions too are of greater importance and certainly in acceptable range.

The coefficient for the influential party seems to be 0.732, 0.689, 0.691, 0.711, 0.742 and 0.647 indicating the acceptable scale denominations. The other party in conflict scale scores an alpha of 0.612, which is of reassuring its subscales. The subscales-conflict nature, gender dimension, age factor, initial responses and the managerial power are all above the cut off of 0.60 and the conflict basics scale accrues the alpha coefficient to the tune of 0.631. This may be indicative that the subscale is of greater assimilating and representative though unidimensionality is yet to be accepted as was reaffirmed by the incorporation of factorial analyses.

Table 5.90: Reliability Analysis

S.No	Module	Dimension	No. of Items	Cronbach's Alpha coefficient (α)							
				HR N1=30	PRD N2=28	MKG N3=15	FIN N4=31	SYS N5=4	FSP N6=7	Overall α N=115	STD. ALPHA
1	Potential source of Conflict	Issue Level	5	0.632	0.751	0.642	0.732	0.647	0.687	**0.695**	**0.832**
		Organisational Level	6	0.663	0.787	0.673	0.762	0.545	0.672	**0.682**	**0.843**
		Procedural Level	3	0.535	0.865	0.674	0.723	0.689	0.732	**0.727**	**0.896**
		Interactional Level	8	0.569	0.673	0.798	0.781	0.691	0.921	**0.713**	**0.835**
2	Conflict and Initial approach	Initial approaches	8	0.879	0.812	0.782	0.721	0.691	0.842	**0.813**	**0.936**
		Satisfaction of past conflict	5	0.781	0.651	0.683	0.677	0.742	0.693	**0.691**	**0.732**
		Conflict and Feelings	10	0.644	0.478	0.563	0.659	0.647	0.563	**0.576**	**0.812**
		Immediate Emotion	11	0.596	0.649	0.634	0.751	0.762	0.764	**0.673**	**0.791**
		Conflict aftermath	14	0.732	0.643	0.638	0.653	0.683	0.753	**0.685**	**0.714**
3	Other Party and Style	Boss/Superiors	8	0.683	0.812	0.782	0.723	0.689	0.764	**0.732**	**0.862**
		Peers/Colleagues	8	0.563	0.651	0.683	0.865	0.674	0.723	**0.689**	**0.723**
		Subordinates	8	0.634	0.478	0.563	0.673	0.798	0.781	**0.691**	**0.812**
		Friend	8	0.674	0.723	0.689	0.812	0.782	0.721	**0.711**	**0.843**
		Woman/Man	8	0.798	0.683	0.812	0.782	0.683	0.677	**0.742**	**0.836**
		Elder/Younger	8	0.782	0.563	0.651	0.683	0.563	0.659	**0.647**	**0.714**
4	Conflict Basics	Nature	4	0.683	0.634	0.478	0.563	0.689	0.751	**0.762**	**0.915**
		Gender Dimension	3	0.683	0.812	0.782	0.689	0.691	0.653	**0.683**	**0.762**
		Age Dimension	3	0.563	0.651	0.683	0.691	0.711	0.691	**0.674**	**0.763**
		Initial Responses	8	0.634	0.478	0.563	0.691	0.742	0.742	**0.693**	**0.813**
		Managerial Hierarchy	3	0.674	0.723	0.689	0.742	0.647	0.647	**0.735**	**0.842**
5	Predominant Conflict Responses	Approach/Avoidance	15	0.798	0.781	0.691	0.751	0.762	0.762	**0.728**	**0.914**
		Confrontation	15	0.782	0.721	0.691	0.653	0.683	0.683	**0.637**	**0.764**
		Public/Private Behaviour	15	0.683	0.683	0.742	0.683	0.743	0.735	**0.726**	**0.882**
		Emotional Expression	15	0.653	0.773	0.813	0.663	0.761	0.731	**0.721**	**0.869**
		Self-disclosure	15	0.762	0.689	0.736	0.689	0.738	0.812	**0.748**	**0.885**

S.No	Module	Dimension	No. of Items	Cronbach's Alpha coefficient (α)							
				HR N1=30	PRD N2=28	MKG N3=15	FIN N4=31	SYS N5=4	FSP N6=7	Overall α N=115	STD. ALPHA
6	Procedural Conflict Handling	Negotiation	9	0.683	0.798	0.781	0.691	0.742	0.637	**0.734**	**0.843**
		Counselling	4	0.746	0.782	0.865	0.674	0.723	0.436	**0.712**	**0.836**
		Mediation	4	0.816	0.683	0.673	0.798	0.781	0.542	**0.602**	**0.762**
		Legal Intervention/Reconciliation	5	0.865	0.563	0.812	0.782	0.721	0.413	**0.732**	**0.846**
		Social Exchanges /Predispositions	13	0.673	0.634	0.651	0.683	0.677	0.531	**0.614**	**0.716**
		Individual/ Combined approaches	12	0.812	0.638	0.478	0.563	0.659	0.689	**0.638**	**0.723**
7	Style Quotient	Controller	12	0.651	0.683	0.673	0.798	0.781	0.691	**0.673**	**0.768**
		Compromiser	12	0.478	0.563	0.798	0.781	0.691	0.742	**0.712**	**0.842**
		Collaborator	12	0.649	0.634	0.782	0.865	0.674	0.723	**0.735**	**0.851**
		Accommodator	12	0.643	0.638	0.683	0.673	0.798	0.781	**0.731**	**0.847**
		Avoider	12	0.798	0.781	0.691	0.742	0.782	0.721	**0.719**	**0.826**
8	Preferred Conflict Mode	Competing/Forcing	25	0.782	0.865	0.674	0.723	0.683	0.677	**0.691**	**0.781**
		Accommodation/Obliging	25	0.683	0.673	0.798	0.781	0.691	0.642	**0.637**	**0.762**
		Collaboration/Integrating	25	0.563	0.812	0.782	0.865	0.674	0.823	**0.716**	**0.793**
		Avoiding	25	0.634	0.651	0.683	0.673	0.798	0.781	**0.684**	**0.796**
		Compromise/Problem-solving	25	0.638	0.478	0.563	0.812	0.782	0.711	**0.663**	**0.784**
9	Global Modules	*Potential sources of Conflict*	4	0.563	0.498	0.381	0.391	0.236	0.331	**0.498**	**0.621**
		Conflict and Initial approach	5	0.634	0.563	0.698	0.681	0.691	0.534	**0.596**	**0.631**
		Other Party and Style	6	0.638	0.634	0.563	0.798	0.781	0.691	**0.612**	**0.693**
		Conflict basics	5	0.581	0.638	0.634	0.682	0.765	0.674	**0.631**	**0.732**
		Predominant conflict responses	5	0.665	0.681	0.638	0.683	0.673	0.798	**0.634**	**0.726**
		Procedural conflict handling	6	0.673	0.765	0.781	0.491	0.742	0.712	**0.702**	**0.793**
		Style quotient	5	0.536	0.673	0.865	0.674	0.723	0.683	**0.432**	**0.521**
		Preferred conflict mode	5	0.432	0.438	0.673	0.598	0.381	0.691	**0.441**	**0.538**
10	**CMI Battery**	**Forty One Dimensions**	446	0.481	0.538	0.783	0.673	0.748	0.681	**0.642**	**0.796**

*HR- Human Resource; PRD- Production; MKG- Marketing &Sales; FIN-Finance & Accounts; SYS- Systems & EDP; FSP- Factory Manager and Special Officials

The scale for assessing the predominant conflict responses attain the alpha of 0.634 and its subscales- Approach/Avoidance (0.728), Confrontation (0.637), Public/Private Behaviour (0.726), Emotional Expression (0.721), and Self-disclosure (0.748) are all passes through the cutoff alpha. In case of procedural conflict handling scale, the sub scales negotiations and legalistic interventions received alpha slightly more than the rest. Further this scale accrued the highest (0.702) among the global modules. The scales- style quotients as well as preferred conflict mode were studded with the lesser alpha, 0.432 and 0.441respectively, though their subscales attained alpha coefficients which are of reliable and representative in nature. The standardised alpha coefficients which are of resultants of the variance analysis was accrued and put into for comparative purposes and considered to be tributary to the analysis. CMI battery had accrued alpha coefficient of 0.642 and the standardised alpha is 0.796. Forty dimensional battery results in a reliable spectrum and can be strengthened by its role integration. Close inspection of the scales reveals that structural factoring of all the sets of items and indices are of greater importance and strengthening the reliability and validity measurable.

Alpha measures the extent to which item responses obtained at the same time correlate highly with each other. Though widely interpreted as such, strictly speaking alpha is *not a measure of unidimensionality*. Rather, alpha is a measure of level of mean intercorrelation weighted by variances or a measure of mean intercorrelation for standardised data, stepped up for number of items. A set of items can have a high alpha and still be multidimensional. This happens when there are separate clusters of items (separate dimensions) which intercorrelate highly, even though the clusters themselves do not intercorrelate highly. Also, a set of items can have a low alpha even when unidimensional if there is high random error. This propel and justifies the cross sectional design of this study as well as the usage of factor analyses, incorporating the principles of multidimensionality. Standardised item alpha is a variant of alpha designed to be used to test k one-item parallel tests and is meant to be interpreted as the average Spearman-Brown-corrected reliability estimate from all possible splits in a series of applications of split half reliability on a single test. It is also the value of computed alpha when all scale items are standardised to have equal means and variances. Both versions usually yield the same substantive conclusions and both versions are widely used. Some argue that the more restrictive standardised item alpha is appropriate when assuming classic parallel tests, otherwise conventional Cronbach's alpha should be used. This study tests the reliability by incorporating both the coefficients and the results are indicating to the confirmatory schemas and assenting in its core.

5.1.13 Projective mapping

Projective or semi-projective techniques of measurement are totally semi structured ways of tapping hidden responses. Individual responses were also content-analysed and/or scored to a predetermined scoring procedure. In semi structured techniques such as in this study, individual empathising process evoked by the case study and or other tributary methods are tapped through a quantitative scoring procedure. Quantification was attempted in all possible ways and the scores are attracted by definite patterns predetermined as represented in tables 5.91 and 5.92. Scales used in this study varies and it necessitates the conversion of multitudinal data into unidirectional. Scales of 1-6, 1-10, forced ranking, and frequency measures are all calculated to this effect and converted to *One to Ten scale*. Mean scores are calculated by incorporating normal and reverse scoring methodology adopted for all the sub scales and accruing the pretended and calculated mid points. Repulsive deviances are identified on both directions from mean scores. Non affirmative and affirmative deviances are valued as type 1 and type 2 respectively. Deviances are of its base in mean score and do not automatically be equated to negative and positive from the conflict management mapping contrives. Deviances are identified and applied to the stratum in three modular ways- upto 25%, 26%-50% and greater than 50%. Conflict management mapping is attempted through this projective technique and the conflict management quotient standard, which is nothing but a crude quantification attempts to help to identify the phased channelisation of global modules of this study. Neutral phase represents the standardised mean scores and the six phases are indicating the deviance denominations in their respective spectrum of operations, which are accrued through quantification of type1 and type2 deviances of this study.

Table 5.91: Conflict Management Quotient Standard

S.No	Global Modules	Neutral Phase	Phase One	Phase Two	Phase Three	Phase Four	Phase Five	Phase Six
1	Potential sources of Conflict	**5.42**	2.06	2.71	4.07	6.78	8.13	8.89
2	Conflict and Initial approach	**4.36**	1.66	2.18	3.27	5.45	6.54	7.15
3	Other Party and Style	**4.24**	1.61	2.12	3.18	5.29	6.35	6.95
4	Conflict basics	**3.96**	1.51	1.98	2.97	4.96	5.95	6.50
5	Predominant conflict responses	**4.64**	1.76	2.32	3.48	5.79	6.95	7.60
6	Procedural conflict handling	**5.26**	2.00	2.63	3.95	6.58	7.90	8.63
7	Style quotient	**3.78**	1.44	1.89	2.84	4.73	5.67	6.20
8	Preferred conflict mode	**2.96**	1.13	1.48	2.22	3.70	4.44	4.86
	CMI Battery	**4.32**	1.64	2.16	3.24	5.40	6.47	7.08

Table 5.92: Conflict Management Mapping

S.No	Module	Dimension	No. of Items	Mean Score/ Frequency*	Respondents' Stratum (in %) N=115					
					Type 1 Deviance from Mean Score			Type 2 Deviance from Mean Score		
					Up to 25%	26%–50%	>50%	Up to 25%	26%–50%	>50%
1	Potential source of Conflict	Issue Level	5	5.143	14.78	13.91	4.35	29.57	20.87	16.52
		Organisational Level	6	4.784	9.57	12.17	6.96	33.91	19.13	18.26
		Procedural Level	3	5.362	12.17	15.65	5.22	29.57	20.87	16.52
		Interactional Level	8	6.732	9.57	12.17	0.00	33.91	25.22	19.13
2	Conflict and Initial approach	Initial approaches	8	4.128	14.78	10.43	6.09	29.57	18.26	20.87
		Satisfaction of past conflict	5	3.268	18.26	6.09	0.00	33.91	19.13	22.61
		Conflict and Feelings	10	4.398	14.78	13.91	4.35	29.57	20.87	16.52
		Immediate Emotion	11	5.231	9.57	12.17	6.96	33.91	19.13	18.26
		Conflict aftermath	14	4.763	19.13	13.91	0.00	29.57	20.87	16.52
3	Other Party and Style	Boss/Superiors	8	3.753	24.35	6.09	6.96	33.91	0.00	28.70
		Peers/Colleagues	8	3.653	14.78	13.91	4.35	16.52	20.87	29.57
		Subordinates	8	4.128	8.70	12.17	7.83	33.91	19.13	18.26
		Friend	8	4.235	14.78	13.91	4.35	29.57	20.87	16.52
		Woman/Man	8	4.238	9.57	12.17	10.43	30.43	19.13	18.26
		Elder/Younger	8	5.432	36.52	13.91	4.35	4.35	20.87	20.00
4	Conflict Basics	Nature	4	4.632	9.57	12.17	6.96	33.91	19.13	18.26
		Gender Dimension	3	3.623	13.04	13.91	20.00	29.57	6.96	16.52
		Age Dimension	3	3.753	9.57	12.17	6.96	33.91	19.13	18.26
		Initial Responses	8	3.432	14.78	13.91	8.70	29.57	16.52	16.52
		Managerial Hierarchy	3	5.324	9.57	12.17	6.96	33.91	19.13	18.26
5	Predominant Conflict Responses	Approach/Avoidance	15	6.421	13.91	13.91	5.22	28.70	21.74	16.52
		Confrontation	15	3.259	8.70	12.17	7.83	42.61	10.43	18.26
		Public/Private Behaviour	15	4.328	12.17	24.35	5.22	29.57	12.17	16.52
		Emotional Expression	15	3.635	9.57	8.70	3.48	33.91	25.22	19.13
		Self-disclosure	15	3.536	23.48	1.74	14.78	20.87	18.26	20.87

S.No	Module	Dimension	No. of Items	Mean Score / Frequency*	Type 1 Deviance from Mean Score			Type 2 Deviance from Mean Score		
					Up to 25%	26%–50%	>50%	Up to 25%	26%–50%	>50%
6	Procedural Conflict Handling	Negotiation	9	5.124	20.00	13.91	4.35	23.48	21.74	16.52
		Counselling	4	4.635	9.57	12.17	6.96	33.91	19.13	18.26
		Mediation	4	4.327	12.17	15.65	5.22	29.57	20.87	16.52
		Legal Intervention/Reconciliation	5	4.321	9.57	12.17	0.00	33.91	25.22	19.13
		Social Exchanges /Predispositions	13	5.364	14.78	10.43	6.09	29.57	18.26	20.87
		Individual/ Combined approaches	12	2.134	14.78	6.09	0.00	38.26	38.26	2.61
7	Style Quotient	Controller	12	2.935	14.78	13.91	4.35	29.57	20.87	16.52
		Compromiser	12	2.364	9.57	10.43	8.70	33.91	19.13	18.26
		Collaborator	12	3.567	19.13	13.91	0.00	20.87	29.57	16.52
		Accommodator	12	5.135	24.35	4.35	4.35	29.57	6.96	30.43
		Avoider	12	3.364	4.35	13.91	29.57	16.52	6.09	29.57
8	Preferred Conflict Mode	Competing/Forcing	25	2.463	19.13	13.91	0.00	20.87	29.57	16.52
		Accommodation/Obliging	25	3.265	24.35	4.35	4.35	29.57	6.96	30.43
		Collaboration/Integrating	25	3.643	4.35	13.91	29.57	16.52	6.09	29.57
		Avoiding	25	3.238	8.70	12.17	7.83	33.91	19.13	18.26
		Compromise/Problem-solving	25	4.324	14.78	13.91	4.35	29.57	20.87	16.52
9	Global Modules	*Potential sources of Conflict*	4	5.423	13.04	22.61	10.43	31.30	4.35	18.26
		Conflict and Initial approach	5	4.357	36.52	13.91	4.35	4.35	20.87	20.00
		Other Party and Style	6	4.235	9.57	12.17	4.35	33.91	21.74	18.26
		Conflict basics	5	3.964	4.35	31.30	4.35	29.57	15.65	14.78
		Predominant conflict responses	5	4.635	35.65	15.65	6.96	4.35	19.13	18.26
		Procedural conflict handling	6	5.264	13.91	13.91	5.22	28.70	21.74	16.52
		Style quotient	5	3.783	8.70	12.17	7.83	42.61	10.43	18.26
		Preferred conflict mode	5	2.963	5.22	13.91	28.70	16.52	3.48	32.17
10	CMI BATTERY	Forty One Dimensions	446	4.316	12.17	16.52	5.22	28.70	29.57	7.83

* Mean Scores and frequencies are converted to the 1-10 scale

5.2 BEHAVIOURAL CASE ANALYSIS

Behavioural case analysis can be expressed as the detailed and intensive analysis of a collection of managerial cases related to the practice of conflict management among the study group. Distinctive situational decisions applied/handled by the representatives of the study group are accrued by employing qualitative tools including the selective appropriation from other modules of the present study. Selective and representative behavioural cases, stratified into ten case modules (10) are analysed primarily for explanation building exercises. To initiate discussion on the case, the researcher proactively requests participants to discuss about various types of conflict which arise through the proceedings in the organisations, their causes, and the manner in which they are handled. The causes of conflict, nature, avoidance/approach leniency, managerial style and efficiency are all explored along the structured domains while collecting the data for the case analysis which indicate the patterns. Disguised referential is maintained throughout the behavioural case analysis to protect the individualistic disclosures as requested by the officials of the textile mills.

The behavioural case analysis presents a unique set of cases that represents the dynamics of conflict management at various organisational levels that are sticks to the workings of the study group and not necessarily revealing the individual identities as per the current academic norms/codes practiced by the organisational research at these levels. The behavioural case study design of the data acquisition part and the usage of available/accrued selection of practices presented prevent major systematic generalisation of the findings. Although the conflictual processes identified cover a broad spectrum, other alternative categories might emerge from a wider, representative sample. In addition, the data does allow us only in a very limited way to draw conclusions regarding the long-term effects of practices transfer, e.g. the renewed eruption of a conflict over a certain behavioural norm despite effective interim conflict handling. A longitudinal study would enable us to observe the incremental evolutionary development of the practices at the local levels and even the potential inverse effects of local practices adjustment on the original organisational practice as applied at organisational system. The present study being academically oriented enables limited variants in the field and the research framework delineates with the understanding of the exploratory cases which are essentially behavioural understanding of the conflict management. In this regard the case analysis only ignites a short trek to the less travelled paths of academic inquest regarding the conflict management.

5.2.1 The Conflict Within–Individual to System Effect

Most organisations have a human resource manager or unit head who often doubles up as a staff counselor. He mentors and trains his subordinates as well as manages a unit or division. Sometimes, he may even end up misusing his authority. Take the case of Mr.Ananth, Human Resource manager, LMN Mills. Instead of assigning duties, instructing his colleagues, counseling and motivating them, his staff ended up in low morale and frustration in many respects. Ananth's problem of *downward* disrespect stemmed from his habit of intimidating his staff. Therefore, despite its success as a business person, the organisation experienced soaring employee turnover rates. Reason can be definitely not the work, but the boss.

Besides, Ananth never delegated work to his juniors but duplicated it by going over what they did, and often, was himself under constant pressure to meet his deadlines. Naturally, he couldn't focus on other important areas of business and ended up threatening his staff with termination of their services. Ananth's staff reacted by being indifferent to their work, much to his chagrin. By now, the Managing Director hired a consultant, Pramod, to work with Ananth. Pramod also had separate sessions with some of Ananth's subordinates and ultimately counseled Ananth to delegate work to his subordinates. In an attempt to set his reputation right, Ananth hired a deputy to oversee and edit the work before he could approve it. A few months later, when his performance was appraised, Ananth's division achieved the highest morale rating. According to Pramod, in his confidential report to the MD, the company could have resolved their problems if the working team had played a more active role by discussing important issues and forcing Ananth to delegate work and trust his staff - a paradigm for all organisations.

5.2.2 Hobbies and conflict management

"I no longer have the enthusiasm, energy or creativity I once had towards my work", says Mr. Raman, Senior manager in KPR mill. Like Raman, employees who once derived pleasure from their work, have begun to lose interest, energy and talent. Though such employees turn in mediocre performance, increased competition and globalisation demand excellence and continuous improvement. *"We direct our efforts to help employees renew and revive the way they once felt about their jobs and most importantly, we cannot ask them to pack their baggage from here. Further the managerial responsibility lies in enabling a lively atmosphere to promote unique work delight"*, says Radhakrishnan, HR Manager. The organisational efforts and initiatives should make an employee feel that the company values his past contributions, and wants him to have a fulfilling

and positive attitude towards work. To prevent boredom, monotony at work, and burnt out employees are eager to pursue hobbies and interests. At times, this can be given more priority and thus effect an individual's concentration at work as practiced by the HRM for dealing with Raman's problems. The capability to identify the various skills in an organisation rests with the managers. Therefore, they have to demonstrate behaviours that help nurture employees' skills. Personal aspirations play significantly influences an individual's performance at work. People tend to work better to fulfill personal aspirations rather than duty or obligation. However, obstacles like ill health or circumstances often prevent the realisation of a dream. People who were successful and were excellent performers may never have had a dream to work towards. Despite success and fame, such employees never have anything more to look forward to. They do not put in the time, energy and talent that they once used to. Resonance makes them reflect on work and how they can make it more meaningful.

5.2.3 Low-conflict organisations and Conflict Management

Low-conflict organisations are not simply characterised by the absence of features possessed by high-conflict organisations. Three mills in the sampled structure are apparently identified intuitively aided with the perceptive assimilation as low-conflict organisations and an attempt was made to pattern the elements that are unique and differentiative with the rest of the group as per the guided revealing from the middle managers in those organisations. The low conflict organisation and its patterns of cooperation can and should be described and discussed in terms of its own practices and internal dynamics. It is also important to note that the low-conflict organisations are not without disputes and differences; rather, the differences, which arise, are managed in a way that avoids extreme rancour, polarisation, and outright violent expressions. Low -conflict organisations have a psycho-cultural environment that is affectionate, warm, low in overt aggression, and relatively untroubled by aggressive and zero sum conflicts. Dispositions established in the earlier phases of organisational life through conscious training and open communication channels build organisational ontology that foster the peaceful management of differences. These dispositions engender a low level of overt conflict, so that there are few models of violent action and reinforcing the idea that nonviolent action can be efficacious. Disputes in low-conflict organisations can be intense and bitter, but they are less likely to escalate into violence and destruction, which make constructive solutions harder to achieve. Certainly anger and frustration may be accompanied by displacement, projection, and externalisation. But in the end these emotions are less intense because conflicts are not felt as threats to the fundamental existence of oneself or the group.

Low-conflict organisations are the most likely places to find constructive conflict management because the psycho cultural dispositions are most conducive to creative joint problem solving and open communication. The chances to find a few low-conflict settings where conflict management is not constructive in these organisations are unavoidable, partially because low levels of conflict can occur when one party is more powerful than the other and the weaker party is unable to press its case effectively. Examination of particular cases reveals important stylistic differences among constructive conflicts in these organisations as well as shared characteristics. A common pattern seems to be that the goals of conflict management are often quite diffuse and subjective. Even while disputants are in conflict, they seem to have a strong sense of linked fate. As a result, conflict management often develops a strong orientation towards the future in which parties do not emphasise short-term concerns as much as long-term relationships. In fact, these organisations seem to resist focusing exclusively on the narrow substance of a dispute and instead pay attention to the larger organisational context in which it is embedded. This provides a way to avoid responding to hostile actions of others with reciprocal, mutually hostile acts that set off escalatory spirals throughout the organisational understanding.

Training and developmental module in these organisations are ever dynamic and it seems that they had an immense effect on the conflict level felt among the organisational elements. This not only shows the training and developmental module acting as per the bookish measures; rather addressing or elevating the issues concerned to the levels of personalised mentoring with its manifold influential spheres. Low level of aggression is promoted by both low permissiveness and strict self-control among the managerial workforce in these organisations. Organisational conformity apparently makes punishment unnecessary, for individuals and groups often monitor themselves in a manner that collectively suits best for the organisation.

Most of the middle level managers connect the low levels of conflict in these organisations to a deep collective sense of responsibility and emphasised the noneconomic aspects of relationships as part of the strong sense of group/ related groups. The sense of psycho-social responsibility is expressed in a variety of ways – a strong emphasis on equality and leveling, attentiveness to group/organisational norms, a great degree of conformity, and a high level of participation even without necessarily high personal commitment. There is, simultaneously, a profound concern for the welfare of others and a certain emotional reserve in personal relations. Tremendous care is taken not to hurt the feelings of others.

Despite their interpersonal sensitivity and reserve, however, the managers in these organisations have little suspicion of top level executives or their fellow subordinates and they do not believe that others will take advantage of them. They perceived that the organisation is there for all, if and when it is needed. Decision-making and the exercise of authority in these organisations are intended to keep overt conflict low and discuss the expressed conflicts in non-confrontative and positive ways. Local/departmental decision-making often involves extensive private/in-group discussion to reach consensus prior to organisational/broader consideration. Broad-based coalitions are valued and regularly sought, and when consensus cannot be reached, matters are often dropped. Finally, managerial advises /interventions make much of legalism and formalism as a way of removing an issue from controversy by standardising the ways in which tasks are performed. What is more, these organisations have not known any upheaval or violent changes in its institutional makeup (they welcomed and rapidly embraced the technical requisites) since the advent of liberalised and globalised scenario from 1991, changes that might otherwise have caused a shift in core values. On the contrary, continuation and tradition plays an important role to promote conscious / quasi-intended conflict managerial momentum.

5.2.4 Core values and behavioural norms

Textile mills are part of wider business sphere of activities among conglomerates in many cases. The centralised managerial culture and the corporate commanding by the parent company or the influential persons of the parent company may cast a deeper impact in the managerial activities of the managers concerned. Middle level managers of KM mills, being part of the wider conglomerate KMR group, faced an academically pertinent conflict situation in recent time. The core values concerning *integrity*, triggered substantial conflict during its transmission from the parent group to the concerned organisation, especially among the managerial workforce. The normative component of this organisational practice demands the abstinence of all employees group wide from any activity that is illegal or violates fair trade. It specifies concrete behavioural rules concerning price fixing, collusive tendering and corruption, and includes, among others, an unwritten but substantially stressed point against the reception or granting of personal gifts to and from customers, suppliers or state/other organisations. Regarding the latter issue, the interviewees (managers) described the value of integrity as clashing with their own local business traditions which are firmly rooted in societal normative institutions.

A long history of the concerned organisation's tradition demands and allows the regular exchange of gifts, sometimes rather valuable items, between partners of a relationship, in this case between the company's sales personnel and local customers and suppliers. The ritual has a high symbolic value for business people/clients. And, in the cultural context of the particular organisation, it is explicitly *not* perceived as being associated with illegal practices or corruption but as an indispensable and socially highly acceptable gesture of politeness that strengthens the bonds between business partners. As such, the practice is interpreted by the managers as being an important basis of good business relationships and as contributing to local business success. Consequently, two highly diverse patterns of meaning and interpretation collide in this practice. As reported by managers, this situation leads to a dilemma for the local sales staff and opens up a double field of conflict. If the sales personnel adhere to the norms set by the parent company, they risk a conflict with their current /potential business partners. In fact, person from the sales team recalls an instance where the prescribed regulation has led to unpleasant debates and embarrassing situation with a particular client who perceived the rejection of gifts offered as being rude and as harming the mutual relationship. If managers in turn sticks with the past tradition and his/her own internalised norms, conflict potential is generated between him and a local/parent upper management which is responsible for implementation of the practice and needs to legitimise its own doings vis-à-vis the corporate headquarter. Even though the threat is perceived as being rather diffuse, noncompliance can, according to the interviewed managers, potentially lead to poor evaluations in management appraisal procedures and thus damage the personal career outlook. The managers perceived the conflict potential generated at the subsidiary to be substantial. It took them more than one year to handle the conflict in a way satisfactory to both parties; the managers, especially from sales team and the corporate headquarters. During this process the original practice associated with the integrity-value has been altered considerably.

Human resource manager with the help of Vice President initiated a series of talks and workshops to identify the exact causes of conflict and to understand the employees' ideas, attitudes and individual interests regarding the core value transferred to the organisation concerned. As a result, the behavioural standards as determined by the parent company have been readjusted through the formulation of a joint interpretation of the value guidelines and compromised amendments regarding acceptability and legitimacy of single, precisely defined activities in local operations.

It was approved in principle that gifts offered to customers or suppliers are acceptable if they are taken from a predefined pool of corporate presents in order to allow for continuation of traditional local rituals. Gifts can be received when they are below a certain value and when they are not brought to personal use of the respective person. Instead, the mill had established an annual procedure where through lottery or auction the presents collected over the year are redistributed among all employees. The issue caused some interim damage to the relationship between the mill and its local environment (customers, suppliers) but, according to managers, the compromise implemented is acceptable to all involved. Intra-personal effects include feelings of insecurity and dissonance between internalised norms and behavioural patterns and those imposed by the parent company during the conflictual period but the structural process effectively helps to reduce these individual uncertainties. The frequency of use and the reporting received by the human resource director indicate a positive reception of the structure by employees. Although the issue was amicably solved, it bears an appropriate application of the unwritten procedure-a loophole that can distort compared to a well written rule or the standard. Further workforce favours guided procedure in this particular case, rather than a well written rule, which always brings elements of vagueness with it because of the uncertainty it got attached.

5.2.5 Quality standards and Active avoidance tactics

In the production department of PFL mills, an interesting conflict occurs when the top level management initiated to impose a quality plan. In this production department, quality is a highly value-infused issue going far beyond mere product specifications. A supreme quality as such is heavily loaded with symbolic meaning, generating pride and identification of the workers involved in its production process. In this unit, this quality orientation has led to an ever improved refinement of product features and the development of specific production technology over time. The recent restructuration into global business units, however, is accompanied by top managerial efforts to globally re-align product specifications and production technologies in order to provide its global customers with exactly the same quality wherever they demand the product and, even more importantly, to reduce costs of technology adaptation and to strengthen the global joint production and delivery system in the long run. For this unit, the introduction of these global quality standards would entail the actual reduction of local product quality in the long run, where the local interests in continuous improvement of quality and its high inherent symbolic value clash with the parent company's interests of global standardisation, conflict is generated.

To handle this conflict the production department, especially production manager and quality control staffs pursued a tactic of deceleration. The issue was infrequently discussed by the company meetings and managers have successfully avoided the implementation of the restructured quality standards. Managers discussed different reasons for this course of events- First, the stable performance of the concerned department as perceived to be a key argument against any enforced changes of local processes. In addition, the geographical distance and peripheral position of the potential buyer and communication system prevents or at least delays direct interference of the official dealings regarding yarn specifications. So far, headquarters have not established any formal platforms for discussion and enforcement of the practice transfer like a task force or special appointee. The departmental staff proved to be right in choosing to adhere to *their* policies which were instrumental to obtain a highly profitable order from a much bigger and long term serving global client who had backed the quality standards solely because of the track record of continuous improvement in production quality and standards of the concerned organisation.

5.2.6 Myth of 360 degree solutions to conflicts

The case of Mr. Ramamurthy, SMP mills provides an opportunity to understand causes of conflict situations in textile organisations, and ways and means of managing such situations. The conflict discussed in the case is not uncommon in a textile mills. Often such conflicts remain unresolved, creating adverse organisational effects. They influence team-work and affect desired outputs. While managerial team would like to find a congenial solution to such conflicts, they are often difficult to handle.

The letter from the production department was very strong. It concluded by observing; *"If this is the attitude of the sales department, we shall have no collaboration with them as of now. Not only do they lack a healthy attitude towards collaborative work, they have often refused to share achievements. Now they want to stifle our work on product specifications, notwithstanding the fact that we have been working on its continuous improvement for over a decade. We would of course continue our work in this area, but without the undue interference of sales department."* Mr. Ramamurthy, Human resource manager, put down the letter and was quite annoyed. He had known that there was trouble between the sales and production departments, or rather between two senior managers of these departments. He had not expected it to reach this level. There had been several instances of conflicts between the managers and their divisions, but the conflicts had never reached boiling point.

They were usually resolved amicably, even before the higher authorities took note of them. Mostly the conflicts arose over allocation of funds for product packaging, budgetary allocations and participation in company representations in external meetings/conferences. However the present conflict is at its face value, without a series motive except the individuals/personal conflict between the two senior managers in the sales and production departments. Further, the conflict between the production and sales departments was different. It was a conflict between two departments which had always collaborated in the past. It was a conflict between two senior managers who had worked together on the same problem over a decade, and had jointly arrived at a solution to improve the products' quality and acceptability. For some strange reason, friends had become foes. In the process, they had vitiated to some extent the environment of the organisation.

Ramamurthy hardly discussed these issues consciously and he perceived that the friendly relations between him and sales manager would become abstemious if he does so. In the mean time, the conflict spreads to greater heights and the two departmental staffs *provoked* by their respective heads, made serious complaints blaming other department to the Managing Director in lieu the rejection of the export order causing time delay. Ramamurthy was at cross roads when the Managing Director put the blame of avoiding the known sparkles of conflict in the past at him and made confrontational meetings with all departmental managers including sales, production. Majority of the managers were seriously disturbed by this confrontational attitude of the authority and blamed in more civilised terms about the aversive/indifferent attitude of human resource department to solve issues like that between *certain individuals*.

Ramamurthy held a series of meetings with sales and production managers individually as well as collectively and put in strong words that the situation was becoming serious and counseled them invoking how they benefitted by their friendly relationship in the past and how they are viewed by their departmental staff as of now. Further he presented the loss suffered by the company because of their strained relationship. A combination of perceived threat with the other, disparities in case of monetary benefit accruals, familial problems related to each other(they being relatives) and a differentiative treatment they are offered by top officials were unfolded among others that points the hidden motives behind the strained relationship. A pragmatic and a touching counsel from Ramamurthy enabled the two managers to put aside the differences and to be their productive heights.

Ramamurthy was satisfied with the results he achieved but asserts that he should have avoided the ugly outburst by staffs and related things that followed by initiating to find a solution in the earlier periods of the interpersonal conflict among the two departmental managers. *"Every conflict cannot be solved. The seeds of potential conflicts are embedded sometimes in the organisational system itself and perpetuated by not only by top officials but also by other employees of the organisation"*, he asserted.

The individual personalities as well as their perceptions, concepts and ideas, emotions, intentions and behaviours are major sources of conflict in this case and Human resource manager's focus here was on the topic and on the task to be performed to amicably settle the issue that he fails to respond in the initial days. For a better handling of the issue, the mutual attitudes of the group members are important, as well as the state of relations between them and the interaction climate, roles and behavioural patterns. Here, techniques of problem solving in a team-such as analytic methods, decision making methods, creativity techniques, formal internal rules for the team and the use of auxiliary means are partially beyond the control of the human resource manager. Further, the way in which information and contacts are cultivated with the rest of the organisation including the rules regarding delegation of work, monetary benefits, if attempted to alter strategically may invite serious issues with various quarters. The best that can be arrived is to provide a decent hearing and active listening by which situation becomes atleast normal if not highly positive. The admixture of conflict management approaches in a theoretical framework starting from controlling the conflict up to reasonably transform or atleast to try to transform the issue got experienced by Ramamurthy and it exposes the most relevant fact that a conflict cannot be completely solved with a 360 degree satisfaction of all the parties as the path of moving from one level of conflict to another/others was experienced by the parties of conflict.

5.2.7 Managing Reactionary impulses

Kumar seems to be learnt a lesson or two from his recent experience which resulted in the reactionary impulses between two conflicting parties and the collateral effects that followed. *"Don't come and try to tell me often what to do!"*– Mani, one of the supervisor bristled when Kumar, production in charge of SRMP Ltd tried to initiate an open dialogue to find a reasonable solution to a conflict existing between Mani, supervisor who has a conflict prone history and a group of workmen including Hari, a sincere and long serving employee. The reason behind the outburst of Mani was well known as he wants to be shifted to another department (quality control/headquarters-testing) and was immensely dissatisfied with his present position. Kumar agreed that Mani had the required exposure and qualification to get a post in his mind but an array of problems persist which can be attributed to vested interests of some higher officials to install another candidate from outside to the same position. In this time, Kumar feels that Mani was not to be blamed and the situation reasonably points fault with Hari among others, he got irritated by a provocative attitude of Mani. In the mean time, Hari and others complained about their supervisor's attitude and dealings with the higher authorities without consulting Kumar. The matter had become serious and exaggerated out of proportion as described by the respondents and Mani was served with a memo by Factory manager, the date when Kumar was on leave.

Kumar was at crossroads and extremely unhappy the way situation was handled by authorities and the parties. He convincingly and assertively reasoned out his displeasure directly to the factory manager and told the dynamics of the conflict in greater detail between the parties. A meeting was convened with necessary departmental staff and the conflicting parties –Hari and Mani. The meeting ended with a stern oral warning to Hari and a well balanced approach that they had taken the concerns expressed by him. Mani had reacted very negatively and indifferent in the meeting, although he expressed his desire to get a transfer that he is qualified and eagerly waits. Further, he apologised for the remarks that he made during his conversations with Kumar. The proceedings called off by the factory manager with a settlement reached. Meanwhile, Kumar insisted that there should be a representation addressing Mani's genuine concerns and all the members agreed the same. Two weeks passed out and on a sudden day Mani came to Kumar's chamber and handed over his resignation letter. Kumar got shocked and enquired about his reason for leaving and Mani explained about non committal attitude of his genuine aspirations and a harsh response he received from the authorities. Kumar took this matter and collateral happenings to the Managing Director along with Human resource manager and find an embarrassing response from him. Managing Director revealed that the company was interested to recruit persons from a particular competitive mill for their quality control department, the reasons beyond explanation and cannot accommodate Mani there and factory manager was directed to accept Mani's resignation. Interestingly, after a few days Kumar got an opportunity to meet Mani in a public place and had a brief conversation while Mani told about his recent job as a quality control specialist in a competitive mill of Kumar's and their organisation is in search for a factory manager with a production background . Kumar in his private conversation told he is still not averse to Mani's information.

Conflict management in these days is shifting from its traditional spheres and middle level managers are at the cross roads. A reasonable facilitative platform to strengthen employees sense of self, to increase their confidence that they are taken seriously by others as beings with a history, an identity worthy of respect and needs that must be addressed and to treat them in ways that honor and support their own resources for making decisions and pursuing solutions to their problems and need-satisfaction is the need of hour in many cases. In this case an ever damaging operational mechanism revolving around the unavailable measures in a satisfactory way can be a serious cause of the attrition. Further, the pattern shows that if it got unaddressed may cause serious damage to the organisational activities. Middle level managers are expected to bridge the conflict managerial measures. The spiraling and multiplex nature of conflicts explained in this case shows that even managers are in great need to address several conflicts effectively and it got vitiated by the unavailability of the organisational procedures and related mechanisms.

5.2.8 Workplace cold wars and hot options

Mahesh took charge as factory manager of GDK (P) Ltd, a job he deserved in his previous mill but was constantly rejected. Being a man from Human resource stream, naturally he started his new operations with the human resource department and arranged a staff meeting with all important staffs from all departments. To his surprise, the meeting was unusually cold and no serious discussions were held between the participants except occasional exchanges of premeditated/crafted words. In later days, Mahesh realised that senior managers in almost all departments are indifferent with each other's affairs and they had only occasional task related interactions. The deeper query points out that relative isolation and an over dose of distorted information of departments were promoted by previous board and Directors. Mahesh discussed the matter in a friendly way with the current Managerial authorities and got a positive feedback from them to enable a wider human participation.

Mahesh convened a meeting with all the important staffs and stressed the need to have a deeper relationship among the departments, besides the task related cooperation that is to be put to new heights. To his utter surprise, human resource manager treated the message as provocative and directly put against him/his inability. It was shot back by the short tempered response from the sales personnel. The situation was controlled by the right intervention from other managers. Mahesh realised that volcano which was silent got erupted and thought about the right steps to put the situation under control.

Mahesh personally met the two problematic managers in their respective chambers and disclosed his real intentions and sternly warns about their misbehaviours. Later, those particular sales personnel along with human resource manager and production manager were put to charge as members of task force to implement quality improvement groups in the mill by Mahesh. Mahesh was particularly tough in the timely introduction of quality groups and extracted good work from all spheres. Factory Manager was perceived as strict and tough to beat by many managers through this process. In his address in one of the review meeting, he showered praises to the task force members and won great acclaim while announcing a token reward to the taskforce. The entire workforce was thrilled as they were unheard of these kinds of gestures in the past and made every effort to enable quality groups a real success.

Although, the company got mixed benefits by the introduction of quality groups, the interaction among the workforce were put into new heights. Mahesh describe that team building is creating a work culture that values collaboration. In a teamwork environment, people understand and believe that thinking, planning, decisions and actions are better when done cooperatively. People recognise, and even assimilate, the belief that *"none of us is as good as all of us. You can, however, create a teamwork culture by doing just a few things right. Admittedly, they're the hard things, but with commitment and appreciation for the value, you can create an overall sense of teamwork in your organisation"*, he added reflecting an aura of transformational leadership in managing conflicts.

5.2.9 Managing conflicts through consensus building

Groups often collaborate closely in order to reach consensus or agreement. The ability to use collaboration requires the recognition of and respect for everyone's ideas, opinions, and suggestions. Consensus requires that each participant must agree on the point being discussed before it becomes a part of the decision. *"Not every point will meet with everyone's complete approval. Unanimity is not the goal. The goal is to have individuals accept a point of view based on logic. When individuals can understand and accept the logic of a differing point of view, you must assume you have reached consensus"*, remarked Mr.Pramod of SKT mills, production in charge an effective team manager. He along with his team members had a tactical guideline to manage conflicts and to build consensus. He usually follows and prescribes these guidelines for reaching consensus -

- Avoid arguing over individual ranking or position. Present a position as logically as possible.

- Avoid "win-lose" statements. Discard the notion that someone must win.

- Avoid changing of minds only in order to avoid conflict and to achieve harmony.

- Avoid majority voting, averaging, bargaining, or coin flipping. These do not lead to consensus. Treat differences of opinion as indicative of incomplete sharing of relevant information, keep asking questions.

- Keep the attitude that holding different views is both natural and healthy to a group.

The most important element is to view initial agreement as suspect and exploring the reasons underlying apparent agreement and make sure that members have really/willingly agreed. There are a few key variables that define conflict management situations and determine which conflict management strategies are likely to be effective. Pramod is of the opinion that time pressure is an important variable–if there were never any time pressures, collaboration might always be the best approach to use. In addition to time pressures, some of the most important factors to consider are issue importance, relationship importance, and relative power-

- The extent to which important priorities, principles or values are involved in the conflict.

- How important it is that you maintain a close, mutually supportive relationship with the other party.

- How much power you have compared to how much power other party has.

5.2.10 In search of creative conflict management mode

The choice of conflict management mode is associated with managerial effectiveness. The ability to creatively manage conflict situations, towards constructive outcomes is becoming a standard requirement. Mr. Rajesh, Human resource manager in NM Ltd agrees that, *"While tensions and misunderstandings are normal and inevitable, if left unresolved they result in hostility, stress and wasted resources in the organisations."* He usually follows a broader approach and mange the conflict situation with pre-meditated phases. Once he had been made aware of a relationship problem, he calls a meeting with the people concerned, and defines the situation as factually as possible. At this initial stage, he agrees that it is usually difficult to define facts, so he keeps things as simple as possible and address the issue but not as a problem. He further stresses to confront the possible negative issues in the relationship. He finds out the problems and constraints the two people/parties involved are dealing with and prepares a ground to share their respective views.

He further encourages parties to look at the possible positive sides to their relationship. People have a tendency to treat perceptions as reality thereby moving a few steps closer to finding out what they are looking for from the relationship. At this stage Rajesh begin to visualise to look for possible solutions to their problems, but without asking for any form of commitment yet. Brainstorm the possibilities. Once he had looked at various options, he starts gaining greater commitment from them and generates to integrate the positive concerns and subsequently minimising the negative ones. Then comes the right time to generate directions (strategies) in order to achieve the listed aspirations and a list of combined plans, actions, objectives and supporting goals were prepared collaboratively.

At this juncture, the unsettled negative factors are dealt and the ground becomes green enough to arrive at amicable settlements and emphasising the parties of conflict to greater care and concentration on positive aspects of their relationships. Rajesh further emphasises on the supporting structure (resources, system) to accomplish the aspirations and selected directions. He emphasises that without this structure no idea can move forward. This may simply be a regular scheduled meeting to follow up on actions. Ultimately, he make a decent estimate/Measure the cost of non-compliance (non-adherence). This means ensuring that they are aware of the cost of not following the solution/s (direction and structure) to the problem, and consequently doing whatever is necessary to get the process back on course.

In the next phase,decisions concerning when and how the parties and others are going to evaluate and re-evaluate the decisions taken and the progress that may or may not have been made that creates accountability. In the final phase, summary of the discussions are prepared with an active promotion of positive aspects. He asserts that the whole process can be a well built one if there is a relatively loosened time pressure.

The above case prescribes that a unique and procedural conflict management scenario brings a framework for an efficient conflict management. Further, the ability to manage conflict is a critical skill in the workplace, and has been identified as a core competency for managers and leaders at all levels. It is ironic, therefore, that companies hesitate to invest time and money in improving employees' conflict management abilities when the cost of conflict in financial and other terms can be enormous.

5.3 HEURISTIC APPRAISAL OF CONFLICT MANAGEMENT CLIMATE

Conscious activation and execution of the research mechanism in terms of data acquisition strategies expressed through the overlapping modules in this study paves way for an exploratory analysis of the data collected in tandem to have a modulating and pragmatic appraisal. Predominantly inclusive analysis inculcating a qualitative exploration stimulated with the error minimisation can be a logical attempt that shall promote an expanded understanding regarding the state of affairs experienced by the study group in organisational settings. Highly interrelated and correlated constituents point to enable summation of a cross-segmental analysis of data acquired through In-depth interviews, Focus Groups, Semi-structured Observations, Content Analysis and Expert/managerial opinions/brainstorming. An appraisal of the *ground reality* through a quasi attempt of scientific triangulations along these lines can be expressed by the term *heuristic appraisal of the conflict management climate.*

In-depth interview sessions with a judgemental sample of human resource clusters from middle-level managers (study group); supervisors and general workers (subordinates of the study group/assistive workforce); corporate executives (superiors/the reporting authority) are sought out in a guided fashion totaling atleast *thirty sessions* representing each clusters. focus group sessions were delineated to the maximum of ten (10) comprising such collections of people as participants from the study group and their organisational co-occupants– top level executives, supervisors, factory workers and others. Prospective participants are approached and those who volunteered for the same were included with a judgemental consideration. Each session got activated for about ninety (90) minutes to the participants ranging between five (5) and nine (9). Every session proceeded adhering to the themes of the research questions with a guided intervention from the part of the facilitator. An active attempt to bridge the gap between the theoretical understanding and the real practices were followed by semi structured observations consciously farmed through out the modules of study. Further content analysis was carried out through permitted organisational documents including reports, diaries /other documentation from the study group and other officials belong to the adorable list of data along the lines of research questions. The predominantly qualitative and explorative data acquired through these modes of operations requires methodological challenge and thus rightly termed as heuristic appraisal of conflict managerial climate, essentially a cautiously optimistic appraisal that helps and attempts to triangulate the resultants asserted through other modes of inquest.

It was observed that the inquired organisations are all long established and mostly situated outside the city premises. Several of them are formerly family owned and family run companies, but today atleast some members of the management teams are all professionally chosen outside the family circles. Most of the participants agreed that they all have extensive linkages with their buyers/suppliers and other stakeholders, including those from international arena. Apart from collecting written data material through opinionaires, the study looked at the action and interaction of key personnel chosen by the authorities/researcher in accordance with the main areas of interest that resonates with the study objectives announced in advance. Members of the top management team together with senior/ operational executives and a range from top managers and department managers to foremen/supervisors and union representatives were all part of the key personnel besides a concentrated effort to analyse the *study group* in-depth. It was made clear to the respondents from the outset that this study considered conflicts a normal part of working life, and as potential areas of conflicts in organisations. Guided factors were obtained regarding conflict management with a view on the dynamics between functional departments, among various organisational components, between boss and subordinates, between individual conflicts in connection with reorganisations and outsourcing.

5.3.1 Conflict experiences and behaviour-initial responses

Asked whether they had conflicts in the organisation, most of the respondents confirmed this point, although some said seldom, and a few would not even admit to there being conflicts from time to time. Some would like to translate the term conflict into euphemisms like problems, discussions, differences of interest or inspiring challenges. In cases of the initial reactions in a conflict situation, the most frequent answer was that they discuss and negotiate, and that usually people would refrain from vehement behaviour, since this is not considered an acceptable form of discussion. However, when deeply discussed about the issue in focus groups, many agreed that conflicts may sometimes turn into shouting, but only very rarely. People with twenty to twenty-five years of working experience would have heard that only a couple of times, and one person explained about a certain loud dispute that *"it was also civilised. .... They shouted and argued quietly"* (Production Manager,), which of course is a contradiction in words. A senior human resource manager, who had eleven years of experience in the company, said in no ambiguous term, that he had heard people shouting at each other a few times. Most of them were indicated that people when feel that they are under too hard psychological pressure, instead of engaging in a loud and heated argumentation, one solution to a severe conflict might be for one of the parties to leave the scene. As one person put it, *"I have seen many times that people stand up and walk out. It is more that they cannot take it anymore; they are afraid that they will say something they will regret, that they might lose control.* (Production Officer).As one Factory Manager put it, *"Me, I never shout, I just get angry in a sort of silent way, and it lasts for a long time. People cannot always see it, I am too good at hiding my anger sometimes, but I try to express that I do not agree."* Obviously, these people exhibit a high degree of self-control and restraint.

In the in-depth interviews, many were of the opinion that the typical way to handle conflicts would be *talks*, talks between the parties including those between managerial workforce involved whether departments, groups, or individuals. They agree that in the initial phase, people would be expected to try to sort out the conflicts between them–themselves, and only if they do not succeed, the senior manager or some person in the garb of mediator need to step in. He needs to talk to the conflictual parties individually and in the next phase try to talk to both of them. Managers agree that the goal would be to reach consensus or a constructive solution (usually resolution / problem solving approach) in the shape of a win-win situation. Only when everything else fails, managers agree to the top level executives to step in and cut through. Both parties would then have to accept the solution and apply it. From the above it is seen that talks, meetings, discussions, and negotiations are the remedies employed to solve/handle conflicts. The idea is to sort out the dispute in a constructive way by the parties themselves and not to push the decision up the hierarchy until all other possibilities have been tried. It can be observed that contemporary psychoanalytic ideas are particularly helpful in thinking about the psycho cultural construction of organisational life. What individuals share is emphasised both affectively and cognitively, whereas deviations from the norm are selectively ignored or negatively reinforced as incompatible with group membership. The dispositions learned early in organisational life are not only relevant on the perceptual level; they are also implicated in specific behavioural patterns which serve one throughout his career especially cases regarding such as, how to respond to perceived insults, when to use physical/verbal aggression, or whom to trust. The translation of dispositional tendencies into behavioural patterns occurs on the individual level but is fundamentally an organisational process; where there is group support for certain types of actions they will be learned and maintained; where they are disapproved of they become less common. The role of culturally shared, profound *we-they* stand, oppositions, the conceptualisation of enemies and allies, and deep-seated dispositions about human action stemming from earliest development is extremely beyond the scope of the present study, whereas the organisational sparkles bears the potential resultants of them in a variety of ways.

Revelations from the managerial population indicates that the conflicts are sometimes just left unsolved, because nothing / nobody can conciliate the two parties, and cases were mentioned where such a situation lasted for years. In one case those involved would go on bickering year in and year out, and in another they chose not to communicate at all. *"...company, at least to my experience, has a fairly soft culture, they care for people, they don't confront people, and that has the consequence that conflicts may live for a very long time"* (Production Manager).Another manager thus hinted, *"There are two other persons here; there is a constant conflict between him/his department and the production department. That has been lasting for about fifteen years or so, and now we are trying to solve it, but it is not that easy. It is much harder now than it was fifteen years ago. Only in the past few years have we realised how deep the conflict really is"* (Operations manager).

5.3.2 Perceptual conflict asymmetry and its Management

Managers are of the opinion that rarely do two people simultaneously recognise a difference in positions or interests in same degree. According to them, perceptual conflict composition is the degree to which one person perceives that a conflict is present compared to the other person involved in the conflict. This concept of asymmetry thus examines the differences in perceptions of conflict among the parties involved in the conflict where one person may perceive that a serious conflict exists while the other party believes there is no or a very low level of conflict present. Perceptual asymmetry of conflict is that in an asymmetrical conflict, party A perceives more conflict than party B. Further managers pointed out that when one party believes there is conflict and the other does not, discomfort and inequity will exist between the parties. If put into the logic, this will cause the parties involved in the conflict to be less satisfied than when symmetrical views of the conflict experience exists. In addition to this managers as well as supervisory cadre employees are of the opinion that if party A believes that his view of the situation is not validated by the other party, or party B, he may question her /his own view of the situation. According to self-verification theory, this may decrease motivation, effort, satisfaction, and performance. Individuals search for coherence in their interactions and organisational environment, and inconsistencies can negatively affect the processes and outcomes of the parties involved. This is considered a meta-conflict construct (conflict about conflict), which can influence outcomes such as commitment, cohesiveness, satisfaction, and individual and group performance.

Mary parker Follett expressed that *"the very act of solving a conflict was not static, but part of the dynamic and continuous pattern of circular response which characterises all human activities"*. In an encounter between A and B, B does not merely react to what A does. He also reacts to his own anticipation of what A may do on his own and of how A may react to what B does. Mary parker Follett's memorable lines could as well be repeated, *"The conception of circular behaviour throws much light on conflicts for now I realise that I can never fight you. I am always fighting you plus me. I have put it this way- that response is always to a relation. I respond not only to you but to the relation between you and me"*.

An asymmetrical conflict structure exists when one party wants to change the status quo, and the other party wants to keep the status quo as it is. The unfairness that individuals feel can cause decreased motivation, depression, and dissatisfaction with the relationship fuelling spiraling conflicts that are often handled with the obsolete human minds. Interestingly, managerial population agrees that in the conflict management process that promotes and effectively handles the situation with heart and brain, there is always a scope for a revaluation of interests and a revaluation of desires leading to a realignment of groups thereby retransformation of conflict potentialities adding plus values to the zero sum game that otherwise opted out in olden days.

5.3.3 Managing Conglomerated Conflict Behavioural Patterns

Most of the participants of the study indicated managing conflict behaviour as an individual's intended or displayed outward reaction to the conflict issue experienced. When a manager combines several kinds of behaviours when handling a disagreement with an opponent and such a handling mechanism is termed as conglomerated conflict behaviour, refers to a simultaneous or sequential aggregation of several behavioural components in varying degrees-in essence the root of the theory of conglomerate conflict behaviour. The theory of conglomerate conflict behaviour is more complex than other models and taxonomies based on Blake and Mouton's (1970) conflict management grid. Most theorists in this tradition use dual concerns (for example concern for own and other's goals), to determine the different behaviours or styles. However, the behavioural styles resulting from these concerns are usually presented as unique and independent, as if a person/manager uses only one 'conflict mode', for example competing. Also, the effects of these modes are typically reported separately for each mode, without considering possible covariating effects (Huismans, 1995).

The theory of conglomerate conflict states that the components of conflict behaviour should be considered as interrelated. That is, mixed motives result not in simple, but in complex behaviour, that is best analysed as a mixture of components. Interpersonal conflicts really are complex situations, in which different motives and concerns about own goals, the relation with the other, others' goals, as well as short and long-term objectives, direct behaviour.

The main reason why managers actually combine different styles, instead of using one single mode, seems that conflict situations are often mixed motive situations. According to many managers, they try to achieve personal outcomes, and try to reach a mutual agreement at the same time- typically combining cooperative and competitive behaviours. Critical for conflict behaviour is how managers think their goals are predominantly linked; these perceptions influence their expectations and actions, and thereby the outcomes of the conflict management. The importance of (perceived) interdependence on conflict behaviour is at the core of conglomeration of conflict behaviour.

As managers perceive more (positive) dependent relations, they agreed that they tend to behave primarily/predominantly cooperative, whereas competitive behaviour is elicited when the relation is experienced as independent or negatively related. These points to the unwritten rule that a conglomerate with relatively more competitive behaviour is related with less perceived interdependency, whereas a conglomerate with relatively more cooperative behaviour is related with a perceived greater interdependence between the parties (be it fellow managers/others). The two different conglomerates that are usually interpreted in contrast with one another, as a more cooperative and a more competitive approach is best suits for the deep analysis to the present study. In a real scenario as expressed by them, the two conglomerates represented offers however mixtures of both, competitive and cooperative behaviours, in rather different forms, not only excluding one another but also combining or supplementing each other. Both conglomerate behaviours are characterised by a fairly low use of avoiding and accommodating and by a relative prevalence of collaborating and competing approaches to the conflict handling.

Effective conglomerates are those that involve a dominant combination of benevolent competing and collaborating styles as indicated by most of the respondents. The scenario requires a deep analysis of the more objective outcomes of conflict handling behaviour that is certainly a possible extension for future research in the present area of study. Therefore, perspectives of parties and of other sources of information are needed in greater accuracy to potentially predict the conflict behavioural dynamics. Further, analysing the interaction between the resulting patterns should help us to understand why certain conglomerates are less or more effective. At the same time, when analysing interaction between the patterns, one can observe the adaptation of one subject to the other party's behaviour. So far, the conglomerate behaviour is an overall description of behaviour. Differentiating in sequences, might shed richer light on the development of conflict behaviour. It is likely that the found/identified conglomerates and their effectiveness differ as a function of context variables, including organisational and occupational culture, the issues at stake, and the relations among parties. It was expressed by few experts who participated in panel sessions that the usefulness of conglomerate conflict behaviour as a way of analysing conflict handling in organisational context can even be attuned with the predominant behavioural pattern though variations can be a possible notion.

5.3.4 Interdisciplinary teams and Conflict management

Almost all the participants in various sessions agreed that interdisciplinary teams comprising specialists from different functional areas (majority being the members of the study group) have the potential for greater creativity in textile organisations. It can be accrued through observation that interactional dynamism among the human workforce in the textile mills convincingly appreciates interdisciplinary teams, usually comprising several departmental elements. Middle level managers are inevitable in every respect to these teams and their actions and responses makes black or white in the success nodes. *"Interdisciplinary teams draw on a wide variety of expertise and divergent perspectives to facilitate the production of creative ideas that are above and beyond the inherent capability of individuals and functionally homogeneous teams"*, expressed by a senior executive of a textile mill. Interdisciplinary teams benefit from differences of opinion about the work being done and improve their decision quality as team members share and adopt each other's new perspectives. The experts are of the opinion that synthesis that emerges from resolving different opinions is generally superior to the individual perspectives themselves. However, it seems that in many cases, despite the diversity of expertise at their disposal, interdisciplinary teams do not necessarily produce creative work because team members do not always share their unique knowledge and perspective. Team members may fear damaging their reputation, appearing incompetent, or they may simply wish to avoid conflict, where conflict in teams is described as awareness by some or all of the members of differences, discrepancies, incompatible wishes, or irreconcilable desires. This is particularly salient in interdisciplinary teams where pride in one's field or specialty area can lead to team members feeling a need to protect their own intellectual territory. Many respondents expressed that interdisciplinary teams to produce creative work, team members must actively voice their unique ideas without fear of encroaching on interpersonal relationships , even if it means being aggressive or stubborn in defending dissenting perspectives to bring about change and improvement.

Regarding the creativity and problem solving, many focus group participants and few expert panel members are of the opinion that when the team is focused on creativity, two key processes are necessary for team performance- divergent and convergent thinking. Divergent thinking occurs when individuals or teams expand the possibilities under consideration by thinking *out of the box.* From a problem solving and reaching common ground perspective, divergent thinking is important because creativity is most usefully applied to ill-defined tasks where the problem is often fuzzy such that both the solution and the path to solution are unknown at the outset. Alternatively, findings from brainstorming research suggest that functional diversity in itself does not guarantee the production of creative ideas. Open dialogues in interdisciplinary team may not always facilitate the generation of creative ideas simply because not all ideas are heard let alone be considered.   By and large, this can be explained by research demonstrating that more often than not, groups have a tendency to actively consider and discuss only information that is commonly shared across members. Functional diversity in interdisciplinary teams is an important resource for the generation of creative ideas, functional diversity in itself does not determine creativity. Instead, the ways in which group processes leverage the knowledge resources provided by functional diversity critically determines the extent to which the potential for creativity is realised in interdisciplinary teams. In most of the organisations studied, either functional creativity oscillates in favour of homogeneous receptivity among the group members or to the dominant creative response/proactive measures initiated by the *first member* of the team.

In an effort to examine the cognitive processes underlying the generation of creative ideas, it was repeatedly found through observations and focus groups that individuals who were motivated to attend to a flow of ideas from others produced more creative ideas than individuals who were not presented any cognitive stimulation. It can be pointed out that the key to knowledge creation is not so much the result of merely sharing information (as common wisdom suggests) but the effective integration of information shared. And perhaps most importantly, a critical aspect of effective integration of shared information is the manner in which teams manage conflict.

Top level officials preferred to say that the type of conflict in interdisciplinary teams and how they manage it is critical to creativity. They further said that in order to manage conflict, team members must be able to distinguish between conflict that is task, relationship, or process focused / dominant. It was observed that teams perform better on collaborating /problem solving and complex tasks when moderate levels of task conflict–conflict driven by differences in opinions or perceptions of the task being performed, is accompanied by low levels of relationship conflict–conflict arises from personality differences, hostility, and annoyance between individuals.

Managers agreed that interdisciplinary teams are particularly at risk for confusing one type of conflict for another. It is observed that the differences in background experience and communication styles coupled with a lack of deep knowledge of teammates make members of interdisciplinary teams relatively more prone to the misattribution of conflict than members of homogeneous teams, (e.g., intradepartmental teams can be considered as homogeneous and tasks that coexist in the organisation with more than one department can be termed as interdisciplinary). Interestingly, in addition to the critical role that minority dissent plays in team creativity, emotions accompanying dissent may play an important role in facilitating creativity in teams as observed throughout the study modes. Interdisciplinary teams experiencing emotional conflict – i.e. conflict arising as a result of dissatisfaction and frustration with the group's state of affairs, are likely to interpret the conflict as an indication that team members remain discontent with whatever solution is at hand and thus persist in their creative efforts to change and improve the status quo.

Managers agreed that positive emotions dampen the possibility of dissent and unique perspectives are never brought up because positive emotion indicates that all is well and there is no need to "discover the problem". This may be a cause of leniency towards maintaining status quo among most of the interactive teams in the studied organisations. In contrast, the presence of emotional conflict in interdisciplinary teams signals a discontentment and dissatisfaction with the status quo and thus motivates members to bring up dissenting views based on their specialised perspectives, visualised by many participants. Further divergent perspectives and dissatisfaction with the status quo are necessary but not sufficient for creativity in interdisciplinary teams. It was accrued that only teams experiencing emotional conflict will become aware of the discontentment and subsequently reveal and actively champion dissenting views. Interdisciplinary teams experiencing positive emotions can even be blissfully ignorant of potentially helpful divergent perspectives because discontentment and dissatisfaction never surface and it can be ascertained that the emotional conflict has a significant effect on creativity and the necessary appropriation of the conflict handling mechanism and the basic approach towards conflict management in organisations in general and teams in particular.

5.3.5 Conflict management and maximising helpful acts

A continuing question in the study of conflict and conflict management is, *"When is conflict helpful, and when it is harmful?"* Most of the focus group participants agree that conceptualising conflict as *simultaneously* containing helpful (conscious broadening and learning) and harmful (negative sentiment related) components in a way would be a right manner to critically analyse the dynamics of conflict management. Participants indicated that both conscious broadening and negative emotion can inhibit or promote future conflict, constituting feedback loops and this implies for conflict over time in terms of the efficacy of collaboration between parties who experience conflict. Traditionally *helpful* conflict has been called task conflict or cognitive conflict, while the *harmful* type of conflict is relationship or emotional conflict. Amidst managerial workforce, task conflict is centered on the group's objectives, or what it should do to solve a problem. It can be animated, but it is not personal. Relationship conflict is personal and emotional and tends to be about clashes of the members of the group. Task conflict, theorised to be positive is found to be negative in many cases of data accrual. Relationship conflict is seen as always negative, but in more humanised fields that deal with the stability of continuing relationships, relationship conflict can sometimes be helpful. It can be ascertained that functional and dysfunctional conflict perception seems to be a high influential factor among the managerial workforce.

Conflict, in addition to bringing about information, is usually experienced as somewhat unpleasant by the managers, and that this will lead to a buildup in negative feelings that over time; can prime people for more conflict. The first link in this had expressed by the expert panel sessions that- when people experience the unpleasantness of conflict, it can build up negative feelings. According to the managers, this happens in relationship conflict where people's personalities are attacked. This is an unpleasant experience that can evoke anger, irritation or annoyance and there may be other negative feelings that build as the result of conflict and to be managed appropriately. When conflict handling is avoided or delayed by protracted difficulties, this can be a frustrating experience. Here it is the inability to get to a reasonable state of affairs rather than anything personal that evokes the unpleasantness, and the particular feeling is one of frustration. In the case of a less powerful person trying to actively manage an important issue; it may be despair rather than frustration that emerges. Further managers opined that some negative feelings may be individual based. A person who simply is conflict avoidant may just experience displeasure as he or she is engaged in the conflict, even a relatively mild one. A person in a high status position may feel affronted that he or she is challenged by a lower status one. Across situations, people, and conflict types the mix of specific negative feelings may change, but in all cases the conflict itself is experienced as unpleasant to some degree, and leaves an emotional residue of feelings that are on the negative side of the continuum. When negative feelings build up, it should increase the likelihood of conflict. There are a number of ways in which negative feelings can provoke conflict. A very simple one is frustration-aggression and frustration has been shown to perpetuate the conflict cycles to come, agreed by most of the participants.

Another is reciprocity, where people who are experiencing something unpleasant can seek to return the unpleasantness in kind, especially if they feel justified. This follows an immediate downfall of ethical heights in the organisation in general and individual relationships in particular. Further, negative emotions crowds out cognitive capacity for other learning and active listening faculties of the parties of conflict. At the same time, emotion can lead one to either selectively attend or encode particular details, thus not comprehending the full story, but only the affect congruent parts (which would be objectively negative to the organisational learning).

Managers agree that all things put aside, with each conflict event; there is some increase in their *conscious expansion* regarding occupational dynamics, and some increase in negative and basically frustrating feelings. If there are more negative feelings than positive expansion of their consciousness, then the information brought about by the conflict event will go unused as people will not learn from each other. This effectively leaves frustration and conflict to spiral unabated as there is no learning to put the brakes on the *conflict-negative feelings spirals*. On the other hand, if conscious development outstrips negative emotion, there will be less conflict, and the unpleasantness of whatever conflict comes up should be overshadowed by the customisation that takes place. Thus there are fewer chances for conflict to produce unpleasantness, and the buildup of negative feelings will be diminished. If too much negative feelings exist among the group members, the scenario usually becomes unpleasant that no one will want to continue in the group and group effectiveness got reduced.

Some of the experts in the management field had revealed that some groups will seek to minimise all conflict and negative feelings. This kind of overzealous desire to have group harmony can be accomplished by inculcating people into the same way of thinking. In this scenario, any conflict would be an occasion for people to learn how to react to each other so that they avoid conflict in the future. The outcome here is groupthink. This was further strengthened and established through focus group, though seldom it occurs perpetually with the frequency it requires in the organisations brings a fact revealed. It can be attributed to the over conscious/cautious zeal among the managers to disassociate themselves from the middle path of compromise that may bring the memoirs of old day continuous streams of wanted and unwanted compromises they were forced to adopt to maintain all the group members equally satisfied.

The right balance in the minds of managers and their coworkers points the optimal situation where the conscious expansion and learning occurs at a high enough rates to control but not eliminate frustration, bringing a general satisfaction to the needy human elements in the organisation. This intuition is consistent with the multi level findings that trust can help increase the usefulness of task conflict, as trust should reduce the unpleasantness of conflict. It echoed in the sentimental expressions of many managers and their immediate occupational participants that people who trust each other may not make negative attributions about the conflict and makes the negativity to a more positive frame of reference adding plus values to the conflict management mechanism. At the practical level, a series of detailed and in-depth research needs to be done on how to find the balance between positive and negative outfits of the conflict management practices.

5.3.6 Culture, Emotion and Conflict management

Focus group sessions and expert panel inputs are lenient towards the new perspective on how organisational culture can shape beliefs about conflict, so much so that it renders them inconsistent with one of the most robust findings in conflict research and with what may appear to be common sense to other organisational/group cultures. One potential downside of the documented conflict literature in textile organisations indicates that the groups containing relationship conflict are automatically handicapped from reaching their full potential. Managers who believe this may refrain from putting together the most qualified team because some interpersonal tension exists between particular individuals. Although the observation findings would not argue that such thinking is imprudent, they do suggest that it is also important to consider what the members think about conflict.

Top level officials stated that if all members who are otherwise parties to conflict agree that relationship conflict does not matter, then perhaps the way in which they interact will turn the beliefs into a self-fulfilling prophecy. From a practical standpoint, different individuals may hold different views about the relationship between conflict and performance and that both may be correct. The more organisation can help all group members be aware of each other's points of view, the better the group can become at knowing when to take advantage of opportunities that on first glance appear doomed and when to stay away from situations that look promising but would ultimately end in disaster.

Most of the sessions indicated that conflicts especially arising out of cultural differences can ofcourse disrupt trusting relationships as well as promote them. Textile organisations, being a forerunner in industrialisation had established synergistic yet traditionally bound organisational culture and the study group seems to be sustainer of the same. Recalling a conflict, managers quite often talk regretfully about losing their tempers or losing their heads and attribute the conflict factor to broader term–*cultural differences*. These colourful phrases aptly characterise the presumed differences that when people are in the middle of a conflict, they behave emotionally often because of the differences exists beyond the occupational understanding. When they discount the influence of emotional factors, they are likely to fail to plan for how they will handle their emotions. This tendency has implications for how managers will respond when they find themselves embroiled in interpersonal conflicts especially the responses they may receive from the other end. An interesting observation was accrued which echoes the pragmatic treatment of this issue. In this case, a manager intends to have a calm discussion with his fellow worker about organisational chores. Beforehand, he knows that he should try to stay calm if he wants to identify a constructive solution to the problem. However, the discussion quickly takes a turn, tempers flare, and an argument ensues.

It was observed that though the manager had every intention of discussing the situation in a reasonable way, he underestimated the degree to which either he or his colleague would react emotionally. In retrospect, the manager regrets having had the argument and believes that they should have talked about the problem more calmly in an effort to identify a solution. Most of the managerial participants agreed that whether thinking ahead to an anticipated conflict or thinking back on a past conflict, emotional reactions will be less prominent than they will be at the time of the conflict. Further individuals' reactions will be more emotional when they are picturing themselves in the middle of conflict than when they are either looking back on a conflict or looking ahead to an anticipated conflict. "Confronted with interpersonal conflicts, it appears that people follow their gut reactions and fail to act in their best long-term interests", expressed by atleast three managers. Managers seem to follow their *hearts* when they respond to conflict to a greater degree than they follow their *heads*. This is especially true when they are in the middle of a conflict. This means that managers who anticipate an interpersonal conflict–particularly when they are thinking about what they want to do in that situation need to be aware that tempers may flare in the heat of the argument. This response is likely to come at the expense of a more thoughtful, rational response, and it may lead to a poor outcome. Moreover, these hot-headed reactions are likely to be the very kind that produces regret, especially in the short-term and continuously affects the relationship or task at hand. Many subordinates of the managerial population indicated that the emotions provide useful signaling information about the importance of the dispute or the significance of the relationship but flaring tempers can easily fuel the conflict and diminish the likelihood of finding a reasonable solution.

Even if parties are able to continue their dialogue, the emotionality of their interaction is likely to prevent them from thinking creatively about potential mutually beneficial solutions. However, that it is negative emotionality that creates the greatest risks to collaborative conflict handling. Positive affect, on the other hand, is associated with cognition and behaviour that increases the likelihood those parties will realise mutually beneficial outcomes, both at the short and long run. Anger or other negative emotions interfere with the ability to manage the conflict effectively; managers may need to plan even more carefully for the interaction. To ensure that cooler heads prevail, managers may need to take steps to limit the emotionality of their responses. They might consider dealing with the other person in a setting in which emotional outbursts would be inappropriate, for instance. Although they cannot predict what the other party may do, they would be wise to consider what the other party might want to do in the heat of the argument influenced by the organisational culture and individual emotions.

5.3.7 Building bridges or be at doldrums

"Never ever remain a middle manager in textile mill; it's the fastest way to spoil you, before your time and energy counts", remarked a factory manager. Nearly a decade ago management thinkers all over the world talked of three factors that effectively motivate middle-level managers. These were–trust, respect and caring, which they stated were an integral part of well-run, successful companies.

Today, most textile organisations studied under this academic query are keen on modernising their strategies to improve employee morale and productivity. But the amount of effort people are willing to put in depends on the degree to which their motivational needs are met. And they have a long way to go as far as trust and respect go. Irrespective of who forms the guidelines and sets the goals it still falls on the middle managers to see that they are successfully implemented. This is because they are in the unique position in the organisations to see and review what works and what doesn't and if doesn't what changes could be made to see that it does. It was observed and accepted by various sessions that in many mills, middle managers are not expected to make executive decisions. Their authority as well as responsibility level is perceived to be low hence they are quite content, being where they are as long as they can pass the work to someone up. However in a few organisations, it's the other way around. Here, the top management is not aware of the day-to-day operations and rely on the middle managers. When things do not go according to plan rather than admit to faulty planning, the middle managers are fired. But despite their hands on experience, most often, the top management pays scant attention to the suggestions or ideas from middle level managers.

They may give a patient ear to his suggestions but as far as implementation of ideas goes the middle manager has to toe the top managerial line. It is frustrating surely when the top management expects middle managers to implement reforms but neither supports their efforts nor acknowledges it. So, what can a middle manager do in this situation? When he knows that it is he who knows his people, he who has the ideas that are workable but his own bosses don't care a howl.

Some of the managers indicated that they can go on doing what they have always done and not care. They forget/forced to forget about making a contribution to the organisation, if they are content to get their pay cheque on time every month, this aspect shouldn't pose too much of a problem in many cases. But, if some manager happens to be one who cares, he had to work out for others and the only way to start is to initiate a dialogue with top management and tell them as it is. It seems that this step could be usually misconstrued by top executives and could be detrimental to the career of middle managers. Perhaps middle level managers may find a pair of friendly ears willing to listen and if they can find a champion for the cause of the organisation, half the battle is won- a fact repeated very often by many managers and their subordinates in various sessions. If not, they have to decide about the repercussions that are going to be bad and a contingency plan.

An important point to remember is that managers don't criticise any plans or actions that they have been asked to implement without having a very good reason as to why they may not work, reinstated by almost all the participants including top level executives. If possible, middle level managers may ask for permission to try out a course of action that they think may work, supplementing past, successful and related attempts. However, managers indicated that they should take every steps to shield themselves be branded as between taking initiative and insubordination. It was observed that, to deliberately disregard a top manager's directive will not be viewed as courageous but as indisciplinary. Whether a person decide to speak up or not if he had decided that enough is enough, should consider all the social, economical, private, and other related issues. There seems that it is indeed thankless and frustrating to be the middle person/ manager— an organisational sandwich between the top management and the bottom-rung employees; painting it as *black* or a *white paper revelation* or still as a *grey mattered one*. But it projections indicated that despite all these constraints or perceived notations, there is a constant and lively expansion among the middle managerial cadre in textile organisations. A senior manager expressed as that *"...we are termed as middle level managers because... we are necessarily in the middle and we may be shifted to top or bottom without consulting the middle portion (I mean heart), and I may not be correct if I add the word 'Unceremoniously' to the above"*, explains tonnes of thoughts that are usually behind every conflict managerial practice exercised by middle level manager.

5.4 INTEGRAL CONFLICT MANAGEMENT-GANDHIAN PERSPECTIVES

In order to ascertain various mechanisms related with the conflict management approaches, a referential scanning of the same was explored in the focus group and expert panel sessions. Most of the focus group participants and expert panel members were unable to differentiate the pattern of conflict management prescribed and practiced by Mahatma Gandhi. In this regard content analysis of Gandhian literature was attempted along the lines of Gandhian approach to conflict management. It can be observed that the integral approach which revolves around the life principles along with various conflict management techniques leads the Gandhian way. Gandhian experiments of integral approach to conflict management were vividly represented in Ahmedabad textile mill struggle in early 1920s.

Mohandas Karamchand Gandhi (2 October 1869 – 30 January 1948) was the pre-eminent political and spiritual leader of India and the Indian independence movement. He was the pioneer of *satyagraha*; resistance to tyranny through mass civil disobedience, firmly founded upon *ahimsa* or total non-violence—which led India to independence and inspired movements for civil rights and freedom across the world. Mahatma Gandhi's thoughts and deeds on human relations and his approach to the conflict handling seem to be one of the guiding lights for modern day managers.

Gandhian approach and the practice of managing conflicts are studded with his own personal situations which sometimes can have its linkages through the elements of history, organisational, industrial as well as greater inner conscience. Conflicts, struggles, and fights—all are words used when two or more people have what Gandhi describes as differing "angles of vision" or underlying principles. Gandhi believed that conflict could be resolved by "satyagraha", or "truth force". This concept by operationally stating that in each confrontation lies, "in some measure, truths from each view". "Satyagraha attempts to find a new position, more inclusive than the old ones, to move into it" as was proclaimed by Mahatma through his words and deeds. This type of handling conflicts synthesises positions and is therefore superior to others such as forced victory, accommodation and compromise, and arbitration and law, because ostensibly there are no losers. However Satyagraha does not offer certainty—it only provides a license to visualise, accept and prepare for truth. A larger discussion of what truth is; violence and struggle, coercion, recalcitrant opponents, strength, and the power of non-cooperation are all greatly intertwined with the situational variables. Gandhi said that the root of every Violence and or Conflict is *Untruth* and that the only permanent solution of Conflict is *Truth*.

The prism of Gandhian principles gives much impetus to the interpersonal conflicts and its management in the organisational sphere of life. In this regard the applications of Mahatma's philosophies on the conflict handling are spiraling in nature with its epicenter on the conflicts perceived by individuals. When interpersonal conflicts arise, whether they be between parties having differing degrees of authority (Boss-Subordinate) or between parties having theoretically equal power (Manager-Manager/Directors, Worker-Worker) the general ways of bringing conflicts to an end are for the parties to attempt to impose their will on each other, for authority figures to exercise their authority, or for one party to give in. The first of these "zero-sum" approaches, tilted towards authoritarian options may produce resentment and hostility in the loser, provide them with little motivation to carry out the solution, requires heavy enforcement, inhibits the growth of self-responsibility, self-discipline and creativity, fosters dependence and submission , and may make the winner feel guilty.

Gandhiji does not want to include the permissiveness into his ideas on handling conflicts. This approach (permissiveness) is of the "Okay-you-win, I-give-up" method of dealing with conflict. In the winner this may foster selfishness and reduce their respect for the loser. For the loser it fosters resentment towards the winner, makes them feel guilty about not getting their needs met and may require the loser to be pushed into an authoritarian approach. In these conflict situations those without power or authority learn to cope by rebelling, retaliating, dishonesty (lying, cheating, blaming others, etc.), submitting or even fantasising and regressing. Gandhiji believed that the use of these zero-sum methods will generally lead the manifest conflicts into non compliance situations or sometimes intensive struggle where the parties have unequal power. Where the parties are of relatively equal power, zero-sum methods often result in bitter stalemates making cooperative methods of solving disputes in these circumstances perhaps even more important. Gandhian approaches which are based upon cooperativeness and principled conflict management avoid these negative outcomes.

The role-reversal technique of switching viewpoints- where each party honestly tries to argue for the other's viewpoint while the other listens, was also explored by Weber. These techniques are also applicable for organisational/industrial situations where there is a sufficient degree of rapport. Further the techniques of 'active-listening' and 'mirroring' could be used until hearing what the opponent in a conflict is saying becomes second nature. The essence of active listening is mirroring back what has been said. This assures the accuracy of listening and also assures the sender that he has been understood when he hears his own message fed back to him accurately. Active listening can help to solve immediate interpersonal conflicts or it can be used by a third party to help one of the antagonists in a conflict situation clarify their own feelings and think creatively about possible solutions.

The visualisations of the management of conflicts were attempted by many practitioners all over the globe. The influence of Gandhian philosophy of Satyagraha, Win-Win and non-zero sum game as well as the proactive conflict dynamics are all fine-tuned for organisational adaptations by Mark Juergensmeyer who had postulated the under mentioned ten basic rules along the Gandhian lines for handling conflicts (Mark Juergensmeyer,2004).

1) Do not avoid confrontation. Avoidance simply prolongs underlying conflicts. Encounters between positions bring clarity.

2) Stay open to communication and self-criticism. Critical perspective is needed to sort out truth from untruth.

3) Find a resolution and hold fast to it. Seize onto harmonious alternatives, but be willing to challenge and change them.

4) Regard your opponent as a potential ally. Do nothing to harm or alienate your opponent. Your goal is to join forces to struggle against untruth.

5) Make your tactics consistent with your goal.

6) Be flexible. Be willing to change tactics, alter goals, and revise notions, including those of your opponent and your conception of truth.

7) Be temperate. Escalate your actions by degrees. Opponents should not feel intimidated, thereby fostering communication rather than defensiveness.

8) Be proportionate. Determine trivial vs. important issues. The basis for judgment is the degree to which life and the quality of life are abused. Mount a campaign of strength equal to that of the opponent.

9) Be disciplined. Especially when involving large numbers for collective action. Make certain your position is coherent, consistent, and committed to nonviolence.

10) Know when to quit. Deadlocked campaigns or ones with negative results may require revision in tactics or a change of goals. Concession, without agreement on principle is not victory. Victory can only be claimed with both sides can say the same.

Conflicts, according to Gandhiji are only a clash of interest and opinions, and are not the real problem. There will always be different thoughts and ideas among organisational citizens. According to him, there is surely a beauty in this. Further he agrees that the question is not conflict itself; it is how individuals handle conflict. And there are only two ways – through violence or through nonviolence. If conflict is handled properly they can lead to growth in institutions, they can lead to growth in personal relationships. Of course Gandhi did not know of these techniques by these names; however, he was fond of emphasising the need for caring and cooperative interpersonal relations that these techniques may aid to achieve. He firmly believed that the home was the training ground of Satyagraha--that it was the world in microcosm and how we reacted to aggression from strangers or handled our disagreement with them depended upon that training. The care and attention paid to small seemingly unimportant conflicts is as important as that given larger disputes, for it will be by those small things that the organisations shall be judged. These techniques can be applied in the modern day business units and its dynamic individuals.

Gandhiji pioneered what is now called as the win-win approach to conflict management and shed some light to evaluate conflict from a win-win perspective. The techniques that he incorporated in his life can then be applied to the goal of demonstrating pitfalls and potential positive outcomes. Winning in the Gandhian sense, requires a transformation of relationships. Win-Win sees life as a cooperative, not a competitive arena. Most people tend to think in terms of dichotomies- strong or weak, win or lose. But that kind of thinking is fundamentally flawed, because it is based on power and position rather than principle. Win-Win means that agreements or solutions are mutually beneficial and mutually satisfying. With a Win-Win solution, all parties feel good about the decision and feel committed to the action plan. In one of his manifold dialogues, Gandhiji equates the winning approaches to the chariot of Rama in Ramayana. The armed chariot that wins the victory of Rama in Ramayana is not of the ordinary kind- "Courage is its wheels; character its banner; self discipline and good will its horses, with mercy and spiritual balance as its reins."

5.5 Mary Parker Follett and integrative paths of conflict management

Managerial in-depth interviews had revealed that conflict management techniques can and should be applied to any one or more of the combination of conflict management approaches in a holistic way. Content analysis was explored regarding the combined conflict management approaches and in this regard integrative conflict management approach prescribed by Mary Parker Follett (1868-1933) was put into analysis. This was supplemented by the inputs from in-depth interview sessions and focus group interviews. It was observed that the multi-track approach, working at different levels has for sometime already been practiced in both micro and meso levels in the organisational sector. Unraveling false perceptions, allowing distorted perception mechanisms to be cleared and hardened concepts to be dissolved is an option to worth considering. By examining alternative modes of action as well as by reviewing one's own patterns of behaviour can also be a positive step towards this direction for the individual concerns. It was observed from various sessions of in-depth interviews that for better managing the content-level conflicts; managers must take step necessary to collect and straightening out the various themes in a conflict and look at them more precisely. Managers must learn rather trained to recognise their own distinct behaviour patterns and role expectations, to review these and to adapt them to the given situation. Good and active cooperation, prescriptive principles and stringent rules should be formulated to avoid any anomalies concerning procedural level conflicts.

Managers indicated that managerial degree of uncertainty should be minimal to the extent. Co-knowledge or co-decisions in co-determination policy issues lessens the conflict that caused by external relations as well as aroused by procedural dynamics of the team concerned. Work in the group environment can be enhanced if the teams and their leaders will participate actively in the process of recognising and identify the higher team dynamics. Managers and team leaders have put forward a number of basic tools in focus group sessions that allow for rapid diagnosis of the strengths and weaknesses of each of the five key levels of team functioning as well as their influence on each other. This work to be done is by its nature interdisciplinary and touches the concepts of major behavioural sciences. The maintenance of the appropriate conflict level in the organisational scenario is carried out by various interventions. One of the major conscious interventions to stimulate conflict level is dialectic method followed in executive and general body meetings. Fostering a debate of opposing viewpoints to better understand an issue is dealt with in this method. Thoughts are taken as thoughts rather than giving undue importance to it as his/their thoughts or my thoughts in its minimal sphere.

Mary Parker Follett expressed that *"the very act of solving a conflict was not static, but part of the dynamic and continuous pattern of circular response which characterises all human activities."* Through her books titled *Creative experience* and *Dynamic administration*, she had advocated that in an encounter between A and B, B does not merely react to what A does. He also reacts to his own anticipation of what A may do on his own and of how A may react to what B does. Mary Parker Follett's memorable lines could as well be repeated, *"The conception of circular behaviour throws much light on conflicts for now I realise that I can never fight you. I am always fighting you plus me. I have put it this way- that response is always to a relation. I respond not only to you but to the relation between you and me."* In the conflict management process, there is always a scope for a revaluation of interests and a revaluation of desires leading to a realignment of groups thereby retransformation of conflict potentialities.

Managers agreed that conflict management at its core enshrines functional cooperation by and through the pooling of organisational talents. May be conflict management refers to all conscious dynamic interventions that enables to promote a sustainable conflict intensity level which stems out of transitional or transformational process at the given settings. Focus group sessions had indicated that this organisational adventure must actively envision, include, respect and promote the human and cultural resources of the organisation. Managers and few executives are also of the opinion that this involves a new set of the understanding through which they do not often see the setting and the people in it as the *problem* and *the solution* as the sole answer. Rather they understand the long-term goal of transformatary values as validating and building on people and resources of textile organisations.

Most of the sessions indicated that conflict is part of every organisation and the managers do recognise it. A conflict manager being a transformational leader has a high level of comfort with managing dissent and conflict in their organisations. These leaders nurture conflict within their organisations believing that out of conflict, innovation occurs. May be a lesson or two from the Gandhian approach of dealing conflicts can serve its purpose for the future managerial interventions. The basis for dealing with conflict and disagreement originate out of a genuine appreciation of the differences between people that our Indian culture is very often sighted for. To become genuine conflict (transformational) leaders, the managers have to undergone self-transformation; rather they are transforming themselves to greater heights and influencing / facilitating transformational values on their followers. In short, conflict managers transformed as value-based leaders creates an atmosphere of trust and openness with his willingness to tell it *like it is* and thereby transforming the conflicts to its rightful managerial heights. Probably self-transformations, value based principles, organisational openness, and consciousness of functional cooperation fits the initial ingredients for the adorable list of conflict management.

5.6 INTEGRATIVE CONFLICT MANAGEMENT AND CONFLICT MANAGEMENT STRINGS

The psychological dimensions of conflict management was repeatedly emphasised by the focus group participants. In case of in- depth interviews, many managers had indicated that there exists a greater need to see the conflict and conflict management from collectivistic and psychological perspectives. They further indicated that there exists the unificatory power of conflict memory which makes the conflict transactions in an organisational life possible. This necessitates to consider all conflict sequences - not just of an individual- is taken to rest on the foundation of a single subjective knower/wisher/doer who playfully proliferates himself into this ephemeral show of fragmentation and then connection, experience and then recall, forgetting and then re-discovery of his own identity.

Through the content analysis of organisational documents as well as the psychological literature concerning self psychology, it can be inferred that conflict perception or direct experience of conflict situations seems to be one thing and remembering and managing it quite something else. Conflict perception of a currently available object of concern or even an introspective enjoyment of a reflexive cognitive or affective state seems to be quite easily separable from conflict memory which is supposed to be concerned with the past and the absent. But this first impression is deceptive. A kind of short term immediate sensory memory through the triggering event is essential for any conflict perception to happen. For perceptual conflict, however instantaneous it may appear, occupies a depth of duration, the illusion of simultaneity being created by rapid successions like a needle going through hundred lotus petals as if at the same time and underlying current of all this is in incalculable multiplicity of conflict memories which are past and absent.

The synthetic functions of cognition, selection, attention, recognition, judgement, hedonic and evaluative assessment are all dependent upon some form of stringing together of individualistic conflict strings in conflict fabric experiences across time and recalling the previous ones. And of course inference, the use of language and other conscious human practices require active use of conflict memory. Even the phenomenal qualia or subjective 'what it is like to be' character of a process of conflict consciousness requires that it feels a certain way for undergo it. And without some narrative implicit episodic conflict memory or atleast recognitional capacity one would not even have a sense of being one self managing conflict.

Expert panel sessions had revealed that in cases of managing the organisational conflicts, conflict recognition and conflict memory need not be bracketed together; since conflict recognition falls under perceptual re-identification of what is currently presented to the senses. Conflict memory is a fresh experience; whereas recollection- which is the chief meaning of conflict memory is always of what is absent and past.

Conflict consciousness intimately involves conflict memory of some form or other. The sense of self, self-continuation and the self-other distinction throughout the conflict managerial plane should be a prerequisite in this regard. The sense of past and hence the awareness of any duration at all should be a strengthening agent to this module. Further the ability to recognise and reidentify objects and other similar and dissimilar entities, ability to form concepts, linguistic capacity, rule following patterns and other emotive denominations including its expressions are all needed to propel conflict consciousness which is of different plane from memory and perception. Managing conflicts needs to focus on expanding the conflict consciousness and strengthening thereby the facets of conflict perception, conflict memory and its denominations. Not just language as a carrier of this expressive domains but all the non verbal cues in particular and any rational practice which involves inference or application of general rules requires that ability to link back with past experiences, their objects and most importantly the ability to synthesise a successive series of experiences under a single unified cognising integral and integrative conflict management-a transcendental unity of apperception must be capable of accompanying all cognitive acts. The essential role played by this linking back or connecting after principles, subjective synthesis can be done by the power of conflict memory.

Many managers indicated that such common day to day practices such as establishing cause-effect relationships, remembering and exposure of error in a previous piece of awareness require a single knower as their foundations. Further it was observed that even all minor popular not so pure activities such as unitary social intercourses and assumptive pure activities like collaborative transformations are possible on the basis of unity of a cogniser. Thus all practices simply live on synthesis. This prepares the organisational entities for a greater creative learning which transcends Pavlovian conditioning, Skinners operants, vicarious learning and even the clean slate theories of learning. *Amygdala*-the currently recognised brain area responsible for emotional reactions and the platform for selective attention are all seems to be building blocks of the greater secrets of conflict managerial understanding and the learning to manage is yet to be unlocked.

Conflict management strings

An attempt was made to postulate a model in this regard with the data accrued through expert panel interviews as well as the content analysis of available conflict literature along the psychological plane. In a typical organisational context, conflict sequences and its responses - not just of an individual can be visualised with the advent of prenotions of the strings of conflict management   which are of unimaginably microcosmic, illusionary yet dynamic packets of energies of managing conflicts. Bionic, psycho-physic-enviro principles, cosmic laws and other quantamised nature of conflict and its management may be attempted to explain with these conflict strings. though it seems to follow a different language of its own.

Infinitively small dissonance- resonance self balance of past and future experienced by a bio-psycho-social microcosmic entity in a time and space influenced by the factors of social, economic, political, technical, industrial, cultural, legal and ecological in origin can be referred as a *conflict management string or SangharshaPrabandhaTantri*- SPT (in Sanskrit this means - strings of conflict management). It necessarily rejects the mechanistic orders of traditional conflict resolution and or managerial approaches. The key features of the SPT model that creatively replaces some of the illustrious decelerating notions of past are thus follows-

- The conflicts experienced in mind-intelligence-consciousness of managers are out of operative conflict management strings-SPT normally in zillions than the pure singular entity causal relationship explored in the past. An SPT can be compared to a small tree in the earth whereas the unitary emotional expression of a social entity to the size of the solar system. This supplements the theories of multiple conflict notions by different managers who are in same organisational set up and calls for integral conflict management which revolves around life principle management.

- The movements of SPTs are in general discontinuous in the sense that action is constituted of indivisible dissonance –resonance balance and its influentials implying that it can go from one state to another, without passing through any states in between. This clarifies the dynamism of conflicts and their strange appearance- disappearance. The helical, spiral, non directional, multidimensional and other conflict movement and mapping can be better explained with this postulation.

- SPTs can show different properties, depending on the environmental context within which they exist and are subject to observation and apperception. This may explain the extrageneous influence and its importance in case of conflict management issues among the managers.

- Conflict management strings-SPTs are peculiar entities which can be called as living from a different sense of its meaning as they self balance, yet they are of non living as a unitary conceptual frame of operation. They are part of greater conflict fabric which is certainly universalistic and single conscious, one without a second in every organisational levels-thus influencing managerial understanding of conflicts and its management.

- Two or more SPTs which initially combine to form a conflict bit, may show a peculiar non local relationship which can best be described as a non-causal connection of elements of conflicts that are far apart. Multiple and multitudinal effects of conflict sources and its management can be explained with this postulation.

- If all human notions are of discrete SPTs, the interactions between different SPTs constitute a single structure of indivisible links, so that the entire conflict has to be thought of as an unbroken whole, each element of conflict that managers can abstract in thought shows basic properties that depend on its overall environment. This in a way is much more reminiscent of how the organs constituting living beings are related, than it is of how parts of a machine interact. In essence organismic nature of conflict is to be adhered so as to manage it. Managers collective mind and their belongingness can be compared as such an incorporated conflict consciousness spectrum which employs tangible and other modes of operations thereby finding a greater amass of synergy in managing conflicts.

- SPTs are self evolving, self managing, metamorphosing, constructively multitudinal, and part of a greater organisational as well as social fabric which can be referred as Mother SPT (MSPT). SPTs are also logically possible to be included in organisational resource-both living and non- living domains too. SPTs create, nourish, sustain and dissemble themselves at their own principles and calls for integrated management of the same for attaining organisational goals by the managers.

- SPTs are temporarily permanent and permanently temporary too all at the same time but not at the space dimensions. SPTs breeds and effectualise parallel SPTs which are tuned to different dissonance- resonance balances, not necessarily be in same time and space. This can be explained with the changing and dynamic nature of conflicts and its various dimensions. Furthermore it necessitates conscious managerial interventions for integrated conflict management.

- SPTs may exist even in supra cortex consciousness or the fourth state of consciousness and all the intuitive conflict management can be attributed to this. Managers do agree that they do take intuitive decisions while managing conflicts.

■ Individual SPTs are deemed to be influenced by karmic (ancient Indian theory of *multi cause-multitudinal*) principles of interconnectivity, integration, multidimensional projection and super positioning and such field is visualised as an energy field which transcends the time and space in its most observational unitarian denominations yet unattached to this in its SPT fabric. This in turn calls for integral conflict management approaches for managers along the lines of life principles studded with ethical and moral dimensions in organisational life.

■ It can be observed and can be postulated that SPTs are managing the dissonance-resonance through various proactive interventions. One among them can be regarded as the ancient Indian politico-ethical methodology of Sama-Dana-Bheda-Danda-Maya-Upeksha-Indrajala domiciles. *Sama* denotes that which brings equipoise or tranquility to the consciousness. It is the art of gentle persuasion and revolves around the conciliatory approach. *Dana* means the usage of giving something in return to achieve managerial purpose and can be denoted as bestowing approach of modern managerial understanding of *carrot and stick*. *Bheda* is the art of aggravating dissension amongst elements opposed to each other and means to create discrimination, make a difference, intentionally creating a gap by following oxymoron. This seems to be similar with the *divide and govern policy* in modern times. If social unit is insensitive even to the difference, then *Danda,* the punishment and or creative destructions happen. *Maya* means the use of managerial illusions or deceit. It seems to be deceptive to the core. *Upeksha* is to deliberately ignore influentials so as to achieve unitary purpose and follows the principles of modern day *active avoidance. Indrajala* literally means jugglery and intend for balancing acts amongst opposing pulls. *Indrajala* brings false manipulations to the conflict situations. Managing dissonance-resonance with this approach can bring integrated conflict management which can creatively deal the conflict situations. This in turn helps to enhance constructive conflict management mechanisms among the managers.

■ SPTs have inbuilt and creative tendencies for win-win approaches as well as zero sum games as they make interactions between or amongst themselves. This indicates that effective conflict management requires much more than the use of specific techniques. The ability to understand and correctly diagnose conflict is essential to managing it. Expert panel reviews had indicated that managers are required to understand the conflicts and after diagnosing the same may take necessary steps for managing the conflicts.

▣ Executives in the textile organisations indicated that conflict management domains are yet to be subjected to laboratory verifications. Constructive conflict management auras, more and more humane as well as intuitive conflict management are some of the possible resultants of well balanced zillions of SPTs. They are omni present in the unitary social intercourse-be it from intra-individualistic, interpersonal or even organisation wide happenings. It recalls the idea that constructive conflict management requires organisation (systems)-wide understanding and managing the conflicts through systematic efforts.

Managers are of the opinion that application of conflict management techniques will highly depend on the nature and causes of conflicts in the organisation. Kottler had rightly observed that conflict management even consists of diagnostic processes, interpersonal styles, negotiating strategies and other interventions that are designed to avoid unnecessary conflicts and reduce or resolve excessive conflict. Furthermore if the conflict is not dysfunctional but it is leading to healthy competition, it can even be encouraged. However, it is unlikely that a conflict is constructive in the absence of proper organisational climate. A major part of organisational climate as relevant to conflict management is built through common goals and proper structural arrangement. This paves way and further necessitates exploring integral and other integrative approaches of managing conflicts. In this regard, above explained SPT model can help a lot to understand the integrative dynamics of conflict management.

5.7 Aura of Conflict Management

According to some expert panel reviews, conflict management approaches can be considered as a conglomeration and multitudinal situational-responses exercised by the parties of conflict. This idea seems to be getting strengthened by systematic observation carried out by the researcher in selected textile mills. The spectrum of managerial options in cases related with conflicts reinforces the multiple preferential mechanisms. This imbibes a culture of extendable and or a combination of under mentioned managerial approaches broadly identified through this study. The managerial understanding about organisational conflicts needs to be rejuvenated so as to mirror the field reality. Many executives and some experts are of the opinion that the definition of theoretical conflict management, when viewed through the prisms of organisational realities needs to be embedded with veracity and requires refurbishment to the futuristic needs.

It can be accrued that conflict management shall refer to all conscious and or unconscious dynamic interventions that enable to promote a sustainable conflict intensity level which stems out of transitional and or transformational process at a given setting. An attempt was made in this regard to define the resultant oriented approaches of conflict management with renewed and more reflective perspectives.

- **Conflict Prevention** - Conflict prevention shall refer to all result oriented strategies for achieving sustainable retrogradation and/or putting an end to the status quo.
- **Conflict Stimulation-** Conflict stimulation refers to those conscious facilitations by accelerating the intensity level of conflict among the target elements.
- **Conflict Mitigation-** Conflict mitigation refers to all balancing and transitional interventions, creating circumstances permitting greater leniency to the net conflict intensity.
- **Conflict Regulation-** Conflict regulation shall refer to all authoritative reconciliatory strategies which direct the conflict energy to the 'right path'.
- **Conflict Resolution-** Conflict resolution refer to all process oriented activities that aim to address the underlying causes of direct, cultural and structural incompatibility and wishes to reframe the conflict as a shared problem with mutually acceptable solutions. It envisages how parties can move from zero-sum game/destructive patterns to positive-sum constructive outcomes.
- **Conflict Resonance-** Conflict resonance shall refer to all dynamic reinforcement or prolongation of constructive conflict harmony thus synchronised by conflict stakeholders and other organisational elements.
- **Conflict Transformation-** Conflict transformation is a continuous process of engaging with and transforming the relationships, interests, transactions and if necessary, the very constitution of destructive conflictual practices. It must actively envision, include, respect and promote the human and cultural resources from within a given setting. This involves a new set of our understanding through which we do not often see the setting and the people in it as the problem and our solutions as the sole answer. Rather, we understand the long term goal of transformatary values as validating and building on people and resources within a given setting.

Probably the concept of conflict management is broad enough to include manifold and realistic situational responses- be it constructive, creatively destructive, cultural, and synthesised or conflict-stakeholder specific. These are certainly to be differentiated from the cosy nostrums of constructive/destructive brandishing conflict management. Furthermore, organisational life and conflicts are intertwined more in these days than ever before. From identifying the positive sparks of the organisational life to the evaluation of the law of karma (Indian concept of *causal - effect*), every elemental influence enshrine with its weightages when deciding managerial conflicts and its channelisation process. Distributive elements of conflict management among the studied population indicate a collection of patterns and selective/integral ones are modelised under the umbrella concept of conflict management.

In a more realistic situation it may not be possible to manage all conflicts experienced by the managers from a mere humanistic bio-psycho-social plane of operations. Higher angel touches are needed which propel the management to more transcendental heights and the heightened conscious will make conflict management. This may sound a close call to spiritualistic side of conflict management. The concepts of self-actualisation (popularised by Abraham Maslow) and Karmic (cause-effect) theories of Indian psyche are all nothing but various shades of principled life style and conscious conflict management. According to some executives, this can be referred as supra conscious conflict management. Interestingly an addendum to supra conscious conflict management is also possible acting diagrammatically opposite to it which can be termed as conflict oppression. The supra conscious conflict management being an active tracker of conflict management- excels in dynamism, varieties and creative solutions. Conflict oppression is essentially an assortment of managing conflicts by destruction and even includes active avoidance. It ranges from simple destruction of a conflict to creative and synthesised destructions.

Balancing *dissonance- resonance of conflict as perceived by managers* seems to be the primary factor which determines the resultant oriented approaches to conflict management as explained above. Organisational life situations channelise the resultant oriented conflict management approaches and present itself as a cyclic phenomenon throughout the conflict management frame.

CHAPTER SIX

MAJOR FINDINGS, SUGGESTIONS AND CONCLUSION

6.1 INTRODUCTION

The present study attempts to identify the practice of conflict management among the textile mill managers. Conflict management as a key component of successful managerial strategy has been researched from different dimensions which relate to the differences in the way managers in a textile organisation handle conflicts. The views managers hold as a homogeneous group about this subject had been identified. The basis of the findings of this study can be expressed as the identified factors regarding attitudinal, integral and stylistic differences about handling conflicts among textile mill managers which are accrued by employing systematic research tools. Major findings of the study are recorded in sections 6.3. Suggestions to strengthen the ideas of conflict management among the textile mill managers got incorporated in 6.4. Potential extensions of the study were recorded in 6.5 and this chapter concludes with a call for re-energised conflict management study.

6.2 RESEARCH OBJECTIVES

One of the primary responsibilities of this academic research resembles to attempt to find a pathway that better expresses the management of conflicts among the textile mill managers from the selected textile mills in the Coimbatore region. The rejuvenation of the managerial ideas and practices concerning the handling of conflicts can be explored in its most intrinsic, integral, in-depth and innovative dimensions.

This study makes modest attempts–

- To identify the major source of occupational conflicts and to assess the preferred conflict handling styles and dominant conflict response pattern among the managers in identified textile mills of Coimbatore district (study group),

- To explore Gandhian and other integrated value systems as an adaptive strategy for managing occupational conflicts,

- To modelise the effectiveness of managing occupational conflicts of the study group.

6.3 MAJOR FINDINGS

This study had identified attitudinal, integral and stylistic differences about managing conflicts among textile mill managers. Major findings along the lines of various domains of conflict management areas had been recorded under respective categories. The profile of the respondents had been explained in section 6.3.1 Major findings of the focused areas of the present study include the identified elements among the textile mill managers along the lines of

- Potential sources of conflict,
- Initial and immediate conflict responses,
- Procedural way of handling conflicts,
- Predominant conflict management styles and
- Conflict management approaches.

6.3.1 Profile of the respondents

Sample survey research was carried out as the method of gathering quantitative/quantifiable data from respondents thought to be the representative of study population, using Conflict Management Inquest (CMI)-an exclusive questionnaire-cum-schedule (*wide reference Appendix*) composed of an array of various structured and open-ended items. Modest attempts along the lines of triangulation are included in the form of essay documentation primarily supplied through the data widely accrued by focus group interviews, supplementary in-depth interviews, behavioural case fundamentals, semi structured observations, content analysis and expert opinions. This exploratory analysis of the data collected in tandem brings a modulating and pragmatic appraisal model to the research dynamics.

All the middle level managers of identified textile mills were approached personally by the principal researcher. Out of the 196 managers from the twenty one textile mills, the responses from 115 managers were recorded and put to further analysis. The average age of the study group was ascertained as 47.92 years and range being 28-58 years. Median of the group can be expressed as 50 years. Standard deviation was 6.71 in years and it indicates that the age of a randomly picked manager's will be 6.71 years from the average 47.92 years. Complete absence of the female strata was another interesting emergent. In case of determining the education level, the highest degree obtained was taken. Forty two (36.52%) respondents possessed professional degrees that better represent their field of specialisation. This includes predominantly in the fields of Business administration, Social Work, Textile and other related Engineering/Technology and a few from Information technology. One doctoral qualified manager in his capacity as special project officer participated in the study. Thirty (26.08%) respondents indicated that they possess post graduate degrees, other than the professional streams mentioned above. The rest of the group- forty two (36.52%) respondents are graduates.

In the departmental stratification, thirty one (26.96%) managers can be expressed as representatives from finance department. Thirty managers (26.09%) belong to human resource department and half of the amount from marketing and sales (13.05%). Twenty eight (24.35%) respondents represented production department, four (3.48%) participants from systems division in their capacity among others offered the profound outreach of the present study. Six factory managers and one special Project officer (6.09%) are representatives of their respective operations and influence in this academic study.

In the case of work experience, average years at present position/designation of the respondents can be ascertained as 9.63 years, range being 1-24 in years and standard deviation to the tune of 6.55 years. The average managerial years of experience of the respondents is 18.57 in years and average years in other related exposure seem to be 4.94 in years. Average work experience accruing the above dimensions seems to be 23.51 in years. The median of the same is 24 in years and the standard deviation being 5.99. These data when translated into a working understanding, reveals that the study group belongs to a highly educated and professionally qualified, managerial cadre personnel with influential understanding about their working know-how generated and or resulted through a high/very high degree of work related experience and exposure.

6.3.2 Findings from Hypotheses Testing

Potential sources of conflicts are explored among the study group and statistical analysis were carried out to test the hypothesis. Multitude of influential and potential factors which acts as sources of conflicts at various levels are perceived differently by the study group and a pattern of ranking preferences operate in organisational life.

Initial approaches towards conflict handling are explored among the study group and statistical testings indicated that there exists partially differentiative apperceptions among the population along eight indicative conflict handling approaches- Negotiate, Force, Compromise, Mediational, Arbitrative, Accommodate, Persuade and Avoid. Furthermore it can be ascertained that managers do prefer a combination of approaches among these eight rather than to follow an exclusive one. The tendency to use the same approach to all situations seems to be more among the managers.

The effectiveness of various procedural mechanisms to manage conflicts and its components are not equally preferred by the managers. The statistical results are all pinpointing vividly a preferential pattern that can be adjudged through the moderate positive correlations operating among procedural ways of conflict management.

There exists a partial multitudinal effect of the preferred styles of conflict management which results in relational preferences of certain conflict management styles among managers. The statistical tests revealed that managerial subgroups- department wise, age and years of work experience are all moderately concurring. It can be ascertained that though there seems to be a little style difference operating among the subgroups regarding conflict management options, they are certainly not significant ones.

Managerial stratum employ five different modes or styles of behaviour in conflict situations - competing, collaborating, compromising, accommodating, and avoiding. The situational responses along these lines of operations got summated to identify the preferred modes or the styles as the case may be of the managerial population and the same revealed that the combinations of these five conflict managerial styles are operational among the managers. The statistical tests revealed that managerial subgroups- department wise, age and years of work experience are all concurring to the group preferential.

6.3.3 Potential Sources of Conflict

Interactional, Issue, Procedural and Organisational variables constitute the sources of conflict among the study group. Work standards to be accomplished, an issue level source of conflict had got the top rank among the studied population, followed by physical working environment, differences in knowledge or expertise, and others. Overall pattern of the studied population was more concordant with that of finance and human resource professionals, followed by other groups. This can be attributed to the dominance of these two groups among the sample.

Issue level conflicts are those which are necessarily occurred out of a single/multiple cause/s of incidental issues of work related concerns and the focus here usually on the topic and on the task to be performed. A combination of work standards to be accomplished, amount of time spent, errors and misinterpretations of orders, differences in basic values, beliefs or opinions plays a significant role in effectuating the potentiality of conflicts. Structural flaw in determining job objectives combined with the judgemental misinterpretations plays vital roles as potential sources of conflict.

Organisational variables are broader in their approach and techniques of problem solving in a team-such as analytic methods, decision methods, creativity techniques, formal internal rules for the team, the use of auxiliary means, besides the way in which information and contacts are cultivated with the rest of the organisation, including the rules regarding delegation of work, etc are all dealt at these levels. Organisational variables like compensation for particular position, hierarchical power differences and general market trends are all indicating the impact of external relations that being enjoyed by the studied population and its effective influence on them to emulate conflicts. The extrageneous influence on the organisational matters, particularly the fixation of wages at market level and related matters combined with the market trends and the internal physical working environment infuses conflicts.

In case of procedural level, flaws/constraints of planning operations combined with less effective performance appraisal mechanism and the technical issues concerning resource allocation are all indicative of the clustered influence of operational deficiency essentially accrued through resource limitation and methodological misappropriations. Thus it presumably acts as a potential source of conflicts among the studied population.

Interactional dynamics among the human workforce at various levels are always potent to act as the source of conflicts. Personality differences combined with the inappropriate/ineffective managerial supervision, direction-control can be a potential source of conflict and these variables share similar features too. The intrapersonal dimensions like differences in basic values, beliefs or opinions combined with interpersonal communication barriers and a higher drive for autonomy are all indicative of a relative intrapersonal influential; particularly the drives and approaches can play a vital role in stimulating conflicts. It was further indicated that drive for autonomy- essentially an intrapersonal variable was expressed through the personal habits and mannerisms, which can if negatively perceived becomes potential source of conflicts.

Perceptual preference of the potential sources of conflict from the respondents are ranked and represented in table 6.1.

Table 6.1: Ranking Preferences-Potential source of Conflict

Rank	Potential source of Conflict	Categorisation levels
1	Work standards to be accomplished (Volume of work expected, time limits, etc).	Issue
2	Physical working environment (Including noise, space, office temperature, ventilation etc).	Organisational
3	Differences in knowledge or expertise.	Issue
4	Compensation for a particular position, power or recognition.	Organisational
5	Resource allocation and related technical issues	Procedural
6	Personal habits or mannerisms (Including dress, way of conversation, etc).	Interactional
7	General market trends and other economic fluctuations.	Organisational
8	Personality differences (Such as cultural background, education, social patterns etc).	Interactional
9	Performance appraisal (Evaluation of task execution, goal attainment, etc).	Procedural
10	Planning of activities (What should be done, how it should be done, who should do it, etc).	Procedural
11	Need for tension release.	Interactional
12	Drive for autonomy.	Interactional
13	Personal dislike.	Interactional
14	Managerial Supervision, direction and control	Interactional
15	Hierarchical differences in status power and rewards.	Organisational
16	Barriers to interpersonal communication.	Interactional
17	Administration of wages, salaries, promotions, sanction of leave etc.	Organisational
18	Organisational policies and procedures.	Organisational
19	Differences in basic values, beliefs or opinions.	Interactional
20	Conflict over job objectives.	Issue
21	Amount of time spent on the job (Not meeting deadlines, arriving late, leaving early, etc).	Issue
22	Errors, misinterpretation of orders, carelessness etc.	Issue

6.3.4 Initial and Past approaches of managers in managing conflicts

Initial approaches towards conflict handling can be differentiative among the population and the same got explored with eight identified variables and factorial derivatives (refer table 6.2). Compromise, avoidance and arbitrative approaches occupied top three slots followed by others. Positive correlation/agreeability of moderately significant for force and compromise, seeking mediation and accommodative, as well as avoidance and force approaches are recorded, explaining their interdependence. Accommodate and force approaches are mutually incompatible and if a manager prefer to follow one he may be inclined to reject the other. Ranking preferences among the groups in the identified eight approaches seems to be tilted towards the acceptance range. Past approaches to handle conflict was significantly similar among all subgroups (departmental, Age, Gender classifications) too.

Table 6.2: Rank-Initial approach

Rank	Conflict and Initial approach
1	Compromise
2	Avoid
3	Arbitrative
4	Force
5	Accommodate
6	Negotiate
7	Persuade
8	Mediational

The combination of the four approaches- force, compromise, persuade, avoid finding opposite preferences with accommodative approaches brings a unique derivative which can be attributed to the more self-centric approaches prevailing among the managers. Combinations of approaches are usually perceived to be operative at all these plains. The gap between avoidance and the other variables shows a shrinking sign and a leniency to avoid rather than compromise, or persuade are tempting to their minds, besides a deep frozen thoughts to accommodate among the studied population. This calls for imparting training to the managers to equip them to take responsibilities rather than to avoid. 58.26% of managerial population indicated significantly low level of satisfaction pertaining to the handling of conflicts in past and all the standard test values rendered significant and rejected normality of the function, indicating the true raw analysis.

The immediate emotions and feelings expressed when a conflict occurred in past as well the immediate conflict responses are ascertained by suitable checklists that allows to not only record the expressed responses but also other responses, if the managers wishes so. Preferential rankings are carried out and tabulated in table 6.3. Positive feelings like strengthening tendencies, etc was recorded by a considerable percentage, though the negative and indifferent feelings about the past conflicts were visibly dominating among the studied population. Interestingly anger was recorded as the top emotion expressed by the group, followed by tension and anxiety. Other disturbing emotions are also recorded and ranked accordingly. It seems that the feelings, emotions and immediate aftermath of conflict situations are all indicative of the heightened negativity of the conflict that prevails among the sampled population.

Table 6.3 Rank—Conflict and Emotion

Rank	Conflict and Immediate Emotion
1	Anger
2	Tension
3	Anxiety
4	Confusion
5	Calm
6	Disturbed
7	Sad
8	Indecisiveness
9	Withdrawal
10	Enmity
11	Outburst

6.3.5 Comparing conflict management styles and the other party in picture

In case of boss/superior, being the other party to the conflict, managers recorded a preferred and or dominant conflict response styles-usually of yielding or accommodating ones. Compromise, avoid and accommodate approaches among others were recorded higher points to those when the other party was younger/elder-presenting the age differentials. It was clearly evident by the points obtained by each stratum that there exists a predominant approach or approaches that highly depend on the other party, hierarchically speaking. The conflict response pattern differentials along the factors of age and the hierarchical positions can be attributed to the cultural denominations existing among the managers. Preferential rankings of the conflict response styles are carried out in this regard and tabulated in table 6.4 (a) and (b).

Table 6.4 (a): Ranking Preferences- Other Party and Style

Rank	Boss/ Superior	Peers/ Colleagues	Subordinates	Friend
1	Yield	Compromise	Compromise	Compromise
2	Accommodate	Yield	Ignore	Collaborate
3	Compromise	Collaborate	Collaborate	Accommodate
4	Collaborate	Avoid	Yield	Ignore
5	Avoid	Compete	Avoid	Avoid
6	Compete	Ignore	Compete	Compete
7	Ignore	Accommodate	Accommodate	Force

Table 6.4 (b): Ranking Preferences- Other Party and Style

Rank	Younger	Elder	Women	Men
1	Compete	Compromise	Compete	Compromise
2	Compromise	Avoid	Compromise	Ignore
3	Collaborate	Accommodate	Avoid	Collaborate
4	Avoid	Collaborate	Collaborate	Yield
5	Accommodate	Compete	Accommodate	Avoid
6	Yield	Ignore	Yield	Compete
7	Force	Yield	Force	Accommodate

Gender differentials were explored through factor derivatives and it establish the fact that managers are highly comfortable managing parties being woman, though they seems to agree to disagree about the fact that women manage more easily than men revealing that gender differentials are highly influential for managing conflicts. The rationalisation if compared with that of the effectiveness of conflict handling between aged and young managers indicate a leniency towards an indifferent approach with younger parties and an assuming effectiveness of handling conflicts by the older persons. Furthermore, conflict as a positive force and unavoidable in workplaces was negatively attributed towards it being a leadership trait or as a destructive one. Interestingly, if it is regarded as a leadership trait then it projects a destructive picture to the organisational understanding.

Emotional and humorist tendencies are more appreciated by managers than using different styles. Anger management, changed conflict styles and a humourist attitude certainly affects the perceived skill denominations and its related excessive emotional expressions. The handling of conflicts and the comfortability are highly related to changed conflict style/usually improved over time and the controlled expression of excessive emotions. Hierarchical differentials vividly prefer improved effectiveness in handling conflicts through ladders (higher designations).

6.3.6 Predominant conflict responses

One of the most influential and expressive responses in managerial conflict situations seems to be that of the approach with which the parties follows and or the tendencies to avoid the conflict intentionally. Conflicts are not perceived to be exciting by the respondents and certainly the arguments do bother them. They are lenient toward waiting to see if the dispute/dissonance resolves itself, rather than to argue with others. They certainly not much appreciate the challenges raised by others against them. When managers do not enjoy the challenging the opinion of the others they feel being drawn into conflicts and or dislike the arguments and vice versa.

The managerial preferences to approach a conflict or to avoid a conflict are greatly influenced by various dimensions like argumentative nature, challenged stature, personal relationships, etc. All these factors indicate an overt reaction through the avoidance approach. Managers may not expect their co-workers to know what was in their mind and they may not feel uncomfortable after a dispute, especially to face the parties of conflict and they agree that they prefer to guess the reason that upset the relationships with others and these dimensions lessen the confrontational expressions exercised by the managerial strata. Managers feel more comfortable having an argument over other modes like telephonic talk or in writing rather than face to face confrontation and this can be certainly influenced by the fact that majority of them dislike about the eye contact during an argument, visibly a projected protective sign. Managers may prefer to wait for the right time to solve issues and in cases express their desire for face to face discussions, bringing down the confrontational leniency.

Managers expressed their hesitation to argue in a public place and it can be perfectly correlated with the facts that they feel uncomfortable seeing others argue in public or even with a friend, when others are there. Managers avoid arguments in public, even that involving strangers in most of the cases and this factor shows negative relationship existing between these and not such uncomfortability with those arguments involving their friendly colleagues. When managers do not bother about the others when they argue, their public behaviour would show visible signs of arguments even with fellow workers and vice versa of this dimension may also happen. Expression of various emotions and responsive or proactive feelings are all seems to be influencing the conflict response pattern. They feel not uncomfortable when emotions are shown during conflicts .The negation of emotional expressions and its recognition may worsen conflicts and they are against to do so. When managers feel that showing their emotions as sign of weakness, they may view being angry too as such and refrain from displaying emotions. When they feel displaying emotions are not as signs of weakness, then this factor may advocate expressing the emotions. In any case, displaying anger was presumably taken as an emotional display at all, though there seems to be a spectrum of emotions that are identified. Emotions are generally perceived to be disturbing in cases dealing with conflicts, though they are not excluded at all.

Open discussions from all quarters are preferred by the managers, though they are less happening. Managers may become silent when others pressurise them or force them to display the emotions during the conflicts. The exact opposite to this may also happen when managers may not become silent and certainly that seems to be a resultant of not pressured situations or compulsions for emotional display, necessarily initiated by other parties of the conflicts.

Managers though not prefer to hide their feelings; they may not let it to know others too. They are comfortable with most of the parties expressing disagreements but they may certainly feel annoyed when they are asked to state their feelings which they do not want to share/express at all. This combination negatively relates with the self disclosure assumptions. Managers opine that though they may prefer not to let the other person/s know what they are thinking, they feel annoyed and disturbed by the fact that the other person/s got upset with them and not expressing it openly. This may also affects the expression of the facts by the managers with them and furthering the dialogues. When the other parties expressed the thoughts and personal feelings in a conflictual situation, they may prefer silence than self disclosure of their real feelings.

6.3.7 Procedural way of handling conflicts and its effectiveness

Negotiation, mediation, counselling, arbitration, other legalistic interventions, etc or a combination of any two or more of these with other approaches may guide the way of handling conflicts into certain directions for the managerial population. The incidental importance will always plays a major role in procedural ways of handling conflicts. Managers seems to disagree that the common interests are seized in a negotiation process, though they agree that there are no hard and fast rules in every negotiation process and this flexibility helps the negotiations to get succeed. In case of negotiation process, there are solid principles and the gender preferential (preferably men rather than women as managers) that are agreed as influentials indicated by the managerial population.

Managers prefer to discuss both positive and other implications of the issue concerned with the parties involved and it strengthens when principled on demand negotiations are not adhered by the organisation policies. To give advice- especially on organisational problems, which are essentially psycho-social determinants are most sought by managerial population. Counselling as an approach got full appreciation and aged and experienced managers seems to be perceived to be effective and preferred in this regard. This can be attributed to the cultural influentials.

Managerial perceptions are tilted towards multitudinal procedural conflict handling and there seems to be more than one procedural way of conflict handling in use by them in their respective organisations. Perceptions regarding procedural ways of conflict handling had been ranked and tabulated in table 6.5.

Table 6.5: Ranking analysis-Procedural ways of dealing conflicts

Rank	Procedural ways of dealing conflicts
1	Mutually Volunteered Agreements
2	Participative Discussions/Dialogues
3	Intra Organisational Counseling
4	Open Negotiation/Bargaining
5	Exercising Organisational Power/Rules
6	Legalistic Interventions
7	Authoritative Organisational Interventions
8	Mediation by a Consultant/Others
9	Industrial Mediations
10	Collective Bargaining
11	Third party intervention by Mutual Consent
12	Collaborative Efforts and Work Execution

Mediation represents a process to enable talk to two separate people or groups involved in a disagreement to try to help them to agree or find a solution to their problems. Managers agreed that organisational mediation not only includes responsive ones but also of proactive too. Managers may be lenient towards accepting a mediatory role that may bring necessary solutions to the dissonance. In an interesting way, they are in no uncertain terms indicated their preference for avoiding the third party mediators from outside the organisation. This may be contra influencing in many ways, though the effectiveness analysis of procedural way of conflict handling in general and that of mediatory roles in particular seems to be beyond the scope of the present study. Legalistic interventions are usually succeeded by a perceived disturbance from managerial population, whereas they accept that forced organisational interventions are part of organisational workflow. Forced organisational interventions are part of managerial life seems to be one of the most influencing facts that make every interventions exercised by the managerial population. In psycho-social plane, when appropriate words and physical responses during organisational dialogues were not exercised by managers, then that seems to be influenced by an array of assumptions by them. It includes, a feeling that no real solution was possible to the conflict, predominant thinking about a physical fight or victimised by physical assault from other parties. The tendency to ignore some frictional relationships among the workforce, sidelining ethical issues in an argumentative bargaining and related physical responses may negatively influence the reconciliatory efforts. Whereas the combination of leniency explained may not be operative when reconciliatory efforts are perceived as important on a particular issue.

6.3.8 Predominant conflict management styles

Managerial dominant conflict style reflects their particular beliefs about conflict, preferences and comfort zone. Secondary choices constitute backups preferences when they find it necessary to abandon their preferences, creating a response pattern or a response hierarchy, as the case may be. Departmental stratification of the conflict management styles was attempted and the same had been ranked (table 6.6 and 6.7). The conflict management style quotients are all indicative of the differential among the textile mill managers regarding the conflict management styles.

Table 6.6: Rank analysis of style quotients

Rank	Group Rank
1	Compromiser
2	Avoider
3	Controller
4	Collaborator
5	Accommodator

Table 6.7 (a): Rank analysis of style quotients

Rank	Managerial Strata*		
	MKG	PRD	SYS
1	Avoider	Compromiser	Compromiser
2	Controller	Avoider	Avoider
3	Compromiser	Controller	Collaborator
4	Collaborator	Collaborator	Controller
5	Accommodator	Accommodator	Accommodator

*Departmental Classification- MKG- Marketing and Sales; PRD- Production; SYS- Systems & EDP

Table 6.7 (b): Rank analysis of style quotients

Rank	Managerial Strata[*]		
	FIN	**FSP**	**HR**
1	Compromiser	Avoider	Avoider
2	Avoider	Compromiser	Compromiser
3	Controller	Accommodator	Controller
4	Collaborator	Controller	Collaborator
5	Accommodator	Collaborator	Accommodator

*Departmental Classification-FIN-Finance & Accounts; FSP- Factory Manager and Special Officials; HR-Human Resource

Preferred situational responses are tabulated below in table 6.8, along the lines of different conflict management styles and it indicate not only the preferred or dominant response patterns but also the combination of options available and exercised by typical managerial decision requiring scenario. Factorial influentials of the conflict modes are explored and the same had been tabulated in table 6.9.

It can be observed that integrating/collaborating style was followed by the managers for dealing with the strategic issues pertaining to an organisation's objectives and policies, long-range planning, etc. It was ascertained that this style seems to be more effective than others in attaining integration of the activities of different subsystems of an organisation. According to the managers, obliging /accommodating style may be appropriate when they are dealing from a position of weakness or believes that preserving relationship is more important. This style had been indicated as useful when a manager is not familiar with the issues involved in a conflict or the other party is right and the issue is much more important to the other party. Dominating/ Competing style seems to be appropriate when the issues involved in a conflict are important to the managers or an unfavourable decision by the other party may be harmful to the managers and is inappropriate when the issues involved in conflict are complex and there is enough time to make a good decision. Avoiding style has been associated with withdrawal or sidestepping situations and used by managers to deal with some trivial or minor issues. Avoiding seems to be inappropriate when the issues are important to the manager indicating self centric approaches followed by the managerial population. Compromising style is normally be used by managers when consensus cannot be reached, the parties need a temporary solution to a complex problem, or other styles have been used and found to be ineffective in dealing with the issues effectively.

Table 6.8: Ranking Preferences of Conflict management styles

Item No.	Situation	Competing/ Forcing	Accommodation/ Obliging	Collaboration/ Integrating	Avoiding	Compromise/ Problem-solving
1	When harmony and stability are especially important.	5	2	1	4	3
2	When quick decisive action is vital- like in case of emergencies.	2	4	1	5	3
3	To gain commitment by incorporating concerns into a consensus.	4	1	2	5	3
4	On issues vital to organizational welfare when managers know that they are right.	1	2	3	4	4
5	When goals are important, but not worth the efforts or potentials of managers.	3	4	5	1	2
6	On important issues where unpopular actions need implementing—enforcing rules, discipline.	1	4	2	5	3
7	When managers perceive no chance of satisfying their concerns.	4	2	3	5	1
8	To find a solution when both sets of concerns are too important.	5	2	1	4	3
9	When potential disruption outweighs the benefits of maintaining an issue.	5	2	4	1	3
10	When opponents with equal power are committed to mutually exclusive goals.	2	4	5	3	1
11	To maintain a deep and personal relationship with a co-worker.	5	1	2	4	3
12	When issues are more important to others than to satisfy others and maintain them.	3	2	5	4	1

Item No.	Situation	Competing/ Forcing	Accommodation/ Obliging	Collaboration/ Integrating	Avoiding	Compromise/ Problem-solving
13	Against people who have lesser expertise in the common field.	1	5	3	4	2
14	To let the people cool down and regain perspectives.	5	1	4	3	2
15	When an issue is trivial, or more important issues are pressing.	5	2	4	1	3
16	To allow subordinates to develop by learning from mistakes.	3	1	5	4	2
17	To achieve at least a temporary settlement to complex issues.	1	3	4	2	5
18	When gathering information supercedes immediate decisions.	5	1	4	3	2
19	When managers find that they are wrong, then to allow others to show their reasonableness.	2	4	5	1	3
20	When managers' objective is to learn and develop professionally.	4	5	2	3	1
21	To arrive at expedient solution under time pressure.	1	4	5	3	2
22	When others can resolve the conflict more effectively than managers.	3	1	2	4	5
23	To merge insights from people with different perspectives.	3	2	1	4	5
24	As a backup when integration of thoughts or forcing a solution may not be possible.	5	2	3	1	4
25	To build social credits among organizational staff for later issues.	4	3	1	5	2

Table 6.9: Factorial influentials of conflict modes

Theoretical Dominant mode is influenced by

Item No.	Situation	Theoretical Dominant mode	Factorial preferences 1					Factorial preferences 2					Factorial preferences 3				
			CF	AO	CI	AV	CP	CF	AO	CI	AV	CP	CF	AO	CI	AV	CP
1	When harmony and stability are especially important.	Accommodating/ Obliging	++		—						—	—	+	++			
2	When quick decisive action is vital-like in case of emergencies.	Competing/ Forcing	+	++		++		+		—		—					
3	To gain commitment by incorporating concerns into a consensus.	Collaboration/ Integrating		+	—		—	++	+		++						
4	On issues vital to organizational welfare when managers know that they are right.	Competing/ Forcing	++		+		++	++	—	—							
5	When goals are important, but not worth the efforts or potentials of managers.	Compromise/ Problem-solving		++	++		++	—		—	+	—					
6	On important issues where unpopular actions need implementing–enforcing rules, discipline.	Competing/ Forcing		+	++	—	++	—	++								
7	When managers perceive no chance of satisfying their concerns.	Avoiding	++			++			+	++		—					
8	To find a solution when both sets of concerns are too important.	Collaboration/ Integrating	—	—		—			—	+	++						
9	When potential disruption outweighs the benefits of maintaining an issue.	Avoiding	++		++				+		—	++					
10	When opponents with equal power are committed to mutually exclusive goals.	Compromise/ Problem-solving		+	++	++		++	+			++					
11	To maintain a deep and personal relationship with a co-worker.	Collaboration/ Integrating	++			++	—		++	—							
12	When issues are more important to others than to satisfy others and maintain them.	Accommodating/ Obliging	++	—			++		—	—							

278

Item No.	Situation	Theoretical Dominant mode	Theoretical Dominant mode is influenced by														
			Factorial preferences 1					Factorial preferences 2					Factorial preferences 3				
			CF	AO	CI	AV	CP	CF	AO	CI	AV	CP	CF	AO	CI	AV	CP
13	Against people who have lesser expertise in the common field.	**Competing/ Forcing**		++	—			–			–	+					
14	To let the people cool down and regain perspectives.	**Avoiding**	++	+	++	+			+			++					
15	When an issue is trivial, or more important issues are pressing.	**Avoiding**	++	+	++		++		+		++						
16	To allow subordinates to develop by learning from mistakes.	**Accommodating/ Obliging**		++	+		++	–		++	++						
17	To achieve at least a temporary settlement to complex issues.	**Compromise/ Problem-solving**	+		+	++	++	+	—	++							
18	When gathering information supercedes immediate decisions.	**Avoiding**		+	—	++		—				++					
19	When managers find that they are wrong, then to allow others to show their reasonableness.	**Accommodating/ Obliging**	+	—	—	+		++			—						++
20	When managers' objective is to learn and develop professionally.	**Collaboration/ Integrating**	—	—	+					+	++	++					
21	To arrive at expedient solution under time pressure.	**Compromise/ Problem-solving**		++	+	++		++				—					
22	When others can resolve the conflict more effectively than managers.	**Avoiding**	—			—			++	—							++
23	To merge insights from people with different perspectives.	**Collaboration/ Integrating**		++	—			+		+	—					++	
24	As a backup when integration of thoughts or forcing a solution may not be possible.	**Compromise/ Problem-solving**	—		++		++		++		++						
25	To build social credits among organizational staff for later issues.	**Accommodating/ Obliging**	—				—		++		—		–	–	++		

+ Positive degree of factorial influence   ++ High positive degree of factorial influence   – Negative degree of factorial influence

— High negative degree of factorial influence

CF –Competing/Forcing AO– Accommodation/Obliging   CI– Collaboration/Integrating   AV– Avoiding   CP– Compromise/Problem-solving

6.4 SUGGESTIONS

The practice of conflict management among the textile mill managers had been assessed by various research tools and the major findings were of indicating the incorporation of necessary steps to improve the conflict management among the managers. Organisational learning along the lines of efficient conflict management can be attempted and the same can be recommended for further treatment. The findings from the study proved that organisational climate and the organisational/predominant individual culture and conflict management styles have the strongest impact on organisational learning. The culture of the organisation can often determine its ability to thrive in a competitive environment. The norms, beliefs, values and practices that pervade an organisation determine the extent and variety of informal and circuitous learning. Organisational practices and social norms and values are the two most important factors that determine circuitous learning and its receptivity. Organisational practices can be expressed as actions that employees perceive as representing the ideas, values and beliefs of the organisation, usually from top to bottom. Social norms and values represent the rules for acceptable behaviour, values and beliefs, generated from within the organisation's employees. Research indicated that an individual's motivation, personality, mental capacity and perceived level of experience affect the circuitous learning. For example, employees who are motivated to learn will learn more than those who are not motivated. Organisations that create a climate of learning and growth are more likely to internalise the value of learning. Circuitous learning can very well affect the predominant behavioural response pattern in cases of conflict situations in turn conflict situations into transformational heights showing glimpses of expertise and leadership. Middle level managers need to possess required skills to position themselves as leaders. These skills include shared and pragmatic vision, assertiveness, skills for conflict management, organisational commitment and adaptability. These skills can help them overcome crises that may perceive in conflict situations. Managers must possess the grit to successfully combat debilitating experiences without losing hope. These qualities spiced with a commitment to grow will make conflicts memorable experiences, rather than a nightmare to the managers.

6.4.1 Managerial essentials for conflict management

- The manager has to address himself to what is important to people from their point of view as well as from his own and make sure he does not confuse the two.

- The manager has to address himself to people's feelings, attitudes and personal background as well as to their general logical motives and purposes.
- The manager has to look at the relationships people have with one another and make sure whether these relationships helps to attain more logical purposes of psycho-social bonding and contributes to the social bonding within the organisational sphere.
- The manager has to reflect himself as more than logical in theory and be creative at times.
- Functionally, the manager being a practitioner of the skills of diagnosis should be at home with the skills of communication and actions.
- A manager who is helping people to feel secure, to learn from their own experience, to reach their own decisions and to become more mature and independent is greatly appreciated by the organisational circles.

6.4.2 Creating plus values by skillful conflict management

The time is now ripe to think of a new whole philosophy of managing the conflicts in the organisation based upon individuals-his desires, instincts, habits and behaviour. In its true sense individual is not treated to be as an individual but as a member of the groups where the same habits and desires float up as in his personal life. True and positive managerial examination of human relationships as the bedrock of business organisations can alone bring the dynamic peace and the highly spoken plus value for the textile organisations.

Managing conflict effectively requires many professional qualities and skills, and changing organisations to be conflict-positive, requires on-going, persistent actions. To become effectively and for appropriately managing conflict, middle level managers must understand the causes, theories, approaches and strategies of conflict management. This requires determining the kind of experiences in conflict management and its adequacy in preparing managers for conflict situations. The study indicates that the preparation in conflict management should start early and body of knowledge should be included along the professional socialisation process from the beginning of every managerial entry levels. It should include, in the first stage, the knowledge of the causes of conflicts, the conflict process and the skills required. Teaching problem-solving and decision-making approaches to cooperative conflict management adding plus values should be together in an integrated fashion. Managers/potential managers should; through planned exercises– be able to negotiate and analyse strategies and tactics for effectively implementing their available power in conflicts. Skill and comfort in using a variety of conflict-handling modes may help to develop a repertoire of conflict managerial skills that are essential in effectively managing the variety of conflict situations. Learning in the work environment can also be done through observations. Superiors may serve as role models. Role modeling can be an effective teaching learning strategy, providing upcoming managers have the skills and abilities required. In addition to the importance of education and skill training when conflict occurs in the unit, managers must deal appropriately with that conflict. Consistently using strategies with *Win–Lose* or *Lose– Lose* outcomes will create disharmony within the unit. The skills desired in enacting the facilitation role in handling intergroup conflict includes counselling, transparent and non violent communication, building better interpersonal relations and the ability for giving and receiving feedback on behaviour.

Only a small percentage of time is spent in true collaboration in the work environment among the textile mills, especially when there is a wide difference in power between individuals or groups involved. Managing effectively conflicts in a unit/department requires using strategies to actively encourage subordinates to attempt to handle their own problems, communicating honestly and openly, ensuring clarity of responsibility of roles, creating policies and changing if needed, and being sensitive to others and offer support.

In these days, managerial understanding is evolving itself through various phases of operations and a manager needs to understand in its most dynamic way the trends and quintessence of managerial appropriations. A word in this regard may help them; *they can't do it by themselves*, no matter how smart they are. Markets move too quickly, technologies grow too complex, and too many smart people are investing too much time and money in innovation. And, by the way, lots of those smart people are working in teams, trying to beat *them* out.

Grey areas of managerial understanding may only be surmounted by the fruits of experience. Managers are real persons with blood and beauty and they need the necessary exposure, expedition and experience to handle the intricacies of emerging scenario. One of the major challenge counted by practicing managers and other stakeholders of contemporary management ethos, is the expressive development of a body of theory to explain why organisational conflicts take the form they do, and why they/others behave as they do, including various stratum of the managerial responses towards conflict dynamics. Outlining some aspects of this emerging line of research on organisations and to call attention to a number of related methodological issues that play an important role in these areas of research – the relation between situational processes, handling strategies and theories, the importance to the research effort of the choice of tautologies and definitions, the nature of evidence, behavioural reengineering, process realignment, organisational preparedness/ adaptability/receptivity and the role of personality-structure interplays among other related domains, enshrine the expanding horizons. Something is *common knowledge* if it is known to each person, and in addition, each person knows that he or she has this knowledge; knows that the other person/s knows the person knows it; and so forth. If in any case, a crevice in this structure entitles a need to acquire the *savoir faire* and to transform the relationship to new heights. It exactly suits for the expanding domains of conflict management studies concerning managers, supervisors, executives and common workers in textile organisations. The current study can be equated with a modest attempt to promote knowledge about conflict management and to share the intricacies of the practice of conflict management with a special emphasise on managerial modalities that brings forth a plethora of opportunities.

6.4.3 Interactionist approaches for better conflict management

The emerging view of conflict, called as interactionist view, reverses many of the cozy nostrums of human relations management in textile mills. The interactionist view of conflict has a broader scope than the traditional notions of unitary and pluralist perspectives which are in a way shy away to address the conflict at all. Interactionist view recognises that in some cases conflict may be helpful, facilitative and functional. The current thought acknowledges the inevitability of conflict and focuses it as a useful tool / vehicle to shake the organisation from stereo type / contention to innovation and creativity. One of the most outstanding aspects of organisational conflict is that it is practically intrinsic to the life and dynamics of organisations. Conflict seems to be present in interpersonal relations, in intragroup and intergroup relations, in strategic decision-making and other organisational episodes. As many authors have pointed out (De Dreu & Van de Vliert, 1997; Pondy, 1967) that conflict is a phenomenon that may give rise to both beneficial and functional consequences, as well as having important positive and negative effects on individuals, groups and organisations. Therefore, it is necessary to exercise managerial aura and to have access to diagnosis and intervention tools that may allow it to handle conflicts appropriately.

The object of conflict management is not the promotion of scientific investigation and discovery of managerial principles, but rather the assimilation and interpretation of that which has been or shall be hereafter discovered, and its application to organisational welfare, especially by the building of the truths of human relations and organisational philosophy into the structure of a broadened and purified management. Such a managerial understanding will greatly stimulate intelligent effort for the improvement of human conditions and the advancement of organisational development in strength and excellence of character. To this end, it is desired that an array of theories and postulates given by men and women in their respective departments – on managerial disciplines, psychology, sociology, ethics; all sciences and branches of knowledge which have an important bearing on the subject; all the great laws of nature, especially of evolution including organisational fruition. And also such interpretations as are in accord with the spirit of the organisation concerned, to the end that the human spirit may be nurtured in the fullest light of the world's knowledge and that organisational human being may be helped to attain their highest possible welfare and happiness upon this earth. The spectrum of conflict management in the textile organisations requires an immediate attention. The buzz word of functional cooperation can be a reality if and only if the managerial decisions are supplemented by the facets of reciprocal relating, integrative unity, law of the situation and cumulative responsibility. A word for the managers-you are not only for what you said and did, but how you said and did it. And that's the quintessence of conflict management.

6.4.4 Imparting training for conflict management

Most of the managers are not really thinking about how they approach conflict. It just happens to them and they do have their preferential domains, normally to avoid the conflicts. When conflict arises, managers agree that they tend to play out their roles like scripts based on their behavioural and conflict management styles. Effective conflict management can only be achieved when a manager begins to really see how her or his conflict management style is actually self-destructive. Managers are required to get exposure in the contemporary conflict management philosophy; especially along the lines of interactionist, integral and integrated ones. Emotional immaturity seems to at its worst during conflict situations as expressed by the managers. In order to change, managers have to *want* to change. Interestingly managers had expressed and the same was revealed by the findings that they want to change and equip themselves with the skills of conflict management. These indicate the need to impart training with an exclusive focus on conflict management skill enhancement among the textile managers. Guided conflict management modules for textile mill managers can be a better suggestive measure and the same is expressed in tabular form in the following section. Further the critical factors to be considered for imparting conflict management training were identified and put forth as suggestive measures.

6.4.4.1 Modules of conflict management training

Effective conflict management is situational. That is, managers must be trained to apply emotional intelligence to deal with each person and situation differently. Conflict management training sessions should be designed the same way. It must include all the right elements to really reach the managers, including humour, role play, direct confrontation, facilitated discussions, exercises and group activities besides the skill sets that are vital for endorsement.

Table 6.10 Contents, objectives and methodology on imparting conflict management skill set

Module Contents	Sub contents	Specific objectives	Training Methodology
1) Concept and sources of conflict 2) Concept of Constructive conflict management 3) Methods of conflict handling and conflict management styles 4) Institutionalised mechanism for conflict management among textile mills, government, associative and legalistic levels 5) Various approaches for conflict management-Integral, Interactionist and Integrated 6) Leadership development on problem-solving, development-oriented attitude and social communication skills 7) Negotiating and active listening skills 8) Counselling skills 9) Assessing Conflict management skills 10) Culture, Consensus and Conflict management 11) Emerging conflict management models	a) Conflict Analysis b) Stakeholder Analysis c) Conflict and early response d) Proactive conflict management e) Gender sensitivity f) Organisational Change and Developmental factors g) Factors of Transformational leadership h) Interpersonal effectiveness and human relations' approach i) Psychometric skills j) SPT model for conflict management	⧈ To identify the sources of conflict ⧈ To clarify the concepts of conflict and Constructive conflict management ⧈ To understand the process of effective conflict management ⧈ To plan collaboration with all stakeholders for Win-Win ⧈ To clarify the institutional set-up and interests of stakeholders in conflict-management ⧈ To identify various approaches of conflict management ⧈ To understand the principles of transformational leadership ⧈ To uplift essential skill sets of conflict management	● Lecture-cum-discussion ● Role-playing ● Brainstorming ● Self-analysis techniques ● Simulation games ● Field visit to success and failure sites ● Story telling and problem-solving ● Case study ● Group-analysis techniques

6.4.4.2 Critical factors to be considered while imparting conflict management training

Multiple and integrated phased training programmes shall be appropriate and effective for skill building on conflict management. Further, the combination of classroom training and mentor-supported field practice can be explored and the same will result in effective learning through practice and increased appreciation of the relevance of conflict management to managers' job responsibilities. Wider participatory group incorporating executives, supervisors, workers etc can be explored in future training sessions. Long term effectiveness of skill building training programmes for conflict management depends on a number of critical factors. These include first and foremost careful selection of participants as well as provision for ongoing support for conflict management processes by textile organisations.

Conflicts are often characterised by considerable social complexity, managing these processes often call for much effort to build rapport for stakeholder engagement, facilitate negotiations, carefully prepared agreements and assistance in the implementation or monitoring of such agreements. Addressing conflicts can be therefore extremely time-consuming, and emotionally draining. Textile organisations in their own capacities require substantial resources for meetings, transport, materials and other logistics. To increase the chances that such processes are sustained, it is worthwhile developing a participant selection process that identifies participants who are already helping parties in organisational conflicts at various levels and have facilitation and field-based experience in conflict management. Ideally, the training group includes participants who are already linked to conflictual parties' social networks and have credibility with the parties or people in authority who can provide assistance. This necessitates not only the water tight managerial group but also transgresses the hierarchical levels. Such a commitment can only occur over an extended period if conflict management is visualised as a priority for the trainee's organisation. Some of the critical factors to be considered while imparting conflict management training are explained below-

- ⌘ Conflict management training sessions will be more effective when it is directed to a group of affiliated people, rather than to individuals. The training of individuals often results in the random application of skills. A cadre of two or more people, however, can work together to mutually support each other in the development of strategies for managing conflicts. Departmental and other stratification can be explored in this case.
- ⌘ Conflict management training may ideally target textile mill managers and other staff together, so that they can coordinate their conflict management activities.

- Conflict management training a small group of people in a small geographic area effectively will be better than training a larger group in a wider area where lack of resources, isolation or inability to impart training modules will reduce the training's effectiveness.

- It will be more effective to train a group of people working in a single textile organisation as this promotes the institutionalisation of procedures.

- Skill-building trainings need to be well integrated in participants' organisations to ensure that participants enjoy the required organisational support for their work.

- New intermediaries in a conflict need support, encouragement and strategy assistance. As an integral part of training, it will certainly be useful to provide periodic mentoring/coaching - via e-mail, telephone and most importantly through field visits and active interaction with the parties of conflict, wherever feasible. Suitable local training institutions should be involved in training and post-training mentoring from the outset, to build local capacity for the replication of training

- New managerial trainees as well as persons who were transferred from technical field to administrative wing should be required to take cases regarding conflict situations, meet stakeholders and conduct conflict management work. It is therefore important that conflict interventions do not have to be abandoned because resources have started to run out. Mechanisms should be put in place to ensure that adequate resources are provided to allow conflict management processes to be sustained over extended periods.

- The contextual understanding organisational conflicts are important. Documented conflict management processes and its outcomes can considerably enhance the material for future training courses. Mechanisms that support the documentation of conflict cases from training - such as coaching and editorial support - should therefore be considered in every textile organisation.

- Effective problem solving requires resources and skills, but it depends even more on the commitments of all parties, including decision-makers, to enable efficient conflict management before conflict grow and escalate into destructive heights. Top level executives need to intervene in a strategic way to enhance the conflict management training mechanism in their organisations.

- Conflict management training can be more effective when it is underpinned by participatory, learning centered and adult education principles.

- Assistance can be provided by various research and training institutions exclusively dealing the textile related issues like Southern India Mills Association (SIMA), South India Textile

Research Association (SITRA), and others. Universities and colleges can also contribute their efforts as like experts in the field of textile and related issues.

⯆ Outcomes of trainings which can be organised and implemented by individual mills and associative partners shall address many of the pressing managerial conflicts. Modest but effectively deployed investment of resources in training may provide and enhance logistical support of even informal conflict management procedures thereby uplifting the face of systematic conflict managerial approaches among textile mill managers.

6.4.5 Emerging approaches of conflict management- Integral and integrated

Modern researches and organisational studies speak of managing the conflicts, the evolution of conflict addressing in organisational life, but management is a word which merely states the situational responses without explaining it. For there seems to be no reason why conflict management should evolve out of material and other elements or mind management out of living form, unless the modern day management gurus explicitly accepts the integrating and all embracing dimensions of it. Modern organisational conflicts are a form of veiled organisational life, organisational life a form of veiled consciousness. And then there seems to be little objection to a farther step in the series and the admission that mental consciousness may itself be only a form and a veil of higher states which are beyond organisational citizenship. The significance of this organisational philosophy applied to the conflict management lies in the fact that it is not speculative in character but is rooted in the theory and practice of organisational conflict management and expounds in philosophical terms the results of the present study in the wider spectrum of organisational consciousness studies. To this the current organisational researchers must accept vestiges of non-computability to be present, at some indiscernible level, in inanimate manner.

An essential ingredient is missing from the present day conflict management picture. This missing ingredient would be needed in order that the central issues of humane approaches in organisations could ever be accommodated within a coherent conflict management world-view. It is a direction that involves an important change in the most basic of our organisational understanding. The resultants of this study are fairly specific about what the nature of the directional change must be and how it might apply to the management of conflicts. Even with the limited present understanding of the nature of conflict management and its missing ingredient, managers can begin to point to where it must be making its mark and how it should be providing one vital contribution to whatever it is that underlies our conscious feelings and actions of organisational life. The precision and scope of principles of management in general and the theories of conflict in particular as presently appreciated is extraordinary, yet they contain no hint of any action that cannot be simulated computationally. Nevertheless, within the possibilities that these management inputs allow us, we must try to find an opening for a hidden non computational action that the functioning of organisational conflict management must somehow be taking advantage of. The present study asserts that managers must look to the phenomenon of quantum scale reduction to see where our present picture of managerial reality must indeed be fundamentally changed. For management to be able to accommodate something that is as foreign to the current physical picture as is the phenomenon of conflict management, organisations must expect a profound change- one that alters the very underpinnings of the philosophical viewpoint as to the nature of organisational reality. For now, organisations may try to ask a somewhat simpler-sounding questions regarding where one might expect that conflict management is to be found in the known organisational world and worlds of common managers.

To obtain an understanding of the relationship of the sources of conflicts and management of the conflicts has, however thus far proved to be extremely difficult and this difficulty has its root in the very great difference in their basic qualities as they present themselves in the organisational experiences. This difference can be expressed with particularity, the sources of conflicts as 'extended substances' and the management of conflicts as 'thinking substances'. Evidently, by extended substances, organisations can infer that those are something made up of distinct forms existing in space, in an order of extension and separation basically similar to the one that managers have been calling explicate. By using the term 'thinking substances', in sharp contrast to the other, managers can infer clearly implying that the various distinct forms appearing in thought do not have their existence in such order of extension and separation, but rather in a different order in which extension and separations have no fundamental significances. The implicate order has just this latter quality and the managers may perhaps anticipate that conflict management has to be understood in terms of an order that is closer to the implicate than it is to the explicate. If sources of conflicts and the management of conflicts could in this way be understood together, in terms of the same general notion of order, the way would be opened to comprehending their relationship on the basis of some common ground. Thus we could come to the germ of a new notion of unbroken conflict management wholeness, in which managing the conflicts are no longer fundamentally separated from the organisational citizenship.

When a bio-psycho-social entity in a time and space (self) of organisational human unit, experience an imbalance due to certain determinable extraneous factors or of intergalactic intractabilities, it is mainly experienced as a conflict of ground-floor desires and the other pro-attitudes. The conflict arises due to reflective self evaluation and quest to regain the balance, in which some target-desire appears evaluatively undesirable to the person/s concerned. That desire or pro-attitude, howsoever compelling it may be, is concerned to be alien to oneself inasmuch as one prefers, on normative grounds to indentify oneself with a character or personality masks from which that desire or pro-attitude must be absent. Alienation of these characters that are naturally formed by ground floor desires and pro-attitudes combined with the underlying transactional stimulants prescribed by transactional theories thus forms a paradigm of being what they really want to be and that expressed as felt conflicts.

Contrastive characterisations of desires or motivations with its constructive/destructive multitudinal influentials are indicative of awareness of and sensitivity to qualitative depth of particular mode of life pattern. Managers are strong evaluators who defines desires contrastively and precisely because they seems to be motivated to cast themselves as persons of certain kind, to live a kind of organisational life shaped by virtues of courage, nobility, integrity, honour and so on.

These evaluative visions draw out for them a preferred mode of organisational life by virtue of qualitative reflection upon the desires and motivations which express and sustain an organisational life of that kind. The felt springs of actions with its conflictual interests matter to them, not so much because of the attraction-repulsion of their consummations, but in virtue of the quality of the kind of organisational life and the kind of character that these desires-conflicts syndromes belong to. Granted that the pertinent viewpoint is that of the reactive attitude when it comes to judging persons or situations, it does not imply that it is always impertinent to adopt the objective attitude and there by finding solutions for innumerous conflicts, whatsoever the human circumstances may be. On the contrary, the participant attitudes in conflictual situations sometimes tend to give place to non participant attitudes, especially when the moral mask of the person is understood to be incapable of participating in ordinary human relationships, whether because of being asymmetrically oriented or because of being much too deranged. This peculiar dimension stimulates to talk about the pertinence of adopting the objective attitude towards the normal and the mature as a way of taking refuge from say the strains of involvement in conflictual situations or simply out of intellectual curiosity.

By the vastness of its extent, the enormity of its achievement, the manner of its invasion of, and the patterns of the influence it has sought to exert over, organisational human life and conduct, the conflict management renders requisite and exigent a revaluation of its central conceptions, and a determination of the scope of its inquiries and the limitations of its techniques. When an organisational human interaction happens, human elements had to re-orientate their minds, to a large extent, particularly to an appreciable extent. Even against the surface-conscience there is an urge from within the depth of every being to find the eternal resonance with the organisations and their environment that they enjoy, whether this is felt perfectly or otherwise. The words of eternal knowledge and the experience shared by management gurus are the ripe fruits of such fine flowers blossomed out in the light of the wisdom. They lead us to the efficient conflict management in organisations, which are but its psychological parts.

The differences among the conceptions regarding the efficacies of the various methods of the transformation and integration of individuals' efforts synchronised with that of the organisational into the higher consciousness (organisational developmental measures) are due to the varying temperaments and grades of experience of those individuals engaged in the task of comprehending the organisational understanding. Each of the ego-centers is different from the other in consciousness and experience. They require higher touches of experience varying in degree, in proportion to the subtlety of the condition of their present state of consciousness.

Management and organisation, likewise, is not an invention of human crotchet or an outcome of fear/greed or even a social necessity but the answer to a living surge of conscious aspiration which cannot be intelligible either to reason or to science. Human nature is not a combination of scientific facts alone or a bundle of physical laws or chemical elements, but manifests in itself a meaning higher than all observable values in the world of mathematics, physics, chemistry or biology. The spirit of management is different from the beaten track of logical philosophy, for it reads an eternal meaning in the temporal structure of the world. It is here that we come face to face with the fact that management is neither a predisposed practice nor a human contrivance but the perennial activity of timeless being and the trail to the universal resonance within. This important factor is forgotten by the modern organisational manager, however much educated he may be. He has refused to walk freely with the workings of the spiritual and integral nature and has attempted his best to centre himself in the state of individualised existence.

The misery of the present-day managerial conflicts and its inefficient management may be attributed to this constrictive tendency in the managers, which is ever trying to block the way of the expansion of the integral consciousness. The case of the half-baked material science and psychology may be specially mentioned here as being one of the forces obstructive to the happy process of Truth-realisation. The ills caused by wrong methods of education, the social and political strife, the individual evils and the world-degeneration are all effected by the one terrible fact that humanity has turned against the law of the spiritual reality. So long as this self-destructive tendency of the human mind is not controlled, and man is not shown the correct way of procedure, the unhappy world has to be contented with its fate. The remedy lies in our being sincere in taking recourse to the direct method of such realisation here and now. A manager has to be cent-per-cent integral.

Occasional and strategic departure from the reactive attitude to the objective/proactive attitude under special circumstances is itself rooted in the organisational citizens' inquest to break the box and make himself more creatively responsible by wearing the more constructive masks of his personality. This explains the possibility of transformative, resonential and other constructive approaches to manage the conflicts. The reactive attitude which defines the personal stance seems to override any switch-over to the complete objective/proactive attitude such that there is no genuine human possibility of our being entirely overtaken by the objective/proactive attitude without losing our human/self identity. This may well explain the usage of comparatively lower intensified transformative, resonential approaches than the elongated fight/flight attitude when it comes to manage conflicts in organisational spheres. The balancing acts of these attitudinal synergies are initiated by inculcating the value system and its various dynamic constituents like ethos, predominant prioritisations of desires, springs of actions, etc. Thus organisational citizens are such that their being is in question in their being. These person contingent features are various specific needs and desires, ways of perceiving things, moods and manners and many other dispositions, all of which make up the ground floor resources of ordinary organisational life with its prenotions of inculcated values and its management. Conflict managerial values represent an internal framework that has the potential to provide meaning to our lives and the way in which we lead them. Knowing and living by the conflict managerial values enriches managerial self-development and leads to an understanding of the purpose of our organisational lives. Conflict managerial values are helpful in maintaining the personal self-esteem in the face of challenge and disappointment. They are the principles by which managers may choose to live in the organisational world.

The idea of strong evaluation of conflict managerial values seems to be an undercurrent in many conflict theories of past– be it from Blake and Mouton, Thomas-Kilmann, Mary Parker Follett, Stephen Robbins, Johan Galtung or Thomas Weber. It seems to be perfectly theorised and put into practice by the likes of Mahatma Gandhi echoed out of ancient wisdom-consciousness of India. The values that inform the value-consciousness of the conflict manager must themselves be objective in the sense that if a value is not objectively there, it is difficult, nay, impossible that there be a value-consciousness at all in the most appropriate proactive situational response mode. The manager of conflicts presupposes the system of values which he is trained to imbibe and manifest in his judgements. The value system of him is rationally and consciously adopted after a process of critical evaluation. The values themselves have a unity and coherence which make them the values of specific value-framework. There is an organic unity which binds them into a system. It is the intrinsic among them which deserve to be central, while the rest can belong to the periphery of the systems enabling dissonance-resonance balancing acts for managing conflicts. Values are not person-centric in the sense an artifact is man-made, but they are deeply ingrained in the human-value-consciousness. For example, the values of non-violence and respect for life are ingrained in the higher order consciousness of human beings as it is the very bedrock of human existence. Values are ideals which set the tones to manage the conflicts and inculcating them to the organisational citizenship itself is a proactive phenomenon exercised by the human workforce in every organisations. Furthermore springs of value wings spreads to every imaginable levels, let be it – intra-individualistic, interpersonal, intragroup, intergroup, organisational-system-wide or to superfluous multitudinal stakeholders of an organisation operating with a value system in time and space thereby expanding the horizons of conflict management domains.

Organisational human beings are natural conflict managers and have the capacity for self-transcendence and the ability to recognise value in others. Their reflective self-transcendence and or transformative approaches to managing the conflicts is certainly a product of reason as was convincingly displayed by Mahatma Gandhi's understanding/ managing the conflicts. Reason gives the human beings the status of constructive conflict managers. It is only humans who recognise the trans-subjective values. The realisation that other beings value themselves as one values oneself and that; it is the same value that is valued by different organisational creatures may lead to the recognition of intrinsic values during conflict management exercises. Rationality, consciousness, self-consciousness, intelligence, a sense of the past and the future, the capacity to relate to other, concern for others are some of the features which an organisational human unit inherit and needs to strengthen the notions of accountability, responsibility, meaningfulness so as to be applied to them all. All these features are gradable and actual organisational units possess these elements in different proportions. The challenge lies in the selection and appropriation of the most suitable ways of explaining these notions from innumerable prenotions that management thinkers had and going to be. It indeed certainly is a distinct human activity with its quest in finding the best situational response. The solution of *One best way* notion, which seems to be consistently rejected by the managerial acumen in past; and in future, management thought may pave way for more integral, integrative yet transformative guided principles for managing the conflicts experienced exclusively by its human constituents echoed from Gandhian schools of wisdom, beautifully crafted from the essence of ancient Indian mind-wisdom-consciousness.

6.4.6 Suggestions in brief

- Middle level managers need to possess required skills to position themselves as leaders. These skill sets include shared and pragmatic vision, assertiveness, skills for conflict management, organisational commitment and adaptability.

- Middle level managers need to address the conflicts; look at the relationships of psycho-social bonding; reflect themselves as more than logical in theory and be creative; should be the practitioner of the skills of diagnosis and communication.

- Middle level managers who are helping people to feel secure, to learn from their own experience, to reach their own decisions and to become more mature and independent is greatly appreciated by the organisational circles.

- Conflict management skills and comfort in using a variety of conflict-handling modes may help middle level managers to develop a repertoire of conflict managerial skills that are essential in effectively managing the variety of conflict situations.

- Managing effectively conflicts in a unit/department requires using strategies to actively encourage subordinates to attempt to handle their own problems, communicating honestly and openly, ensuring clarity of responsibility of roles, creating policies and changing if needed, and being sensitive to others and offer support.

- One of the major challenge counted by practicing managers and other stakeholders of contemporary management ethos, is the expressive development of a body of theory to explain why organisational conflicts take the form they do, and why they/others behave as they do, including various stratum of the managerial responses towards conflict dynamics. This calls for the sharing of the knowledge regarding conflict management for common goodness and benefits. Various universities, textile associations and research institutions can play a better role in this regard.

- Conflict managerial values are not person-centric in the sense an artifact is man-made, but they are deeply ingrained in the human-value-consciousness. The values of non-violence and respect for life are ingrained in the higher order consciousness of human beings as it is the very bedrock of human existence and need to be inculcated among the textile mill managers.

- To become effectively and for appropriately managing conflict, middle level managers must understand the causal-effects, theories, approaches and strategies of conflict management.

- The interactionist view of conflict management has a broader scope than the traditional notions of unitary and pluralist perspectives and the same is to be promoted. Further this can be strengthened by inculcating the principles of integral and integrated conflict management. In this regard Gandhian approach along the lines of Win-Win and built upon life principles need to be actively promoted. Integrated approach as propagated by Mary Parker Follett and can be accrued from various sources of body of knowledge including ancient Indian scriptures need to be ascertained.

- The need to impart training with an exclusive focus on conflict management skill enhancement among the textile managers seems to a pressing one. Guided conflict management modules for textile mill managers can be a better suggestive measure and the same can be utilised for further enhancement. The critical factors to be considered for imparting conflict management training were identified and put forth as suggestive measures. Training for efficient and constructive conflict management can be imparted not only for the managers but also for executives, supervisors and even for common workers.

- Management thought may pave way for more integral, integrative yet transformative guided principles for managing the conflicts when all the constituents of managing the conflicts were taken into consideration. Current models, theories and approaches of conflict management need to be creatively utilised for the same as they possess vital links to understand the hidden aspects of conflict management from the past.

6.5 POSSIBLE EXTENSIONS OF THE STUDY

Managing conflicts with others can be enervating, tedious and exasperating but can become a fascinating challenge if and only if the manager shows his real mental stature, guts and forbearance during the process. In handling the conflict situation, much depends upon the strategy and the tactical inputs that are redeemed by the managers dealing with other human elements in the organisation.

It appears that two kinds of organised learning are involved in managerial dealing with the organisational life. One is phylogenetic learning, in the sense that during organisational evolution-both the individualistic as well as system wide operations evolving very sophisticated machinery for perceiving and making inferences about the real world. In other words an organisational citizen approaches conflict perception a priori. What is a priori for an individual is a posteriori for the organisational units like groups, departments etc. The second kind of organisational learning involved in dealing with the world is ontogenetic learning, namely the lifelong acquisition of cultural, linguistic and scientific managerial knowledge. Thus the organisational members see the world through multiple pairs of glasses; some of them are inherited as part of physiological apparatus, others acquired from direct experiences as they proceed through organisational life. Interestingly, a priori and a posteriori are relative terms, thoroughly intertwined with the phylogenetic and ontogenetic processes. Presumed common biological-phylogenetic heritage is so vast that it may lead the organisational thinkers to believe that all the members think and perceive and function in the same ways, but of this there can be no certain proof. Further the ontogenetic ways expels this wrong perception and strengthens the possibilities of conflict to occur more within and with others from individualistic perspectives of every social unit-be it an individual, group or even organisations.

The quest to find solutions to all possible answers start by strategising the patterns and attempting to find the commonness underlying through the advocacies of various theories and the practical exposures. Modern conflict management theories from various domains of knowledge seem to be of greater use and their assimilative nature enables every potential researcher fetch himself to superior heights and consciousness. Be it from psycho dynamic theory, transactional analysis, and psychomotor-psychosocial theories, all are indicating the commonness which itself reveals in uncommon ways. It may even get strengthened by the inclusion of propulsive theories like game theory or organisational learning theory. Amalgamation, assimilation, integration and amassing the knowhow which we gained through various paths of wisdom are to be the keywords for the future conflict management theories. In organisational spheres, micro-meso as well macro scientific experimentative studies is the need of the hour, apart from diagnostic and or descriptive research on conflict management. Indian organisations can play a vital role in this regard as they are propounded in these principles. Presence of ancient wisdom with the latest technologies is the indomitable component of our business organisations.

Psychometrics and extensions of the philosophy of the conflict management enriched by postulations like conflict management strings (SPTs) are going to be a challenge and much depends upon the creative appropriation of such important instrumental applications in this field. Structural and procedural ways are also to be explored in its highest levels including associative institutions, research organisations as well as governmental machineries. Though academic in its origin, the resultants of this study can act as in valuable inputs along with other dimensions for reframing, revaluing and refining conflict management studies at this juncture.

In organisational plane of operation, each manager's sense world is strictly private and not directly accessible to anyone else. That inexorable, absolute division between spheres of conflict consciousness and their total and impenetrable exclusion of each other is always organised chaotic, yet falls under the nature's law of management. In spite of all this, there is the possibility of some degree of communication between the individuals and a surprising degree of commonality in the pictures of the world they separately create. The logical lines of thinking and acting can carry the organisational thinkers only so far, they peter out at some point, but they do indicate something beyond even though they cannot carry to there. Thus it can be said that the notions of all conflict consciousnesses are really one and the organisational conflict management needs to address the conflict consciousness management in its ever widening umbrella.

6.6 CONCLUSION

Middle level managers represent the infinite dynamics among the organisational understanding. To equip themselves, they are required to consciously evolve their thoughts into the harmonious tunes of this universe. An integral experience necessitates an integral approach, a transformation of the integral personality. The differences among the conceptions regarding the efficacies of various methods of the transformation of managerial personality into the higher consciousness (essence of conflict management) are due to the varying temperaments and grades of experience of those engaged in the task of realising the organisational affiliations and in some way their own existence. Each of the ego-centers (human psyche) is different from the other in consciousness and experience. They require higher touches of experience varying in degree, in proportion to the subtlety of the condition of their present state of consciousness while bringing organisational profits.

Organisational destructions, back biting, obliteration, and annihilation is not the purpose of organisations. Growth, evolution, constructive activity, and purposeful movement towards the ultimate affiliation and attachment, is the aim of the modern organisation. Hence, there exists a need to share knowledge, feeling, emotion and work among organisational workforce. Managers need to discover themselves and others in its true spirit and that can be only happening if managers by way of the description of knowledge, will, emotion and action attempts to do so. It leads to the integral development of the humanistic collective psyche and to the synergetic goals in every organisational sphere of life can be achieved. It is here that this study comes face to face with the fact that managerial understandings of conflict management are not one time organisational practice nor human contrivances; but the perennial activity of integrated and integral as well as 360 degree conflict management.

Management gurus were quick to appreciate the necessity to appeal to the various sides of human nature and to alter the method of teaching in adjustment with this need. Reality and creation in textile organisations are not to be regarded as two facts or problems to be encountered but two ways of witnessing the same thing. The managerial mind is composed not only of the rational powers but also the emotional and the instinctive elements which feel the presence and working of certain truths that rationality cannot explain adequately.

Contemporary understanding of conflict management necessitates the theorisation of the practice of conflict management. This study gives suggestive measures towards integral, integrated and interactionist approaches of conflict management. Conflict management string model evolved through this study and the training modules ascertained by need based analysis are all part of futuristic projection for enabling the assessment of the practice of conflict management among the managers.

To bring effective positive change among textile managers regarding conflict management, it requires accepting many transcending organisational practices than merely reading and talking about conflict managerial values. Managers need to consider practical ways of weaving them into the fabric of everyday actions in their respective organisations. The initial ingredients rendered towards in this direction should start with the likes such as - openness, truthful interactions, humane and process-centric, free from exploitations, integrative inclusiveness, reciprocal relating, integrative unity, law of the situation, cumulative responsibility, functional cooperation, etc. And certainly this list may not get constrained itself to a comparatively smaller target research group of this study, but certainly may expand its wings to those unimaginable heights which are of made up to manage the dissonance-resonance balances in every spectrum of organisational life forms where managerial interventions are possible. Furthermore, the last word in conflict management is that there is no last word in conflict management.

Referential notes and other major works including the textual references are highlighted in this section. To enable a better communication of the most relevant components which was constantly referred throughout the present study, it would be most appropriate to present a list of selected referential components. Further, an exhaustive referential module in a way or other would bring more flimsiness to this section. Thus, present list only bears signs of advanced/sustained references and assumes the pre-worked basic textual and other references in the issues fundamental to the study points.

Alam, O. G., and Srivastava, R. 1981. Punctuality as a function of alienation and ego strength. *Perspectives in Psychological Researches*, 4(11): 29-31.

Allport, F. 1955. *Theories of perception and the concept of structure*. New York: Wiley.

Allport, G. 1956. *The Nature of Prejudice*. Cambridge MA: Addison Wesley.

Allred, K. G. 1999. Anger and retaliation: Toward an understanding of impassioned conflict in organizations. In R. J. Bies, and Lewicki, R. J. (Ed.), *Research on negotiations in organizations*, Vol. 7. Greenwich, CT: JAI Press.

Alper, S., Tjosvold, D., and Law, K.S. 2000. Conflict management, efficacy, and performance in organizational teams. *Personnel Psychology*, 53: 625-642.

Amabile, T. M. 1996. *Creativity in context* (2 Ed.). Boulder, CO: Westview.

Amason, A. C. 1996. Distinguishing the effects of functional and dysfunctional conflict on strategic decision making: Resolving a paradox for top management teams. *Academy of Management Journal*, 39(1): 123-148.

Amason, A. C., and Sapienza, H. J. 1997. The effects of top management team size and interaction norms on cognitive and affective conflict. *Journal of Management* (23): 495-516.

Ansari.M. 1990. *Managing people at work: leadership styles and influence strategies*. New Delhi: Sage Publications.

Argote, L., Gruenfeld, D. H., and Naquin, C. 2001. Group learning in organizations. In M. E. Turner (Ed.), *Groups at Work: Advances in Theory and Research*: 369-411. Mahwah, NJ: Lawrence Erlbaum.

Argyris,C. 1964. *Integrating the individual and organization*. New York: Wiley.

Argyris,C. 1970. *Intervention Theory & Method: A Behavioral Science View*: Addison-Wesley.

Argyris, C. 1971. *Management and Organization Development*. New York: McGraw-Hill.

Athreya, M. B. 1997. Business Values for the 21st Century: HRM. *The New Frontiers*, 3(3): 7–10.

Axelrod, R. 1984. *The Evolution of Cooperation*. New York: Basic Books.

Babu, T. 2004. *A study on Conflict Resolution in Industrial Disputes – A Gandhian Approach*. Unpublished PhD Thesis: Gandhigram Rural Institute, India.

Bandura, A. 1977. Self-efficacy: Toward a unifying theory of behavioral change. *Psychological Review*, 84: 191-215.

Bandura, A. 1986. *Social foundation of thought and action: Social Theory*. Englewood Cliffs, N.J: Prentice Hall.

Barbara, B., and Rubin, J. Z. 1995. *Conflict, Cooperation & Justice*. Palo Alto: Jossey-Bass.

Barlingay, S. S. 1966. *A Modern Introduction to Indian Ethics*. New Delhi: Penman Publishers.

Barnett, M. E. 1990. The Relationship Between Personality Type and Choice of Conflict Resolution Mode. *Dissertation Abstracts International*, 51(5): 1504-A.

Baron, R. A. 1984. Reducing organizational conflict: An incompatible response approach. *Journal of Applied Psychology* (69): 272-279.

Ben-Yoav, O., and Banai, M. 1992. Measuring conflict management styles: A comparison between the MODE and ROCI–II instruments using self and peer ratings. *International Journal of Conflict Management*, I (3): 237–247.

Berk, R. A. 2003. *Regression analysis: A constructive critique*. Thousand Oaks, CA: Sage Publications.

Berkowitz, L. 1982. Aversive conditions as stimuli to aggression. In L. Berkowitz (Ed.), *Advances in Experimental Social Psychology*, Vol. 15: 249-288. New York: Ac. Press.

Berkowitz, L. 1993. *Aggression: Its Causes, Consequences and Control*. Philadelphia, PA: Temple University.

Bhaskar, K. R., and Mehrotra, A. . 1998. Managerial Values: A Study of Selected Organisations in India. *Personnel Today*, 18(4): 29–34.

Bies, R. J. 1987. The predicament of injustice: The management of moral outrage. *Research in Organizational Behavior* (9): 289-319.

Blake, R. A., and Mouton, J.S. 2006. *The New Managerial Grid*. New Delhi: Jaico Publications.

Blake, R. R., and Mouton, J.S. 1964. *The Managerial Grid*. Houston: Gulf Publishing Co.

Blake, R. R., Mouton, J.S., and Shepard, H.A. 1964. *Managing Intergroup Conflict in Industry*. Houston: Gulf Publishing Co.

Boryshenko, J. 1993. *Fire in the soul: A new psychology of spiritual optimism*. New York, NY: Warner Books, Inc.

Boulding, K. E. 1962. *Conflict and defense: a general theory*. New York: Harper & Brothers.

Boulding, K. E. 1963. Conflict Management as a Key to Survival. *American Journal of Orthopsychiatry*, 33(2): 230-231.

Bower, G. H., and Forgas, J. P. (Ed.). 2001. *Mood and social memory*. Mahwah, NJ: Lawrence Erlbaum Associates.

Brett, J. M., Shapiro, D. L., and Lytle, A. L. 1998. Breaking the bonds of reciprocity in negotiations. *Academy of Management Journal* (41): 410-424.

Brewer, M. B. 1996. When contact is not enough: Social identity and intergroup cooperation. *International Journal of Intercultural Relations* (20): 291-303.

Burton, J. W. 1997. *Violence Explained: The Sources of Conflict, Violence and Crime and their Prevention*. Manchester: Manchester University Press.

Bush, R. A. B., and Folger, J. P. 1994. *The promise of mediation: Responding to conflict through empowerment and recognition*. San Francisco, CA: Jossey-Bass.

Byrne, D. 1971. Attitudes and Attraction. In L.Berkowitz (Ed.), *Advances in Experimental and Social Psychology*. New York, NY: Academic Press.

Chakrabarty, S. 2002. Evaluation of Rahim's Organizational Conflict Inventory as a measure of conflict-handling styles in a sample of Indian salespersons. *Psychological Reports*, 90: 549-567.

Church, A. H., and McMahan, G.C. 1995. Key Characteristics of OD in Rapidly Growing Firms. *ASTD OD Newsletter*, Fall/Winter: 7–8.

Churchman, D. 2005. *Why We Fight: Theories of Human Aggression and Conflict*. Lanham, MD: University Press of America.

Cohen, H. 1980. *You Can Negotiate Anything*. Secaucus, NJ: Lyle Stuart.

Cornelius, H., and Shoshana, Faire. 1989. *Everyone Can Win: How to Resolve Conflict*. Sydney: Simon & Schuster.

Cosier, R., and Rose, G. 1977. Cognitive conflict and goal conflict effects on task performance. *Organizational Behavior and Human Decision Processes* (19): 378-391.

Crawley, J. 1992. *Constructive Conflict Management: Managing to Make a Difference*: Nicholas Bealey Publishing.

Dalton, E. M. 1979. *Management: foundations and practices* (5ed.).New York: McMillan Press

Das, G. S. 1987. Conflict management styles of efficient branch managers: As perceived by others. *ASCI Journal of Management*, 17(1): 30–38.

Dayal, I. 1970. *New concepts in management*. Bombay: Lalvani Publishing House.

Dayal, I. 2002. Group and intergroup relations. *Indian Journal of Industrial Relations*, 37(4).

De Dreu, C. K. W., Nauta, A., and Van de Vliert, E. 1995. Self-serving evaluations of conflict behavior and dispute. *Journal of Applied Social Psychology*, 25(23): 2049-2066.

Denzin, N., K. and Yvonna, Lincoln. 2003. *Strategies of qualitative inquiry* (2 ed.). Thousand Oaks, CA: Sage Publications.

Deutsch, M., and Robert M. Krauss. 1960. Effect of Threat on Interpersonal Bargaining. *Journal of Abnormal and Social Psychology* 61(2): 181–189.

Dollard, J. 1980. *Frustration and Aggression*. Westport, CT: Greenwood.

Donohue, W. A. 1992. *Managing Interpersonal Conflict*: Sage.

Druckman, D. 2005. *Doing Research: Methods of Inquiry for Conflict Analysis*. Thousand Oaks: Sage.

Dwivedi, R. S. 1981. *Dynamics of Human Behaviour at Work*. New Delhi: Oxford and IBH Publishing Company.

Dwivedi, R. S. 2001. *Human relations and organisational behaviour*. New Delhi: Macmillan India ltd.

Eisenhardt, K. M., Jean L. Kahwajy, and., Bourgeois, L .J. III. 1997. How management teams can have a good fight. *Harvard Business Review*, 75(4): 77–85.

Fernandez, G., Pattanayak, Dhar, Ravishankar. 2000. *For one and all Human skills*. New Delhi: Himalaya Publishing House.

Finkelstein, S. 2003. *Why smart executives fail*. New York: Portfolio.

Fisher, R., and Ury, William. 1987. *Getting to Yes: Negotiating Agreement Without Giving In* (2 ed.). London: Arrow.

Follett, M. P. 1924. *Creative Experience*. London: Longmans.

Forgas, J. P. 1995. Mood and judgment: The affect infusion model (AIM). *Psychological Bulletin* (117): 39-66.

Fraser, N., and Hipel, K. 1984. *Conflict Analysis: Models and Resolutions*. Amsterdam: Elsevier Science.

French, W. L., and Bell, C.H. 1973. *Organization Development: Behavioural Science Interventions for Organizational Improvement* Englewood Cliffs, N.J: Prentice-Hall.

Frey, L. R. (Ed.). 1995. *Innovations in Group Facilitation*. New Jersey: Hampton Press.

Friedman, R. A., Tidd, S.T., Currall, S.C., and Tsai, J.C. 2000. What goes around comes around: The impact of personal conflict style on work conflict and stress. *International Journal of Conflict Management*, 11: 32-55.

Fryman, S. 2006. *The Psychology of Prejudice*. New York: Penguin Publications.

Fucilla, R. 2001. *The influence of cultural and individual level variables on conflict avoidance behavior: A cross-cultural study of U.S. and Latin American professionals*. Unpublished Master's thesis, University of Wisconsin-Milwaukee.

Gandhi, M. K. 1900. *Fellowship of faiths and unity of religions*. New Delhi: GB House.

Gandhi, M. K. 1940. *An Autobiography or The Story of My Experiments With Truth*. Ahmedabad: Navajivan.

Gandhi, M. K. 1932-36. Editorial and other selected articles, *Harijan*.

Gandhi, M. K. 1959. *The message of the Gita*. Ahmedabad: Navajivan.

Gandhi, M. K. 2000. *Thought for the day*. New Delhi: Publication Division, Ministry of Information and Broadcasting, Government of India.

Gangadhara, R., and Surya, P. Rao. 1996. *The Dynamics of Group Behaviour*. New Delhi: Kanishka Publishers.

Gangrade, K. D. 1998. *Gandhi's Autobiography: Moral lessons*. New Delhi: Gandhi smriti and darshan samiti, Rajghat.

Gangrade, K. D., Kothari, L.S., and Verma, A.R. 2005. *Concept of truth in Science and Religion*. New Delhi: Gandhi Smriti and Darshan Samiti, Rajghat.

Ganguli, B. N. 2000. *Gandhi's social philosophy, perspective and relevance*. New Delhi: National Gandhi Museum.

George, R., and David, Walchak. 1986. *Working: Conflict and Change* (3 ed.). New Delhi: Prentice Hall.

Ghosh, D. 1993. Risk propensity and conflict behavior in dyadic negotiation: Some evidence from the laboratory. *International Journal of Conflict Management*, 4: 223–247.

Goel, S. L. 2000. *Modern management techniques*. New Delhi: Deep and Deep Publications.

Gottshalk, J. 2002. *Crisis Management*. New York: John Wiley and Sons.

Gross, M A., and Guererro, L. K. 2000. Managing conflict appropriately and effectively: An application of the competence model to Rahim's organizational conflict styles. *International Journal of Conflict Management*, 11(3): 200-226.

Hall, L. (Ed.). 1993. *Negotiation: Strategies for Mutual Gain*: Sage.

Hammond, J. S., Keeney, R.L., and H. Raiffa. 1999. *Smart choices: A practical guide to making better decisions*. Harvard: HBS Press.

Hingorani, A., T. (Ed.). 1971. *Teaching of the Gita, Gandhi*. Bombay: Bharathiya Vidya Bhawan.

Holman, D. J., and Wall, T.J. 2002. Work Characteristics, Learning-Related Outcomes, and Strain: A Test of Competing Direct Effects, Mediated, and Moderated Models. *Journal of Occupational Health Psychology* (7): 283-301.

Husain, A., S. 1969. *Gandhiji and communal unity*. New Delhi: Orient Longman.

Janis, I. L. 1997. Groupthink. In R. L. Vecchio (Ed.), *Leadership: Understanding the dynamics of power and influence in organizations*: 163-176. Notre Dame, IN: University of Notre Dame Press.

Jehn, K. A. 1995. A multimethod examination of the benefits and detriments of intragroup conflict. *Administrative Science Quarterly* (40): 256-282.

Jehn, K. A. 1997. A qualitative analysis of conflict types and dimensions in organizational groups. *Administrative Science Quarterly* (42): 530-557.

Jehn, K. A., and Mannix, E. A. 2001. The dynamic nature of conflict: A longitudinal study of intragroup conflict. *Academy of Management Journal* (44): 238-251.

Joseph P. Folger.Scott, M., Poole., and Randall, K. Stutman. 1996. *Working through Conflict: Strategies for Relationships, Groups and Organizations* (3 ed.): Harper-Collins.

Joshi, K. 2002. *Philosophy of value-oriented education: theory and practice.* New Delhi: Indian Council of Philosophical Research.

Katzenbach, J. R., and Smith, D. K. 1993. The discipline of groups. *Harvard Business Review*, March-April, 71(2): 111-120.

Kautilya. 1912. Arthashastra. In T. Ganapathi Sastrigal (Ed.), Vol. 1-3. Mysore: Mysore Oriental Library.

Kay, E. 1974. *The crisis in middle management*. New York: Amacom.

Kilmann, R. H., and Thomas,K. W. 1982. Four Perspectives on Conflict Management: An Attributional Framework for Organizing Descriptive and Normative Theory. In V. J. Kelly and Baba (Ed.), *The New Management Scene*. Englewood Cliffs, NJ: Prentice-Hall.

Kissinger, H. 1994. *Diplomacy*. New York: Simon & Schuster.

Kothari, C. R. 2006. *Research Methodology* (2 ed.). New Delhi: Wishwa Prakashan.

Kruskal, J. B., and Wish, M. 1978. *Multidimensional scaling*. Beverly Hills, CA: Sage.

Kurtz, E., and Ketcham, K. 1993. *The spirituality of imperfection*. NY: Bantam Books.

Laird, W. M., and Gary,P.Latham. 1996. *Skills for managerial success-theory,experience and practice*: Irwin Publications.

Lallan, P., and Banerjee,A.M. 1981. *Management of Human Resources*. Jaipur: Sterling Publishers.

Lawley, D. N., and Maxwell, A. E. 1971. *Factor analysis as a statistical method*. London: Butterworth and Co.

Levitt, S., and Steven, Dubner. 2005. *Freakonomics*. New York: William Morrow.

Lewicki, R. J., Saunders, D. M., Minton, J. W., and Barry, B. 2002. *Negotiation: Readings, exercises, and cases*. New York: McGraw-Hill/Irwin.

Lipman-Blumen, J., and Leavitt, H. J. 1995. Hot groups. *Harvard Business Review*, July-August 73(4).

Lorenz, K. 1974. *On Aggression*. New York: Harvest.

Louis, E. B., and David,L.Kurtz. 1992. *Management*. New York: McGraw Hill Inc.

Luthans, F. 1998. *Organisational Behaviour* (8 International ed.). New York: McGraw-Hill.

Machiavelli, N. 1513, 2003. *The Prince*. London: Penguin.

Maitra, S. K. 1963. *The Ethics of the Hindus*. Kolkata: Calcutta University Press.

Maslow, A. H. 1954. *Motivation and personality* (2 ed.). New York: Harper & Row.

Mathur, H. B., and Sayeed,O.B. 1990. Application of conflict management strategies as perceived by the manager for himself and for his supervisor. *Indian Journal of Social Works*, 41(2): 163-169.

McGrath, J. E. 1984. *Groups: Interaction and performance*. Englewood Cliffs, NJ: Prentice Hall.

McKenna, E. 2000. *Business psychology and Organisational Behaviour* (Students' ed.). New York: Taylor and Francis Inc.

McWhorter, J. 2005. *Winning the Race*. New York: Penguin.

Mills, R. D., and Smith,L. 1985. Conflict handling and personality dimensions of project management personnel. *Psychological Reports*, 57(3): 1135-1143.

Mishra, P., and Dhar,Upinder. 2002. Leveraging functional conflicts. *Indian Journal of Industrial Relations*, 38(1).

Murnighan., J. 1991. *The Dynamics of Bargaining Games*: Prentice Hall.

Nalini, V. D. 1997. *Vedanta and Management*. New Delhi: Deep and Deep Publications.

Nandini, S. 2000. *Top Management Team and Organizational Performance: The Moderating Role of Differentiation & Integration Processes and Managerial Discretion*. Indian Institute of Management , Calcutta.

Narayan, B., and Sharma,Bharathi. 2004. *Behavioural science in management*. New Delhi: Omsons Publications.

Nicholson, Michael.1970 *Conflict analysis* London: Unibooks p.53

Nicotera, A. M., Smilowitz,M. and Pearson,J.C. 1990. Ambiguity tolerance, conflict management style and argumentativeness as predictors of innovativeness. *Communication Research Reports*, 7(2): 125-131.

Nizam al-Mulk. ca 1095, 1978. *Siyasatnama (The Book of Government or Rules for Kings)*. London: Routledge.

Pareek, U. 1982. *Managing conflicts and colloboration*. New Delhi: Oxford-IBH.

Pareek, U. 1982. Managing conflicts through negotiation. *Bombay Psychologist*, 3(1): 5-16.

Pareek, U. 1994. *Beyond Management*. New Delhi: Tata McGraw-Hill.

Park, R., Ezra and Ernest, W. Burgess. 1921. *An Introduction to the Science of Sociology*. Chicago: University of Chicago.

Patricia Hayes Andrews and Richard, T. H. 1997. *Organisational communication-Empowerment in a technological society*. Delhi: A.I.T.B.S. Publishers and Distributors.

Pelled, L. H. 1996. Demographic diversity, conflict, and work group outcomes: An intervening process theory. *Organization Science*(7): 615-631.

Pinkley, R. L. 1990. Dimensions of conflict frame: Disputant interpretations of conflict. *Journal of Applied Psychology*, 75: 117-126.

Porter, M. 1998. *Competitive Strategy*. New York: The Free Press.

Prasad.L.M. 2004. *Organisational Behaviour* (1 Reprint ed.). New Delhi: Sultan Chand and Sons.

Pruitt Dean, G. 1972. Methods for Resolving Differences of Interest: A Theoretical Analysis. *Journal of Social Issues*, 28(1): 133–154.

Radhakrishnan, N. 1995. *Gandhi: the quest for tolerance and survival*. New Delhi: Gandhi smriti and darshan samiti and Gandhi media centre.

Radhakrishnan, S. 1926. *Hindu View of Life*. London: Allen and Unwin.

Rahim, M. A., and Bonoma, T.V. 1979. Managing organizational conflict: a model for diagnosis and intervention. *Psychological Reports*(44): 1323-1344.

Rahim, M. A. 1980. Some contingencies affecting interpersonal conflict in academia: A multivariate study. *Management International Review*, 20(2): 117–121.

Rahim, M. A. 1983. A measurement of styles of handling interpersonal conflict. *Academy of Management Journal*(26): 368-376.

Rahim, M. A. 1997. Styles of managing organizational conflict: A critical review and synthesis of theory and research. In R. T. G. M. A. Rahim, and L. E. Pate (Ed.), *Current topics in management*, Vol. 2: 61–77. Greenwich, CT: JAI Press.

Rahim, M. A. 2001. Managing organizational conflict: Challenges for organization development and change. In R. T. Golembiewski (Ed.), *Handbook of organizational behavior*, 2 ed.: 365–387. New York: Marcel Dekker.

Raiffa, H. 1982. *Art and Science of Negotiation*. Cambridge: Harvard University.

Rapoport, A. 1960. *Fights. Games and Debates*. Ann Arbor, MI: University of Michigan Press.

Richard E. Walton, Joel, Cutcher-Gershenfeld., and Robert, B. McKersie. 1994. *Strategic Negotiations : A Theory of Change in Labor-Management Relations*. Boston: HBS

Robbins, S. P. 1974. *Managing Organizational Conflict: A Non-Traditional Approach*. Englewood Cliffs, N.J: Prentice-Hall.

Robbins, S. P. 1998. *Organisational Behaviour*. New Delhi: Prentice Hall of India Pvt.Ltd.

Robbins, S. P. 1998. *Organization theory structure,design and applications* (3 ed.). New Delhi: Prentice Hall of India.

Robert, A. B., Donn Byrne, Blair,T.Johnson. 1998. *Exploring Social Psychology* (4 ed.): Allyn and Bacon Publishers.

Robert, B. L., and Zhengsen. 1998. *Organisational Psychology-foundations and applications*. London: Oxford University Press.

Roger Fisher, E. K., and Andrea Kupfer Schneider. 1994. *Beyond Machiavelli : Tools for Coping with Conflict*. Cambridge, Mass: Harvard University Press.

Rogers, C. 1961. *On Becoming a Person: A Therapist's View of Psychotherapy*. Boston, MA: Houghton Mifflin.

Rosenberg, S. 1982. The method of sorting in multivariate research with applications selected from cognitive psychology and person perception. In N. H. a. L. G. Humphreys (Ed.), *Multivariate applications in the social sciences*: 117-142. Hillsdale, NJ: Erlbaum.

Ross, L., and., Nisbett, R. E. 1991. *The person and the situation: Perspectives of social psychology*. Philadelphia: Temple University Press.

Ross, R. 1989. Conflict. In R. Ross, and Ross,J. (Ed.), *Small groups in organizational settings*: 139-178. Englewood Cliffs, NJ: Prentice Hall.

Roy, D. 1997. Values in Management: Present Scene and Future Needs. *Management Accountant*, 32(8): 592–596.

Saiyaddhin, M. S. 1988. *Human Resources Management*. New Delhi: Tata McGraw-Hill.

Samantara, R. 2003. Management of superior-subordinate conflicts: an exploration. *Indian Journal of Industrial Relations*, 38(4).

Samantara, R. 2004. Conflict management strategies and organisational effectiveness. *Indian Journal of Industrial Relations*, 39(3).

Sayeed, O. B. 1990. Conflict management styles: relationship with leadership styles and effect of esteem for coworker. *Indian Journal of Industrial Relations*, 26(3): 227-243.

Sayeed, O. B. 1993. Leadership effectiveness and managerial response to conflict strategies. *Productivity*, 34(1): 99-108.

Schein, E. H. 1992. *Organizational culture and leadership*. San Francisco: Jossey-Bass Publishers.

Schellenberg, J. A. 1996. *Conflict Resolution: Theory, Research, and Practice*. Albany: State University of New York.

Schneider, B. 1985. Organizational Behavior. *Annual Review of Psychology*, 36: 573-611.

Schweiger, D. M. 1989. A meta-analysis on the comparative effectiveness of devil's advocacy and dialectical inquiry. *Strategic Management Journal*(10): 303-306.

Schwenk, C. R. 1990. Conflict in organizational decision making: An exploratory study of its effects in for-profit and not-for-profit organization. *Management Science*, 36(4): 436-448.

Shapiro, D. L., and Rosen, B. 1994. An investigation of managerial interventions in employee disputes. *Employee Responsibilities and Rights Journal*, 7(1): 53-72.

Sharp, G. 1999. *Gandhi as political strategist, with Essays on ethics and politics.* (Indian ed.). New Delhi: Gandhi media centre.

Sherif, M. 1967. *Group Conflict and Cooperation: Their Special Psychology*. London: Routledge, Kegan Paul.

Silva, M. O. S. 2000. *Conflict source and conflict management style at Notre Dame of Greater manila as perceived by grade school and high school administrators and teachers, school year 1998-1999*. Unpublished Master's thesis, Ateneo De Manila University, Philippines.

Simmel, G. 1955. *Conflicts*. New York: The Free Press.

Simons, T. L., and Peterson, R. S. 2000. Task conflict and relationship conflict in top management teams: The pivotal role of intergroup trust. *Journal of Applied Psychology*(85): 102-112.

Singh, P. 1979. *Occupation Values and Styles of Indian Managers*. New Delhi: Wiley Eastern.

Sowell, T. 1987. *A Conflict of Visions*. New York: William Morrow.

Stiglitz, J. 2003. *The roaring nineties: seeds of destruction*. London: Allen lane.

Sudan, A. S., and Naveen Kumar. 2004. *Organisation effectiveness and change*. New Delhi: Anmol Publications Pvt.Ltd.

Suresh, S. 2004. Conflicts: types, causes and resolution strategies. *Paradigm*, 8(1).

Tabachnick, B.,G. and Linda, S. Fidell. 2001. *Using Multivariate Statistics*(4 ed.). Boston: A&B

Textiles, M. o. 2004-2007. Annual reports. In M. o. Textiles (Ed.).

Thomas, K. W., and Kilmann, R. H. 1974. *The Thomas-Kilmann conflict mode instrument*. Tuxedo, NY: Xicom.

Thomas, K. W., and Kilmann, R. H. 1977. Developing a Forced-Choice Measure of Conflict-Handling Behavior: The "Mode" Instrument. *Educational and Psychological Measurement*, 37(2): 309-325.

Thomas, K. W. 1979. Conflict. In S. Kerr (Ed.), *Organizational Behavior*: 151-181. Columbus, OH: Grid Publications.

Thomas, K. W., and Tymon,W. G. Jr. 1985. Structural Approaches to Conflict Management. In R. Tannenbaum, Margulies,N., and Massarik,F. (Ed.), *Human Systems Development*: 336-366. San Francisco: Jossey-Bass.

Thomas, K. W. 2000. *Intrinsic Motivation at Work: Building Energy and Commitment*. San Francisco: Berrett-Koehler.

Thomas, K. W. 2004. Conflict and Negotiation Processes in Organizations. In M. D. Dunnette, and Hough,L. M. (Ed.), *Handbook of Industrial and Organizational Psychology*, 2 ed., Vol. 3: 651-717. Palo Alto, CA: Consulting Psychologists Press.

Ting-Toomey, S. 1997. Intercultural conflict competence. In D. W. Cupach and Canary (Ed.), *Competence in interpersonal conflict*: 120-147. New York: McGraw-Hill.

Tjosvold, D. 1985. Implications of controversy research for management. *Journal of Management Science*(11): 21-37.

Tjosvold, D. 1997. Conflict within interdependence: Its value for productivity and individuality. In C. K. W. D. D. a. E. V. d. Vliert (Ed.), *Using Conflict in Organizations*, 2 ed.: 651-717. Palo Alto, CA: Consulting Psychologists Press.

Tucker, A. 1950. Prisoners' Dilemma: Unpublished lecture delivered at Stanford University.

Upadhyay, D. P. 1985. Value, People and Organisations. *Indian Management*, 24(12): 31–34.

Ury, W. 1991. *Getting Past No: Negotiating with Difficult People*. New York: Bantam Books.

Van de Vliert, E., and Kabanoff, B. 1990. Toward theory-based measures of conflict management. *Academy of Management Journal*, 33: 199–209.

Van de Vliert, E. 1997. *Complex interpersonal behavior: Theoretical frontiers*. Hove, UK: Psychology Press.

Venkaiah, V., and Rao,V.S.P. 1991. Organisational conflicts: concepts,models,types and resolution strategies. In V. S. P. Rao (Ed.), *Organisation Development*: 3-41. New Delhi: Discovery Publishing House.

Verma, R. 2001. *The spiritual basis of satyagraha*. Ahmedabad: Navajivan Publishing House.

Wanasiri, W. 1996. Interpersonal Conflict Handling Styles of Private Vocational School Principals in Thailand. *Dissertation Abstracts International*, 57(8): 2315-A.

Weber, T. 1992. *Gandhian way of conflict resolution*. New Delhi: Gandhi peace foundation.

Weber, T. 2001. Gandhian Philosophy, Conflict Resolution Theory and Practical Approaches to Negotiation. *Journal of Peace Research*, 38(4): 493–513.

Weider-Hatfield, D. 1988. Assessing the Rahim Organizational Conflict Inventory–II (ROCI–II). *Management Communication Quarterly*, 1: 350–366.

Weider-Hatfield, D., and Hatfield, J. D. 1995. Relationships among conflict management styles, levels of conflict, and reactions to work. *Journal of Social Psychology*(135): 687-699.

Welch, J. 2001. *Jack: Straight from the gut*. New York: Warner Business Books.

Wilkinson, L., Blank,G. and Gruber,C. 1996. *Desktop Data Analysis* Upper Saddle River, NJ: Prentice-Hall.

William Baskaran, M. 2004. *Indian Perspectives on Conflict Resolution*. Thiruvananthapuram: Gandhi Media Centre.

Wilmot, W., and Joyce, L. Hocker. 2005. *Interpersonal Conflict*. New York: McGraw-Hill.

Wittenbaum, G. M., and Stasser, G. 1996. *Management of information in small groups*. Thousand Oaks, CA: Sage Publications.

Wittenbaum, G. M., Hollingshead, A. B. et al. 2004. From cooperative to motivated information sharing in groups: Moving beyond the hidden profile paradigm. *Communication Monographs*, 71(3): 286-310.

Wolfe D. M.and Kolb, D. A. 1980. Beyond specialization: the quest for integration in midcareer. In N. C. Derr (Ed.), *Work, family and career*. New York, NY: Praeger.

Worchel, S., and Simpson, J.A. (Ed.). 1997. *Conflict between People and Groups*. Chicago: Nelson-Hall Publishers.

Xie, J., Michael Song,X. and Anne Stringfellow. 1998. Interfunctional Conflict, Conflict Resolution Styles, and New Product Success: A Four-Culture Comparison. *Management Science*, 44(12): 192-206.

Zhou, J., and George, J. M. 2001. When job dissatisfaction leads to creativity: Encouraging the expression of voice. *Academy of Management Journal*, 44(4): 682-696.